FOR KING AND OTHER COUNTRIES

FOR KING AND OTHER COUNTRIES

The New Zealanders who fought in other services in the First World War

GLYN HARPER

with Christine Clement and Rebecca Johns

MASSEY UNIVERSITY PRESS

To all the New Zealanders who served in the First World War

CONTENTS

FOREWORD

For *King and Other Countries* tells the hitherto unchronicled story of the significant number of New Zealanders who fought in the Great War for nations other than their own. To our twenty-first-century sensibilities, it may seem a little odd that many New Zealanders who saw active service opted to enlist elsewhere and fight under foreign flags. We need to remember, though, that in 1914 nationalist feelings in New Zealand and indeed in the other dominions were relatively weak. During the First World War, the king and his empire were under threat, and if you happened to be elsewhere in *his* empire, then, for many, enlistment there and then was the natural patriotic act. Though it may appear strange to us, for the generation who witnessed the onset of the 'war to end all wars', a call to serve the king was above all else.

In the early years of the twentieth century, travel abroad was slow and expensive, and yet there were a surprising number of New Zealanders overseas when war broke out. Most of them were middle-class or well-to-do and either visiting family or attending university in England. As with the later war, they leapt at the chance to join the fighting and often sought commissions in the more attractive British regiments. These early volunteers went to France with the 'Old Contemptibles', the small British Regular Army, and by the end of the first year of the war, most of them were dead.

In later years there continued to be a small but measurable cohort who preferred to enlist in the British army rather than in the New Zealand forces. In addition, if you preferred the war at sea, or in the air, then the Royal Navy or the Royal Flying Corps were the only opportunities. Otherwise, plain old-fashioned snobbery, a better chance of promotion and sometimes old family connections were motive enough for those who fought in other services. Eventually this led the New Zealand authorities, short of good officers, to impose tight controls on those who chose to fight elsewhere.

Young New Zealand women had also travelled to England or were in Europe in large numbers when war erupted. Most had joined British nursing organisations, some braving the risks at sea to get to Britain and join up. They undertook work caring for the wounded in France and often travelled even more widely than the soldiers, nursing in not only Egypt and Gallipoli, but also Italy, St Petersburg, Mesopotamia (now Iraq) and India.

Next to Britain, Australia naturally attracted the largest number of New Zealand enlistments: perhaps 5000 soldiers and at least 48 women in the nursing service. Most joined because they were in Australia when war broke out, though better pay and Australian manpower shortages also helped propel their decision-making. The Australians were less fussy about age restrictions, and many recruits who were below the minimum age managed to enlist — along with a 51-year-old. Interestingly, those with criminal convictions could get away with using false names, and some managed to enlist several times over.

In the view of the British commander, Douglas Haig, the Australians were the unruliest of the imperial forces, with the highest rates of indiscipline and venereal disease. There seem, too, to have been more 'bad characters' who made the most of their chances, and their adventures are detailed in an entertaining chapter in this volume. Though one New Zealander rose to the rank of brigadier in the Australian forces, other New Zealand recruits seem to have troubled the Australian authorities at least as much as did their own men.

In Canada, two nurses and more than 400 men enlisted from New Zealand, of whom 80 did not survive the fierce battles on the Western Front. Travellers passing through accounted for 40 recruits in South Africa and 30 in the United States. About 40 New Zealanders fought for France, mainly in the Foreign Legion, where a different nationality, or other drawbacks, were no bar to joining up. Harold Gillies, the pioneer of modern plastic surgery, was one of these men, as was James Waddell, who fought both on Gallipoli and at the Western Front and was to become one of France's most-decorated soldiers. The Indian army, which expanded rapidly to become the 'largest all-volunteer army in history' and deployed to East Africa and Palestine as well as Gallipoli and the Western Front, also offered attractive commissions to New Zealanders.

Some New Zealanders ended up in unexpected places. While we are aware of the occupation of Sāmoa, it is not widely known that the Ceylon Planters Rifle Corps included three New Zealanders. The saintly Suzanne Aubert — French-born, but domiciled in New Zealand — nursed war-wounded and earthquake victims in Italy; Christina Hunter and three others worked in Russia; the novelist Jane Mander, trapped in France by the war, joined the American Red Cross; and the deputy matron of Christchurch Hospital concluded her war in Constantinople. A major in the Royal Marines went to Ethiopia on a trade mission and, amazingly, three New Zealanders fought for Germany, one being awarded the highly regarded Iron Cross.

The authors' meticulous research has uncovered many of their names and their interesting, and at times unbelievable, stories. Surprisingly, the numbers of New Zealanders who served in other forces turns out to be much higher than historians have expected. Almost 12,000 New Zealanders helped the war effort elsewhere, of whom just over 1400 died. While a database of names will be available on a future website, many readers will recognise names and perhaps family members from the stories in this book.

Overall, this is a sad story, and one of enormous loss and grief. Alongside the names, we read a constant refrain — missing in action, died of wounds, died of enteric (typhoid) fever, died in hospital sometimes months after the end of the war. From mothers and wives, too, there are anxious appeals to the War Office or unit commanders for news of whether a loved one might have survived or at least of how he died.

Many will read this as a testimony to the futility of war. Indeed, it would be fair to say that going to war never recovered its 'glamour' and sense of adventure after this huge industrial-scale struggle. But futility is not the only emotion aroused by this conflict. The young who lied about their age and scrambled to enlist wherever they happened to be were not only after adventure and comradeship. They also believed that this was the only honourable thing to do.

When we read about the men and women in this book we are affected in a way we would not have been had they lived to lead long and fulfilling lives. The story of loss is also a story of courage and self-sacrifice, and this has become part of our national community and spirit. Perhaps, in this regard, the best epitaph for any war dead was composed for the Spartans who died at Thermopylae: 'Stranger, tell them at home that we lie here keeping their trust.' Those New Zealanders who lie in so many different uniforms and places around the world kept our trust, and we honour them still.

Giselle Byrnes and Gerald Hensley
Co-chairs, Centenary History Governance Group
November 2018

LORD KITCHENER AT FORBURY
No 3,
PROT 18.2.1

INTRODUCTION

LARGELY FORGOTTEN

previous pages
Prior to 1914 New Zealand was quite a martial society. In 1909 a Defence Act made military training for boys and young men compulsory, and New Zealand's elite high schools and colleges had a long tradition of military training. Here Lord Kitchener, veteran of the South African War and former commander in chief in India, reviews the Otago cadets in February 1910 before presenting the colours. OTAGO BOYS' HIGH SCHOOL MUSEUM, C754, 18053012

In New Zealand during the years of the First World War, many young men were desperate to serve, but age or ill health stood in the way. In 1915 Gustav Victor Berg (Bergh) of Southbridge, a small settlement of 369 people in the 1916 census and some 28 miles (45 kilometres) south-west of Christchurch in Canterbury, was 18 years old and working as an apprentice printer for the local paper, the *Ellesmere Guardian*.[1] Late that year he boarded a ship for Sydney and made his way to Adelaide via Melbourne to enlist in the Australian Imperial Force (AIF), the army the Australian government had raised to support Britain's fight against Germany and its allies.

Gustav Berg had tried to enlist in the New Zealand Expeditionary Force (NZEF) several times, in various parts of the country including in the North Island, but each time he had been rejected because he was too young.[2] He wrote to his former employer on 14 January 1916:

> There was no hope of being accepted in New Zealand, and I could not stay there and see my mates go away as though I was suffering from 'cold feet', so I had to come over here. I do not know anyone here except the acquaintances I have made since coming into camp. We have a fairly good time and the only things that trouble me are the heat and the flies, both of which are very trying.[3]

On his AIF papers Berg gave his true age as 18 and a half.[4]

During his four years with the AIF, Berg wrote home regularly to his parents, who passed his letters on to the *Ellesmere Guardian*. The paper printed them as letters from 'a Southbridge boy' and always mentioned that Berg was 'formerly of the "Guardian" staff'. A letter that appeared in the paper on 18 March 1916 was written after Berg had spent nearly a week guarding the wireless station at Abberton, South Australia. There were about 40,000 Germans in South Australia, he said, and they had 'been causing some trouble up country'. The wireless station was seen as an obvious target.

Berg had just completed his final training and was soon to depart for the front. He assured his family, 'I have had a good time so far and am enjoying the life.'[5] The next news to appear in the *Ellesmere Guardian* was an extract from a letter written on 25 May, by which time Berg was in Egypt and, apart from the heat and flies, was 'enjoying the best of health and . . . the military life was suiting him first rate'.[6] Berg's other letters, printed in 1916, would not be so cheerful.

In Australia Berg was initially posted into the 48th Infantry Battalion, but three weeks after arriving in France he was transferred to the 12th Brigade Machine Gun Company.[7] He enjoyed being with the machine gunners and found learning all the parts that made the work 'very interesting'. But the letter to his parents informing them of his transfer, written from a dugout in the trenches, was much darker than those he had written before. He was still 'having a good time', but:

> The only thing that troubles me is the poisonous gasses the Huns use, and we have to be very alert. I have had some experiences with it. They send it along with the wind and it is of a yellowish colour and comes in a thick cloud. A couple of mouthfuls is enough. The shells are buzzing over our heads all day and you can hear them a good way off. They generally try to shell us on account of doing so much damage with our machine guns. We can fire 500 rounds of ammunition in a minute. The rats are very plentiful in our trenches, there being some very big ones. I have not had any letters from New Zealand for over five months. They must be going astray.[8]

Gustav Berg was one of a considerable number of New Zealanders who fought in the war on the same side as New Zealand but under another flag. For the first time, this book tells their story.

New Zealand's military contribution to the First World War is generally accepted as being a massive effort for such a small country. For the first time in its history, New Zealand despatched a large expeditionary force to serve abroad that was centred primarily on a complete infantry division and a mounted rifle brigade. By the time the Armistice came into effect on 11 November 1918, 124,211 men had enlisted for military service: 91,941 volunteers and a further 32,270 men conscripted under the Military Service Act. New Zealand's population was just over one million people, and some 42 per cent of the country's male population of military age had served with the NZEF during the war.[9]

The figure most often quoted about New Zealand's war effort is that, from October 1914 through to October 1918, just over 100,000 New Zealanders embarked for military service overseas.[10] This figure included individuals who were Imperial Reservists and those who served in the Royal Flying Corps and some other services. It excludes, however, the thousands of New Zealanders who served with the AIF and with British army units. Also missing are the men who served in the Indian army, the Canadian Expeditionary Force and the French Foreign Legion, and the considerable number of women who served with other nations' medical organisations.

Those who served with other nations are, of course, far outnumbered by those who served in the NZEF, but their contribution to New Zealand's war effort should be recognised. This book aims to outline where and when these New Zealanders served and to tell some of their stories.

It does not cover the experiences of those New Zealanders who joined the Royal Flying Corps — the Royal Air Force from April 1918 — or those who served with British naval units.

A studio portrait, taken in March 1916, of 18-year-old Gustav Berg (Bergh) in the Australian Imperial Force uniform which Berg sent to his sweetheart in New Zealand. CORRIE HUGHES COLLECTION

Their service in the First World War is the subject of other volumes of the Centenary History series. Further, defining who is included as a New Zealander is no easy task given that New Zealanders also regarded themselves very much as being 'British' in 1914. The men and women who are the focus of this book were born in New Zealand and spent their formative years here. Also included are those who were born elsewhere but spent a considerable part of their early lives in New Zealand. The experience of British reservists living in New Zealand will be briefly touched on especially as the New Zealand government paid for some of their salaries and allowances after the war.[11] Excluded from the book are those who served in the war prior to moving here, and those whose connections to New Zealand could be best described as tenuous.

Another aim of this book is to come as close as possible to reaching a figure for the numbers involved. It is clear that to date the estimated numbers have been far too low. Early estimates put the figure for New Zealanders serving with British units as less than 1000. A 2016 publication stated that 'more than 3000 men and women would [fight] in imperial units during the war'.[12] This was a threefold increase on the existing estimates, but the research for this book has revealed that it was also far too low. After all, close to 850 New Zealanders alone served in the RFC or RAF during the war, and more than 4000 New Zealand-born soldiers served in the AIF.[13] It is likely that the total figure could be more than 12,000 people.

This figure derives from the extensive and ground-breaking work of genealogist Christine Clement, who has spent years compiling a database of all New Zealanders known to have served during the First World War. Her work has been confirmed and enhanced by a wide-ranging trawl through *Papers Past*, given that many newspapers reported regularly through the war on where New Zealanders were serving. Added to this has been a general search for information at the British National Archives in Kew, the British Library, the Australian War Memorial, and the state libraries of New South Wales and Victoria. The service records of soldiers in the NZEF and AIF, now freely available online, were also heavily utilised. From these and many other sources, new information has emerged to challenge our existing knowledge. Many people provided fresh material that greatly assisted the research process. As part of this book's publication, a database of names has been compiled and will be placed on appropriate websites for easy access.

Another figure largely taken as read, and not interrogated until this publication, is that more than 1400 New Zealanders died while serving with the military forces of other nations. (The names of those known at the time of writing are recorded in the Roll of Honour at the end of this book.) This is a staggering figure and, to date, a significant omission from New Zealand's war history.

Why would so many New Zealanders serve with other nations' military forces? The most obvious answer is that their decision reflected the circumstances of the time. In 1914, thousands of New Zealanders were travelling or living abroad. These men and women enlisted quickly where it was most convenient, and they were very comfortable serving with their adopted militaries. For others, though, it was a deliberate choice to serve with British military units rather than join the NZEF. A small number of New Zealanders deliberately opted to transfer from the NZEF to either the British or Indian armies. Their reasons for doing so, and the process and numbers involved, are examined later in this book.

Then there is the fact that in August 1914 many New Zealanders were already serving in the British army, a handful were in the Indian army, and a very small number had enlisted in the French Foreign Legion. British ex-servicemen who had migrated to New Zealand but were still on the reserve list, which could be for a period as long as nine years, were under an obligation to return to service. In 1914, reservists were called up and many migrants had to travel back to the United Kingdom to rejoin their former military units.

Of course, the reverse of this trend happened, too: many people born in the United Kingdom or Australia served in the NZEF. Moreover, Canadians, Australians, Indians and others who were travelling in New Zealand in August 1914 did not hesitate to join the NZEF if the mood took them. This clearly demonstrates how interconnected the British Empire and its dominions were in the early twentieth century. Men and women from the various dominions could freely serve in one another's forces and did so without compunction. They could also serve in units of the British or Indian armies. In addition, it reveals what a truly global struggle the First World War was. As this book shows, New Zealanders served in a staggering array of places, in parts of the world that would have been unknown to them and to their compatriots when war was declared in 1914. New Zealand's current fixation on Gallipoli, and to a lesser degree on the Western Front, means that the global nature of the war is often overlooked, and our collective understanding of it needs to be much broader.

The first chapter examines the experience of those New Zealanders who joined the British Expeditionary Force (BEF) in 1914 and found themselves part of the 'Old Contemptibles'. Their experience was different to anything that followed in the war. For the BEF in France the five months of fighting in 1914 were costly and traumatic. Those New Zealanders who joined or transferred to the BEF after 1914 are the subject of a different chapter, as are those who served with the AIF. Since there were so many New Zealanders in the AIF, with such a diverse range of experiences, they are given two chapters. Other chapters look at those New Zealanders who served in the Indian army, the Canadian Expeditionary Force, and with the French military, including its Foreign Legion. A chapter has been allocated to those New Zealanders who either defy categorisation or who have interesting and often unusual stories. This includes a very small number known to have fought for Imperial Germany.

Finding details on the individuals in this book required extensive research in New Zealand, Australia and the United Kingdom. While the details of several hundred New Zealanders appear in this book, they are representative of many thousands of others who could not be included.

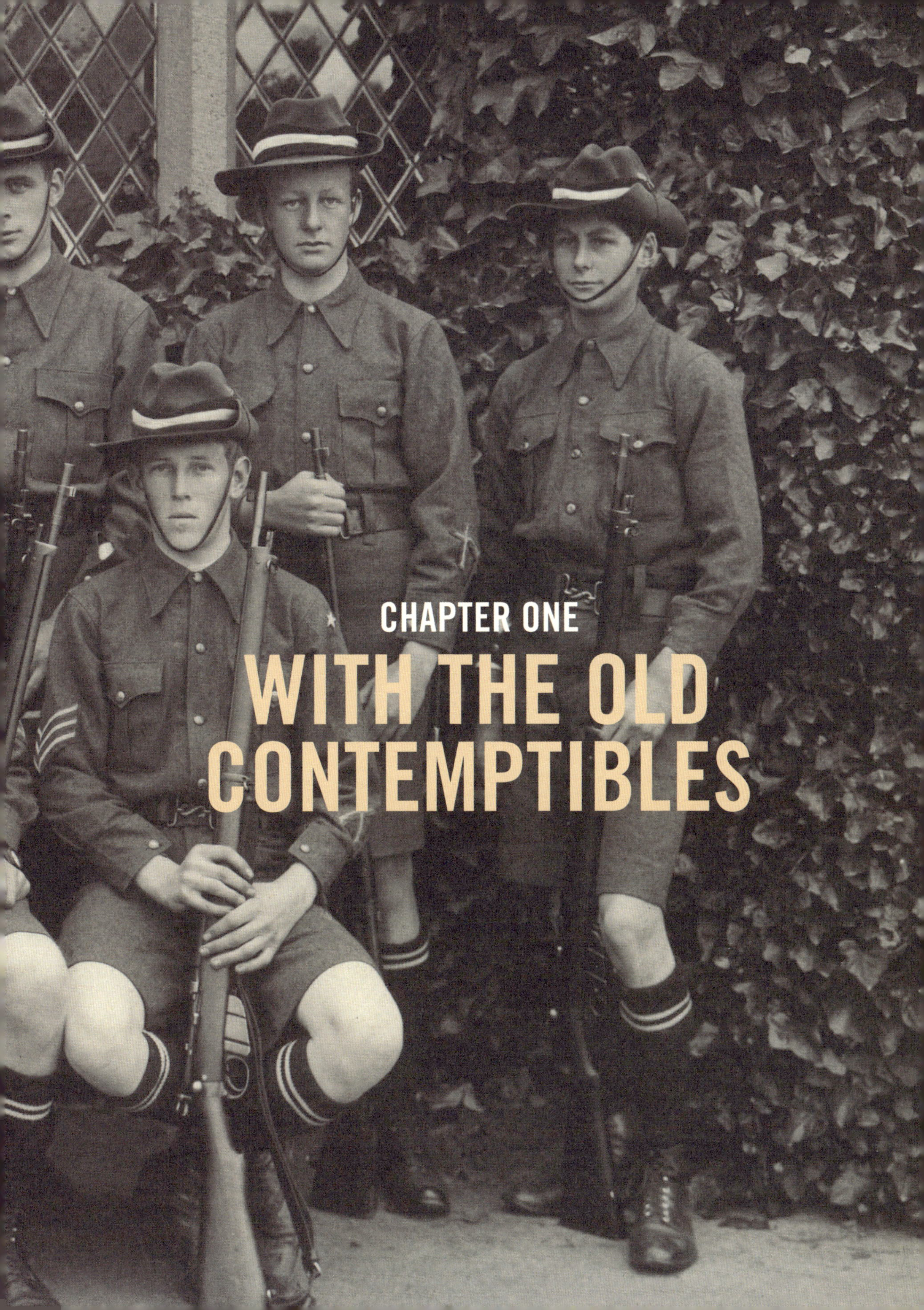

CHAPTER ONE

WITH THE OLD CONTEMPTIBLES

Previous pages
In the early twentieth century, the well-established New Zealand secondary schools had strong military traditions, including school cadets and rifle clubs. This is the Christ's College shooting team in 1913, wearing their newly introduced slouch Mounted Rifles hats. The member at far left, seated, is John William Pinckney who, just over a year later, received a commission in the fashionable 1st King Edward's Horse.
CHRIST'S COLLEGE ARCHIVES, CCST//1913/1

The British army's routine orders for 24 September 1914 contained an extraordinary piece of information, which has since passed into military folklore. Those who heard the orders read aloud, or who read them later, were informed that the German Kaiser was not very impressed with them. In what was purported to be an intercepted communication with one of his generals issued on 19 August, the kaiser is alleged to have said:

> It is my Royal and Imperial command that you concentrate your energies, for the immediate present, upon one single purpose, and that is that you address all your skill and all the valour of my soldiers to exterminate, first, the treacherous English [and] walk over General French's contemptible little Army.

The routine orders, issued after Mons and Le Cateau, made the laconic statement that '[t]he answer of the British army on the subject of extermination has already been given'.[1]

Some historians have disputed whether Wilhelm II actually issued any such order, but its effect was immediate.[2] Displaying the dark humour that was such a feature of the wartime BEF, the regular soldiers of its first formations began referring to themselves as the 'Old Contemptibles'. The phrase soon became a badge of honour and an enduring legacy. According to one of the BEF's officers, there was no 'prouder thing' than being able to say you were one of the Old Contemptibles.[3]

In 1914, the British Regular Army, compared with its European allies and rivals, was tiny. It consisted of just 10,800 officers and 236,632 other ranks. Of this latter figure, the distinguished British military historian Richard Holmes noted it was 'easily exceeded by the 265,379 officers commissioned during the war'.[4] Such a small force enabled the establishment of only one cavalry and six infantry divisions in August 1914. (A seventh infantry division of regular soldiers would be sent in October.) By comparison, the Germans committed 1077 infantry battalions, the French 1108 and the Belgians 120 at the start of the campaign in August, whereas the BEF could field just 52.[5] This small force of regular soldiers that made up the BEF for most of 1914 comprised the Old Contemptibles. And yet, as British historian Lyn MacDonald has pointed out, 'the Kaiser was referring to the size of the British Expeditionary Force, and not its quality'.[6]

Indeed, the BEF of 1914 was not only 'the best equipped Britain had ever sent to war', but its high standard of training also made it 'man for man . . . the finest Army in Europe'.[7]

Fine it certainly was, but quality could not prevent heavy casualties. The Old Contemptibles' time was tragically short — just four months. With severe fighting in several critical battles of 1914, including at Mons, on the Marne and at the First Battle of Ypres, casualties amongst the BEF at the end of the year reached almost 90,000. The original BEF had numbered just on 120,000.[8] Little wonder that one officer who wrote of his experiences in 1914 described the November battle of First Ypres as 'the Last Stand of the Old Army'.[9] The original BEF had been all but destroyed. The casualties had been so high among the aristocratic officer class that Debrett's *Peerage* could not be published in the spring of 1915 because the editors had insufficient time to revise it.[10] MacDonald concluded her study of 1914 with these words:

> Hard battles lay ahead, but they would be fought by other men. The Old Army was finished. The battles of Mons, Le Cateau, the Marne, the Aisne and Ypres had already passed into history — and most of the men who had fought them were dead and gone.[11]

Those who were 'dead and gone' and those who were too badly injured to fight again were primarily from the British Regular Army. This loss of trained, experienced manpower so early in the war 'was to haunt the British army for the entire conflict'.[12]

The poet Robert Service, often described as the 'Canadian Kipling', wrote of their passing:

> Oh, weren't they the fine boys! You never saw the beat of them,
> Singing all together with their throats bronze-bare;
> Fighting-fit and mirth-mad, music in the feet of them,
> Swinging on to glory and the wrath out there.
> Laughing by and chaffing by, frolic in the smiles of them,
> On the road, the white road, all the afternoon;
> Strangers in a strange land, miles and miles and miles of them,
> Battle-bound and heart-high:
> The gallant old 'Contemptibles'! There isn't much remains of them,
> So full of fun and fitness, and a-singing in their pride;
> For some are cold as clabber and the corby picks the brains of them,
> And some are back in Blighty, and a-wishing they had died.[13]

More than 300 New Zealanders fought as part of or alongside the Old Contemptibles in 1914. This included about 15 women, who also offered their services to the BEF in 1914. Their stories form the rest of this chapter.

New Zealanders became part of the Old Contemptibles in several ways. First, there were a small number serving in British regular units in August 1914. These men had chosen to make a career serving with British imperial units either in the United Kingdom or in parts of the British Empire, often because it was a family tradition. They included men like Frederick Andrews in The King's Liverpool Regiment, Robert Gee (Wiltshire Regiment), Frederick Houston (York and Lancaster Regiment) and Robert Masefield (Shropshire Light Infantry). In the mid-1880s the British government initiated a scheme that offered commissions in the British army to officers of the colonial defence forces if they could pass the demanding examination required. The first New Zealander to do this was Albert William Andrew from Christchurch who, in 1886, passed the examination and accepted a commission in the Devonshire Regiment. While serving with his regiment in India, Albert Andrew transferred to the Indian army and served with it as a senior officer during the First World War.[14] His story will feature in a later chapter.

Walter Russell, the only surviving son of Hawke's Bay landowner and politician Sir William Russell, was serving in the Northamptonshire Regiment in 1914. He was not the only New Zealander in the regiment. The three sons of Captain Christopher Garsia of Canterbury were serving in the British military and all were on active duty from August 1914. Lieutenant Oliver Durham Melville Garsia served in the Duke of Cornwall's Light Infantry, while his brother Captain Willoughby Garsia was in the Hampshire Regiment. The youngest brother, Lieutenant Rupert Garsia, had opted for the Royal Navy instead. Rupert served for a time on HMS *New Zealand*, but in 1914 joined the Royal Australian Navy ship *Sydney*. When escorting dominion troops to Egypt in September 1914, the vessel had encountered and destroyed the German light cruiser SMS *Emden*.[15] Lieutenant Oliver Garsia would be one of New Zealand's earliest casualties of the war. His story will feature later in this chapter.

Charles Watts, who had secured a commission by examination from Nelson College in 1906, was also in the Northamptonshire Regiment. Nelson College had quite a tradition in providing officers for the British army; this dated back to 1883, when William Glasgow became the first old boy to gain a commission by examination. Glasgow officially retired from the army in August 1914, but offered his services as one of the many 'dugouts' — officers of the regular force who were retired in 1914 but were called back to serve during the war years. Glasgow had become a brigadier general by the end of the war. From April 1916 he commanded 50th Brigade, which was part of 17th Division. William's brother Alfred Glasgow arrived in France in October with the Indian Contingent. He, too, would be promoted to the rank of brigadier before the war's end, commanding 58th Brigade in 19th Division. This was the only instance of two brothers serving as brigadiers in the British army for New Zealand.

South African War veteran Oliver Steele, an accountant from Auckland, obtained a commission in a British regiment, the Royal Berkshire, and spent eight years with it stationed in India. When war broke out, Steele had been in Britain attending a military course. He returned to his regiment and was soon on active service with it in France. Two months later, on 25 October, he was killed in action near Zonnebeke in Belgium. He was aged 32.[16] Following his death, in what would become a familiar pattern, Steele's family wrote to the War Office

'Old Contemptibles' but also New Zealanders. Clockwise from top left: William Glasgow, Alfred Glasgow, Charles Watts and Walter Russell. The Glasgow brothers both commanded British Expeditionary Force brigades during the war — a unique record. NELSON COLLEGE (WILLIAM AND ALFRED GLASGOW, CHARLES WATTS); AUCKLAND WAR MEMORIAL MUSEUM ONLINE CENOTAPH, KINDLY DONATED BY FAMILY (WALTER RUSSELL)

seeking further information about how he had died. The response, which would be repeated to other families thousands of times before the war was over, was that 'no further information has yet reached the War Office'.[17]

Harold Williams from Napier had also obtained a commission in the British army after serving in the South African War. He was with the Dorsetshire Regiment when war was declared. On 23 August, in the first clash of arms between the BEF and the Imperial German Army, Captain Harold Williams 'would earn the dubious distinction' of being one of the first New Zealanders wounded on the Western Front.[18]

From Palmerston North, Bertie Albert Follas was the youngest son of John and Elizabeth Follas. While he was still a teenager Bertie had travelled to England, where he enlisted in the Welsh Regiment. His battalion was stationed in India when war broke out, and it was immediately sent to the Western Front. The 1st Welsh arrived in time to take part in the retreat from Mons. In the fighting that followed, Bertie Follas was twice wounded. He recovered in time to take part in the Second Battle of Ypres the following year. Follas described the fighting in this battle as 'murderous' . . . 'the ground between the opposing forces was covered with dead and badly wounded Germans after this big attack, and there was no way of removing them as it was sudden death for anyone to go out in front'.[19] In the conclusion to a letter to his parents, Follas observed a profound truth: that 'the war was all luck'. So much artillery was being used that it was not always possible to find shelter. Therefore, 'if a man lived to see the war right through, it was luck and nothing more'.[20] Twenty-four-year-old Bertie Follas' luck ran out during the Battle of Loos in autumn 1915. He was reported missing on 2 October and was never seen again. He was subsequently reported as 'now concluded dead'.[21]

Several New Zealand officers were on duty in the United Kingdom in 1914, most of them attending military education courses. The most senior of these was South African War veteran Brigadier-General Richard Hutton Davies. A former civil engineer and surveyor, Davies had spent the last five years in the United Kingdom, where he held a number of senior appointments, including four years in command of the 6th Infantry Brigade, stationed at Aldershot. Davies' initial posting to the United Kingdom had been for a year only, but he had so impressed the imperial authorities that they offered him this plum role.[22]

An experienced commander, Davies was regarded by the New Zealand defence minister, James Allen, as the logical replacement for Alexander Godley as commandant of the New Zealand military forces.[23] When war was declared, it would have been too disruptive to recall all of the dominion officers serving with the British military, so Davies began preparing his brigade for active service and sailed with it to France as part of the British 2nd Division. The 6th landed in France on 12 August 1914; the first regular infantry brigade of the BEF to do so. Davies would be the first New Zealander to command a brigade, and later a division, on active service.[24]

Davies' military service in this war was chequered. He was not well in 1914; nor, at 53 years of age, was he young. His UK service record indicates that he 'had a serious illness before the war',[25] confirmed in a letter he wrote to Allen: 'I was very ill indeed . . . shortly before the war started, & had not properly recovered when we went over.'[26] The strains of active service, especially the withdrawal from Mons, left him and his soldiers 'absolutely exhausted'. Davies had not been happy soldiering and wrote of his fatigued men: 'I hope never in my life to see such a sight again.' As he explained to Allen, 'This is now a most peculiar war in many ways . . . In fact, now it is a war for sappers, garrison and heavy gunners. The poor Infantry have a poisonous time in the wet and cold trenches.'[27]

Back in Britain, Davies transferred to the imperial forces at their request in order to command a division. The United Kingdom was desperate for experienced, competent officers, and in February 1915, Davies was promoted to major general and given command of 20th (Light) Division, one of the new formations raised as part of Kitchener's Army. He was given three months' rest prior to assuming his new command.[28] It followed the previous pattern of his brigade appointment, in that in January 1916, while commanding the division on the Western Front, Davies was again mentioned in despatches. Just two months later, however, strain and sickness struck again.

His corps commander, Lord Cavan, wrote a secret and confidential memorandum that was read to Davies prior to being sent to the BEF's new commander, General Sir Douglas Haig. The memorandum opened with this assessment of Davies' poor health: 'He is a man of strong character, but would, I am convinced, break down with the strain of commanding a Division in the Summer campaign.' Cavan therefore considered his 'duty in the interests of the 20th Division to recommend that he be relieved of his command, but that his valuable knowledge and experience be utilised to the full at home'.

In his defence, Davies noted his 'very serious illness' before the war, the strain of the Mons battle and the fact that he had recently suffered 'two bad bouts of influenza'.[29] Haig had Davies removed from his command and sent back to the United Kingdom to recover. Haig, writing to the War Office, considered Davies to be 'physically unfit to withstand the strain of commanding a Division in the field', but, like Cavan, recognised his other strengths and recommended he be employed 'to the fullest advantage' at home.[30]

Davies later complained to Allen:

> I did not agree with the way certain parts of the line were held with regard to ground & did not hesitate to explain my views . . . I considered very many men could have been saved & more damage done to the enemy by certain slight alterations of position, & am still convinced of it.

He described divisional command in the trenches as 'a poisonous job & one is simply a glorified ganger . . . I would rather keep a shop.'[31] Although Davies was mentioned in despatches for his part in the Battle of Mons, Haig had not been impressed with his performance, later telling Godley that Davies 'had no nerve even from the start'.[32] Godley, who knew that Allen saw Davies as his logical replacement, used his position to undermine Davies. He wrote to Allen in December 1916:

Richard Hutton Davies was the first New Zealander to command a brigade and then a division on active service. His military service in the First World War was marred by ill health. Worn out by the war, and depressed, Davies took his own life in May 1918.
AUCKLAND WAR MEMORIAL MUSEUM ONLINE CENOTAPH, KINDLY DONATED BY FAMILY

> I do not think that Davies will ever come back to New Zealand. He takes no interest in New Zealand affairs out here, and none of us have ever seen or heard of him since the war began.[33]

Allen was in sporadic correspondence with Davies and knew how busy Davies was in his command appointments and that he was a proud New Zealander. Just after Allen received this barb from Godley, Davies had written to Allen, 'I hear on all hands how splendidly the men have done, & you know I always said, & wrote, that they were the best material in the Empire of which to make soldiers.'[34] In reply to Godley's December letter, Allen observed: 'I feel sure that [Davies] still does take an interest in New Zealand affairs.'[35]

Still in poor health, Davies commanded a number of base camps until mid-1918, when he was informed that he was to be placed on the Retired List for Officers. Depressed by this news, with money worries caused by his transfer to the British military, and suffering from influenza, malnutrition and insomnia, Davies was admitted to a Special Hospital for Officers at Palace Green, London. He seemed to require nothing more than a period of rest,[36] but it had all become too much for him. On the third day after his admission, on 9 May 1918, Davies 'self-inflicted with a razor, a severe wound on his throat' and died almost immediately.[37]

His son Henry Cornwall Davies, a surveyor from New Plymouth, had transferred from the NZEF in 1915 to serve as a captain with the Royal Engineers. He was given leave to attend his father's full military funeral complete with gun carriage, pipes and drums, and eight non-commissioned officers from the Grenadier Guards acting as bearers.[38]

Several other New Zealand officers on duty in the United Kingdom in 1914 also served with the Old Contemptibles. They included artillery officer Major Murray Menzies Gard'ner and lieutenants John Lancelot Harcourt Turner and Henry Arthur Davies. Officers in the New Zealand Staff Corps included three captains: Rayner Barrington Smythe, Charles William Melvill and Robert Oswald Chesney. All these officers were posted into British military units in 1914 and served with the Old Contemptibles. Those who did not get to France in 1914 were posted to home defence units. Gard'ner and Smythe were attached to coastal defence units, while Chesney found himself attached to the War Office.[39] Both Chesney and Smythe later served on Gallipoli: Chesney with the New Zealanders, Smythe as a staff officer (GSO 3) with the Anzac Corps.[40]

Charles Melvill was the son of a holder of the Victoria Cross. During the Anglo-Zulu war of 1879, his father, Teignmouth Melvill, had been killed in the action at the battle of Isandlwana while trying to prevent his regiment's colours from being captured by the victorious Zulu. Though born in England and commissioned into the British army in 1897, Charles Melvill emigrated to New Zealand in 1907 to take up the life of a gentleman farmer in the Otago province.[41] The appeal of a sedentary life must have worn off, given that in March 1911 Melvill joined the Staff Corps as one of New Zealand's few full-time officers. In 1914, he was on the staff course at Camberley in Surrey when war was declared. He immediately rejoined his old regiment, the South Lancashires, with which he had served for nine years from 1897. He was posted into the regiment's 3rd Battalion, and in August 1914 the unit sailed to France, where he rejoined his old battalion, the 2nd South Lancashires. Melvill was wounded in November

1914 at Richebourg St-Vaast and sent to England to recover.[42] From January until October 1915 he performed 'light duties' in the United Kingdom, including two stints as a chief instructor — first at the Signalling School, and then at an officers' training school.[43] At the end of October Melvill sailed for Gallipoli, where he transferred to the NZEF. He finished the war commanding one of the New Zealand Division's infantry brigades. In 1924, he was promoted to major general and appointed commandant of New Zealand Military Forces. He died in September 1925 while serving in this role.

New Zealand regular force artillery captains John Turner and Henry Davies were in the United Kingdom in 1914 attending the gunnery staff course. They both mobilised with the Royal Field Artillery and crossed to France in September with the 6th Division. Turner, born in Christchurch in 1891, was stationed in Farnborough in Hampshire at the beginning of the war. After serving 18 months with the BEF with the 40th (Howitzer) Battery, Royal Field Artillery, during which he was awarded the Military Cross, Turner sailed to Egypt to rejoin the NZEF in February 1916. Posted to the New Zealand Field Artillery, he left with the New Zealand Division for France on 5 April 1916. On 14 July, just over three months later and after being mentioned in despatches, he was killed in action near Armentières.[44]

Davies, from Whanganui, served with the BEF in France for six months with the 34th Battery, Royal Field Artillery, before transferring to the NZEF. He left for the Dardanelles in mid-April 1915 and served with the New Zealand artillery on Gallipoli. When the New Zealand Division was formed in Egypt in early 1916, he was posted to the 12th Battery of the 3rd Field Artillery Brigade and sailed to France with his unit on 7 April 1916. Five months later, on 15 September, Davies, who had also been mentioned in despatches, died of wounds near Delville Wood on the Somme.[45]

In January 1914, the British Army Council had advised the New Zealand government that 'in the event of mobilisation' it would be responsible 'for the collecting of all Army Reservists residing in the Dominion and for their despatch to whatever place at the time may be ordered'.[46] With Britain's declaration of war in August 1914, those on the reserve lists received their call-up notices. The *Evening Post* reported that, excluding naval reservists, there were 190 British army reservists then living in New Zealand. The paper worried that those reservists who were married would leave their families 'in distressing circumstances'. Of the 190 men, 60 were married and these unions had produced 89 children. The meagre pay and allowances offered by the imperial authorities meant that 'a hard financial blow is inflicted upon their families, unless they happen to have a decent bank balance, which is very rarely the case'.[47] It would be left to the New Zealand government to make up the difference in pay rates after the war.

However, some were keen to assist. In May 1915 the *Sun* newspaper reported that when war broke out 'two Imperial Reservists from the Wellington Police Force left for England to answer the Empire's call'. Both rejoined their units, the Irish Guards and the 91st Heavy Battery, Royal Garrison Artillery. In their absence, members of the Wellington Police Force 'voluntarily agreed to devote a portion of their pay to assist the families of their two brother constables'. The generous gesture was greatly appreciated by both men.[48]

The navy reservists were sent to Wellington, while those in the army went to Awapuni

Camp in Palmerston North. The first army reservists to leave New Zealand to return to active duty sailed from Wellington on board the *Corinthic* on 7 October 1914. They reached London on 20 November, and many were soon fighting with their units in France.

This first batch of reservists numbered 140 men and included seven officers. Their ages ranged from 20 to 40 years, although most of them, some 99, were aged between 24 and 30.[49] They had been out of uniform for various periods of time, but their military skills remained sharp. On a Saturday in September 1914, the Manawatu Rifle Club challenged the reservists at Awapuni Camp to a shooting contest. Shooting at the Hokowhitu Rifle Range at distances of 200 and 300 yards, the reservists, 'comprising men from most of the best known Imperial regiments', defeated the local shooters by 46 points.[50]

It was not just the British reservists who received their call-up in August 1914. The ships' complements of the first transport vessels to leave New Zealand recorded that not only was the Main Body leaving New Zealand, but some of their allies were on board, too. Sailing with the Main Body in October 1914 were 13 imperial officers and 120 other ranks, returning to their units, and 12 French reservists. In addition, Lieutenant Voevolod Pentke, a reserve artillery officer in the Imperial Russian Army, was also sailing to war.[51] Two French reservists had left New Zealand earlier on the SS *Mamari*: Reni Bielecki and Godefroy Galitzenstein arrived in London on 23 September and immediately crossed the Channel to France.[52]

With many British reservists joining their units and being immediately committed to action in France, casualties were inevitable. Of those who sailed on the *Corinthic* on 7 October, William Tait was killed in action fighting with the King's Own Scottish Borderers. On 19 January 1915, the *Poverty Bay Herald* reported that three army reservists from the region had been killed in action in France and another seriously wounded. Of the four, three were brothers: Sam and William Todd were killed, and R. Todd had lost a leg.[53] All four men had worked for the railways and were described as being 'staunch members' of the Poverty Bay Railway Construction Workers' Union.[54] Private John Walinck, who had left a wife and child in Petone to rejoin his regiment, was killed in action in March 1915. It was the start of the long casualty lists that haunted New Zealand for the duration of the war.

New Zealand civilians who were in the United Kingdom in August 1914 formed another large group who signed up for early service with the BEF on the Western Front. Some had been living in Britain at the time, while others were there temporarily as travellers or students. They were part of the general rush to 'join up' in 1914. As one British unit history recorded of this 'wonderful response' to the call to arms: 'From England, Scotland, Ireland and Wales, from the far corners of the earth, wherever the British Flag waved, men flocked to the recruiting offices.'[55] While technically not part of the Old Contemptibles, some of the New Zealanders who flocked to recruiting offices in the United Kingdom certainly served alongside them.

The Reverend Cuthbert Trelawder MacLean, a curate at a church in Stoke Newington, London and a former New Zealand Territorial Force officer, immediately volunteered in August

Charles William Melvill, a member of the New Zealand Staff Corps, was on a course of instruction in the United Kingdom in 1914. He immediately joined his old unit, the South Lancashires, and served with them in France until his wounding in November 1914. In October 1915 Melvill was sent to Gallipoli, where he transferred back to the New Zealand Expeditionary Force. He later commanded one of the New Zealand Division's brigades on the Western Front. TE PAPA TONGAREWA O.009481

Prior to the introduction of compulsory military training for young men, the volunteer movement was strong in New Zealand. Many of those who joined the British Expeditionary Force in 1914 had been members of the volunteers; Frederick Andrews is one example. These members of the Palmerston North Rifle Volunteers are taking part in a drill competition at the 1909 military tournament, held at the Palmerston North Agricultural and Pastoral Showgrounds. MANAWATŪ HERITAGE, 2010P_A4_004495

1914. MacLean obtained a commission in the Royal Fusiliers and arrived in France in September as part of the regiment's 4th Battalion. In this unit was a fellow New Zealander, Ivan Douglas Scott Orbell, who had been studying architecture in Britain and who had also received a commission in the Royal Fusiliers.

Rhodes scholar Frederick Fisher Miles had just graduated with an MA from Balliol College, Oxford when war was declared. He joined up in September 1914 and obtained a commission in the 9th Battalion of the Gloucester Regiment. Rather than serve with the Old Contemptibles on the Western Front, Miles served with his Gloucestershire battalion from September 1915 to January 1919 in the sideshow of the Salonika campaign.[56]

A year after arriving in Salonika Miles was admitted to No. 29 General Hospital suffering from 'shrapnel wounds in left arm and shoulder'. After treatment there he was declared 'fit for Active Service' again.[57] Frederick Miles survived the war, and at the end of 1920, he and his wife returned to New Zealand as Miles had been offered a teaching position at Wanganui Collegiate School.[58] His request to the War Office to assist with the passage back to New Zealand was turned down.[59]

Former Wanganui Collegiate students William Edward and Rainsford Balcombe-Brown were studying at Oxford University when war was declared. Using the influence of their family, which had strong British army connections and a history of military service, they both secured commissions in the Royal Field Artillery. William was killed in action on 30 June 1915 while serving with his unit in Belgium. Rainsford received a telegram from the War Office informing him of his brother's fate, and was deeply touched by Lord Kitchener's expression of sympathy at the loss of a 'beloved brother'.[60] Rainsford transferred to the Royal Flying Corps in 1916 and was awarded the Military Cross for his services; by autumn 1917, promoted to major, he was commanding 56 Squadron, RAF.[61] When he died in an aerial dogfight on 2 May 1918 Rainsford Balcombe-Brown was the highest-ranking New Zealand airman killed on operations during the war.[62] The historian of New Zealand's air war wrote that 'his death was a severe loss for the squadron'.[63]

Most of these volunteers were successful in obtaining commissions, reflecting their often well-connected middle-class backgrounds. William Oswald Berryman, a young sheep farmer from Oxford, North Canterbury, certainly fell into this category. Berryman was in the United Kingdom with two thoroughbred horses. He used his connections with General Sir Ian Hamilton, who had visited New Zealand as inspector-general of overseas forces in early 1914 and who would command the ill-fated Gallipoli campaign a year later, to secure a commission in the 2nd Dragoons (Royal Scots Greys).[64] John Hugh Allen took a similar path. The son of Minister of Defence Sir James Allen, John was a graduate of Cambridge University and was working as a barrister in London when war was declared. On 25 August he joined the Inns of Court Officer Training Course, and after only a few weeks' training obtained a commission in the Worcester Regiment.

It was 'a great grief' to John Allen that he did not deploy with his battalion to France in 1914 or 1915. Instead, with six other officers, he was sent out to Gallipoli and attached to other units there. Allen was serving with the 1st Battalion of the Essex Regiment and had only been a fortnight on the peninsula at Cape Helles when he was killed in action on 6 June 1915.[65] The New Zealand High Commissioner in London wrote twice to the War Office seeking further information about his death. Its second letter stated that 'numerous enquiries are being made at this Office touching [on] the death of Lieut. J. H. Allen', and that the High Commissioner 'would be glad to receive as early as possible any information which the War Office is kindly able to supply'.[66] The War Office, though, was unable to assist further.[67]

Only about 10 per cent of the New Zealand volunteers in 1914 served in the ranks.[68] Among them was Michael Ryan, who had given up trying to obtain a commission and had joined the King's Liverpool Regiment. Having served with the volunteer unit the Otago Hussars, he originally wanted to join a cavalry regiment, but was told he was too tall and should join a line or infantry unit instead.[69] On arriving in France, Ryan served as a corporal in the 6th Infantry Brigade under Brigadier-General Davies. Another was Joseph Rutledge from Christchurch, who joined the 7th Reserve Battery, Royal Field Artillery as a gunner. His brother George, who had studied engineering at Canterbury College, received a commission as an engineer-lieutenant in the Royal Navy.[70] In July 1915 Joseph at last received a commission in the Royal Field Artillery. Just days later, on 31 July, he was killed in action. His name is recorded on the Menin Gate Memorial to the Missing in Ypres (Ieper), Belgium.[71]

Edmund Boulnois also joined the Army Service Corps in September 1914 as a private soldier. Boulnois served in the ranks until he obtained a commission in the 21st (Service) Battalion, West Yorkshire Regiment, in May 1916.[72] He was killed in action on 23 October while serving

Well-connected New Zealanders easily secured commissions in the British Expeditionary Force. Clockwise from top left: John Allen, Edmund Boulnois, William Edward Balcombe-Brown and Rainsford Balcombe-Brown. All four were killed in action during the war. SELWYN LIBRARY (EDMUND BOULNOIS); AUCKLAND WAR MEMORIAL MUSEUM ONLINE CENOTAPH, KINDLY DONATED BY FAMILY (JOHN ALLEN, WILLIAM EDWARD AND RAINSFORD BALCOMBE-BROWN)

in France.[73] Four years later the New Zealand government and the Boulnois family were still trying to sort out his war gratuity payment.[74]

Boulnois was not the only New Zealander to serve in the ranks with the Old Contemptibles before obtaining a commission. Claude Gladstone Robinson had served as a corporal in a reserve signals company of the Royal Engineers, where he had been a motorcycle rider. He had even provided his own vehicle: a Douglas two-speed motorcycle.[75] Commissioned into the 7th Battalion South Wales Borderers on 15 January 1915, Robinson served with his battalion in France and was killed in action near Amiens on 20 October.[76]

One New Zealander who joined the Old Contemptibles went on to have a distinguished, if short, military career. A Mataura publican and Canterbury representative rugby player, Cecil Frederick George Humphries had been on holiday in Britain with his mother when war broke out in 1914. He immediately joined up as a private soldier in the Army Service Corps, a key support element of the BEF. Although he had no prior military experience, Humphries excelled in his new calling. Within a week he was promoted to lance corporal, and by the end of August he was in France with the rank of sergeant.

On 26 September Humphries transferred to the 1st Manchesters, which had just arrived in France from India. To join a line infantry battalion Humphries had to relinquish the rank and pay of sergeant and start as a private soldier again. He explained the reasons to his commanding officer: 'I am a New Zealander and I want to go back to New Zealand, but I would be ashamed to have to say I had stayed fifty miles behind the firing line.'[77] Humphries must have impressed the British regulars because after six weeks with the 1st Manchesters he was once again a lance corporal. It was just the start. For his bravery at Givenchy in December 1914 Humphries was awarded the Distinguished Conduct Medal (DCM), the first to be awarded to a New Zealander in the war.[78] Humphries was lucky to survive this 'bust up', as he called it, as he was hit several times but not hurt. Humphries wrote to a friend in Waimate:

> I have sent my shirt to the mater [his mother] as a souvenir. It has eight holes in the tail (please don't think I was running away), but I happened to be leaning over a poor chap who had 'stopped one,' when they turned the machine gun on to me, and God knows how I am here with a whole skin.[79]

After this action Cecil Humphries received a field promotion to the rank of sergeant.

Humphries was wounded in the fighting at Neuve Chapelle in March 1915, and while recovering in hospital he was recommended for an officer's commission. In June that year, commissioned as a second lieutenant, Humphries was posted to the 12th Battalion of the Highland Light Infantry (HLI); in September he was promoted to the rank of captain. Fighting with his battalion on the Somme in August 1916, Humphries was shot through the muscles of his right arm. His recovery took some time and he was posted to recruiting and service units in late 1916 and 1917. As an officer in 10th Labour Company, he was recognised for saving a burning ammunition train at Kemmel Hill in Belgium on 7 June 1917. For this 'remarkably gallant piece of work . . . carried out under a hail of shell and fragments' Humphries was awarded a Military

Cross.[80] He received his award from the king at Buckingham Palace on 31 October.

Humphries served most of 1917 with 10th Labour Company but was eventually transferred to the Duke of Cornwall's Light Infantry (DCLI), and served with this battalion in Italy. Back on the Western Front from April 1918, Humphries was promoted to the rank of major and received a bar to his Military Cross. He was promoted again, to acting lieutenant colonel, and remained in that rank with the DCLI for two months. In mid-1918 he was ordered to take command of the 1st Battalion of the Norfolk Regiment. On 21 August 1918 the 1st Norfolks took part in a successful attack that captured the high ground in front of the village of Achiet-le-Petit, a prized position that overlooked much of this new Somme battlefield. The battalion's war diary recorded the Germans' response: 'Enemy bombardment of the position very heavy and his Machine Guns very active about 12 noon.' The next entry reads: 'Lt Col C. F. G. Humphries M.C., D.C.M. and Capt G. C. Tyler (adjt) wounded by shellfire and died one hour later.'[81]

Cecil Humphries was posthumously awarded the Distinguished Service Order, which added to his MC and bar, DCM and four mentions in despatches. He may also have been recommended for the Victoria Cross.[82] He was one of the most decorated New Zealanders to serve on the Western Front. Little wonder that Humphries' brigadier wrote in a letter of condolence to his mother, saying that her son 'was without exception the bravest man I ever saw'.[83] Writing about New Zealanders in the Second World War, historian Michael King made the observation that there were 'hundreds of examples of mild-mannered civilians who discovered that, faced with wartime conditions . . . [they were] possessed of great courage and considerable military skills'.[84] This was also true for the First World War, and Cecil Humphries is a prime example.

Ropata Kereti's experience was most unusual. He had gone to Britain with Makereti (Maggie) Papakura's 40-strong Māori troupe for the Festival of Empire celebrations in 1911. When 17 members of the troupe returned home in June 1913 after what the newspapers described as 'a rather unfortunate experience', Kereti was one of many who stayed on in the United Kingdom.[85] The troupe's misfortune included the death of one of its members, and the whole venture was 'beset by financial problems'.[86] In 1914, Kereti joined a Middlesex Regiment battalion and served with it on the Western Front. He survived the experience, and in May 1918 the *New Zealand Herald* reported that he was returning to New Zealand with other returned soldiers.[87]

Many New Zealanders joined King Edward's Horse (The King's Overseas Dominions Regiment) with the expectation of getting into the action in France very quickly. They were to have a frustrating wait, as the regiment, which had been formed as a unit of the Imperial Yeomanry for service in the South African War, was a unit of the Special Reserve in 1914. It did not leave for France until April 1915.

One young New Zealander could not wait that long, and his impatience would cost him his life. James Dilworth Mossman from Gisborne was visiting England when war was declared and immediately enlisted with King Edward's Horse. Not content to sit around in England, Mossman transferred to another unit in the BEF and, after training at Bulford on Salisbury Plain, was sent to Egypt. While in Egypt Mossman somehow managed to have himself attached to the Auckland Mounted Rifles and served with them on Gallipoli.[88] Reaching the peninsula in May and fighting as infantry, Mossman became one of the unit's first casualties when he was

above Cecil Frederick George Humphries was on holiday in the United Kingdom with his mother when war was declared. He immediately joined the British Expeditionary Force. Despite having no previous military experience, Humphries excelled as a soldier and rose from private to the rank of lieutenant colonel. Humphries was killed in action leading his battalion on 21 August 1918. ARCHIVES NEW ZEALAND, TE RUA MAHARA O TE KĀWANATANGA, F1782

right Lieutenant John William Pinckney of Christchurch went missing in action on 9 April 1918. He was last seen almost single-handedly defending a bridge during a German advance. In September 1919, the British War Office concluded that he had been killed in action. CHRIST'S COLLEGE ARCHIVES

killed in action on 19 May. There was a further tragedy for the Mossman family that year. While he was in Egypt James had met his brother Thomas, who had left New Zealand with the Second Reinforcements. Thomas Mossman, serving with the Otago Mounted Rifles, died from disease in Egypt on 12 April 1915.[89] The fatal illness was reported as bronchitis and pneumonia.[90]

In France, King Edward's Horse was used as divisional and corps cavalry and its first military action was at Loos. The regiment drew almost entirely on men from the British dominions, and by December 1914 its ranks included 45 New Zealanders. They included the newly commissioned Cheviot Dillon Bell, son of the first New Zealand-born prime minister, Francis Bell. Guy Russell was another New Zealander commissioned in the regiment, while Lionel Martyn Abraham from Palmerston North joined as a corporal.[91] As one historian has pointed out, King Edward's Horse was

> [a] chic regiment made up almost wholly of young gentlemen who had been studying at Oxford or Cambridge. Forty or more other young moneyed men from the dominion were in the regiment, ranging from two sons of the Hellaby family of Auckland all the way down the length of the islands to a son of the landed Pinckney family of Southland.[92]

While Cheviot Bell later transferred to the 10th Hussars and then the RAF, his brother, the former member of Parliament William Henry Dillon Bell, also joined King Edward's Horse. In the fighting around Passchendaele Ridge the regiment was used as the cavalry arm of 18 Corps, and William was killed in action during a German counter-attack. Another New Zealand officer, Lieutenant John William Pinckney, was killed in the fighting around La Bassée Canal in April 1918. The former Christ's College old boy went missing in action, having been 'last seen defending a bridge during the German advance when they broke through the Portuguese'.[93] It was not until 30 September 1919 that the British Army Council was able to conclude that Pinckney was 'dead, and that his death occurred on or since the 9th day of April 1918'.[94]

New Zealander Major Guy Russell was awarded the DSO and mentioned in despatches three times while serving with King Edward's Horse. He also commanded the regiment when the commanding officer was on leave or other duties. In November 1918 the regiment was providing a cavalry screen for three army corps and prided itself that it 'was actually the last British unit engaged with the enemy when the "bell rang"'.[95] One New Zealander, Trooper Samuel Roy Williams from the Waipawa district in Hawke's Bay, also a Wanganui Collegiate old boy, had been studying science at Cambridge in August 1914. He immediately joined King Edward's Horse and served with it throughout the war, then in 1919 returned to Cambridge to complete his degree.[96]

Another New Zealander who joined King Edward's Horse in 1914 was sheep farmer Theodore Arthur Izard. Despite having graduated from Sandhurst Military Academy in 1901 and having 10 years of service with Mounted Rifles units in New Zealand, Izard was initially appointed as a lance corporal.[97] The situation was soon remedied, and on 6 December 1914 Izard was appointed to the rank of second lieutenant. He served with the 1st Regiment, King Edward's Horse until April 1918 when, having relinquished the rank of acting captain, he transferred to the Machine Gun Corps and served with this formation until the end of the war.[98] In early 1919, after surviving a bout of influenza and jaundice, Izard applied to the Colonial Office for employment as a public servant.[99]

Two sons of the prominent and wealthy Remuera Hellaby family, who had made their money in the meat and abattoir industry, joined King Edward's Horse. A third son, Frederick Allan Hellaby, took another route. A married university student in 1914, Frederick joined the 1st Battalion of the Devonshire Regiment,[100] and served with this standard line infantry battalion until the end of 1915, when he transferred to the Machine Gun Corps. His service record was impressive. He was awarded the MC and would be twice mentioned in despatches. Frederick Hellaby ended the war as a temporary major, second in command of 63 Battalion, Machine Gun Corps.[101] He was demobilised in the United Kingdom in February 1919.

Several New Zealanders also joined a formation especially created for service in the First World War: the Royal Naval Division (RND). Raised and organised primarily by First Lord of the Admiralty Winston Churchill, the RND consisted of two brigades of volunteers and a brigade of Royal Marines, and it offered one of 'relatively few opportunities for volunteers to get into active units quickly at the beginning of the war'.[102] Like King Edward's Horse, the RND could be regarded as a 'chic' formation, given that it attracted men from the intellectual and social elite, including poet Rupert Brooke and Arthur Asquith, third son of British prime minister H. H. Asquith. Major George Richardson, who since 1913 had been the New Zealand representative at the War Office, was the RND's initial deputy adjutant and quartermaster-general. He was promoted to lieutenant colonel.

It was Churchill who helped New Zealander Bernard Freyberg, a Wellington-educated dentist and future war hero, secure a commission in the RND. As Freyberg's biographer notes, this commission was 'the turning point of Freyberg's life'.[103] Bernard's eldest brother, South African War veteran Oscar Freyberg, was also commissioned in the RND in September 1914, but would die of wounds inflicted on Gallipoli in the Third Battle of Krithia on 4 June 1915. On that day Oscar's Collingwood Battalion suffered more than 500

When war was declared in 1914 New Zealand did not have any permanent military camps.Local racecourses provided the most easily converted accommodation, and Awapuni at Palmerston North was used in this role for the duration of the war. This postcard shows soldiers exercising at Awapuni in 1915. MANAWATŪ HERITAGE, 2007P_A93_WAR_0017

casualties, including 16 officers killed and eight more wounded. By the evening of 4 June, 'the Collingwood Battalion literally ceased to exist'.[104]

Many years later, after a 12-day visit to New Zealand in early 1940 preparing another New Zealand division for war service, Freyberg reflected on his departure for Gallipoli in February 1915. In his farewell speech, which was broadcast on radio, Freyberg described the unique make-up of the RND:

> War is a hard and an unpleasant business. No amount of talking can make it otherwise. If you must go to war, it is important to pick your comrades well. I believe I am the luckiest man in the world. I remember going out to Gallipoli in February 1915 on the troop ship *Grantully Castle*, and I had probably the most distinguished lot of young officers that any company commander ever left the shores of Great Britain [with]. I had Charles Lister, a great classical scholar who would have risen to the highest positions in the diplomatic service. I had Patrick Shaw-Stewart, possibly one of the greatest classical scholars for a century, a young man who at the age of 27 was Managing Director of Barings Bank, of whom Mr Asquith and Lord Balfour said, 'If this man lives, there's nothing to stop him, he'll be Prime Minister of England'. And my third subaltern was our great national poet, Rupert Brooke. And those three men were all killed early on in the war.[105]

When he addressed the pupils of Wellington College on an Anzac Day after the Second World War, the war hero was reduced to tears by the memory of the loss of his brother and friends on Gallipoli.[106]

Other New Zealanders to join the RND in 1914 included South African War veteran D'Arcy Chaytor and Wellington department store manager Albert Corrigan. In September 1914, the Royal Marine Brigade was deployed to Belgium, and Chaytor was its base commander at Dunkirk. Major Albert Corrigan was deployed on a staff mission with the Belgian Cycle Corps and was there when the initial German thrust through Belgium was checked by the French and Belgian armies at Nieuport. Corrigan described Nieuport after its shelling by German heavy artillery as 'a picture of desolation. Its cobble streets were torn with shells, its buildings wrecked, and it was totally deserted by the inhabitants.'[107] Albert Corrigan was undoubtedly the first New Zealander to come under heavy artillery fire. It was an unnerving experience and 'fearful to look at'. He was also one of the first to witness the new role of aircraft in this war. He later recalled: 'The buzz of aeroplanes never ceased the whole day long. They circle overhead unceasingly in great flocks.'[108] Corrigan's war did not last long. In May 1909 the *New Zealand Free Lance* featured an article on 'The Genial Skipper of the D.I.C. Wellington' alongside a sketch of the portly, middle-aged Albert Corrigan.[109] After just two months' service on the Western Front, cut short probably by ill health, he was discharged and on his way back to New Zealand.[110]

The rest of the RND joined the marines in the attempt to defend the important fortress city of Antwerp during early October 1914. The naval brigades had received very little training, and they lacked engineers and vital equipment such as signals, artillery, field ambulances and even

Oscar Freyberg (above), like his famous younger brother Bernard (below), was commissioned into the Royal Naval Division. Oscar was killed in the fighting around Krithia, Gallipoli, on 4 June 1915. In a single day of fighting, his battalion 'literally ceased to exist'. Bernard Freyberg was awarded the Victoria Cross for holding the village of Beaucourt against fierce German counter-attacks in November 1916. WEEKLY NEWS, 24 JUNE 1915; NATIONAL MUSEUM OF THE ROYAL NEW ZEALAND NAVY, APP0007

a divisional headquarters. Emphasising the ad hoc nature of this venture, the two brigades had received just 10 hours' notice to move. They would be the first British non-regular troops to see military action in the First World War. During the fighting at Antwerp, Bernard Freyberg received the first of his many war wounds when he was badly burned on one hand after touching electrified barbed wire. The injury was painful but not life-threatening, unlike some of his later wounds. His Admiralty service record described the wound as 'slight', but the scars from the burns and lacerations 'stayed with him the rest of his life'.[111] Freyberg later served with the RND on Gallipoli, where his 'conspicuous gallantry during the landing operations' resulted in the award of the first of four DSOs. In the fighting on the Somme in November 1916 Freyberg earned the Victoria Cross for what his commanding general described as 'probably the most distinguished personal act of the war'.[112] Despite being wounded four times, Freyberg had led the remnants of two shattered infantry brigades to capture and hold the village of Beaucourt against determined German counter-attacks. On Gallipoli Freyberg had been wounded twice. The second, incurred on 20 July 1915, was recorded as 'a severe shrapnel wound in abdominal wall'.[113] Its rupture in July 1963 would cause his death.[114]

The defence of Antwerp, one of Churchill's bright if impractical ideas, was a forlorn attempt. It was costly, too. The RND had 900 men taken as prisoners by the Germans and a further 2000 interned in neutral Holland. One of those to suffer this relatively fortunate fate was New Zealander Arthur Richardson, whose active war effort lasted less than the two weeks' training he had received. Richardson had been part of the Collingwood Battalion, which had reached the Dutch border 'worn out from want of food and sleep'. In Holland the internees were well looked after, with the Dutch providing them with plenty of food, and arranging football matches and film shows twice a week.[115] They stayed in Holland for the duration of the war.

Another New Zealander to serve with the RND was Anthony Frederick Wilding, who crossed the Channel on 6 October as part of a makeshift unit of armoured cars. Wilding, described by historian Stevan Eldred-Grigg as the 'tall blond son of a well-to-do Canterbury family and one of the leading tennis stars in the world', had been in the United States in August 1914 competing with his tennis partner in the Davis Cup.[116] When he returned to the United Kingdom as an international sportsman Wilding came under immense pressure to join up and play 'the greater game'. He willingly accepted an invitation from Churchill to join the fledgling RND, even though he expressed some misgivings about the patriotic fervour and the social pressure on young men to enlist. 'I verily believe that it would take a braver man to stand down than become a soldier,' he wrote to his mother in late September.[117]

Despite getting to France early, and at a desperate time for the BEF, Wilding's armoured cars were an orphan unit that he described as 'nobody's children'. The cars did some reconnaissance that Wilding found to be 'the most intensely interesting work I have ever done'. He 'love[d] this life' and described himself as 'feeling very fit'. The good times ended, however, with the development of trench warfare. Wilding wrote at the end of 1914 that the stalemate was 'a little dull' and, given the static positions, that there was 'no work at all for armoured cars'.[118] A week's leave in March 1915 offered some respite. At the end of it he wrote to his mother: 'I quite look forward in a way to getting back though the whole war disgusts me to death.'[119]

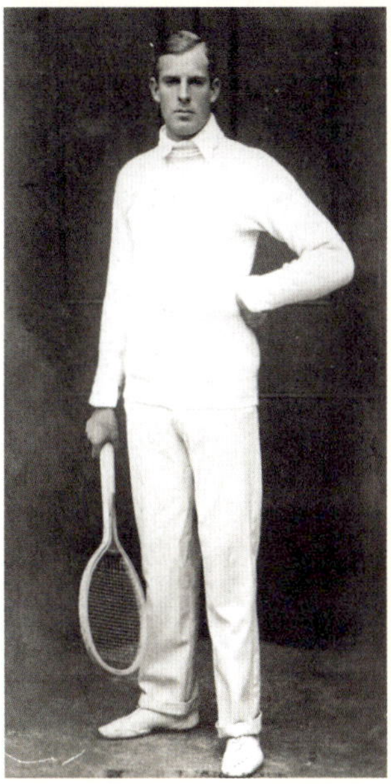

clockwise from top Tennis star Anthony Wilding had serious misgivings about the war, but came under immense pressure to join up. He served with an armoured car unit of the Royal Naval Division and was killed in action at Aubers Ridge, near Arras, in May 1915. Here he is shown driving a Rolls-Royce armoured car at Dunkirk, France, in April 1915; on a motorcycle at Land's End in 1912; and in his tennis whites circa 1910. ALEXANDER TURNBULL LIBRARY, 1/2-049756-F, 1/2-049754-F, MNZ-0971-1/4-F

One of New Zealand's most gifted athletes, Wilding was killed by shellfire at Aubers Ridge on the evening of 9 May 1915. The battle was an unmitigated disaster for the BEF: he was one of more than 10,000 British dead at Aubers 'without an inch of territory gained'.[120]

A number of New Zealand doctors and medical students were in the United Kingdom in 1914, and many immediately offered their services once war had been declared. An article in the *Press* in May 1915 claimed that 'the honour of being the first New Zealander in France' belonged to Colonel Henry Owen Knox of the Army Service Corps. It also drew attention to 14 doctors serving in the Royal Army Medical Corps (RAMC) who had sailed with the BEF in August 1914. Of these, William Henry Johnston and Harrolde Bedford George Russell crossed to France with the first detachment of the BEF to help staff No. 1 General Hospital. Among the 14 were Cyril James Anthony Griffin, Charles William Littlejohn, Andrew Robert Dillon Carbery and Arthur Anderson Martin, who 'were all very early in the field'.[121]

Martin was one of the most notable examples of these doctors. A veteran of the South African War, he was the senior surgeon at Palmerston North Hospital and one of New Zealand's leading cancer specialists. In early August 1914 Arthur Martin was in Aberdeen, Scotland, attending the annual general meeting of the British Medical Association. The delegates knew something was seriously amiss when their German colleagues were suddenly withdrawn from the meeting after being ordered to take an urgent passage home.[122] The British declaration of war soon followed, and the next day Martin travelled to London to offer his services to the War Office.

Martin was offered a commission as a temporary lieutenant in the RAMC. Though disappointed with and slightly offended by his lowly rank, the 38-year-old accepted the commission and was soon working in France with the 15th Field Ambulance. He observed firsthand the battles of the Marne and First Ypres, and he witnessed the aftermath of several German atrocities committed in France and Belgium, which he described as 'hellish deeds [of] nauseous and disgusting frightfulness'.[123] While in France Martin served at a casualty clearing station near Béthune and then served as a specialist surgeon at Rouen.

Martin was shocked by the sheer destructiveness of modern warfare and by how badly prepared the British military medical authorities were to meet this new challenge. The field ambulances lacked most vital equipment and the knowledge of how best to treat serious war wounds. He could not believe that in 1914 the RAMC was still using horse-drawn ambulances, just as it had done during the wars against Napoleon a century earlier. Indeed, the medical corps went to war in 1914 without a single motor ambulance. Had they been used, 'Many lives would have been saved, and much suffering would have been avoided,' he wrote.[124] Not one to tolerate this inefficiency and incompetence, he soon made himself unpopular by lobbying for change. He wrote to several influential people in the United Kingdom, especially stressing the need for modern equipment, such as motorised ambulances. One of his letters eventually reached Lord Kitchener, the British war hero and, from August 1914, Britain's secretary of state for war. Motorised ambulances and other essential equipment were soon on their way to France.[125]

It probably came as some relief to the RAMC when, in early 1915, after eight months of

Dr Arthur Anderson Martin was a senior surgeon at the Palmerston North Hospital and a South African War veteran. In August 1914, Martin was in Scotland attending a general meeting of the British Medical Association. On the outbreak of war he immediately offered his services to the Royal Army Medical Corps and was given a temporary commission. The outspoken Martin soon made himself unpopular with his criticisms of outdated medical procedures and obsolete equipment used by the RAMC.
MANAWATŪ HERITAGE, 2007P_PI244_WAR_0024

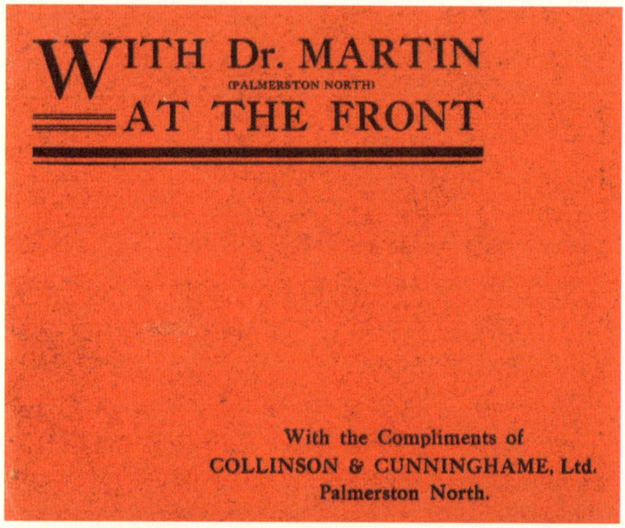

above Dr Arthur Martin was something of a local hero in Palmerston North. The town's department store, Collinson & Cunninghame Ltd, published a booklet about Martin's experiences at the front. It was given free to their customers. MANAWATŪ HERITAGE, 2018PA_A175_483_024572

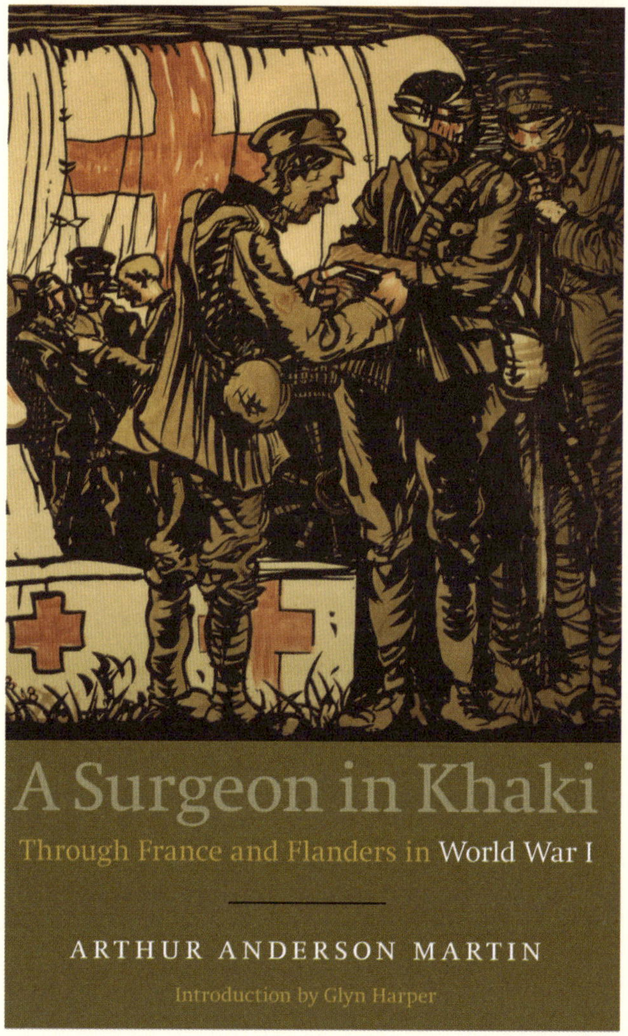

right After being released from the Royal Army Medical Corps, and while travelling back to New Zealand, Arthur Martin wrote a detailed account of his time with the British Expeditionary Force. Published in 1916, the year he was killed in action, *A Surgeon in Khaki* is regarded as a classic account of frontline medical conditions in the early months of the war. This is the cover of the 2011 edition. NEBRASKA UNIVERSITY PRESS

service in France and Belgium, Martin was discharged home. Between the time of his release from the RAMC and his arrival in New Zealand, he wrote an account of his experiences as a wartime surgeon. *A Surgeon in Khaki*, published in 1916, was an immediate success, and is still regarded as 'a classic account of frontline medical conditions and battlefield surgery in the early months of the First World War'.[126]

Back in New Zealand, Martin was appointed the medical member of a commission investigating conditions at Trentham Military Camp in Upper Hutt, which had experienced several outbreaks of disease that had killed more than 30 soldiers. After this investigation was completed, Martin returned briefly to Palmerston North before he again sailed for France, now as a senior major with the 3rd Field Ambulance, attached to the New Zealand Rifle Brigade.

In *A Surgeon in Khaki* Martin stressed the need for having modern equipment and surgical capability as close to the battlefield as possible; the first treatment given to a seriously wounded man, he believed, was critical to his chances of survival. This doctrine was certainly correct, but on 15 September 1916 it was to cost Martin his life. He was mortally wounded while treating wounded soldiers in the front line near Flers village. 'He was bold, resolute, resourceful and brave to a fault . . . we could ill afford to lose him,' noted the New Zealand medical history of the war.[127] Martin was one of five medical officer casualties in the New Zealand Rifle Brigade that day, and consequently the senior medical officer of the division issued orders countering Martin's doctrine. Doctors were to avoid unnecessary risk and were not to proceed beyond their advanced dressing stations except under special circumstances.[128] It was a more cautious approach, but men of Martin's skill, dedication and courage were hard to replace.

Arthur Martin was one of at least 16 New Zealanders to serve with the RAMC in the early months of the war.[129] Others included Edward Aitkin Seagar, Ivan Stuart Wilson, Andrew Carbery (later the historian of the NZEF medical services), William Johnston and Charles Cochrane Iles. Johnston, a graduate of Otago University who had practised for a time in the Wairarapa, was in Edinburgh in August 1914. A September letter to his parents records his sense of shock at the high number of casualties being suffered and the severity of the wounds. He described the British casualties as being 'enormous so far — 18,000 in six weeks'. The casualties among the Germans were also 'awful. The soldiers say it makes them sick to see the way they fall.' Johnston recorded the reality of conditions on the Western Front with remarkable frankness: 'Life is cheap. Blood is spilt like water,' he wrote.[130]

Among the medical volunteers was 39-year-old ophthalmologist Angus McNab (sometimes spelt MacNab). When war was declared, Invercargill-born McNab, whose brother was a Cabinet minister in William Massey's Reform government, immediately volunteered for military service. His tragic fate will be covered later in this chapter.[131]

New Zealand women also joined various medical organisations, including those sponsored by well-connected and well-resourced private civilians. Two New Zealand nurses, Jessie Elizabeth McLeod and Theresa Butler, and medical student Eric Croft were part of a 41-strong party that crossed the Channel on 15 August with the St John Ambulance Association. All three were taken prisoner when the Germans entered Brussels, and for a time they nursed wounded German soldiers. They were kept prisoner for two months before the intervention of the US ambassador secured their release. They returned to England 'after a dangerous and exhausting journey that included detention by a German commander convinced they were spies and an appalling Channel crossing'.[132] It also meant travelling 'a very circuitous route' through Belgium, Germany, Denmark, Norway and Sweden.[133] Four days after reaching London, Croft, with three others, was sent to work at an army hospital near Ypres, where he remained until November; in December he was working at an Indian Hospital in France.[134]

In September 1915, Croft was commissioned into the Royal Field Artillery and served on the Western Front. The following June, he was awarded the Military Cross for his gallantry in helping capture a German raiding party of 36 men.[135] Early in 1917 Croft was posted to serve with the Mediterranean Expeditionary Force, where he was promoted to the rank of captain. In November of that year he was wounded and suffered 'severe gas shell poisoning',[136] and was sent back to the United Kingdom to recover. His health on the mend, Eric Croft became engaged to Iris Jardine, the daughter of a prominent British member of Parliament. Two days before his wedding Croft had dinner at the Piccadilly Grill Room in London with two friends from his medical student days. Climbing some stairs after dinner, he slipped and fell. Eric Croft died of his injuries at the Charing Cross Hospital some hours later.[137] An Otago paper headline summed up the incident succinctly: 'CAPTAIN ERIC CROFT, M.C. A Tragic End in London.'[138]

Jessie McLeod, who had been born in Invercargill and had trained as a midwife at Dunedin Hospital, had also been held prisoner with Croft in 1914. Upon reaching England and after a brief holiday in Scotland, McLeod joined Queen Alexandra's Imperial Military Nursing Service Reserve (QAIMNSR) on 6 January 1915 and served with it until her contract terminated in February 1919. She spent most of this time in France, where she nursed in very stressful conditions. During the Battle of Neuve Chapelle in March 1915 there was not even time to change bedsheets between patients. McLeod wrote of this ordeal:

> I cannot describe the awfulness of those days. The moaning, the groaning, the shrieking, when the dressings were being done were simply appalling. You understand that these men, besides being badly wounded, were in a shocking nervous state. They tried so hard, too, to keep quiet, poor fellows, but it was too much for most of them.[139]

Theresa Butler (in window) was in Belgium in August 1914 nursing with the St John Ambulance Association. Two other New Zealanders were serving in her unit, and all three were taken prisoner when the Germans captured Brussels. It took two months for the US ambassador to secure their release. AUCKLAND WAR MEMORIAL MUSEUM TĀMAKI PAENGA HIRA, PH-2017-2-2-P28-4

As New Zealand nursing historian Sherayl McNabb has acknowledged, McLeod's horrific experience deeply 'affected her and she saw the futility of the war'.[140]

In April 1918 McLeod was trained in the administration of anaesthetics at No. 3 Canadian General Hospital and at No. 64 Casualty Clearing Station in France, where she was assessed as 'competent to act as an Anaesthetist'.[141] This made her part of a select group of only seven New Zealand nurses who were specifically trained as anaesthetists. McLeod returned home at the end of 1919 and continued to nurse until her retirement in 1938. Her last 15 years' nursing were as the assistant matron at the Cashmere Hills sanatorium in Christchurch.[142]

Another New Zealand nurse, Muriel Edna Bartlett, went to Namur in Belgium with a group of nurses organised by the Duchess of Sutherland. Beatrice Eleanor Dormer Maunder, from the lower Rangitīkei, also went to Belgium and worked with refugees in Ostend before the German advance forced a move to Rouen, where she set up a hospital for wounded Belgian soldiers. Other New Zealand nurses working in France and Belgium in 1914 included Gertrude Amy Fisher (Red Cross) and Nurse Beasley (Women's Emergency Service Corps). Margaret Hitchcock, Lily Lind, Ella Kate Cooke and Mary Audley Eaddy all served with the French Flag Nursing Corps, which had been established by the French War Ministry in an attempt to help staff the overworked French military hospitals. Agnes Barclay and Nina May Palmer served in civilian hospitals. Others joined British military organisations. Laura Elizabeth James was the first serving with the QAIMNSR. She crossed to France in late August 1914 and served with the No. 12 British General Hospital at Rouen. Eva Clare Jordan also joined the QAIMNSR and worked at a casualty clearing station. Another New Zealand nurse, Edith Maud Fairchild, served at a hospital near Boulogne and then on hospital trains taking British wounded back home.

Medical military service was not confined to the Western Front. Dr William Allan Chapple MP, born in Alexandra in Central Otago, was appointed a temporary major in the RAMC. In 1914, he was in charge of a 10-coach train and 14 staff who distributed the wounded docking at Southampton to various military hospitals in the United Kingdom. Chapple's medical train included bathrooms, a pharmacy and an operating room, and up to April 1915 it allocated more than 5000 wounded men to hospitals between Plymouth and Aberdeen.[143] This was not an isolated example, either. In 1914 Dr Roy McIntosh Muir of Wellington was appointed the senior casualty surgeon at the Royal Infirmary Home in Hull, where batches of wounded from the Western Front were arriving each day. When Muir arrived at the Infirmary Home, he was surprised to learn that four of the five medical staff there were from New Zealand. The other three were house surgeon Dr Louis Levy, house physician Dr Leslie Fraser Eiloart Jeffcoat, and junior house physician Dr Frank Johnston.[144] With so many wounded arriving, the medical staff at the Infirmary Home were working 16 to 18 hours a day.

The heavy casualties in the first months of the war were 'profoundly shocking' both to those doing the fighting and to their home communities.[145] While the BEF's 1914 casualties were vastly outnumbered by those of Germany, France, Austria, Russia and Serbia, they were nevertheless immensely significant to the United Kingdom and its dominions. By the end of 1914 the BEF had deployed 270,000 soldiers to the Western Front. Since August 1914 it had lost 16,200 officers and men killed and 47,707 wounded, with a further 16,746 missing or taken prisoner.[146] These were sobering figures for an empire used to small wars, policing actions and limited casualties, with most killed by disease rather than enemy action. *Catastrophe*, the title of historian Max Hastings' book about 1914, aptly evokes the mood. With so many untrained and inexperienced New Zealanders offering their services in the first months of the war, it was to be expected that some, especially those serving in frontline units, would not survive.

The first New Zealand casualties occurred during the fighting in August around Mons. This dubious distinction belonged to Captain Harold Sutton Williams from Napier, who was serving with the Dorsetshire Regiment, and Corporal Michael Thomas Ryan from Ophir, with The King's Liverpool Regiment. Both were wounded. The *Poverty Bay Herald* was adamant that Ryan was 'the first New Zealander wounded in the war'. At Mons on 23 August Ryan was 'one of the first hit — a shrapnel bullet passing through my left calf'. The wound was big enough to insert two fingers into it, and the sensation was like 'a blow with a hot piece of iron' — but Ryan was still able, with some assistance, to march the 10 miles to Pont au Sommes, where he was sent by train to a field hospital at Rouen.[147] He wrote back to a friend in New Zealand that he was 'very lucky' to have only a flesh wound as 'several of our people are having their last sleep in the cornfields of Northern France and Belgium'.[148]

Lieutenant Algernon Donald Douglas McLean, from a prominent Hawke's Bay family, served with the 1st Battalion of the Cameron Highlanders. During the fighting in the First Battle of Ypres in Belgium he was shot through the leg, the bullet entering just below his knee. Held prisoner by the Germans overnight, McLean was lucky not to be killed. A German officer threatened to shoot him, but a German private, who had been a college professor, 'was exceptionally kind'. McLean and the other wounded of his battalion were recovered the next morning when the British recaptured the lost ground. McLean's Cameron Highlanders had 'a particularly bad time' during First Ypres. By the end of the battle, all but one of its officers had become casualties.[149]

One New Zealander serving with the Old Contemptibles was taken prisoner in October 1914 and remained in captivity for the duration of the war. He was Captain Thomas Edmund Sotheron-Estcourt, who was serving with the famed 2nd Dragoons of the Royal Scots Greys. After the war, the Army Council investigated the circumstances of all BEF officers captured during the war to ascertain whether they had surrendered too easily or could be otherwise blamed for what happened. In his statement to the Army Council, Sotheron-Estcourt explained the circumstances of his capture. When carrying out a reconnaissance of the village of Rebais, his troop was cut off from his cavalry brigade and surrounded by German infantry and a squadron of German cavalry. Sotheron-Estcourt tried to escape, but in vain:

> Owing to the enclosed nature of the country round REBAIS it was impossible to proceed across the country. The village square at REBAIS was livid with German dismounted troops. I decided to gallop through the square, hoping the Germans would not be able to fire for fear of hitting their own men on the opposite side of the square. In this I was

> right, as several Germans were thus hit. About ½ way across the square my horse was hit & came down. I lost consciousness owing to the fall, & my right knee was also injured. On recovering consciousness I found myself being pulled up by 2 Germans, one of whom in English summoned me to surrender, which I did, escape under the circumstances being impossible.[150]

The Army Council agreed, concluding that 'no blame attaches to him in the matter'.[151] No other finding was possible, but Sotheron-Estcourt resigned his commission two months later.[152]

The severity of the fighting caught New Zealander Lieutenant Patrick Kinloch Campbell, who was serving in the 1st Battalion of the Black Watch. During the First Battle of the Aisne in September 1914, Campbell was wounded three times, his battalion's commanding officer and two other officers were killed, and a further 11 officers were wounded. Campbell's servant, or batman, was also badly wounded.[153] Lieutenant Oliver Garsia, who was serving in the Duke of Cornwall's Light Infantry, died of wounds on 18 September.[154] His unit had deployed so quickly to France that in early August he had been forced to buy boots for some of his men 'out of my own pocket' and to seek reimbursement later.[155] Oliver Garsia was probably the first New Zealand fatality on the Western Front.[156] Two more fatalities soon followed: Privates Robert Henry Lewis from Westport, serving in the 1st Battalion of The King's Liverpool Regiment, and William Donovan from Dunedin, 1st Battalion of the Devonshire Regiment.

Others who were killed in action or died of wounds in 1914 include: Lieutenant Frederick George Andrews, 4th Battalion, The King's Liverpool Regiment; Lieutenant Edward Wynne Chapman, 3rd Dragoon Guards; Second Lieutenant Gilbert Colin Cunninghame Ferrier, 7th Battalion, Royal Fusiliers; Second Lieutenant Robert Francis McLean Gee, 3rd Battalion, Wiltshire Regiment; Second Lieutenant Ivan Orbell, 7th Battalion, Royal Fusiliers; Captain Walter Russell, 2nd Battalion, Northamptonshire Regiment; and Captain Oliver Steele, 1st Battalion, Royal Berkshire Regiment.

Most were killed over the course of six days in late October, during the murderous First Battle of Ypres. First to die was Frederick Andrews, who had previously held a commission in the Christchurch Rifle Volunteers for four years, and was reported killed in action on 21 October.[157] Andrews had named his sister Laura as his next of kin. In what is a very common feature of the files of New Zealanders killed while serving with another nation's military, Laura wrote to the War Office pleading for more information about her brother's death: 'If any further particulars should come to hand later on I shall be most grateful if you will inform me.'[158] The War Office assured Laura that any new information would be communicated to her, but nothing more was heard.

There was anguish, too, for the family of Ivan Orbell, who was reported missing in action on 30 October.[159] In early 1915 Orbell's sister Ruth wrote to the War Office, asking what steps had been taken to trace the fate of those who went missing. 'It seems very hard,' she wrote, 'that one should give their dearest and best and never know whether he be alive or what has become of him.'[160] Ruth's enquiries were joined by those made by the New Zealand High Commissioner in London, who informed the War Office that the Orbells were 'a highly respected New Zealand family and that the High Commissioner trusts you will be able to communicate some news regarding the missing officer'.[161] The War Office made a 'special enquiry', which confirmed that it was likely that Orbell had been killed in action.[162]

But the matter did not end there. The High Commissioner made further enquiries about Orbell in 1915, noting that the 'suspense is naturally very trying to his mother', and also sought to obtain Orbell's possessions for the family, which had only received a returned letter.[163] In August 1915 Ruth wrote again to the War Office, saying that after 10 months without news 'I know if my poor brother were alive I should most certainly have heard from him long ere this'. She wrote that the family was now 'anxious to get his affairs settled as we shall be returning to New Zealand shortly'.[164] The War Office agreed to assist the family. The office could not provide a formal death certificate, but it wrote stating that after such a period of time and with one witness statement about the severity of Orbell's wound 'the Army Council are regretfully constrained to conclude that this officer is dead and that death occurred on or since the 25th day of October 1914'.[165]

New Zealander and Old Contemptible Frederick Neville Houston, who had been wounded in 1914 and again in 1915, went missing on a day of infamy: 1 July 1916, the opening day of the Battle of the Somme.[166] He was last seen 'crossing towards the German Trenches gallantly leading his company & cheering the men on'.[167] The news was devastating for Houston's wife, Ellenor, who wrote to the War Office in July offering a photograph to be circulated in Germany and describing her condition as 'so anxious'. She wrote again in early August seeking an explanation for why her husband's body had not been found. 'Surely they ought to have found his body if he were dead,' she pleaded.[168] She wrote again that month: 'It is now two months ago since my dear husband . . . was wounded & missing. Have you heard any further news? I am so sorry to worry you, but, Oh, it is weary waiting.' The War Office responded that it made enquiries through the American Embassy in Berlin, but 'no further news of Captain F. N. Houston . . . has been received since he was reported missing — believed killed — on July 1st'.[169] The Army Council formally concluded in February 1917 that Houston must be dead.[170]

Second Lieutenant Robert Gee was mortally wounded on 18 October. He was sent to a UK hospital with a 'gunshot wound of head, dangerously ill and unconscious' and he died there on 27 October.[171] He had just turned 20. As well as having to cope with the loss of a son who was 'under age at the time of his death', Gee's father had the added stress of trying to retrieve the sword Robert had taken to France. Gee senior explained: 'He was sent out very hurriedly and the sword was borrowed from a friend as one could not be purchased at the time.' The sword in fact belonged to the Reverend F. S. Williams, headmaster of Eastbourne College in East Sussex.[172]

More New Zealanders were killed in the last months of 1914. Major Robert Masefield died on 24 October serving with the Shropshire Light Infantry south of Armentières, and Lieutenant Edward Chapman, serving in the 3rd Dragoon Guards, 'died from wounds received in action' at No. 19 Field Ambulance near Ypres on 17 November.[173]

The Reverend Lieutenant Cuthbert MacLean was severely wounded in the First Battle of Ypres when he was hit in the back by an artillery shell that burst over his head. After receiving medical treatment, MacLean returned to the fighting to take command of his battalion, as most of the other officers had been casualties too, and he received further gunshots in the leg and through his side. He wrote to his mother:

> I am enjoying the rest, as I have been fighting hard now for over two months. An officer in the Royal Fusiliers has a strenuous time of it, as we have been in the thick of the fight all the time.[174]

For his gallantry during these early months of the war MacLean was awarded the Military Cross. After recovering from his wounds, he joined the Royal Flying Corps, and in 1918 was serving as a lieutenant colonel in the Royal Air Force.[175] In August 1918 he was awarded the French Légion d'honneur for his skill and daring when leading the 10th (Army) Wing that year.[176]

Another young New Zealander who would receive this award was James Lloyd Findlay, the Wellington-born son of politician Sir John Findlay. In 1912 James Findlay had travelled to England with his younger brother Ian to study at the Imperial Service College in Windsor. He was an impressive student, in 1914 winning the prestigious Blue Ribbon prize, and was the College Captain.[177] As soon as war was declared in August 1914 Findlay joined the British army as a private soldier, and soon obtained a commission in the East Surrey Regiment. While fighting with his regiment in France at the Battle of Loos in 1915 he so distinguished himself as to be awarded both the Military Cross and the Croix de Chevalier of the Légion d'honneur.[178] He had just turned 20. Findlay was seriously wounded at the Battle of the Somme in July 1916. After recuperating, he joined the RFC as a pilot and served in this role for the duration of the war. He later had a distinguished career in the Royal New Zealand Air Force.[179]

Ian Calcutt Findlay was not as fortunate as his older brother. Ian was studying at Jesus College, Cambridge and was a student of Inner Temple, London in 1914. He obtained a commission in the 2nd Battalion of the York and Lancaster Regiment and was killed in action in Flanders, Belgium on 10 August 1915.[180] He was just 18 years old.

The month-long First Battle of Ypres completed the destruction of the old army. While the Allies achieved a notable victory here, it had come at too high a price. As Max Hastings has written, 'the inventory of misery and tragedy was so large for victors and vanquished alike that few men afterwards felt minded to celebrate the battle'.[181] Hastings is correct to highlight the losses on both sides. While First Ypres was the death-blow for the Old Contemptibles, for the Germans it was the *Kindermord*, the massacre of innocent youth. While slightly older than the *Kinder* victims of the battle, First Ypres was Adolf Hitler's first military action and he was lucky to survive it. His Bavarian Reserve Infantry Regiment 16 (better known by the name of its first commander as the 'List Regiment') comprised mainly 'raw recruits'. Fighting on the Menin Road near Ypres reduced its strength in four days from 3600 to just 611 men. The regiment's commander, Colonel List, was one of the casualties.[182]

As the trench lines became static, artillery fire and snipers continued to take a toll. New Zealanders killed at the end of 1914 included Glenrowan Edward Champion (Gerry) Rawlins, of the 28th (The Artist Rifles) Battalion, who died while cutting enemy barbed wire on 11 December. On 19 December a German sniper shot Wellington-born doctor Charles Cochrane

The Reverend Cuthbert Trelawder MacLean was a curate at a London church in 1914. He immediately volunteered and accepted a commission in the 4th Battalion of the Royal Fusiliers. He fought in the deadly Battle of First Ypres in 1914 and, at one point, was in command of the 4th Battalion as its only surviving officer. MacLean was severely wounded during First Ypres and received the Military Cross for his gallantry. He later transferred to the Royal Flying Corps. ROYAL AERO CLUB TRUST

Captain James Lloyd Findlay of the East Surrey Regiment was awarded the Military Cross for his gallantry at the Battle of Loos in 1915 and the Legion of Honour for 'great gallantry' at the Hohenzollern Redoubt in March 1916. He had just turned 20. ARCHIVES NEW ZEALAND TE RUA MAHARA O TE KĀWANATANGA, AALZ902, F1113

Iles, who had been the medical officer of the 2nd Battalion, East Lancashire Regiment. He died of 'wounds received in action' at No. 25 Field Ambulance later that day.[183] On 19 December, Captain Charles Harold Reynell Watts was killed in action with the 2nd Battalion, the Northamptonshire Regiment, at Neuve Chapelle.[184] Aucklander Lieutenant Eric Hardwick Tayler of the 1st Battalion of the York and Lancaster Regiment died of pneumonia at the military hospital at Hazebrouck in February 1915.[185]

On 31 October, in fighting around Messines, New Zealand-born doctor Angus McNab, brother of a Cabinet minister, was killed in action in an incident that could only be regarded as a war crime. McNab was a highly distinguished medical practitioner who had been educated in Berlin and Vienna and served in the South African War as a civilian attached to the Scottish Hospital in the Cape Colony.[186] A specialist eye surgeon at the Charing Cross Ophthalmic Hospital in London, also with a Harley Street practice, the multilingual McNab had published a text on the eye and had translated the leading German work on the same subject.[187] On the outbreak of war, McNab immediately offered his services and was commissioned into the Royal Army Medical Corps. Presumably because of his heritage — both his parents had been born in Scotland — McNab was posted as medical officer to the 14th County of London (London Scottish) Regiment of the Territorial Force.[188]

The London Scottish was one of the first territorial battalions sent to France, and it would be the first to see military action. On 31 October 1914 its men, wearing 'hodden grey' kilts, fought just north of Messines in what was part of the First Battle of Ypres.[189] It was a disastrous day for the gallant battalion, which lost 278 of just over 800 men in just two days of fighting.[190] A history of the battalion described the action:

> With no preparatory training, ignorant of the ground and without maps, with defective rifles and without their machine guns, the London Scottish had met the enemy in overwhelming numbers and denied them the road to Ypres.[191]

The battalion's defective rifles were an unpleasant shock, and exacerbated the casualty numbers. A note in the London Scottish war diary recorded with some alarm:

> During the action 31st Oct/1st Nov the rifles Mark I was proved to be very [word illegible] and nearly 50% are useless for rapid firing owing to faulty magazines. An inquiry is being made and it is expect[ed] that fresh rifles will be obtained if possible.[192]

Eleven officers of the London Scottish were killed, among them McNab, who was bayoneted by the Germans.

In November *The Times* reported on the 'Exploits of the London Scottish' and, as would be expected, had a lot to say on the German bayoneting of wounded men. The report reprinted a letter written to the headmaster of the High School for Boys at Croydon by a former pupil who was a survivor of the battle:

> The behaviour of the Germans was awful . . . All our wounded at hand were bayoneted, and they actually bayoneted a medical officer while he was bandaging a wounded man. He was found afterwards quite dead.[193]

Another letter by a motorcycle despatch rider gave more detail:

> Their [London Scottish] medical officer, a Harley-street specialist called McNab, was actually bayoneted in front of their eyes whilst down attending to two wounded men. It was bright moonlight, and he had a white badge and red cross on his arm, and even a blue tunic on, so as to be unmistakable, and was of course, without arms of any sort. The Germans behave like inhuman fiends: every wounded man they bayonet at once.[194]

There is little doubt that the brutal killing of wounded men and their doctor was an atrocity and a war crime. However, it was far from one-sided. The despatch rider's letter also recorded that on learning of the fate of their wounded, the London Scottish gave the order of 'no prisoners'. In the fighting that followed '[t]hey drove the Germans back eventually, giving no quarter, and getting none'.[195]

Angus McNab, 39, left a widow and two small children. His name appears on Panel 56 of the Menin Gate Memorial to the Missing at Ypres.[196] This memorial records the names of more than 54,000 soldiers from the British Empire who fell while fighting in the Ypres Salient and who have no known graves. Inside the monument, the New Zealanders are jointly commemorated with a simple plaque, while the names of the individual New Zealand missing are recorded on memorial sites nearer to where they fell in battle. In the Ypres Salient these are at the Buttes New British Cemetery, near Polygon Wood; the Messines Ridge British Cemetery; and on the walls of the memorial at Tyne Cot, close to where the disastrous attacks on Passchendaele Ridge took place.[197] The only New Zealanders commemorated on the Menin Gate are those who served with other nations of the British Empire, and McNab's is one of more than a hundred New Zealanders' names etched on its stone face.[198] The names of the New Zealanders on this memorial feature in Appendix 2 of this book.

As this chapter has demonstrated, many New Zealanders were actively involved in the First World War from its earliest days. They performed in a variety of roles and many served with or alongside the Old Contemptibles of 1914. Some, like Angus McNab, Oliver Garsia and Charles Iles, paid the ultimate price for this early involvement. The exact number of New Zealanders who served with the BEF in 1914 may never be known. In February 1915 the *Otago Daily Times* featured a list of all those New Zealanders then serving 'At the Front'. It noted that 'New Zealanders abroad have not been slow to tender their services in defence of the Empire' and that its list was likely to be incomplete, as it did not include New Zealanders who were serving in distant parts of the empire. It was a substantial list nonetheless, featuring the names of 301 men and 15 women who were then known to be serving with British military units and other organisations involved in the war effort. The women were serving in a range of medical appointments with the British and French Red Cross, with various British military hospitals in the United Kingdom and France, and with the St John Ambulance in Belgium.[199]

In another indication of the numbers involved, the *Evening Post* in early 1920 reported that King George V had approved the wearing of a clasp attached to the 1914 Star to designate those who had actually served under fire in France and Belgium. The clasp had an extremely narrow date range, being issued to those who were on the Western Front between 5 August and 22 November 1914. As the paper noted: 'Quite a number of New Zealanders are entitled to wear this clasp as well as a number of officers in the British army who are known [to be] in New Zealand.' That number, which included Melvill, Freyberg, Richardson, Chaytor and Garsia, totalled 80 Old Contemptibles or men who had fought with them.[200] The 316 New Zealanders 'At the Front' and the 80 entitled to wear the clasp are significant numbers, especially for a nation as small as New Zealand was in 1914. It demonstrated the strong patriotic response of New Zealanders, whose national identity was firmly embedded as part of the British Empire. This was only the start, though, and their allegiance to empire would be severely tested over the next three years.

CHAPTER TWO

WITH THE BRITISH ARMY AND BRITISH MEDICAL ORGANISATIONS

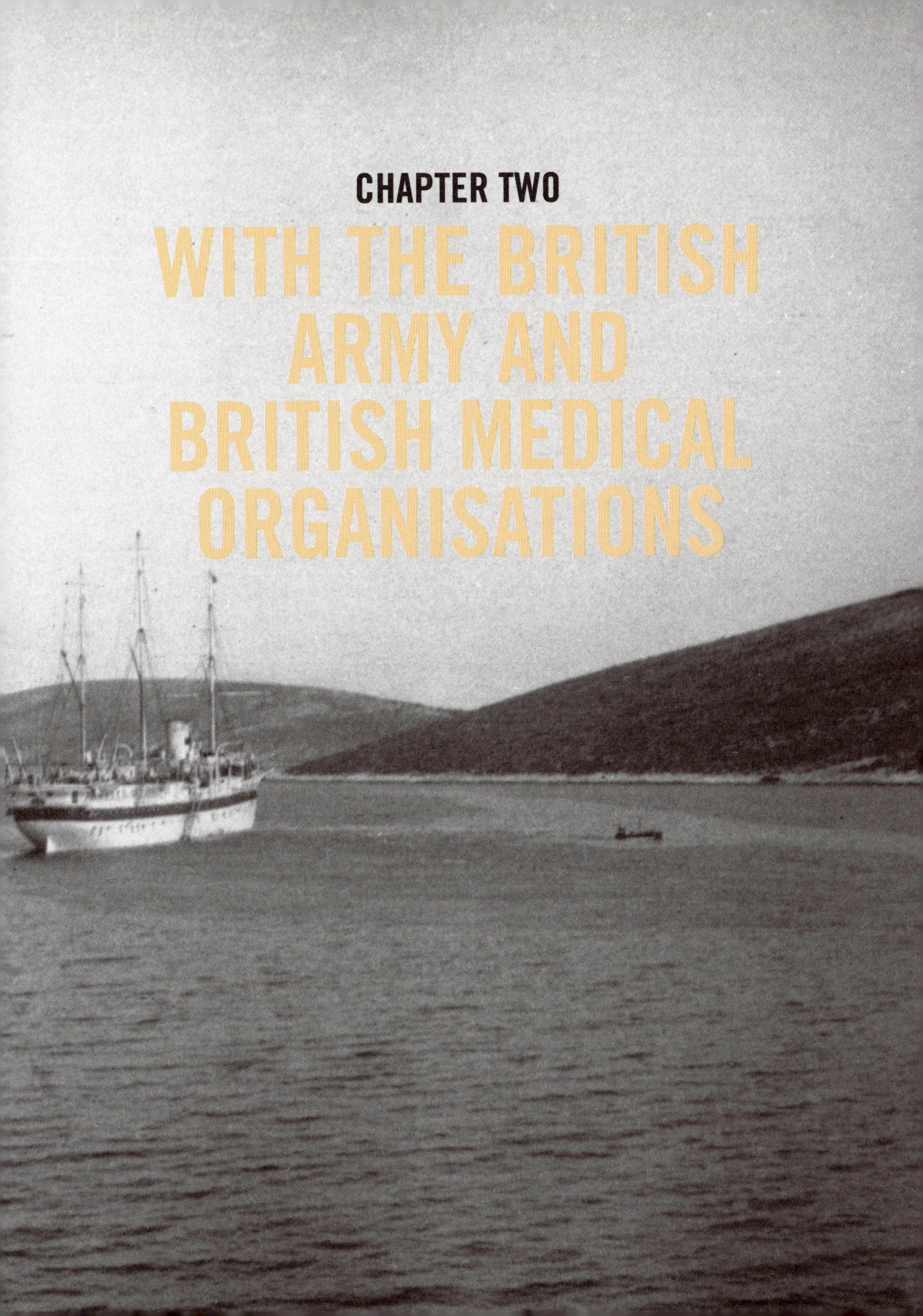

Previous pages
A photograph taken from the fo'c'sle of the SS *Grantully Castle* near Stavros, Greece, on 23 April 1915. *Grantully Castle*, built at Glasgow in 1910, was converted into a 552-bed hospital ship in May 1915. Prior to this she was a troopship and landed men on the Gallipoli Peninsula on 29 April 1915. On this vessel Bernard Freyberg's wartime comrade, the poet Rupert Brooke, contracted a fatal illness while sailing to Gallipoli. The ship in front is a French hospital ship. IMPERIAL WAR MUSEUM, Q61114

By mid-1916 the New Zealand government had become opposed to New Zealanders serving with the British army, and it began to tightly control the number of transfers from the NZEF. In a reply to a parliamentary question in July about the desirability of young New Zealanders seeking British army commissions, the government was 'emphatic' that such enlistments should be discouraged except in exceptional circumstances. 'All the suitable men are required for service in the New Zealand military forces.'[1]

Despite the government's concerns, New Zealanders continued to enlist in British military forces for the duration of the war, and there were two ways to do this: enlist directly and process through the British recruiting system, or transfer from the NZEF. New Zealanders keen to experience powered flight and to fight in the air war had to enlist in or transfer to the Royal Flying Corps, the Royal Naval Air Service (RNAS) or, from April 1918, the Royal Air Force. Similarly, New Zealanders wanting to participate in the war at sea needed to join the Royal Navy or even the Royal Australian Navy. (The experiences of the New Zealanders fighting in the air war and the war at sea are the subjects of separate volumes of the Centenary History.)[2]

It is harder to ascertain the motives of those who travelled to enlist in or transfer to British army regiments. After all, the men and women who did this had a choice. For most of the war, and for the first time in its history, New Zealand had a complete infantry division on active service as well as a mounted rifle brigade. Even before the New Zealand Division was formed in Egypt in early 1916, the Gallipoli campaign had consumed so many New Zealand soldiers that there was always a demand for more men. Those New Zealanders who joined British army colours rather than those of New Zealand units had made a deliberate choice to do so. Why?

For New Zealanders who were resident in the United Kingdom or travelling through it, joining a British regiment was an easier option. It offered the prospect of seeing active service much sooner than waiting for the chance to join the NZEF. Joining the NZEF from the United Kingdom was certainly possible, and some New Zealanders did so,[3] but this was a more bureaucratic and lengthy affair, and many young men and women were impatient to serve. It was quicker to join the British regiments that welcomed suitable young men warmly. Some New Zealand women, through choice or circumstance, joined various British medical organisations. Then there were the New Zealand families with established military traditions;

some opted to join the regiments of their forebears rather than serve with the new and untested New Zealand military units.

It is difficult to ignore social class when seeking an explanation for why so many New Zealanders served in British army regiments, given that it took a certain amount of wealth, education and confidence to join a British regiment, especially if one wanted to serve as a commissioned officer rather than in the ranks. As Stevan Eldred-Grigg has written: 'Warlike sons of well-to-do households not wishing to join dominion regiments hastened to the motherland,' where they joined old, new or 'chic' British regiments. These men were the 'sons of the well-heeled and wealthy'.[4] According to Eldred-Grigg, more of the sons of the Canterbury landed gentry were sent to serve in the British army than to the NZEF.[5]

When Leslie Heron Beauchamp, the brother of the writer Katherine Mansfield, was seeking a commission in the British army in early 1915 he came armed with a letter of recommendation from Sir Thomas Mackenzie, the New Zealand High Commissioner in London (and, briefly, a former prime minister). It noted that Beauchamp was 'a member of a well-known and highly respected New Zealand family, his father being Chairman of the Bank of New Zealand'. Mackenzie also noted that young New Zealand men applying for commissions in the United Kingdom were at a considerable disadvantage because they lacked suitable connections and networks: 'I think this fact should be taken into consideration when they apply for commissions, especially if they come of good stock and are well-conducted, capable men.'[6] Those who lacked these credentials certainly had a harder time obtaining a commission in the British army. Leslie Beauchamp's story is covered later in this chapter.

Ernest Cyril Branson was another from 'good stock' and 'a highly respected family'. A company manager from Dunedin, Branson enlisted as a gunner in the Royal Horse Artillery (RHA), in spite of the fact that his father had served as an officer in the elite 1st King's Dragoon Guards.[7] Armed with three letters of recommendation from the High Commissioner's Office, and despite being removed from an officer cadet school for being 'not likely to make an efficient Artillery officer', Branson achieved his goal of obtaining a commission in the British army.[8] He ended the war as a second lieutenant in the Tank Corps and was discharged on 21 February 1919.[9]

Auckland lawyer and Wanganui Collegiate old boy Trevor Holmden sailed with the New Zealand Main Body in October 1914 as a sergeant in the Auckland Battalion, but, shortly after arriving in Egypt, he successfully applied for a transfer and a commission to the British army. In his unpublished autobiography Holmden explained his reasons:

> There seemed no chance of getting a commission in our New Zealand forces and I had no desire to remain in the ranks a moment longer than necessary and besides there was a certain glamour attached to 'Imperial Commissions' and on the eve of our troops departure for Gallipoli Sergeants Bigwood, Oliphant and Holmden were fallen out on parade and informed that they were to remain with the base details and await orders.[10]

Holmden and the two other New Zealand sergeants were gazetted as temporary second

Trevor Holmden was a New Zealand NCO and one of the first to transfer to the British Expeditionary Force. Along with seven other compatriots, he received a temporary commission in the BEF in April 1915, and served with the Worcestershire Regiment on Gallipoli and the Western Front. Holmden later explained that there was 'a certain glamour' in being an officer in the BEF where, unlike the New Zealand Expeditionary Force, one met 'charming fellows to soldier with'. ARCHIVES NEW ZEALAND TE RUA MAHARA O TE KĀWANATANGA, F944

lieutenants on 19 April 1915. Along with 80 other temporary officers, including seven New Zealanders, Holmden spent May attending an officers' training camp at Zeitoun run by a Grenadier Guards colonel. It was a pleasant experience for Holmden and he found his classmates 'charming fellows to soldier with . . . they were a relief after the jat one was forced to associate with in the ranks of the New Zealand Army'.[11] Holmden passed out second in this class of 80 and applied to serve with the Worcestershire Regiment, choosing this 'most famous line regiment' because one of the other New Zealanders had a family association with it.[12] Holmden served on Gallipoli with the 9th Worcestershire Battalion, which was then part of the British 13th Division. When he and fellow New Zealander Wilfred Bigwood joined the 9th Worcestershires as second lieutenants on 21 August 1915 its ration strength was just 50 men and there were no combatant officers left.[13] Holmden survived Gallipoli and spent some time recuperating in Cairo, where he enjoyed the nightlife that the city had to offer. He later served in France with his regiment and was awarded the Military Cross.[14]

A small number of New Zealanders served in the British and Australian forces after being rejected for military service with the NZEF. John Upton Gaskell Slack, a property owner and animal breeder from the Manawatū, for example, was rejected twice for military service by New Zealand, most likely through failing the medical examination. So determined was he that he sold his property and travelled to the United Kingdom with the express purpose of going to war. The British military authorities were obviously not so fussy, and Slack was enlisted into the RHA as a gunner in March 1916.[15] He must have proved quite a soldier: in December that year Slack obtained a commission with the Machine Gun Corps. He served as a machine-gun officer in France for the duration of the war, and in 1919 was part of the BEF's army of occupation in Germany.[16] It was certainly New Zealand's loss.

Another whose route to a commission was smoothed by good connections was sheep farmer and Wanganui Collegiate old boy Daniel Henry Strother Riddiford, who had no problems obtaining a commission in the Grenadier Guards in November 1915. The regimental colonel even provided a special letter of recommendation:

> Although this gentleman is over 30 years of age, I beg to recommend that the application may receive special consideration as I am most anxious to obtain the services of Mr. Riddiford in the Regiment under my Command, and I consider him most suitable to hold a Commission.[17]

Riddiford's service was plagued by ill health; particularly muscular rheumatism.[18]

Another who travelled to the United Kingdom after being discharged from the NZEF due to illness was Percy Ashton Elworthy, whose family were prominent in South Canterbury. Elworthy had joined the Samoan Relief Force on 5 January 1915 and was discharged for health reasons at the end of the month.[19] He was suffering from duodenal ulcers, described in his British army file as a long-standing illness.[20] In May 1915 Elworthy travelled to the United Kingdom for 'a serious surgical operation' that would make him fit for active service.[21] Once in England it was discovered that an operation was not necessary, and he was able to obtain a commission in the elite 1st Battalion of the Life Guards. He served with his unit in France, and it was reported at the end of the year that he had 'been at the Front for a month, and was quite well'.[22] However, his file reveals an ongoing struggle with his health, which deteriorated to such an extent that in April 1917 Elworthy was informed that he was 'permanently unfit for any duty' and could no longer serve.[23] He refused to accept this decision, and two months later appeared for examination by his regiment's medical officer with a medical certificate from his private doctor. The medical officer agreed with Elworthy's doctor that he was now 'physically fit for service'.[24] He rejoined the 1st Life Guards and was promoted to the rank of captain. However, in 1918 a recurrence of his gastric problems saw him classified as 'fit for Home Service' only.[25]

For some, service in the British military offered a second chance and the possibility of redemption from previous military service that had not met their expectations. Frederick Holford from Gisborne was one who sought redemption of this sort. In early 1915 he had been returned to New Zealand from Egypt along with 14 other men for refusing to be inoculated against typhoid. The inoculations were painful, requiring an injection in the arm and chest, and men were sore for days afterwards. There was also a fear that the injection caused rather than prevented illness.[26] The 15 objectors were promptly discharged upon their return. Holford was discharged on 22 January 1915 after 157 days with the NZEF.[27] He then travelled to the United Kingdom in mid-1915 and enlisted in the Royal Engineers. He later served with a divisional signal company on the Western Front.[28]

Robert Heaton Livingstone, a Timaru-born law student at Canterbury College, was another example. He joined the NZEF on 14 August 1914 and served with the Canterbury Infantry Battalion on Gallipoli as a lance corporal. He was shot in the shoulder at Suvla Bay and, after spending nearly two months at the Australian hospital at Heliopolis, returned to New Zealand on the *Willochra* on 30 October 1915. He was discharged from the NZEF on 25 February 1916, having been declared 'medically unfit for active service'.[29] It would later be revealed that Livingstone was suffering from shell shock, now better known as post-traumatic stress injury (PTSI).[30]

Livingstone was not prepared to let his military service end with his discharge from the NZEF. At the end of 1916 he was in the United Kingdom, where he obtained a commission in the 4th Battalion of the South Staffordshire Regiment. He served with this battalion in France and on 15 May 1917, at Bullecourt, he was wounded in action. His medical report described the gunshot wound as 'superficial at back of neck'.[31] Livingstone spent the rest of 1917 recovering and trying to join the Royal Flying Corps. Unfortunately, the stress of trying to learn to fly and his wounding triggered another attack of PTSI. One of his medical reports describes some classic symptoms:

> he complains of headache after every flight . . . States he has bad dreams on those nights following the days he has flown. Tremors of fingers & eyelids — reflexes brisk — Pulse 90. Tension fair — only fairly sustained. Has applied to be allowed to cease flying and return to Infantry. The Board confirms its finding of 5.2.18.[32]

That finding confirmed that Livingstone was 'Permanently Unfit For Service as a Pilot or Observer'.[33] In early April 1918, despite having been assessed as suffering from PTSI, he was ordered to rejoin the South Staffordshire Regiment 'forthwith', this time in its 3rd Battalion.[34] Upon arrival in France in September, Livingstone was promoted to temporary captain and seconded as adjutant to an administrative command in charge of railheads. During the remainder of 1918 and early 1919 he was posted to a number of administrative jobs with various depot units and labour groups, and to a company responsible for handling prisoners of war.[35] He was discharged from the British army in May 1919.

Even this military service may not have satisfied him. When another war broke out two decades after his discharge, the 48-year-old Christchurch solicitor again offered his services. He was posted to the 3rd Battalion National Military Reserve, a home defence unit based in Christchurch, initially as its intelligence officer and assistant adjutant. Livingstone served with the unit until his discharge and transfer to the Retired Officers' Supplementary List in May 1943.[36]

It is easy to ascertain the motives of Hugh Miller Christie Robertson Ludlow in joining the BEF in 1916. From Balclutha, South Otago, the son of Frederick and Jane Ludlow, Hugh was aged 16 in 1914. After being rejected by the NZEF because of his age, Ludlow managed to convince his mother to allow him to travel to the United Kingdom in order to enlist there. With no sailing experience and not yet 17, Ludlow signed on with a Norwegian sailing ship bound for Copenhagen via South America. At Buenos Aires, he fell into the hold while trying to secure some hatches and was rushed to hospital. While he recovered, the British consul arranged for Ludlow to be paid out by his Norwegian skipper and granted free passage for him to travel to England.[37] When he finally reached England, after being inoculated twice and having two bad teeth removed, Hugh Ludlow was initially enlisted into the 14th Gloucestershire Battalion. This was a 'bantam' battalion, consisting of men who normally would have been too short to join the BEF. Their heights ranged from five foot to five foot and three inches; at five two, Ludlow would have been one of the taller members.[38] During training at Chiseldon Camp in Wiltshire, Ludlow distinguished himself by winning the eight-mile race by an impressive one minute and 45 seconds' lead. For this he received the prize of a 10-guinea cup, presented by the colonel's wife.[39]

Ludlow served with the 3rd Battalion of the Gloucestershire Regiment on the Western Front, from where he described sitting in the trenches at Neuve Chapelle as 'nothing but shells, bullets and bombs flying about and bursting around us'.[40] During a retaliatory German bombardment a shell burst on the parapet above Ludlow's position, killing two men and wounding three more. Ludlow was hit by shrapnel on the side, shoulder and leg. A harrowing journey to an advanced dressing station followed. 'I was soaked through with blood and water and covered with mire,' he wrote.[41] Better treatment followed at several hospitals and included a 10-day period of sick leave in London.

By now, understandably, the young Private Hugh Ludlow had had enough of the war. It was far from the 'adventurous experience' reported in the New Zealand newspapers. His medal card for the Gloucestershire Regiment indicates that after he had deserted from his unit on 22 August 1916 his medals had been forfeited. At his court martial he was sentenced to 90 days of Field Punishment No. 2.[42] The British military authorities, however, implemented a humane and practical solution. In November 1916 Ludlow wrote to his parents to say that he had been transferred to the Royal Navy. He made no mention of his court martial, but instead claimed that it had been discovered that he was 'evidently too young to be in the Army', hence the transfer.[43] Still on light duties after his wounding, Ludlow expected to be serving in the North Sea very shortly. It is not known whether he served out the 90 days of Field Punishment No. 2 prior to the transfer.[44]

Hugh Ludlow joined the Royal Navy on 31 August 1916 for an engagement period of more than five years, but it was not to be. After a stint at HMS *Vivid*, the Royal Navy barracks at Devonport in Auckland, and then aboard the *Juno*, a second-class cruiser, his naval service ended abruptly on 5 February 1917. On his Admiralty record, the column recording reasons for discharge from the service has only one word: 'Run'.[45]

Wanganui Collegiate old boy Reginald Victor Deacon, an articled law clerk who was finishing a study tour in the United Kingdom in 1914, rose from the ranks after serving with a British territorial unit. His military service was remarkably varied. Deacon, who listed his previous military service with the 'Rough Riders' (the Canterbury Yeoman Cavalry), joined the Welsh Horse as a private soldier in August 1914.[46] Unlike other middle-class New Zealanders, Deacon wanted to serve with the NZEF, but his colonel refused to approve the transfer. According to Deacon: 'He [his CO] regretted that he couldn't spare me. Consequently I have throughout the last four years stuck to the Imperial Forces,' this despite being 'a born New Zealander, with my Home and Mother in New Zealand'.[47]

Deacon served with the 1st Battalion Welsh Horse Guards on Gallipoli and in the Sinai campaign, and in August 1916 he transferred to the Machine Gun Corps (MGC) as a lance corporal. In early 1917 Deacon was sent to France with the MGC, and in September that year, after attending an officer training school, he received a temporary commission as a lieutenant with the MGC in France for a full year. In September 1918, though, he was discharged from the army, his service record stating that Deacon was '[t]o relinquish [his commission] on account of ill-health contracted on active service — Grant Hon rank & King's certificate (France)'. A further note recorded his illness as 'shell shock'.[48]

Rather than a King's Certificate (which in effect was an honourable discharge), what Deacon really wanted from the War Office at the end of 1918 was a passage home. He wrote to the office twice in 1918 to make this request, noting that his circumstances were not good. The war had left him with 'limited resources', which were 'fast eking out', and bad headaches prevented him gaining employment.[49] Furthermore, his mother in New Zealand was seriously ill. Little wonder that he informed the War Office that 'I should be indeed grateful if I could get home at the earliest opportunity'.[50]

Another lawyer to fit the pattern of middle-class enlistment in British military units was Leonard Poulter Leary CMG, MC, QC, who was born in 1891 in Palmerston North and whose father had established and owned the only chemist shop in town. Not only did Leary's chemist shop dispense medicines, but gold and black letters on the windows informed the public that here was the place for eye tests and to have 'teeth carefully extracted'.[51] It was a prosperous, thriving business until Leary senior died unexpectedly in 1901. Nonetheless, the family was still well enough off to have travelled to the United States, the United Kingdom, France and India while Leonard and his brother were young boys. In August 1914 Leonard Leary was finishing his law degree at Victoria College in Wellington. Within a week of the declaration of war both he and his brother, Ernest Richard Leary, had joined up and were on their way to German Sāmoa as part of the makeshift, ill-prepared force that would seize the colony from Germany. It was not an experience they enjoyed, and Leonard was soon back in New Zealand suffering from an infected mosquito bite.

Both brothers were 'disgusted at being side-tracked to Samoa' and decided to go to England 'to make sure of getting somewhere'.[52] Leonard, who after the war had a distinguished legal career in New Zealand, explained in a radio interview in 1982 why he and Ernest felt the need to join the BEF in 1915:

> My brother and I thought that we might get marooned again as we had in Samoa and we weren't going to be fooled a second time. So we decided to go to England and we would then be quite sure about getting some action. Everybody thought the war would be over in a few weeks and we didn't want that to happen without us getting into it.[53]

By mid-1915 both Leary brothers had received commissions in the British army; Ernest as an infantry officer in the York and Lancaster Regiment and Leonard as an artillery officer in the field gunners. Their experience was not unusual. Of the total of just over 1400 men who made up the Samoa Expeditionary Force in 1914, 1115 served again. While most of these men served with their fellow New Zealanders, 45 went into British (imperial) forces and 13 joined the Australian Imperial Force (AIF). Some 229 of them, just over 20 per cent, never returned to New Zealand. They were killed in action or died of wounds, accident or disease.[54] They died in some unusual places, too. Lieutenant William Baldwin Busby, who had been discharged from the Samoa Expeditionary Force on 15 April 1915 for 'domestic reasons',[55] was serving with the 12th Battalion, Worcestershire Regiment when he was killed in action on 15 February 1917 on the banks of the Tigris River in Mesopotamia.[56]

After joining up in mid-1915 Leonard Leary was to see his brother for only one 'fleeting moment'. He learnt the art of gunnery and, equally important, the art of managing horses at Woolwich, and was then sent to Egypt in preparation for a stint on Gallipoli. At the same time, Ernest joined his regiment in France. Leonard, too late to fight on Gallipoli, was soon back in England, recovering from pneumonia and dysentery contracted while in Egypt.[57] Upon his arrival Leonard received a letter from Ernest, a brotherly attempt to cheer him up but also containing a premonition of his fate. In it Ernest advised his brother to '[t]ake my tip and stay in Blighty for a while'. Ernest, now a second lieutenant, wrote that preparations for the Somme battle were well under way and '[y]ou can see from the papers that there is something happening out here now'. Ernest thought he would 'come thro' alright somehow', but he informed Leonard that 'in case anything happens to me which it won't' Leonard was to have his revolver and their mother was to have his sword and Sam Browne belt. Ernest signed

above Second Lieutenant Leonard Leary, at right rear, with officers of A Battery, 177th Brigade Royal Field Artillery, just prior to the Battle of Messines in June 1917. Leary was awarded the Military Cross for his service in France. He was wounded during the fighting around Passchendaele and later suffered from post-traumatic stress injury. After the war, he returned home to establish himself as a lawyer; he was described as one of the most prominent advocates in New Zealand's legal history. L. P. LEARY, *NOT ENTIRELY LEGAL*

left Ernest Richard Leary, Leonard's brother, was commissioned into the York and Lancaster Regiment. In July 1916 Ernest wrote to Leonard with the news that he had been hospitalised with 'a bit of a scratch'. Two days later, he died of his wound; he was just 21 years old. L. P. LEARY, *NOT ENTIRELY LEGAL*

the letter 'Cheery oh and Kia ora' and added a postscript: 'Hope you have been cheered up a bit on your sick bed by this.'[58]

In mid-1916 another 'cheery letter' from Ernest, then fighting on the Somme, informed Leonard that he was in hospital with 'a bit of a scratch'. This was a considerable understatement: a gunshot wound to the buttocks had penetrated through to the bladder area.[59] Two days after writing to his brother, on 23 July 1916, Ernest Leary died. As Leonard wrote: 'The youngster I had fought with, laughed with and grown up with was gone, and a few regimental buttons and a sword were all I had left of him.'[60]

Leonard Leary finally reached France in early 1917. He served with a battery of field artillery during the Battle of Messines in June, and a meeting with fellow New Zealanders there reveals much about why Leary joined the British army. As well as 'getting somewhere', he wrote that at Messines '[s]ome of them [New Zealanders] came to see me and roared with laughter at saluting a man they had last seen driving a water cart in Samoa'.[61] Prospects for obtaining an officer's commission were certainly better in British (imperial) regiments. Having experience with horses and being reasonably proficient at mathematics had been enough for Leary to demonstrate to the recruiting officer that he was 'the very type I want'.[62] He was later awarded the Military Cross for his service in France in 1917.

A wound in the fighting around Passchendaele ended Leonard Leary's active military career. Suffering from post-traumatic stress injury, he was posted to training establishments in the United Kingdom for all of 1918. In early 1919 he was back in Wellington accompanied by his English war bride, 'a charming young nurse . . . whom I had met in Egypt'.[63] A move to an Auckland law firm soon followed, but the marriage was not a success and his wife later returned to England.[64] Leonard Leary, who became a QC, was knighted in London in 1973. While there, he took the opportunity to cross the Channel and revisit the battlefields of France and Belgium. He particularly sought out his brother's grave and described in his memoirs what it was like to find it:

> There he was. First his regimental crest, the Yorks and Lancs, then rank, name and date of death. Aged twenty-one. Below was inscribed *Festivus cecidit*. This was almost a surprise. I had forgotten that years ago when, for uniformity, they replaced the plaque I had put there, they had inquired whether there was any inscription I would like. As he went gaily to the war, and I heard of him laughing just before he died, I felt that 'He died gaily' was a happy phrase.

Leary admitted that he 'mused long at the graveside' and was deeply affected by the visit.[65]

One of the young New Zealanders to enlist in a British regiment early in the war was Leslie Beauchamp. The only son of self-made and highly successful businessman and Bank of New Zealand director Harold Beauchamp and his wife, Leslie was the much-loved younger brother of New Zealand's most famous writer, Katherine Mansfield (Kathleen Mansfield Beauchamp). In 1908 Katherine described her brother, known as 'Chummie', in a letter to a cousin:

> I have never dreamed of loving a child as I love this boy. Do not laugh at me when I tell you I feel so maternal towards him. He is intensely affectionate and sensitive — he reads a great deal — draws with the most delicate sympathetic touch — and yet is a thoroughly brave healthy boy.[66]

Leslie Beauchamp arrived in the United Kingdom in February 1915, aged 21, and after completing an officer training course he was commissioned into the 8th Battalion, South Lancashire Regiment. Prior to his departure for France in September 1915 he managed to spend a short period of leave with his sister, who wrote to him shortly after expressing her love and pride:

> Ever since last Sunday you are close in my thoughts. It meant a tremendous lot, seeing you and being with you again and I was so frightfully proud of you — you know that — but I like saying it . . . This is not a letter. It is only my arms round you for a quick minute.[67]

Leslie Beauchamp did not have a long war, and it is doubtful he ever fired a shot at the enemy. On 5 October he wrote his last letter to his sister:

> Dearest Kate
> No time for a letter am frightfully fit and full of beans! We are up and doing at last. The trenches are beastly wet owing to the big bombardment going on. So far have remained scathless so that's all right! I can't describe my sensations during all this business — everything is wonderfully simple and elemental — still about 7 years old.
> Good night darling. Write to me.
> Ever yours — Chummie [68]

Less than a month after arriving on the Western Front, he was killed the day after writing the letter as the result of a hand-grenade accident during training at Ploegsteert Wood.

Needless to say, the Beauchamp family was distraught at the news of his death. They were also upset at the way he had died and the paucity of information provided by the War Office. An official telegram had informed them that Leslie Beauchamp had been 'killed accidentally on 7 October' and that Lord Kitchener expressed his sympathy.[69] Clearly, this was not enough, and the family, through the Bank of New Zealand and the office of the High Commissioner in London, pressed the War Office for more information.[70] A report on Beauchamp's death, written by his commanding officer, was received at the end of October and some of the information was reported to the New Zealand authorities. The report is brief, typed on just one page of a field service notebook, but it contains the full, tragic account of Leslie Beauchamp's last moments:

> In accordance with your S.C. 105 of to-days date, I beg to report as follows:
> On the afternoon of the 6th inst 2/Lieut L. Beauchamp, Bombing Officer of this Battalion was

above Stretcher-bearers near Ploegsteert Wood, known by British Expeditionary Force soldiers as 'Plugstreet', in the Ypres salient of Belgium. Katherine Mansfield's brother Leslie Beauchamp was killed in a training accident near here. ALEXANDER TURNBULL LIBRARY, 1/2-012899-G

right Leslie Beauchamp, known as 'Chummie', was killed in October 1915. ALEXANDER TURNBULL LIBRARY, A-006-001

instructing a party of Officers N.C.O's in the use of Bombs. About 3 p.m. I and Major Menzies were on our way back to Bn Hd Qrs when we came to the party in a field. Lieut Beauchamp had a 'Nobel Lighter' Grenade in his hand explaining the method of firing it. I asked several questions about it which he answered. The questions were all about the lighting of it. About 3.10 p.m. he and the Bombing Sergt No 15000 J. Holden went forward about 15 yards to a small pond in the field as he said he would throw it in there for safety's sake. He took the Sergt with him as he informed us it required 2 to light the grenade. What happened then none of us could see as the two had their backs to us. Almost directly after they stopped near the pond an explosion occurred and they both fell to the ground. We all ran up and gave 1st aid and sent for the doctors. The Sergt died in about 10 minutes and 2/Lieut Beauchamp in about ½ or ¾ of an hour. The first Medical Officer to arrive was one from the 4th Canadians and then one from the 11th Cheshires soon afterwards. The Battalion Medical Officer had gone to the trenches to find out about the arrangements necessary for the Bn when it went up into the trenches. This Officer saw the bodies before burial.

9.10.15

A.G.A. Lang

Lieut Colonel.

Commanding 8th Bn South Lancashire Regt.[71]

While it was undoubtedly a terrible tragedy for the Beauchamp family, such training accidents were all too common. On 15 June 1916 at Trentham Camp, for example, bombing instructor Captain Antonie Beekman was demonstrating bomb-throwing to the governor, Lord Liverpool, and his officials. Captain Beekman 'held the bomb too long in his hand and was killed'. Another officer, Lieutenant Richard Francis Bale, was seriously wounded 'and it is surprising that others were not hurt'.[72]

Mansfield never recovered from the loss of her beloved brother. In November 1915 she wrote in her diary: 'Yes, though he is lying in the middle of a little wood in France and I am still walking upright, and feeling the sun and wind from the sea, I am just as much dead as he is.'[73] The war, and in particular her brother's death, fragmented the world Mansfield had known before the war and its effects remained with her, 'undiminished', for the rest of her years.[74] According to one of her biographers, Mansfield 'dedicated the remainder of her life to recreating and immortalising both him [Leslie] and the world they had shared'.[75] During the period regarded as her most productive, from July 1921 to February 1922, over half her stories featured a character modelled on her brother, who was constantly on her mind and even in her dreams.[76] At the end of 1922 Mansfield wrote one of her last letters to her father, describing how Christmas was enjoyable only because of its 'childish associations' but how such memories now were painful. She wrote:

I remember us all going to St Paul's and Mother's enjoyment of 'Hark the Herald Angels Sing'. And that makes me think of darling Leslie still a child enjoying everything. Such memories do not make for gaiety.[77]

Nine days later, Katherine Mansfield died of tuberculosis at the age of 34. Both Chummie and Mansfield are casualties of the war.

Oliver Wakefield was another from a well-established New Zealand family. His father, Edward Wakefield, had been a member of Parliament, and Oliver was the nephew of Edward Gibbon Wakefield, founder of the New Zealand Company, which had been responsible for the first waves of immigration to New Zealand from 1840 onwards. Oliver Wakefield had served in the South African War with the Canterbury Mounted Volunteers and had been 'very badly wounded' in that conflict.[78] Once he had recovered, he studied to become an Anglican clergyman, and from 1911 had been working as one of the Archbishop of Canterbury's representatives in western Canada. On the outbreak of war he offered his services to the British military and received a commission in the 7th Hussars. He later transferred to the Life Guards and then to the Household Battalion.

During the Battle of Arras in April 1917, the Household Battalion lost 600 men and Lieutenant Oliver Wakefield was again wounded. He recovered from his wounds in time to lead his men in the ill-fated battle of Poelcappelle, near Passchendaele, on 9 October 1917. He was attempting to rally his men when a large German shell landed nearby. A New Zealand newspaper reported that Wakefield fell to the ground 'and never regained consciousness his steel helmet having been pierced and his head crushed'.[79] Back in New Zealand, his father received many letters of condolence, including one from the king and queen.

These examples demonstrate the incredible degree of stress and heartache felt by New Zealand families when one of their members was reported as missing in action. The uncertainty about a loved one's fate often lingered for years and it tormented family members. One of the saddest cases was that of Lieutenant John Nevill Ritchie, who served with the 3rd Battalion, Seaforth Highlanders in Mesopotamia. Born in 1879, Ritchie had attended Otago Boys' High School and St John's College, Cambridge.[80] He attempted to join the NZEF, 'but he was always rejected' on medical grounds.[81] After undergoing an operation Ritchie was passed medically fit and gazetted into the Seaforth Highlanders at the end of 1915, joining them in the field on 29 March 1916 when the unit was part of the attempt to break through to the besieged force at the town of Kut-al-Amara in Mesopotamia. A garrison of 13,000 British and Indian troops had been trapped at Kut since late 1915 after advancing up the Tigris River and being heavily defeated at Ctesiphon. The siege at Kut lasted 147 days before the Allied force finally surrendered on 29 April 1916. In their several attempts to break the siege, the British army in Mesopotamia suffered 23,000 casualties, much more than the number of soldiers actually trapped in Kut.[82]

Ritchie was one of the casualties. Fighting on the banks of the Tigris on 22 April, he was last seen leading the few survivors of his platoon 'in a futile effort to hold a second line trench which held five feet of water'. Wounded in his shoulder,[83] Ritchie was never seen again.[84] The official telegram to his wife, Eviene Ritchie, gave grounds for hope, advising that 'this does not necessarily mean that he is killed or wounded'.[85] Appeals to the Turkish government through the American Embassy produced no further information. The New Zealand government also made enquiries with the War Office in mid-1917 but was informed that since Ritchie had gone missing, 'no further news has been received concerning him'.[86] In November the Army Council

above The siege of the town of Kut-al-Amara, 160 kilometres south of Baghdad, in what was then known as Mesopotamia, was one of the worst disasters of the war for the United Kingdom. Not only was the entire besieged garrison of 13,000 taken prisoner, but the British also lost another 23,000 men trying to break the siege. IMPERIAL WAR MUSEUM, Q25254

left Rejected from the New Zealand Expeditionary Force on medical grounds, John Nevill Ritchie underwent a major surgical operation, then travelled to the United Kingdom to accept a commission in the Seaforth Highlanders. Ritchie went missing on operations in Mesopotamia in April 1916 and was declared dead by the British Army Council 18 months later. OTAGO BOYS' HIGH SCHOOL MUSEUM, C754, 18053012

wrote to Ritchie's wife asking whether she had heard anything and whether she was willing to accept that Ritchie was now dead.[87] She replied:

> I have received no further news that has led me to believe him alive, any reports as to his fate leaving little hope that he could have survived in the action on the date specified . . . I have realised from other unofficial evidence that there could be no more hope of his being alive, and I can only thank you very much indeed for your kind message of sympathy.[88]

Just over a month after receiving Eviene Ritchie's letter, the Army Council announced its conclusion that Lieutenant Ritchie was 'dead, and that his death occurred on, or since the 21st day of April, 1916'.[89]

The First World War gave nurses of the British Empire a prime opportunity to use their skills to save lives, a task that they had made their life's work. It also offered nurses from the various British dominions a certain independence and 'the freedom to travel around exotic areas they would have been unlikely to visit otherwise'.[90] Prior to the war, international travel in relative comfort was something for the wealthy. During the conflict, however, New Zealand women served in a multitude of places in an incredible range of tasks. As well as the 550 who served in the New Zealand Army Nursing Service (NZANS), more than 100 New Zealand nurses served with British or French nursing organisations.[91] In her impressive and comprehensive history of New Zealand military nursing, Sherayl McNabb records the names and details of 108 New Zealand nurses who served overseas during the war with other military and civilian organisations.[92]

McNabb also records the names and details of 11 New Zealand women who worked as part of the Voluntary Aid Detachment (VAD) for various British medical organisations. The VAD provided nursing care for military personnel in the United Kingdom and in various theatres of war. The crucial difference for VADs was that they were civilian volunteers who, prior to the war, had had limited or no nursing experience. The VAD system had been founded in 1909 and by the summer of 1914 there were over 1800 VADs in Britain with a membership of 40,000 people.[93]

These VADs served in France, Serbia, Salonika and England.[94] Thirty-six-year-old Mary Herbert (Molly) Tripp from Canterbury, for example, worked as a VAD in a military hospital near London. She made 'a particular point' of seeking out Australians and New Zealanders and found her work as a VAD rewarding.[95] Other New Zealand women who travelled from New Zealand, paying their own way, to work as British VADs included Harriet Simeon and Mabel Gertrude Hyde. Both Simeon and Hyde worked as VADs in Egypt, while Maud Bowerbank travelled to Britain to work there. Harriet Simeon later worked as a VAD on a hospital ship and then served in France at No. 25 Stationary Hospital and No. 5 General Hospital, Rouen. In 1918 Simeon joined the Women's Royal Air Force, 'in which she held responsible positions in different parts of Britain with the rank of major'.[96] Her papers, held at the Auckland War

Harriet Simeon paid her own way from New Zealand to the United Kingdom to work as a British VAD; she performed her duties with the Voluntary Aid Detachment in the UK, Egypt and France, and on hospital ships. She later joined the Women's Royal Air Force. AUCKLAND WAR MEMORIAL MUSEUM TĀMAKI PAENGA HIRA, PH-1987-2-1

Memorial Museum, include many tributes from some of the soldiers for whom she cared. One written by a young British lieutenant in May 1916 is typical:

> The Noble and self-sacrificing spirit of the British Empire's Womanhood has been amply proved in this great conflict by the devoted bands of voluntary workers tending the sick and wounded.
>
> Among these Angels of Mercy is my great pleasure to number Sister Simeon of faraway New Zealand, whose sympathy & kindness to me whilst a patient at 19th General Hospital Alexandria I shall never forget & for whose welfare I shall always pray.[97]

A newspaper article about Harriet Simeon and her husband George, a major serving in the New Zealand Rifle Brigade, declared that theirs was 'A Unique Record', with 'a record of war service that is, to say the least, out of the ordinary'.[98]

In 1915 Taplin (Lin) Allman was working for the New Zealand Express Office in Palmerston North. She had completed a first-aid course with the St John Ambulance Association when she offered her services to the British Red Cross and was immediately commissioned as a VAD. She worked as a VAD in military hospitals in Britain and France as well as working at an enteric (typhoid) camp and in a prisoner-of-war hospital.[99] Eveline Frances (Evelyn) Smith, from Marton in the Rangitīkei, passed the Red Cross exams that allowed her to become a VAD in military hospitals in the United Kingdom. Working in a surgical ward, she found that she 'liked it very much' and that her soldier patients 'are very good and help me as much as they can'.[100] Another VAD, Mary Theodora Joyce (Dora) Wilcox, from Banks Peninsula, worked in the 200-bed King George's Military Hospital in Stamford Street, London, where she cared for soldiers from all over the British Empire.[101]

Elsie Gertrude Dimock from Silverstream, near Wellington, had a similar experience working for four months as a VAD at a hospital for officers in Kensington. Dimock must have found this work a bit mundane as she left after a few months in order to complete a tool-setting course at the London School of Engineering. She later worked as a foreman tool-setter at the Austin Motor Company in Birmingham.[102] In early 1918, Elizabeth Marion (Bessie) Ernest of Auckland was awarded the Royal Red Cross for her work as a VAD in British military hospitals on the Western Front. Such a high award to a lowly VAD attracted the ire of NZANS chief Hester Maclean, who believed that 'the title of nurse has been abused in its assumption by VAD workers'.[103] Despite this petty jealousy, the award was undoubtedly well earned, and probably many more VADs should have received them. Mary Victoria Cracroft-Wilson from Culverden, North Canterbury, worked as a British Red Cross VAD in an auxiliary hospital in Roehampton for three years. She later became New Zealand's fourth female member of Parliament.[104]

New Zealander Jean Campbell worked as a VAD in Britain and France before parental pressure forced her back to safer work, stripping down aeroplane engines in Cheltenham. Two months before the end of the war she married Gallipoli veteran and childhood friend Spencer Westmacott.[105]

The nurses and VADs were women who were already overseas when war broke out or who could not wait for the New Zealand government to decide on its policy of providing a military nursing service. Their experiences were often remarkable, and some of them are recorded below.

On 12 April 1917 the *New Zealand Herald* ran a feature on 'Fighting Families'. The first family mentioned in the article was the household of Peter Robertson of Avondale, Auckland. Readers were informed that Mr Robertson had three sons and two daughters 'engaged in war work'. Of the sons, Lieutenant Gordon Robertson was serving as an engineer for the naval air service in the United Kingdom, Private Norman Robertson was serving with an Australian machine-gun company and Private Benjamin Robertson had enlisted in a New Zealand Reinforcement contingent. The two daughters were in the United Kingdom: Nancy was a nursing sister in the Lord Derby War Hospital at Warrington, and Susan, who had recently qualified from Edinburgh University as a doctor, had volunteered to serve in France.[106] It was certainly a remarkable record of service, but it was also notable that only one of the Robertson children was serving with New Zealand military forces.

Nancy Marion Robertson trained at Auckland Hospital and graduated as a nurse in June 1915. Her name was recorded in several New Zealand newspapers as one of 25 nurses who passed the state examinations for the registration of nurses with a pass mark of 75 per cent or higher.[107] In 1916 she applied to join Queen Alexandra's Imperial Military Nursing Service Reserve (QAIMNSR). It must have been an impressive application because in early November Robertson heard from the matron-in-chief that her services were 'likely to be needed at an early date', and was requested: 'Please state the earliest date that you can join for duty.'[108] Robertson worked at hospitals in Britain but served most of 1918 in France with No. 5 Casualty Clearing Station, with which she remained until March 1919 in charge of the acute medical wards. Her report from this unit recorded that Robertson 'proved a very capable nursing sister and . . . worked very hard'. She was described as 'very even tempered and reliable and well-liked by her fellow sisters'.[109]

Nancy Robertson was not the only New Zealand nurse to serve in the QAIMNSR. The first New Zealander to join was Hokitika-born, Wellington-trained nurse Laura Elizabeth James, who was living in London in 1914 and had been nursing at British army hospitals since 1910.[110] She was mobilised on 17 August 1914 and was on active duty in France a week later. She initially worked with No. 12 British General Hospital at Rouen, where she had the unnerving experience of a forced evacuation in her first week. When settled back at Rouen, No. 12 General Hospital treated the severely wounded Old Contemptibles, and James was dismayed by what she saw and heard:

> Some of the wounds are beyond description and the men tell us appalling stories of things that have happened. Surely this ghastly war cannot last long.[111]

Over the course of the war, she served at several British stationary and general hospitals as well as at three different casualty clearing stations.[112] In early 1917 James was in charge of a special hospital attached to No. 37 Field Ambulance near Arras and had a staff of 50 people. Located in a chateau right on the front line, the hospital treated severe abdominal, chest and head wounds, often in the most trying of conditions. James admitted that when the German artillery shook the walls she had 'a horrid little quaking feeling'.[113] She was later sent to Italy as matron in charge of the large No. 11 General Hospital. In June 1918 James herself briefly became a patient at this hospital after she contracted influenza. She served there until April 1919, when illness forced her to take three months' sick leave.[114] For her war service, Sister Laura James was awarded the Royal Red Cross, the Military Medal, the 1914 Star, the General War Service Medal, the Victory Medal and the Allies' Medal. She had also been mentioned in despatches twice. As the *Star* newspaper wrote: 'This is a splendid record for a New Zealand girl and one her countrywomen might well be proud of.'[115] It was a splendid and extraordinary record for anybody. After the war, James nursed in military hospitals in the United Kingdom, Gibraltar and Malta. She ended her career nursing British soldiers in India.[116]

Following closely behind Laura James was Mildred Gertrude Rees from Waitaki. Rees, who trained at Wellington Hospital, had also been working in the United Kingdom since 1910. After a six-week stint in Belgium, she returned to England in September 1914 to join the QAIMNSR and spent the next 12 months working at hospitals in Rouen before returning to London to recuperate from the effects of influenza. Back in France in 1916, Rees worked at a stationary hospital before nursing for five months on Barge 192 of British No. 4 Ambulance Flotilla. This work involved ferrying badly wounded men down the River Somme to various hospitals along the way. Rees described the river as 'very swift' and 'full of turns and twists' and the number of patients aboard as 'awfully heavy'.[117] Rees, who was in her late forties, continued to serve in France until she was demobilised in April 1919. She was awarded the 1914 Star and the Associate Royal Red Cross, and was mentioned in despatches.

The daughter of a former soldier and landowner, Nursing Sister Louisa Higginson, who had been the matron at Wairoa Hospital prior to the war, also eventually became a member of the QAIMNSR. Her friend Sister Mary Nora Collins, who was from Ross on the South Island West Coast and who had previously worked at the Cambridge Sanatorium and the Wairoa Hospital, joined her. Both paid their own passage to the United Kingdom, arriving early April 1915. With the help of the New Zealand High Commissioner, Sir Thomas Mackenzie, they tried to join the QAIMNSR. Offered a position with the British Red Cross instead, Higginson and Collins sailed for Malta on 9 May. During the voyage the nurses thought something had 'gone wrong with the ship' as it increased speed and carried out several strange manoeuvres at top speed. They were later 'very pleased' to learn that they had escaped from the German submarine that had been following them.[118]

On arrival in Malta, the group of nurses learned from the matron-in-chief that 'we were not wanted here & yet they are crying out for nurses'. Higginson was 'not very impressed with [the matron's] manners'.[119] Despite this initial setback, the two women were soon working at the Maltese hospital of Hamrun, treating Australian and New Zealand wounded from Gallipoli, and they received considerable praise for being 'good and practical'.[120] But the work took its toll. After the death of a 17-year-old patient, Louisa Higginson wrote that 'it is so dreadful to see all the suffering'.[121] When a letter from New Zealand arrived with the news that her father was very ill, and suffering stomach problems herself, she wrote in her diary, 'I wish I had not left New Zealand. It is the first time I have felt so far away.'[122]

Both Higginson and Collins were desperate to join the NZANS and made several applications to do so. Collins explained their reasons in a letter to Sir James Allen on 18 July:

> I wondered if Miss Higginson and I would have a chance of, even now, being employed by the N.Z. Government, & having our passage money refunded, the pay given by the Red Cross or the War Office is very small, and I'm afraid we would stand little chance of getting back to N.Z. on it.[123]

She later also wrote to the matron-in-chief of the QAIMNSR explaining that she and Higginson were 'most anxious to be with our own people'.[124] Despite the intervention and support of both Allen and Mackenzie in London, internal and external nursing politics prevented them from joining the New Zealand service. In fact, the bad feeling that arose between QAIMNSR and NZANS provoked the matron-in-chief of the NZANS to write to her QAIMNSR counterpart that 'as I feel they [Collins and Higginson] have not been candid in this matter, I decline to have any further dealings with them'.[125] This must have been a considerable disappointment. Higginson especially, according to historian Hannah Clark, 'was taken aback by how she was treated by fellow British nurses and military commanders, as neither she nor many other New Zealanders viewed themselves as "colonials" and thus of inferior skill and rank'.[126] She wrote that, compared with Australian and New Zealand medical personnel, 'These English people, they haven't got the spunk of a flie [sic], they seem afraid of everyone above them.'[127]

Higginson and Collins served with the British Red Cross in the Mediterranean theatre, including Egypt, for a year. Back in London in November 1916, they resigned from the Red Cross to join the QAIMNSR and served with it for the duration of the war, starting with 12-month postings to hospitals in the United Kingdom. 'The days seem long & lonely,' Higginson wrote in her diary.[128] During a stint at the Belmont War Hospital at Sutton, near London, she treated German prisoners of war, and it was not an experience she enjoyed. After her arrival at Belmont in June 1917 Higginson wrote in her diary:

> I feel so disgusted & ashamed to think I have to nurse Huns. This is what I paid my fare & came 16,000 miles for . . . It is a beautiful place and should be used for our boys, of course we only do dressing & just what is necessary no more.[129]

During her months there her attitude remained unchanged.[130] 'How I loathe being here, when I think I could be nursing our own boys & when I think the way the beast [sic] behave,' she wrote in her diary. But she did concede that '[o]f course they are good patients'.[131]

In September 1918 Higginson and Collins were about to do a third posting, this time with a British hospital ship.[132] Higginson was eventually posted to the hospital ship *Grantully Castle* as its matron.[133] She was later transferred to the *Carisbrooke Castle*, which was returning wounded South African soldiers to their homeland.[134] Both nurses returned to New Zealand in August 1919. 'Can't believe I am nearly home,' Higginson wrote on sighting Cape Brett; 'I wonder what are the changes after four & half years.'[135] After an eventful and at times difficult war she had to wait another two days until she could set foot on her homeland. 'On the boat, so near & yet so far,' she recorded.[136] Higginson went on to run and own her own private hospital in Whangarei.[137]

New Zealand gained another connection with the Belmont Hospital when Wellington nurse Edith Maud Fairchild, serving with the QAIMNSR, was appointed its matron in mid-1918.[138] Edith Fairchild had a very active war. When the conflict broke out in 1914, she was working at the Royal Hospital, Woolwich. She was soon posted to a British base hospital in France. While in France she worked at the large military hospital at Boulogne, was matron of a field hospital and, for a time, was attached to one of the ambulance trains bringing wounded from the field hospitals back to the United Kingdom.[139] In August 1920, New Zealand newspapers reported on her recent visit to family in Wellington: 'Miss Edith Fairchild, R.R.C., Q.A., A.I.N.S. was only recently in New Zealand after being on active service during the whole of the war.'[140]

Another New Zealand nurse to serve in the QAIMNSR met a tragic end. In 1914, Aucklander Ella Kate Cooke was travelling with her sister Lily to the United Kingdom via Canada and the United States. Arriving after the declaration of war, Ella Cooke offered her services to the British medical authorities, but was informed she would not be needed. Not one to wait around, Cooke crossed the Channel in November 1914 and spent the next six months nursing on the Western Front with the French Flag Nursing Corps at Bernay.[141] She returned to England in May 1915 and again offered her services to the British military. This time she was accepted into the QAIMNSR and was soon nursing at the Connaught Hospital at Aldershot. But she was disappointed not to be serving abroad, and unimpressed by the way she was treated by the British army nurses. The work was 'frightfully hard & we've a ridiculously small staff', she wrote. At night on duty Cooke was responsible for 240 patients. The constant bickering and bitchiness of the staff wore her down. She wrote to a friend in July:

> I can't call some of these women anything else, they are cats of the deepest dye . . . Eaddy [Nurse Mary Audley Eaddy] and I were happier in France with foreigners than being here with our own flesh and blood . . . It's a wonder we're allowed to breathe. Some of these dreadful women would like to alter the whole universe — they're proper fiends to have anything to do with.[142]

At the end of September 1915 Cooke's wish to serve abroad was granted. She was transferred to No. 17 General Hospital in Alexandria. Here she was very happy and soon became a 'very great favourite' of the patients.[143] Two years after she arrived in Egypt, Ella Cooke was hurrying to have dinner with a friend. She went to take a shortcut at a busy intersection on a tramline, but stepped straight into the path of an oncoming tram and was killed instantly.[144] She was buried in the Alexandria (Hadra) War Memorial Cemetery with full military honours.[145] She shares her last resting place with 52 other New Zealanders.

Eva Clare Jordan from Tauranga was another New Zealand nurse to serve in the QAIMNSR. Trained in Auckland, Jordan was nursing in Honolulu when war broke out. She paid her own way to England, and on arrival in November 1914 she immediately joined the British Red Cross. For the first month of 1915 Jordan was helping run a small Red Cross military hospital at Newbury while trying to join the NZANS. In early 1915, with no immediate prospect of linking up with her own country's military nursing service, Jordan, along with eight other New Zealand nurses, signed on for a year's service with the QAIMNSR.[146] Jordan was immediately sent to France to nurse at No. 3 Casualty Clearing Station, just a few miles behind the front line. The work was hard and the winter conditions harsh.

In April 1915 she was working at a hospital at Poperinghe in Belgium when the Germans launched an offensive to remove the Ypres Salient. This Second Battle of Ypres was an arduous time for the medical staff in Flanders. Jordan's hospital, under constant shellfire, was soon swamped with wounded Canadian soldiers. She described them as 'a splendid lot of men, awfully plucky, and very modest about their deeds'. Jordan described to her uncle what it was like to be nursing on the front line during a battle:

> They were strenuous times, and there was so much to do, and all so important, that one hardly knew where to start first. The medical officers were just 'bricks' and I never wish to have better helpers than my night orderlies. Often they worked 20 hours out of 24 and the medical officer on duty at night was always up 24 hours with no chance of getting to bed. Sometimes the whole medical staff would be working half the night. Sometimes we had it quite slack, but that was before Ypres began.[147]

By July 1915 Jordan was working at No. 11 General Hospital in Boulogne, where she must have impressed the military medical staff as that year she was promoted from staff nurse to sister and had been mentioned in despatches. She finally managed to join the NZANS, but not until the war had finished. Typical of the penny-pinching New Zealand military authorities, she had to drop a rank to do so.[148]

Other New Zealand nurses served in the QAIMNSR, on hospital ships, in the British Red Cross, in British hospitals, and on hospital trains. In early February 1915 the *Dominion* newspaper ran an article titled 'New Zealand Nurses at the Front' that featured the names of 22 New Zealand nurses serving in 10 different medical organisations.[149] Three New Zealand nurses who found themselves nursing in Serbia had a very different experience to those in Britain. One was South African War veteran Sister Emily Jane Peter. Fifty-six years old in 1914, Jane Peter travelled to England, joined the Red Cross and was sent to Serbia as part of Lady Leila Paget's Serbian Relief Fund military hospital, the first of several Allied medical organisations to serve in the Balkans and predating the arrival of the British–French forces at Salonika by almost a year.[150] Peter worked for two months at Lady Paget's hospital at Uskub and later moved to nurse at Vrnjačka Banja. When she contracted typhus, which had reached epidemic levels in Serbia, she had to return to Britain. Peter, who was decorated for her service in Serbia, greatly admired her Serbian patients, describing them as 'nice, grateful quiet people [who] bear pain marvellously'. The countryside reminded her of New Zealand.[151]

Nurse Mabel Atkinson from Christchurch also served with Lady Paget's unit in Serbia, staying on when the hospital was captured by Bulgarian soldiers. She was repatriated to England with Lady Paget and the remnants of her medical unit via Romania, Russia, Sweden and Norway, but she soon returned to work for two years at the Serbian Relief Fund Hospital in Salonika until the Armistice.[152] Back in England after the war, she nursed Serbian orphans at a school at Faversham, Kent, and then travelled to Czechoslovakia to nurse convalescing Czech soldiers.[153]

Another New Zealand nurse to serve in Serbia would be honoured for her bravery there. Ethel Mary Lewis had been a district nurse at Ōtaki but was in England when war broke out. She joined a British medical unit on 1 September 1914 and four days later was working in a Belgian Field Hospital that had been set up by a British colonel.[154] After nine weeks at Antwerp, the hospital was evacuated just as the Germans entered the city. The medical unit returned to England, and was then sent to Serbia, attached to the Serbian Second Army fighting on the Bulgarian frontier. While nursing near the front trenches, Sister Lewis received a slight shrapnel wound to her shoulder. Later, she received a bravery award, presented to her by King Peter of Serbia for saving an officer's life. When the German army overran Serbia the medical unit had to evacuate to Salonika via a forced march of about 130 miles, an ordeal that Lewis described in a letter home:

> Have just reached England, safe and sound, except for a frostbitten knee. It has been a truly awful time. I have lost absolutely everything. We walked through snow, etc., 129 miles in five and a half days with nothing to eat but black bread, and very little of that. We were simply starving when we reached Salonika; had only slept on cobble stones and a little straw for six weeks.[155]

In spite of the frostbite, upon her return to England Lewis was soon nursing at the New Zealand hospital at Walton-on-Thames. Not even a broken arm, a repeat of an earlier injury, prevented her from turning up for duty.[156]

Ethel Lewis returned to New Zealand for a brief visit in October 1916 but did not remain long. She joined the NZANS and left for overseas service with the 33rd Reinforcement aboard the *Athenic* on 31 December 1917. Lewis served in France, where she claimed she was again recognised for her bravery, and back in England at No. 3 New Zealand Hospital, Codford. The intrepid nurse returned to New Zealand in May 1919. A New Zealand newspaper wrote that her five decorations and gold wound stripe were 'records of her honourable service abroad in the interests of the fighting men'.[157] There is no doubt Ethel Lewis had been dedicated to the service of sick and wounded during the war. There is growing doubt, though, over the veracity of some of the eight decorations she claimed to have received. These were the Légion d'honneur (France); Médaille Militaire (France); Croix de Guerre (Belgium); 1914 Star Trio; Order of St Sava, 3rd Class (Serbia); Order of White Eagle (Serbia); Royal Red Cross (Serbia); and Retreat Medal (Serbia).[158]

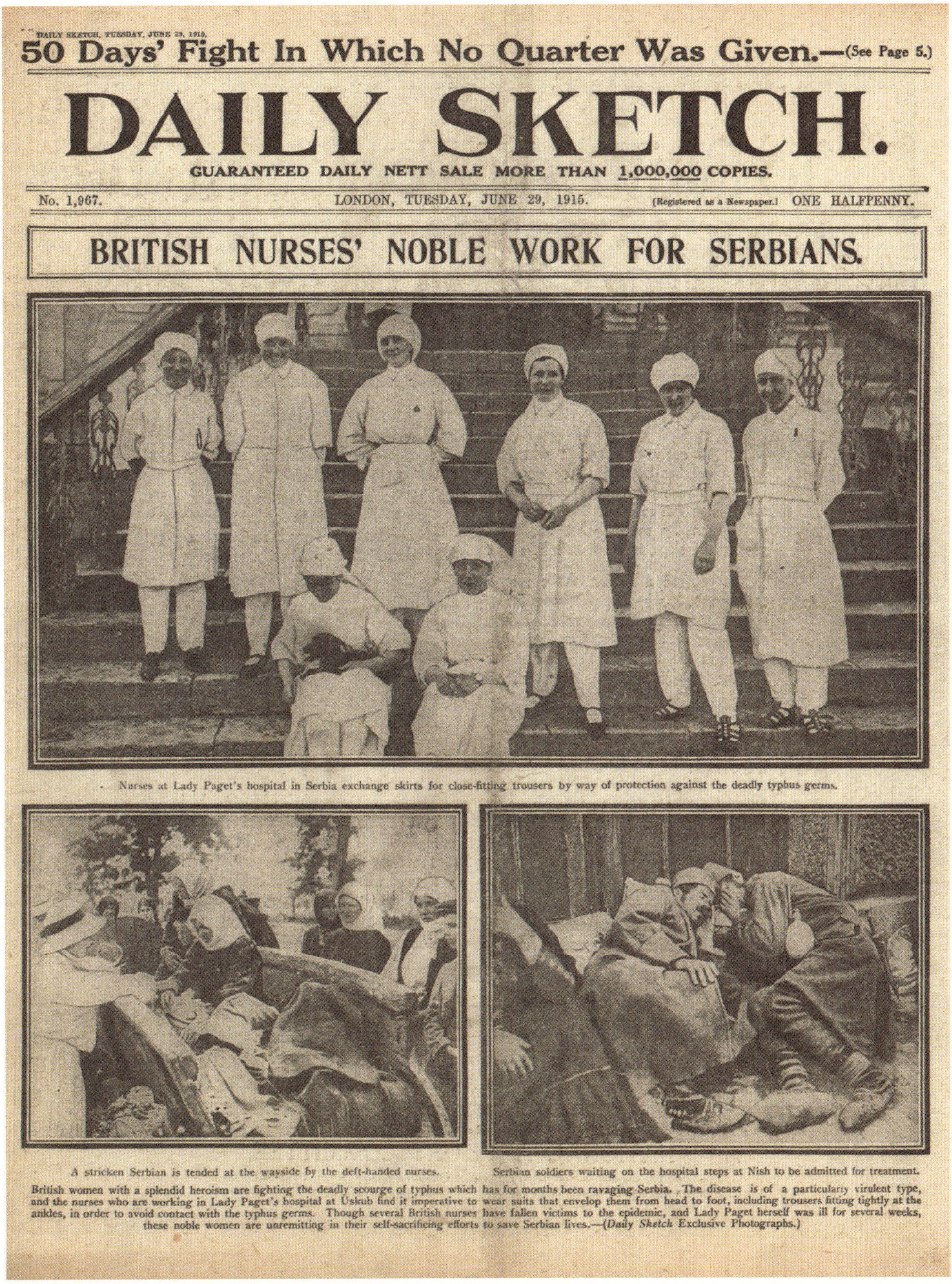

DAILY SKETCH, TUESDAY, JUNE 29, 1915.

50 Days' Fight In Which No Quarter Was Given.—(See Page 5.)

DAILY SKETCH.

GUARANTEED DAILY NETT SALE MORE THAN 1,000,000 COPIES.

No. 1,967. LONDON, TUESDAY, JUNE 29, 1915. [Registered as a Newspaper.] ONE HALFPENNY.

BRITISH NURSES' NOBLE WORK FOR SERBIANS.

Nurses at Lady Paget's hospital in Serbia exchange skirts for close-fitting trousers by way of protection against the deadly typhus germs.

A stricken Serbian is tended at the wayside by the deft-handed nurses.

Serbian soldiers waiting on the hospital steps at Nish to be admitted for treatment.

British women with a splendid heroism are fighting the deadly scourge of typhus which has for months been ravaging Serbia. The disease is of a particularly virulent type, and the nurses who are working in Lady Paget's hospital at Üskub find it imperative to wear suits that envelop them from head to foot, including trousers fitting tightly at the ankles, in order to avoid contact with the typhus germs. Though several British nurses have fallen victims to the epidemic, and Lady Paget herself was ill for several weeks, these noble women are unremitting in their self-sacrificing efforts to save Serbian lives.—(*Daily Sketch* Exclusive Photographs.)

This front page of the *Daily Sketch* described the work of Lady Paget's hospital in Serbia. Several New Zealanders worked in this hospital, including Mabel Atkinson and Jane Peter.
ALAMY, F22WKA

Like many other New Zealand nurses serving abroad, Sister Ethel Mary Lewis had a remarkable record of service. She nursed wounded and sick soldiers on the Western Front, in Serbia and in the United Kingdom (including at Walton-on-Thames, shown above). While her courage is unquestioned, some of the decorations she claimed are doubtful. In the image (right) she wears many campaign and medal ribbons. In later years she was photographed wearing as many as 10 medals, including the French Legion of Honour and the Belgian Croix de Guerre. However, her name is absent from the master list of recipients of the Legion of Honour, and researchers in New Zealand have not been able to verify the Belgian medal, either. THE VOLUNTEERS, NEW ZEALAND MILITARY HISTORICAL SOCIETY; OTAKI MUSEUM

One of the awards Sister Lewis claimed and wore was the Knight's Cross of the Légion d'honneur. This would have made her the only New Zealand woman to receive the medal for war service. However, the Grand Chancery of the Légion d'honneur has no record of her being awarded the honour.[159] There is some doubt as to the veracity of some of the other awards, too, especially the French Military Medal and the Belgian Cross of War.

Two other New Zealand nurses also served in Serbia. Agnes Dorothy Kerr and Mildred Stephens had arrived in Egypt with the Volunteer Sisterhood, a makeshift, largely unpaid organisation that owed much to the drive and energy of its founder, Ettie Rout. While in Serbia, Kerr and Stephens worked with another remarkable woman, the pioneering New Zealand doctor Agnes Bennett, who was then in charge of the 7th Medical Unit of the Scottish Women's Hospital.[160] From February 1917 Kerr worked at the No. 1 Southern General Hospital in Birmingham, where she was described a year later as 'a good nurse, hardworking and trustworthy'. However, her deafness prevented her from being given 'any work of a very responsible nature'.[161] In October 1918 Kerr was transferred to the nearby Stourbridge Military Hospital, where she was described in her first annual report as 'having proved herself a capable and conscientious staff nurse, well trained and methodical'. The report did note that '[a] certain degree of deafness would probably be a bar to promotion'.[162] However, the disability did not prevent her from continuing to serve as a staff nurse with the British Territorial Force Nursing Service until she reached the compulsory retirement age in February 1930.[163]

Eileen Nelson arrived in Egypt with the first group of Ettie Rout's Volunteer Sisterhood. The Sisterhood comprised New Zealand women volunteers who, like Rout herself, were determined to serve in the war despite government hostility, harsh living conditions and little remuneration. Months after arriving in Egypt, Nelson found herself nursing at No. 32 British General Hospital at Amara in Mesopotamia in June 1916. The journey to Amara had been a nightmare in itself, involving cramped accommodation on a dirty paddleboat, bad food and 'ravenous mosquitoes'.[164] To the strains of her nursing duties were added the intense heat — '110 degrees F in the shade' — and attacks of the debilitating sandfly fever.[165] Nursing conditions in the various theatres of war are a key theme of *With Them Through Hell*, the medical services volume of the Centenary History written by Anna Rogers.[166]

Despite all these challenges, only two New Zealand-born nurses lost their lives during the war. The fate of Ella Cooke has been detailed above. The other nurse to die was Elise Margaret Kemp, a QAIMNSR nurse attached to No. 37 Casualty Clearing Station in Flanders, who was killed in an air raid on 20 October 1917 along with three patients and three orderlies.[167]

The efforts and experiences of the 100-odd New Zealand nurses who served with British medical organisations were extraordinary and have been overlooked for far too long.

The contributions of women doctors have also been long overlooked. According to author Jane Tolerton, 'at least 25 New Zealand women doctors worked overseas in the war effort'.[168] As with the New Zealand-born nurses discussed above, these doctors performed outstanding service in unusual places. In November 1915, for instance, Dr Mary Alice Blair of Wellington arrived in Salonika as the commanding officer of a unit of the Scottish Women's Hospital.[169] Her unit was attached to the Serbian army, which had just completed its long retreat from

Serbia. Dr Agnes Elizabeth Lloyd Bennett, also of Wellington, served with this unit, too, as did Dr Jessie Ann Scott, who had grown up on a farm in Canterbury.[170] Agnes Bennett and her friend Dr Grace Matilda Hetty Russell were 'the first women doctors to work in a British army medical unit'.[171] They both began the war working at the Egyptian Army Hospital at Abassia.

There is little doubt that the work of New Zealand medical personnel outside of the NZEF was a significant contribution to the British war effort. Moreover, this service often took a heavy toll. New Zealand doctor George Redpath, from Gisborne, was a prime example. Redpath served with the Royal Army Medical Corps in France in 1915 and 1916 and later served in Italy in 1917.[172] Before he enlisted in the RAMC, Redpath did not drink; a fellow medical student and doctor was 'quite certain' of this.[173] But to the immense despair of his young wife and family, Redpath returned to New Zealand a hopeless alcoholic. A local doctor in Gisborne tried to help the family have George sent to the military hospital at Hanmer Springs 'to endeavour to break him of the habit'. The doctor's recommendation detailed a family tragedy. In 1920 Redpath was 'a confirmed drunkard' who got 'helpless on every occasion'. It was the doctor's opinion that his patient 'got shell shocked etc & the resulting neurasthenia has evidently forced him to take to the bottle'. It was 'an exceedingly sad case', but it was certainly not an uncommon one.[174]

In February 1967 the radio station 1YZ in Rotorua recorded an interview with Thomas Remi Morrison of the Arawa Returned Services Association League. In the interview Morrison, who had enlisted in the NZEF shortly after his sixteenth birthday, reflected on his time serving with the New Zealand Pioneer Battalion. One of his memories was of a soldier named Sonny Breeze (or possibly Brees), who was also from Rotorua. Brees had joined a British regiment very early in the war and was proud of the fact that 'he belonged to the great Guards of the British Army' rather than the NZEF. Morrison believed that Brees was 'the only Maori to join the British Army' in the First World War.[175] Sonny Brees later transferred to the New Zealand Maori (Pioneers) in France. However, the claim that he was the only Māori to join the British army in the war was incorrect. The previous chapter has already mentioned another: Ropata Kereti, who joined a Middlesex Regiment battalion and served with it on the Western Front.

Moreover, there were others, including Alexander Ormond. Of Ngāti Rongomaiwahine and Ngāti Kahungunu descent, Ormond was born in May 1890 and spent his early years in Māhia in the northern Hawke's Bay, where his family had extensive farm holdings. From 1903 to 1910 he attended Wanganui Collegiate, 'where he excelled in both academic and sporting pursuits'.[176] At Canterbury Agricultural College he was vice-captain of both the First XI and the First XV. He graduated with a diploma in agriculture in 1913 and was awarded a special prize for taking second place in the graduating class.

In September 1915, Ormond gave up managing one of the family farms and sailed for England, where he immediately joined the Inns of Court Officer Training Corps with the intention of gaining a commission in the BEF. In July 1916 he was commissioned as a second lieutenant into the 27th Battalion of the Manchester Regiment. On his attestation form Ormond had made it

Agnes Bennett graduated from the University of Edinburgh and held senior roles in hospitals in Wellington before becoming the first female commissioned officer in the British army in 1915. As a captain she worked as a medical officer in war hospitals in Cairo, and in 1916–17 she was in charge of a unit of the Scottish Women's Hospitals on the Serbian front. IMPERIAL WAR MUSEUM, Q108182

clear that he was not 'of pure European descent', but nonetheless was — with echoes of the 1840 Treaty of Waitangi — 'British by birth'.[177] A month later, he was attached to the regiment's 11th Battalion and sailed with it to the Western Front.

In September 1916, the Battle of the Somme was entering its third deadly stage and the 11th Manchesters were sent to a position near Pozières, north-east of Amiens and in the very centre of the Somme battlefield. The New Zealand Division was fighting nearby at Flers. The battalion successfully defended its position, but on the evening of 30 September, just before his battalion was to be relieved, Ormond was hit by an artillery shell fragment and killed. He was 26 years old. Following his death, the Ormond family received a letter from an officer in his battalion who stated that, although he had not known Alexander long,

> I never wish to go into action with a braver man or better officer. He was perfectly cheerful under the heaviest fire, and I can't speak too highly of the way he commanded that bombing section . . . he will be very much missed.[178]

Alexander Ormond's name is on the Thiepval Memorial to the Missing of the Somme. It is also on the Māhia Soldiers' Memorial erected by his parents in 1922 and on the Roll of Honour of Lincoln University. Two of his brothers, William Ormond and John Ormond, served with the New Zealand Pioneer Battalion. They both survived the war and returned to New Zealand.

Charles Edward Anketell holds the dubious record of serving in all three services of the British military during the First World War. He must have been a bit of a character: according to a laconic note on his military file, enquiries to the New Zealand High Commissioner's Office in London revealed that 'the officer was well known to them'.[179] From Napier, Anketell began his military career in the New Zealand branch of the Royal Navy Volunteer Reserve (RNVR) as an assistant engineer.[180] He transferred to the Royal Navy but deserted some time in 1915.[181] It cannot have been military service that Anketell was avoiding, as he joined the army's East Surrey Regiment and was promoted to NCO rank. It was erroneously reported in New Zealand, probably at his instigation, that Anketell had been awarded the Military Medal for his service in France with the East Surreys.[182]

On 26 August 1917 Anketell was commissioned into the 12th Battalion of the Royal Fusiliers. He did not serve long with this regiment before transferring to the Royal Flying Corps at the end of November. Anketell spent two of his three months with the Royal Fusiliers being treated at various field hospitals for 'ringworm'.[183] A medical board report of early 1918 revealed that Anketell was in fact suffering from gonorrhoea and that he needed further treatment at a VD hospital.[184] Anketell eventually served as an observer in the newly created Royal Air Force, but was killed in action on 11 May 1918, aged 23. He had certainly crammed plenty of experience into his short life.

Henry Norman Spence, a farmer from Pukekohe, had obtained a commission in the 10th Battalion of the Border Regiment. On 10 November 1916 Spence was captured in the Somme

A gifted athlete with a strong academic record, Alexander Ormond was one of a number of Māori to serve in the British Expeditionary Force. Killed during the 1916 Somme battle, he is one of the Somme 'missing', and his name is recorded on the Thiepval Memorial to the Missing of the Somme. LINCOLN UNIVERSITY LIVING HERITAGE: TIKAKA TŌKU IHO

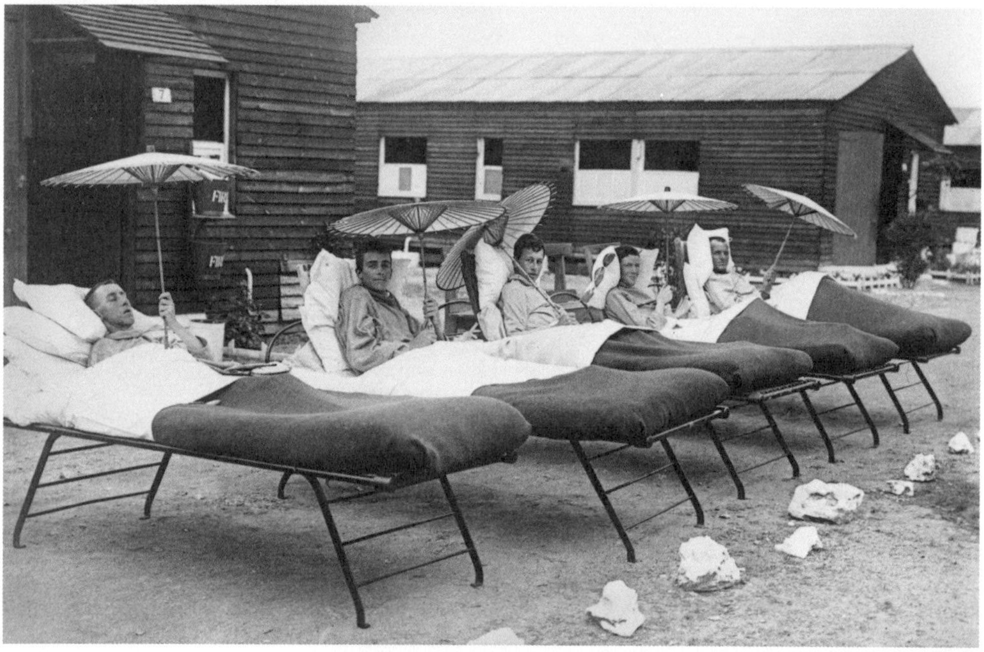

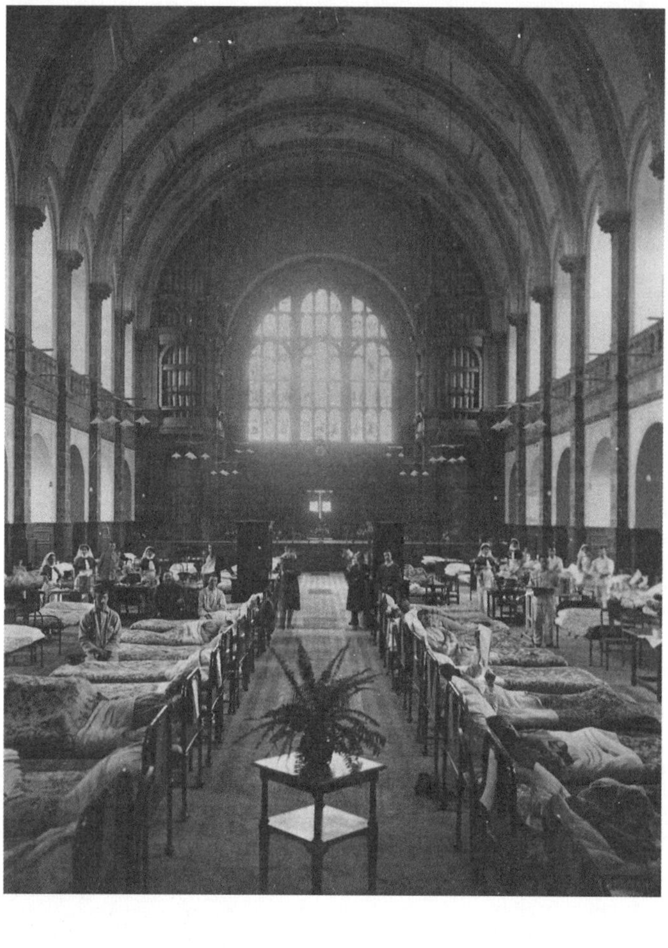

above Wounded British soldiers convalesce at a base hospital in Rouen. This is likely to be the No. 12 General Hospital, where several New Zealand nurses worked and which was taken over by the US army in June 1917. IMPERIAL WAR MUSEUM, Q2339

right The No. 1 Southern General Hospital occupied Birmingham University's Great Hall. New Zealand-born nurses and other medical personnel worked at many British military hospitals during the war. CADBURY RESEARCH LIBRARY: SPECIAL COLLECTIONS, UNIVERSITY OF BIRMINGHAM, UC10I4

region of France and spent the rest of the war as a prisoner in Germany. After the war, the British War Office investigated the circumstances of all officers who were taken prisoner to ascertain whether other options had been open to them. Henry Spence's first, brief, statement stressed that his platoon 'got cut off and surrounded'.[185] The War Office demanded to know what sort of resistance had been offered, the size of the enemy force, whether the ammunition had been exhausted and the number of casualties sustained. Spence's reply was also brief: three of the questions received a one-word reply. It was enough, though, the War Office later informing Spence 'that no blame attaches to him in the matter'.[186]

It is difficult to know exactly how many New Zealanders served with the BEF during the war, but, as in the case of the Australian Imperial Force (AIF), it must run to several thousand. New Zealand newspapers frequently reported news about various New Zealanders serving in British military units. Their reports were headed: 'On Service. New Zealanders Abroad: Appointments and Promotions'. Individuals were mentioned only if they had been recently appointed or had received a promotion. A report in August 1917 in the *Evening Post* featured news about 43 New Zealanders, and at the end of the year it mentioned another 96.[187] In mid-1918, a further 32 New Zealanders were reported on. The New Zealanders had endured many challenges joining the British army and medical unit.[188] Not a few were irked by the strong class system they found, and resented being regarded as inferior 'colonials'. While they were still proud to belong to the British Empire and to claim British citizenship, their experiences also helped foster an emerging New Zealand national identity.

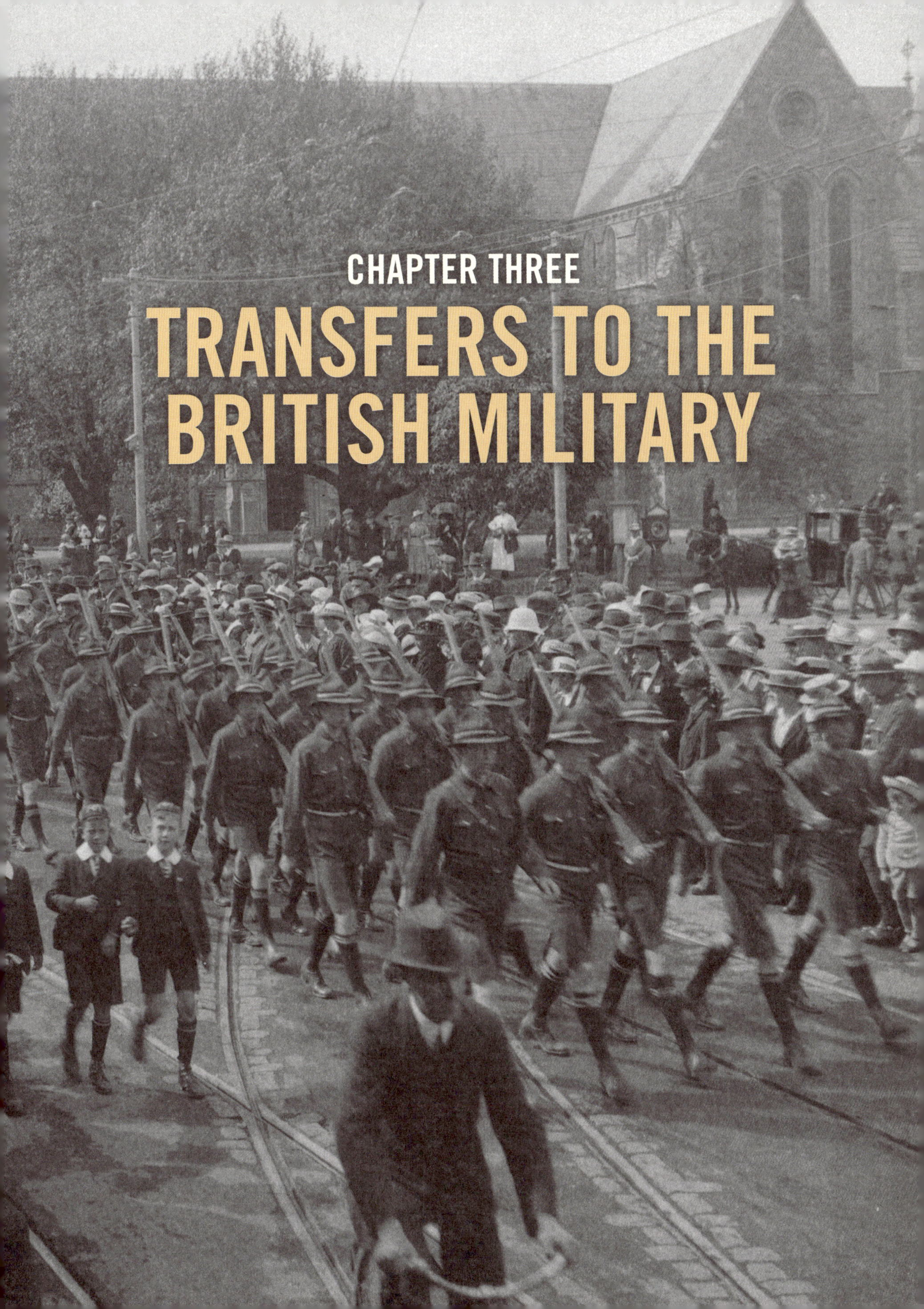

CHAPTER THREE

TRANSFERS TO THE BRITISH MILITARY

Previous pages
First World War soldiers march through Cathedral Square, Christchurch, in 1914. While most local soldiers joined the New Zealand Expeditionary Force, many from the established private schools such as Christ's College opted to join British units instead. At the time this photograph was taken, many New Zealanders were already serving with the British Expeditionary Force in France and Belgium.
ALEXANDER TURNBULL LIBRARY, 1/1-017665-G

Beginning in April 1915 and continuing for the duration of the war, several members of the New Zealand Expeditionary Force (NZEF) transferred to British military forces, causing considerable concern for the New Zealand government and its military leaders in the process. In a total war, when manpower was stretched to its limits and good junior leadership on the battlefield was paramount, it made no sense to allow experienced and talented soldiers to leave.

Nevertheless, many did leave. The exact numbers may never be known, but Lieutenant-Colonel John Studholme's *Record of Personal Services During the War*, published in 1928, is a useful guide. Studholme begins by listing the names and number of NZEF commissioned officers who 'transferred to other forces'. This number is quite small: just 20 people. Six of these officers, three of whom had been awarded the Military Cross, transferred to the Indian army. Another five transferred to the Royal Flying Corps (RFC) or Royal Air Force (RAF). Of the remainder, three joined the Royal Naval Reserve (RNR), five joined British army units and one transferred to the Australian Imperial Force (AIF).[1] The number of non-commissioned officers (NCOs) and men who transferred to receive commissions in the British forces is significantly higher. Studholme's *Record* lists the names of 341 men who did so. Of these, 132 transferred to the Royal Navy, another 132 transferred to the British army, 67 joined the various flying services, and another 10 served with the Indian army.[2]

While a total of 361 transfers is small — barely half of 1 per cent of the NZEF's total personnel — they do represent a drain on the pool of talent. As a result, Lieutenant-General Godley imposed very tight controls on the number of transfers that would be permissible. Godley first raised the issue with the New Zealand government in July 1915, after learning that some New Zealand wounded who had been sent to the United Kingdom to recover were applying for commissions in the vastly expanding BEF. He wrote to the New Zealand defence minister, Sir James Allen, arguing that this development was 'most undesirable', and that the men concerned 'should return here as soon as possible to their units where they will have ample chance of promotion, if deserving'.[3] He considered the opportunity for those in the United Kingdom to obtain commissions was 'most unfair' on those who remained fighting on Gallipoli, and that 'these men should stick to their own force into which they have enlisted'. Given the expected heavy casualties, 'everybody will be wanted'.[4] The New Zealand government was equally alarmed by the development. Allen asked the governor, Lord Liverpool, to inform the War Office that 'we do not approve of commissions being granted in such cases except in any extraordinary circumstances'.[5]

Godley's concerns were justified. When the New Zealand Division was formed in early 1916, he had informed Allen: 'I have been very thoroughly and carefully into the question of officering . . . with Russell, and have found that it is a great difficulty and that we are very short of officers.'[6] He also admonished the New Zealand High Commissioner in London, Sir Thomas Mackenzie, for facilitating transfers to the British forces. 'I have consistently refused all such applications even when recommended by yourself,' he informed him, adding that the notion that the NZEF had enough officers 'is altogether erroneous . . . I should be glad if you would correct the wrong impression referred to as far as possible.'[7] He instructed the senior New Zealand officer in London not to allow any officer transfers from the NZEF to the BEF. He noted that 'Australians are very stiff about this, and will not allow any transfers'.[8]

Allen was primarily concerned to keep control in Godley's hands. He was especially uncomfortable that Mackenzie, a former political opponent, was involved in the process, and in mid-1916 he wrote to Godley:

> I note you say you have taken the High Commissioner's recommendations in one or two cases for the Imperial Commissions, and I hope that you are exercising your own judgement in this matter, uninfluenced by the fact that recommendations have been sent by [the] High Commissioner and I trust that you will make certain that everything is right from the New Zealand point of view regarding these commissions. They do not always play the game in the High Commissioner's office and we rely on you that nobody secures a commission, either in our Force or in the Imperial Force, unless that commission is thoroughly justified and that it is secured without influence and without favour.[9]

In reply, Godley was quick to reassure Allen that Mackenzie had not influenced his selection for transfers 'in the least'.

Lieutenant-General Alexander Godley speaking to New Zealand soldiers in July 1917. Godley was concerned about the number of New Zealanders transferring to the British Expeditionary Force in 1915 and implemented a strict policy to control this, believing that 'these men should stick to their own force'.
ALEXANDER TURNBULL LIBRARY, 1/2-012809-G

No applications for commissions were considered without a commanding officer's endorsement, so that 'there is no possibility of favouritism about it'.[10] In consultation with Allen, the War Office and the New Zealand military authorities in London, Godley initiated a policy in early 1916 to approve only five nominations for imperial commissions per month.[11] This tight restriction was relaxed only for specific requests, such as artillery officers in early 1917 when that corps expanded, and in the last year of the war.[12]

Why was such a severe constraint necessary? There are several reasons. First, New Zealanders in 1914 regarded themselves very much as British citizens. Nearly all those New Zealanders who enlisted in British military units during the war described their nationality as 'British'. Even Alexander Ormond, one of the few soldiers of Māori descent, had stated proudly in his attestation form that he was 'British by birth'.[13] Serving in a British military unit, then, was not such a foreign concept.

Probably the signal reason, however, was the rapid expansion of the British army from a pre-war strength of 733,514 men in the regular army and reserves to a strength of close to four million in March 1918.[14] This created a high demand for commissioned officers, and 'dugouts' from retirement could not meet it. For New Zealand men who were reasonably well educated, articulate and confident, commissions were therefore much easier to obtain in the BEF than in the NZEF. There was also a degree of glamour and adventure associated with joining the British armed services. The NZEF would be concentrated in just two theatres of war, but British army formations 'were more scattered and diverse'.[15] By November 1918 British army divisions were deployed in the United Kingdom, India, Italy, Macedonia, Egypt, Palestine and Mesopotamia, and on the Western Front. New Zealanders served in nearly all of these divisions.

Finally, there was the issue of payment. New Zealand soldiers were well paid, but NCOs and officers were not, especially in proportion to the responsibilities they carried. Godley left it until the end of the war to advise Allen that, in comparison with officers from the BEF, Australia and Canada, 'the inequality is so glaring'. Godley explained that 'the New Zealand officer is paid considerably less than any of the three, except in the most junior of ranks'.[16] Why Godley had not tried to remove this glaring inequality during the war remains a mystery. It must have provided an additional incentive for commissioned officers and potential officers to seek employment where their skills and talent would be better remunerated.

As with those New Zealanders who enlisted directly into the British army, those who transferred served in a wide range of units and locations. They also had more than their share of tragedy, as will become evident later in this chapter.

In October 1919 the *New Zealand Free Lance* reported that Major George Dacre Hamilton had just returned to New Zealand 'after a long period of active service'.[17] George Hamilton's long service had also been extraordinary. A civil servant from Karori, he served with the New Zealand Mounted Rifles in Egypt, but transferred to the New Zealand Pioneer Battalion in March 1916. He fought with the Pioneers on the Western Front until 6 September 1917, when he transferred to the British army as an officer in the Royal Engineers.[18] In this capacity, he had

top The Christ's College First XV in 1907. The young man lying on the right and listed as C. Rich is Geoffrey Gordon Rich, who left New Zealand with the Main Body in October 1914 and served with the Canterbury Mounted Rifles. At the end of 1916, Rich transferred to the British army, with the 1st Lancers and, later, King Edward's Horse. More than 40 New Zealanders served in this latter, fashionable, unit. CHRIST'S COLLEGE ARCHIVES, CCXV/1907/1

below Henry Eugene Voyce (left) and George Willoughby Hadfield Marshall. Voyce transferred to the Worcestershire Regiment on commission and was killed on Gallipoli during the August offensive. Marshall obtained a commission in the York and Lancaster Regiment and was killed in action in France on 21 March 1918. KETE CHRISTCHURCH (HENRY EUGENE VOYCE); AUCKLAND WAR MEMORIAL MUSEUM ONLINE CENOTAPH, KINDLY DONATED BY FAMILY (GEORGE WILLOUGHBY)

a stint of 'special duty' with the Forestry Department and served as a staff officer at the army's general headquarters.[19] Hamilton spent the final six months of his war working with the staff of the Independent Air Force preparing a fleet of four-engined Handley Page V/1500 bombers to raid Berlin. Because the first raid had been planned for 12 November 1918, a day after the Armistice, these large bombers were not used.

Geoffrey Gordon Rich, a farmer from Canterbury, left New Zealand with the Main Body of the NZEF in October 1914. He served as a sergeant in the Canterbury Mounted Rifles before transferring to the British army at the end of 1916.[20] As befitting a Canterbury landholder and Christ's College old boy, Rich initially joined the 1st Reserve Regiment of Lancers before transferring to King Edward's Horse. Geoffrey Rich must have felt at home with the other New Zealanders in this chic unit. His service was exemplary: he was awarded the Military Cross in April 1918 and promoted to full lieutenant two months later. At the end of August Rich was given a period of leave in New Zealand.[21] On 10 December, he wrote to the War Office requesting to resign his commission, explaining that 'my father has a very serious illness & is only expected to live a few months'. As the only son, Geoffrey was needed at home to keep the farm running.[22] He was officially demobilised on 1 February 1919.

Another who had an interesting and varied war was George Gordon de Courcy Drury, a clerk with the Bank of New Zealand in Christchurch, whose grandfather had been a major general in the Royal Marine Light Infantry.[23] A Main Body man, Drury served as a lowly gunner with the New Zealand Field Artillery; after service on Gallipoli and the Western Front he transferred to the British army in April 1917, obtaining a commission in the 3rd Battalion, Royal Scots Fusiliers.[24] In October that year he transferred to the King's African Rifles and served in East Africa until the end of the war, and then on until his discharge on 14 November 1920.[25] At that point, Drury disappeared from official records, and attempts by the War Office to locate him produced no further information. In 1935 his father's obituary listed him as living in Kakamega in Kenya.[26]

A commission in the British army may have offered many more opportunities, but it was far from a soft option. Officers, as with their dominion counterparts, were far more likely to be killed or wounded than ordinary foot soldiers.[27] Leading men in combat greatly increased the risk to those who did it. Death in any theatre of war was arbitrary, owing as much to bad luck as to any skill or experience, and many New Zealanders paid the price for their service in all of the armies in which they chose to serve. And the grief, suffering and anxiety felt by the families of those listed as missing were just the same.

The story of John Willoughby Hadfield Marshall, who transferred as a private from the 1st Wellington Battalion in April 1917 and obtained a commission in the 3rd Battalion of the York and Lancaster Regiment, is indicative of those soldiers who were listed missing. On 21 March 1918, the opening day of the German 'Michael' offensive on the Western Front, John Marshall was reported as 'killed in action'.[28] That was the extent of the official information the family, living in the Rangitīkei, received about his final hours. In May 1918 Marshall's uncle, who lived in London, wrote to the War Office enquiring about his nephew on behalf of the family in New Zealand, which had received updated news from the regiment that 'Jack's Captain reports him prisoner, wounded'.[29] The War Office responded that 'no details respecting the death of 2nd Lieutenant J.W.H. Marshall . . . has been received at the War Office' and directed the uncle to write to Marshall's commanding officer for further details.[30] In early September, the New Zealand Records Section asked the War Office to make enquiries to the York and Lancaster Regiment about the possibility that John Marshall was a prisoner of war. They attached a statement from Marshall's company commander, who had placed Marshall in a protected culvert and had been speaking with him 'just before the enemy broke our line'. Marshall was wounded but still alive, and his company commander was 'perfectly certain that the Boy's wounds were not serious enough to cause his Death'.[31] In reply, the War Office referred to an eyewitness statement from Corporal S. Bradford, an officer in Marshall's company:

> I saw the dead body of 2/Lt. Marshall lying on a stretcher in an arch, which led to the trench down some steps at Lagnicourt on March 21/18. I looked at him and recognised the body as belonging to 2/Lt. Marshall, but as we were retiring it had to be left. He was not my Pl. officer but belonged to my Coy. (C) and I knew him well. He had been killed by a shell.[32]

The War Office communicated this information directly to Marshall's father, stating, 'The Military Secretary fears that there can be no doubt as to the nature of this report.'[33] Nevertheless, there was still much left unknown about John Marshall's fate, and the family needed to know more. In mid-1919, the New Zealand High Commission wrote to the War Office asking about his death and where he had been buried. It stated that Marshall's father was travelling from New Zealand to obtain this information firsthand and visit his son's grave.[34] The War Office promptly and rather bluntly pointed out that 'the details of the circumstances under which an officer meets his death in action on the battlefield are not officially required of Commanding Officers' and that 'no report has reached this Department of his burial'.[35] John's father most likely made an unproductive but undoubtedly emotional journey.

Henry Frederick Roy Messenger, like Trevor Holmden (see pages 68–69), left the NZEF early in the war. He had been a sergeant at Divisional Headquarters but transferred from it on 18 April 1915.[36] He received a commission in the 6th Battalion of the Yorkshire Regiment and served with it on Gallipoli. During the fighting around Cape Helles in the August offensive, Messenger was reported as wounded and then later as 'wounded and missing'.[37] Anxious family members and the New Zealand government wrote to the War Office seeking further information, but in response the Military Secretary could only 'say that nothing further has been heard of 2nd Lieutenant H.F.R. Messenger, 6th Yorkshire Regiment since he was reported "missing"'.[38] One letter to the War Office pointed out that

> [h]is poor old mother had no other means of support but her lost son & as she can get no word of him, cannot receive any of his pay, & and is struggling to keep up his insurance money.[39]

In June 1918 the Army Council, after considerable prompting from the New Zealand government, which wrote five times for news of his fate, officially concluded that Henry Messenger had died of his wounds on or since 22 August 1915.[40] In 1920 the government was still finalising the details of Messenger's estate, nearly five years after he had been reported missing.[41]

The fate of Henry Eugene (Harry) Voyce was much more clear-cut. Voyce, a sapper in the New Zealand Engineers, had transferred from the NZEF at the same time as Holmden and Messenger.[42] He was one of the few New Zealanders serving with the British to list his nationality as 'New Zealand' rather than 'British' or 'British-born'.[43] Like Holmden, he received a commission in the Worcestershire Regiment and served with its 4th Battalion on Gallipoli, where he was killed in action during the start of the August offensive.[44] As was the case with so many of the New Zealand casualties incurred in British service, the family wrote to the War Office for information. In particular, they wanted to know whether Voyce had been killed instantly or 'lay wounded'.[45] The War Office wrote back giving no further details and recommending that the family write to his commanding officer. The War Office also assured them that '[w]hen any information is received it will at once be communicated to his next-of-kin, his mother'.[46] No further information about Voyce's death was ever received.

Canterbury farmer Anthony Darley Russell Rendle was a corporal in the 2nd Canterbury Battalion when he transferred from the NZEF in February 1917.[47] He took a commission in the 9th Battalion of the Devonshire Regiment and served with it on the Western Front. Rendle was killed in action in Belgium on 11 October that year,[48] and was buried in the Hooge Crater Cemetery, Zillebeke, to the south-east of Ypres. Once again, the New Zealand government wrote to the War Office, asking about Rendle's death. Once again, the War Office could offer no further information, redirecting enquiries to the 9th Battalion's commanding officer instead.[49] In what had become a familiar pattern, the government was still settling Rendle's estate some years later.[50]

British-born William Caithness Talbot, a bank clerk from Dunedin, served as a private in the Wellington Battalion before transferring from the NZEF in July 1915.[51] He obtained a commission in the 6th Battalion of the Leinster Regiment,[52] and served with his battalion in Egypt, in Serbia (including the forced retreat from that country) and in Salonika. Malaria was endemic in Salonika, and after a severe bout in June 1916 Talbot was sent back to New Zealand to recuperate.[53] Recovery took almost a year.[54] He was passed fit at the end of July 1917 and sailed for the United Kingdom with the 29 Reinforcements on 17 November. Presenting himself to the War Office ready for duty on 9 January 1918, Talbot now joined the RFC. Aged 26 and the only son in the family, he was killed in a training accident in England on 20 July.[55]

Another New Zealand casualty of a transfer was Brian Gerald Mahoney. An Otago Boys' High School old boy and graduate of Otago University College, Mahoney joined the NZEF as a private soldier in the Auckland Battalion and had reached the rank of sergeant when he transferred from the NZEF at the end of 1917.[56] Given that he listed his nationality as Irish in his application form, it was natural that Mahoney received a commission in the 1/2nd Battalion of Royal Munster Fusiliers.[57] He died on 3 September 1918 while attached to the RAF;[58] newspapers in New Zealand reported that, like Talbot, Mahoney had been 'the victim of a fatal aeroplane accident in England'.[59] The reports also revealed the extent of the Mahoney family's suffering. Two of his brothers, Ulric and Edmund, had been killed in action on Gallipoli and in France respectively. A fourth brother, Ernest, who served with the British army, had been seriously wounded and was reported to be 'dangerously ill' at the end of 1918.[60]

Frank George Massey, son of New Zealand prime minister William Massey, also served in an Irish unit during the war. Captain Frank Massey, a self-employed lawyer from Auckland, joined the NZEF at the end of April 1915. He proved to be quite a soldier. He joined the 1st Battalion of the New Zealand Rifle Brigade as a private, but within two months had been promoted to sergeant, and six months after that he was commissioned as an officer in the 2nd Battalion of the New Zealand Rifle Brigade.[61] The politically astute Godley was aware that a straight transfer might be used to damage the government, but he knew that a Northern Ireland connection would be deeply pleasing to the Massey family. He came up with a formula that kept everyone happy, telling Allen:

> The Prime Minister's son has had a most meteoric career lately, and is now commanding a British Battalion. I had better let you know the circumstances of the whole thing, as I suppose some people will say it is because he is the Prime Minister's son. He was, in the ordinary course of events, like many other promising young officers, attached to a British Brigade to learn Staff work. In this Brigade there happened to be an Ulster battalion of the Royal Irish Rifles, to which I suppose, from the nature of his antecedents, he was particularly attracted. Anyhow, they asked if he might be transferred to the regiment and appointed Second-in-Command, to which I would not agree, as I said I thought he ought to stick to the New Zealand Forces. He was still attached to the Staff of this Brigade during the battle of Messines, and did so well that he got a Military Cross, and they then asked if he might be allowed to stay on and be employed with a battalion. To this I agreed, on the distinct understanding that he was not in any way transferred to the British Army, and that he was only lent temporarily and whenever we wanted him back we should have him. The result is that he is now commanding a battalion. But he is only lent, and we can have him back whenever we like. They had no idea till they were told that he was the Prime Minister's son, and his success, I need hardly say, has been entirely on his own merits and with no help from anybody.[62]

Frank Massey was indeed awarded the Military Cross 'for acts of Gallantry in the Field' at Messines in 1917, and the following year he received the Distinguished Service Order 'for conspicuous gallantry and devotion to duty'. He was also twice mentioned in despatches by General Sir Douglas Haig.[63]

Godley may have described the arrangement with the British army as a 'loan', but although Frank Massey returned to the NZEF he never again served with the New Zealand Rifle Brigade. Leaving the brigade on 1 February 1917 for eight months' service as a staff officer at Divisional Headquarters, he was then seconded to the British army on 8 September, initially with an Ulster battalion. On 23 March 1918, however, Frank Massey was seriously wounded while leading a battalion of the Lancashire Fusiliers in action and was immediately transferred back

above Brian Gerald Mahoney transferred from the New Zealand Expeditionary Force to the British Expeditionary Force and was commissioned into the Royal Munster Fusiliers. He later transferred to the Royal Flying Corps and was killed in an air accident in England in September 1918. Two of Mahoney's brothers were also casualties of the war. OTAGO BOYS' HIGH SCHOOL MUSEUM, C754, 18053012

right Frank Massey, son of Prime Minister William Massey, was loaned to the British Expeditionary Force and commanded a battalion. He proved to be an excellent soldier and was awarded the Military Cross and the Distinguished Service Order and was twice mentioned in despatches. When he was seriously wounded on 28 March 1918 it was the end his active military service. SIR GEORGE GREY SPECIAL COLLECTIONS, AUCKLAND LIBRARIES, AWNS-19150603-50-1

to the NZEF.[64] His service file records that on 28 March he was at Walton-on-Thames Hospital 'ser ill . . . GSW chest'.[65] The New Zealand newspapers were more revealing, reporting that Major Massey, while 'serving with the British Army . . . was dangerously wounded, being shot through both lungs'. A news report of September 1918 added that Massey, by then recuperating at Brockenhurst Hospital, was 'very unlikely' to be 'permitted to return to the Western front, owing to this injury'.[66] It was an astute assessment. After months in hospital Frank Massey returned to New Zealand in October 1918, and was discharged from the NZEF on 2 December.[67]

One officer has been difficult to place in any category. Arthur Tahu Gravenor Rhodes was an officer in the elite regiment of the Grenadier Guards, but was in New Zealand in August 1914. He was subsequently 'loaned' to the NZEF, given a New Zealand service number and posted into Divisional Headquarters.[68] Arthur Rhodes landed on Gallipoli on 25 April 1915 and served there as Godley's aide-de-camp (ADC). He excelled in this role, for which he would be mentioned in despatches by General Sir Ian Hamilton. General Godley wrote in the citation for this award:

> I cannot speak too highly of the services this officer has rendered to me. Since the landing he has incessantly accompanied me wherever I have gone, as a personal staff officer and proved invaluable and made himself quite indispensable.[69]

Godley later learned he would have to cope without Rhodes, who was evacuated sick to Egypt in July, and then again to Malta in September. His military record noted the September illness as influenza. It must have been a serious case; from Malta, Rhodes was sent by hospital ship to London and admitted to hospital there. On 2 March 1916 Arthur Rhodes was discharged from the NZEF 'for reasons of ill health'.[70]

Rhodes recovered sufficiently to rejoin the Grenadier Guards, serving out the war with his old regiment. He would later be awarded the Serbian Order of the White Eagle with Swords, 5th Class, by the king of Serbia for 'distinguished services'.[71] In early 1916 Rhodes married the Honourable Helen Cecil Olive Plunket, eldest daughter of Lord and Lady Plunket, at the Guards Chapel in Wellington Barracks, London. The *Press* described the occasion as 'a very pretty military wedding'.[72] After the war, Rhodes took some tests for the New Zealand Permanent Air Force, but the family moved to the United Kingdom in April 1927. Arthur Rhodes died at Maidstone, Kent in 1947, aged 53 years.[73]

CHAPTER FOUR

IN THE INDIAN ARMY

Previous pages
A woman pins a flower onto a soldier's tunic during a march-past of Indian soldiers. IMPERIAL WAR MUSEUM, Q70214

Joining the Indian army was another way 'British' soldiers could serve in the First World War. The army was an unusual military organisation — one that traced its origins to the private armies of individual Indian rulers and the native regiments of the powerful East India Company (established 1599), which traded in (and effectively ruled) parts of India for Britain until 1858, when Britain assumed control of the entire country under the British Raj.[1]

By the early twentieth century there were two main components of the Indian army. First, there were regiments of the British Regular Army, usually cavalry or infantry regiments, which served in India as part of their regular posting cycles. The term of this posting was usually for a period of three to four years, but in some cases it stretched to more than 25.[2] To distinguish them from the other main component of the Indian army, these units carried the prefix 'HM' in front of their regimental number.

The other, larger, constituent part of the Indian army was the local or native Indian units, most named for the area from which they had been raised: the Bengal Fusiliers and the 20th Punjabi Regiment, for example. The men of these local regiments came predominantly from the so-called martial races of India: the Sikhs, Pathans and Dogras. While these local members could obtain the rank of an NCO or junior officer, most of the senior NCO appointments and crucial administrative roles, such as adjutant or quartermaster, and all the senior officer appointments were held by British officers of European descent. The Indian regular soldier was known as a sepoy in the infantry and a sowar in the cavalry. He remained its backbone. As Richard Holmes has commented, the British soldier was always in a minority in this British–Indian army, and so its successes and failures rested firmly on the performance of the sepoys.[3] Yet the best a sepoy (or a sowar) could hope to attain in his regiment was the honoured rank of subadar-major in the infantry or risaldar-major in the cavalry, which was roughly equivalent to the rank of captain and made him the senior Indian officer in the regiment.[4]

At the outbreak of the First World War the Indian army numbered 239,561 men, almost double the size of the British Regular Army. It was, in fact, 'at that time the largest all-volunteer army in history',[5] and by 1918 its numbers had risen to 1,440,437, an expansion that has been described as 'one of the great administrative achievements of the war'.[6] In terms of manpower alone British India (which comprised India, Pakistan, Sri Lanka, Burma and Bangladesh, with

Nepal also contributing troops to the Indian army) 'made the largest contribution to the war effort . . . of any of the colonies and dominions of the British Empire'.[7] It is estimated that more than 70,000 Indian soldiers died during the First World War.[8]

The Indian army was a critical part of the British war effort, with its regiments serving in five theatres, including the Western Front, East Africa, Gallipoli and Sinai–Palestine. In addition, the Indian army provided most of the fighting men for the campaign in Mesopotamia. With most of the key officer appointments in the Indian army reserved for British Europeans and with such a rapid expansion during the war years, there were many opportunities for men of the 'right' colour and class to easily obtain a commission, and a select number of New Zealanders did so.

Prior to the war, the Indian army's reputation was patchy. Its officers were 'seen as only interested in sport and regimental duties'.[9] However, a series of reforms had aimed to bring the army onto a more professional footing. In 1903, when he was commander in chief in India, Lord Kitchener abolished the Indian Staff Corps and renumbered all the Indian regiments. He also organised the army into two distinct tactical formations: the Northern and Southern armies. In 1907 the Indian Staff College was established at Quetta to improve the education of senior officers, and in 1909 a General Staff was established, bringing the Indian army in line with the British War Office organisation. Lieutenant-General Sir Douglas Haig oversaw this later reform. Of special significance was the policy to standardise training and doctrine with that of the British army. The War Office capstone manuals *Field Service Pocket Book* and *Field Service Regulations* became the standard doctrine for both the British and Indian armies.[10]

While much had been achieved prior to 1914, the Indian army, like its British counterpart, was in no way equipped for the total war ahead of it. Nevertheless, both had the ability to learn from their mistakes and improved greatly as the war progressed. Certainly, the British army could not have prevailed in this global conflict without the efforts of the Indian army. In 1914 the commander in chief in India was General Sir Beauchamp Duff. He was replaced on 1 October 1916 by General Sir Charles Monro, who had also been in command of the final months of the Gallipoli campaign. The Northern and Southern armies together comprised 10 divisions and three independent brigades with a total of 39 cavalry regiments, 138 infantry battalions (including 20 Gurkha battalions), three engineer regiments and 12 mountain artillery batteries.[11] This was a substantial military force.

Before looking at some of those New Zealanders who served in the Indian army during the First World War, it is worthwhile considering why British Europeans would join its ranks. Ignoring the family tradition, which saw many British and Indian families providing generations of soldiers for the Indian army, and which rarely applied to New Zealanders, there were two main reasons. First, there was a strong element of the colonial mystique about India. It was the jewel in the crown of the British Empire, an exotic location that offered adventure and opportunity. A British First World War general, Lionel Dunsterville, recalled that the family tradition of serving in the Indian army began with his grandfather, who had attained high rank in the service of the East India Company. The senior Dunsterville had gone to India 'in those palmy days when the pagoda-tree stood so invitingly on India's coral strand, awaiting just the

above The Indian army served in most of the United Kingdom's main theatres of war including the Western Front and the Middle East. Here, Indian soldiers use a pole-mounted Lewis gun as an anti-aircraft weapon. The photograph was taken in Palestine in 1918. ALAMY, AC5Y51

below Sikh soldiers of the Indian army on Gallipoli, August 1915. At the outbreak of the war, the Indian army was the largest all-volunteer army in history, and several New Zealanders served in it. AUSTRALIAN WAR MEMORIAL, C02711

gentlest shake to pour its golden fruit into the lap of fortune-hunters'. Lionel Dunsterville did note, however, that his grandfather, like so many of the fortune-hunters attracted to India, 'died possessed of very moderate means'.[12] Money was another primary motivator. Unlike a commission in many British army regiments, no private income was required to hold an equivalent commission in the Indian army. Lionel Dunsterville reached the rank of major general in the Indian army, as both his father and grandfather had done. He had, however, originally joined a regular British army regiment, the 2nd Battalion of the Royal Sussex Regiment, where his entire pay plus an allowance of £100 a year from his father 'fell far short of my Mess-bill'.[13] After three years of financial struggle, he transferred to the Indian army, where his salary as quartermaster of the 24th Punjabis was more than enough to live on.[14]

At the outbreak of war in August 1914 a small number of New Zealanders were already serving in the Indian army. The exact number will never be known but it included the commissioned officers Albert William Andrew, William Gilhome Selby of the Indian Medical Service, Hardwicke Holderness of the 1st Gurkha Rifles, Archibald Francis Hamilton of the 61st Pioneers, and Kenneth Sinclair Thomson of the 21st (Frontier Force) Cavalry. Frank James Medley, who served with the 2nd Madras Sappers and Miners, and Reuben McCarthy Newman, who served with the 2nd Gurkha Rifles, joined up during the war on a temporary (wartime only) commission. Solomon Netheim Ziman initially tried to join a unit of the BEF but, when finally given permission to enlist, he was commissioned into a famous cavalry regiment of the Indian army.

As mentioned in an earlier chapter, the first New Zealander to pass the entrance examination for a commission in the British army was Albert Andrew from Christchurch. Andrew took the examination in 1886 and accepted a commission in the Devonshire Regiment, but later transferred to the Indian army. During the 1899 South African War, he was seconded to the New Zealand military forces and subsequently commanded the Sixth and Tenth New Zealand contingents. A gifted linguist and military theorist, Andrew published several books on military matters, something many of his contemporaries would have found disturbing. Serious study of military theory was discouraged and was treated with suspicion by the British and Indian armies prior to 1914. Andrew was still serving in the Indian army in 1914 and again distinguished himself during the First World War. He commanded an infantry brigade group in Mesopotamia, one of the handful of New Zealanders in other forces to reach the rank of brigadier general. He did not put a foot wrong in this command. For this service Andrew was made a Companion of the Order of St Michael and St George (CMG) and was mentioned in despatches five times.[15] Andrew retired from the Indian army in 1920 and returned to his home city of Christchurch.

The first New Zealand-born recipient of the DSO was a member of the Indian army during the First World War. Surgeon Captain William Selby was a medical practitioner from Dunedin. In 1894 Selby joined the Indian Medical Services as a lieutenant and served on the North-west Frontier in 1895 and 1897. It was for his services in the later campaign that he received the DSO, the citation appearing in the *London Gazette* on 20 May 1898. He was also mentioned in despatches that year.[16] Selby was still in the Indian army in August 1914. In 1915 he went to

Gallipoli, but very little is known about his service there. Lieutenant-Colonel William Selby died on 8 September 1916, aged 47, after a motorcycle accident in Lucknow, and was buried at the Lucknow Cantonment Military Cemetery at Madras.[17]

Kenneth Thomson, born in Wellington in 1886, was educated at Wanganui Collegiate and at the Otago Medical School, which he attended for a year before heading to St John's College, Cambridge. While at Cambridge Thomson obtained a commission in the King's Colonials and became more interested in the military than a medical career.[18]

After taking a bachelor of arts degree with honours in 1909, Thomson obtained a commission in the Indian army. He left in February to join the 21st (Frontier Force) Cavalry. He returned to New Zealand on leave for six months in 1913 and visited his old school in Whanganui. Thomson did not have a long war. When British forces landed in Mesopotamia in November 1914, most of the fighting troops were from the Indian army. Having been attached for service to the 16th Cavalry, and put in command of a machine-gun section, Thomson was involved in the fighting around Basra in early 1915. He died on 3 March — the first New Zealand-born member of the Indian army to be killed in action.[19] His two younger brothers also served in the war: Colin Sinclair Thomson served as an officer in the Royal Navy and survived the war. Captain George Alastair Thomson of the Argyle and Sutherland Highlanders died of wounds in France on 21 July 1916, aged 24.[20]

Hardwicke Holderness was born in Christchurch in 1879 and attended Christ's College. In 1902 he joined the 1st Gurkha Rifles, a unit of Gurkha soldiers of Nepalese origin. The 1st Gurkhas was one of the first Indian army units deployed in the war. It served on the Western Front in 1914 and 1915, and earned distinction for its performance at Neuve Chapelle and during the Second Battle of Ypres. At the end of 1915 the unit was shipped off to Mesopotamia, where it took part in attempts to lift the Ottoman Turk siege of Kut-el-Amara. After two years in Mesopotamia, the 1st Gurkha Rifles was sent to fight in Palestine in early 1918 and finished its war campaigning there. Hardwicke Holderness served with the battalion throughout the war and was awarded a DSO for his actions during the Battle of Megiddo in September 1918, at the end of the Palestine campaign. After the war Holderness continued to serve with the Indian army, and commanded the 1st Battalion of the 1st Gurkha Regiment from 1923 to 1927. He retired in the rank of colonel in 1932 and lived the rest of his life in the United Kingdom.[21]

Archibald Hamilton was born in Nelson and attended Nelson College, where he successfully applied for an imperial commission into the Indian army's 61st Pioneer Battalion. The 61st Pioneers was one of the units involved in the disastrous Battle of Tanga, fought in East Africa in November 1914. The unit continued to serve in East Africa, where Major Hamilton was awarded the Military Cross for his services.[22] Hamilton's large family obviously valued the imperial connection. Of its nine sons, six served in the war, but only half with the New Zealanders. Alan Hamilton was a doctor with the Royal Army Medical Corps. Hugh Hamilton, a trooper with the New Zealand Mounted Rifles, was wounded on Gallipoli; following his recovery in the United Kingdom, he took a commission in the Royal Flying Corps.[23] In mid-1917 it was reported in the New Zealand press that three of the brothers had 'a noteworthy reunion' in the United Kingdom; Archibald and Alan 'had not met for nearly fifteen years'.[24] After the war,

Archibald Hamilton saw further active service with the Indian army in Afghanistan in 1919 and Waziristan in 1923. He was promoted to lieutenant colonel in 1929 and commanded the 2/1 Madras Pioneers until his retirement to the United Kingdom in 1933.[25]

Frank Medley was born in Southland in 1888. A qualified engineer, he joined No. 12 Company of the Madras Sappers and Miners as a commissioned officer and served with them in Mesopotamia during the war. He remained with the Indian army until 1931 and on their reserve list until 1939. Medley later returned to New Zealand and became a tobacconist in Mataura, Southland.[26]

Solomon Ziman's case was unusual. Ziman, a student at Auckland University College, was the New Zealand Rhodes scholar in 1907, the first Rhodes scholar from Auckland.[27] After studying mathematics at Balliol College, Oxford, he entered the Indian Civil Service and was stationed in the Bombay Presidency. When war broke out, Ziman applied to join his old university regiment, King Edward's Horse, but was not permitted to resign his post. From 1916, Indian civil servants were permitted to apply for commissions in the Indian Army Reserve of Officers because of an acute shortage of quality men. Solomon Ziman joined the 35th Scinde Horse as a lieutenant and, after garrison duty at Jubbulpore and Kashmir, he spent most of 1918 as a staff captain in a cavalry brigade at Miranshah on the Afghan border. After the armistice with the Ottoman Turks, he returned to his post in the civil service.[28] His brother, Louis Isaac Ziman, served with the NZEF for a year before transferring to the Royal Navy in March 1918 in order to accept a temporary commission.[29] After the war Louis also secured a commission in the Indian army.

Another who entered the Indian army from the civil service was Gordon Cunningham from Christchurch. Educated at Christ's College and with an engineering qualification obtained in the United Kingdom, in 1906 Cunningham travelled to India, where he joined the Bengal Nagpur Railway as an assistant locomotive superintendent. In early 1917 he enlisted with the Mesopotamia Expeditionary Force and served with it for the next two years, assisting with building and running a railway between Kut and Baghdad. Cunningham was 'responsible for the equipment and organisation of the temporary shops at Kut and for the reconditioning there of rolling stock'.[30] He must have been good at his work: he was promoted to major, mentioned in despatches for his work at Kut, and later awarded an MBE.[31] One of his brothers, Norman Cunningham, served as an officer with the Royal Field Artillery and was decorated for distinguished service, while a sister worked as a forewoman in the Woolwich Arsenal, London during the war years.[32]

After the war, Gordon Cunningham returned to his post with the Bengal Nagpur Railway and completed 25 years of service, retiring as the company's chief mechanical engineer in April 1931.[33] He did not get to enjoy a long retirement. While visiting Glasgow he suffered a severe bout of meningitis and died suddenly on 8 January 1932, aged 55.[34] He had married only two years earlier.

Reuben Newman joined the Indian army in October 1917. Born in Dunedin, he attended Otago Boys' High School and later Wellington College. Newman was one of the first volunteers for the NZEF and sailed in August for Sāmoa; he spent the first months of the war in the garrison

Kenneth Sinclair Thomson in the cavalry uniform of the 21st Frontier Force. Thomson was the first New Zealand-born member of the Indian army to be killed in action, in March 1915.
WANGANUI COLLEGIATE

of this newly won British territory. After his discharge from the Samoa Expeditionary Force in April 1915 he re-enlisted and was for some months deployed as a guard on Somes Island, in Wellington Harbour. In early January 1916, now a sergeant, Newman sailed from New Zealand as part of the Ninth Reinforcement of the NZEF.[35] Upon his posting to the 2nd Otago Battalion in March 1916 he reverted to the rank of private, but a month later was promoted to sergeant. He served with the battalion in France for a year before he transferred to the 4th New Zealand Infantry Brigade as a warrant officer. Six months later, on 19 September 1917, Newman was 'selected for appointment to the Indian Army Reserve of Officers by the Secretary of State for India in Council'. Following the transfer on 8 October 1917, he served with the 3/2nd Battalion of the Gurkha Rifles.[36] The regimental history of the 2nd Gurkha Rifles makes a revealing reference to Second Lieutenant R. M. Newman:

> During the hot weather of 1918 at Peshawar an incident worthy of record occurred. A detachment of one company garrisoned Jamrud Fort, and when drawing water one day from a deep well in the fort, Rifleman Prem Sing Bisht fell into it. Second Lieutenant R.M. Newman in command of the detachment, hurried to the scene, and in spite of the fact that he was a big man, descended three times into the well by a thin rope at great danger to himself to try and rescue the man. This officer was granted a certificate by the Royal Humane Society.[37]

On 23 November 1918, aged 24, Lieutenant Reuben McCarthy Newman died on active service in the North-west Frontier province of India.[38] He had been hospitalised with illness at the Abbottabad Officers' Hospital and succumbed to either influenza or enteric fever.[39]

For some unexplained reason Newman is absent from Lieutenant-Colonel John Studholme's list of NZEF personnel who received temporary commissions in the British and Indian armies (see chapter three). Studholme records the names of six officers and 10 NCOs and other ranks who transferred from the NZEF to the Indian army during the war. Five of the officers transferred in October 1917; the sixth, Captain Reuben James Bird, did so in January 1918 after some delay.[40] The ranks of the NCOs ranged from lance corporal to warrant officer. Four private soldiers were among those selected for commissions. Of the 10 men who transferred to the Indian army, two did so at the end of 1917, three in February 1918 and two more in September of that year. The remaining three received their commissions in December 1918, after the Armistice.[41] A total of 16 New Zealanders transferring from the NZEF to be commissioned into the Indian army was not a large number; it is likely that Studholme has omitted some (among them Newman), although this number is likely to be small too. The New Zealand official record of these transfers reveals that even dealing with such a small number caused considerable administrative problems.

First, even though the numbers permitted to transfer were low, not enough men came forward to fill the quota. In October 1917 four officers and four NCOs were invited to submit their names for a transfer to the Indian army. After examination by a medical board, two from each category would be given the final approval to transfer. Only five men put their names forward.[42] Of these, only one was a commissioned officer: Captain Reuben James Bird of the

above Archibald Hamilton as an officer in the 2nd Royal Scots. It was typical for those who wanted to join the Indian army to spend some years attached to a British regiment in order to gain some command experience. NELSON COLLEGE

left Solomon Netheim Ziman was the first Rhodes scholar from Auckland. After studying mathematics at Oxford University, Ziman joined the Indian Civil Service. In 1916, he joined the Indian army and served with the cavalry unit the 35th Scinde Horse. His brother Louis Isaac Ziman was also commissioned into the Indian army after transferring from the Royal Navy. SIR GEORGE GREY SPECIAL COLLECTIONS, AUCKLAND LIBRARIES, 1504-42

Wellington Mounted Rifles. But even Bird's application was a problem, as he was 'ineligible for an appointment to a permanent commission in the Indian Army on account of his age': he was 30 at the time, and regulations stated that '[c]andidates must not be more than 28 years of age at the date of application'.[43] When the need is acute, however, rules can be waived, and Bird was duly transferred to the Indian army on 1 January 1918.[44] Even after a transfer was approved, it took some time for the paperwork to catch up. Quartermaster Sergeant John Robertson was transferred to the Indian army on 12 November 1917. He sailed for India the next day, but on his arrival found that 'the Military Authorities in India have received no advice whatsoever regarding me'.[45] He would have to stay at the rest camp in Karachi 'indefinitely'. It could have been worse.

The New Zealanders who served in the Indian army were not immune from the suffering and privations of war. William Henderson Gibb, an architect from the Waikato, had considerable military experience in the New Zealand Volunteers and in the British Territorial Force. In September 1914, aged 28, he received a commission in the 3rd Battalion of the Black Watch (the Royal Highland Regiment) and he served with this battalion in some of the hardest fighting of 1914 and 1915, including First Ypres and Fromelles in 1914 and Neuve Chapelle, Fromelles and Festubert in 1915.[46] This took its toll, and from 25 May 1915 and well into 1916 Gibb suffered from severe post-traumatic stress injury. His medical records repeatedly note that he was depressed, nervous and having trouble sleeping. One medical report noted these symptoms, but also recommended a possible cure:

> There is little change in his condition. Not troubled as much by insomnia. Knee jerks still exaggerated. Anxious expression. The climate is against him here. He might improve in a warmer locality. Service in a tropical battalion should suit him.[47]

The recommendation was accepted, and on 21 February 1916 Gibb sailed for India with the 1st Garrison Battalion of the Scottish Rifles. Garrison battalions were raised from men deemed too old or medically unfit for full military service. They garrisoned dangerous or remote areas, typically in Egypt or India, leaving regular battalions free to fight in the key theatres of war. Gibb spent most of the rest of his war in India at a training camp in Bangalore, where his illness did not prevent further promotion to captain. He served at Bangalore as adjutant, company commander, battalion commander and depot commander. In 1919 Gibb was still serving in India as the commander of the Allied rest camps in Bombay.[48]

Another New Zealand officer plagued by ill health during his time in India was Algernon Donald Douglas McLean. From Maraekākaho near Hastings in Hawke's Bay, Algernon McLean had enlisted early in the war when he received a commission in the 3rd Battalion of the Cameron Highlanders. He served with this battalion in France and was evacuated back to England on 25 October 1914 after being wounded in the left leg.[49] While recovering from this wound, McLean, now promoted to captain, underwent surgery for 'aggravated varicose veins of the right leg' in April 1915.[50] (He had been previously operated on for varicose veins in London in 1909.) In October 1915, though, McLean was declared 'fit for light duties' and attached to the 1st Garrison Battalion of the Scottish Rifles, the same unit as William Gibb, and sent with the battalion to India.[51]

In India McLean's varicose veins worsened to the point that at the end of 1916 he could neither march nor stand still for any length of time. Two more operations in India followed in April, but his condition did not improve. In November 1917, McLean left Bombay for Southampton for six months' medical leave.[52] It is unlikely that his health ever recovered from his war service. He died in New Zealand on 5 November 1923, aged 31.[53]

Some New Zealanders left a chequered record of service in India. Wanganui Collegiate old boy Frederick Adrian Maunsell Jenkins was one. Jenkins joined the Army Service Corps in May 1915 and later transferred to the 2nd Battalion of the Dorsetshire Regiment and served with it in India. He faced a court martial at Deolali in May 1918 for being absent without leave (AWL) for nearly a week. Jenkins entered a plea of guilty, for which he received a 'severe reprimand'.[54] This blemish did not prevent him from being placed in command of an infantry company in the battalion in November 1918, and again in February 1919. By then the battalion had been posted to Kantara in Egypt, where in February 1920 Jenkins was again court-martialled for being AWL. This time the sentence was a severe reprimand combined with a forfeiture of seniority of rank.[55] Jenkins was demobilised three weeks later.

Another to fall foul of the military authorities was the well-connected Stuart Maxwell Deans. A member of the Riccarton, Christchurch Deans family, he was an old boy of Waitaki Boys' High School in Ōamaru and had graduated from Sandhurst Military Academy in May 1916. He received a commission in the elite 16th (The Queen's) Lancers, served with his regiment in France in 1917 and 1918, and was promoted to lieutenant in April 1918. In 1920 Deans was still serving in the 16th Lancers, which was then in Egypt awaiting a posting to India before the end of the year.

On 1 July 1920 Deans was granted six months' paid leave to visit New Zealand, and in early 1921 he was expected to rejoin his regiment in India. But he sent a cable, dated 28 January, to his commanding officer saying: 'Regret resignation necessary. Explanation follows.'[56] But a letter of explanation did not follow until 12 July 1921.[57] Needless to say, the military authorities were far from impressed with Stuart Deans. The War Office regarded his absence from this battalion as 'an aggravated case of absence without leave of a regular officer'.[58] The commander in chief in India 'did not consider the explanation satisfactory in any way' and told New Zealand's Governor-General that Deans' actions were 'highly reprehensible, and in the absence of any explanation from him it is impossible to accept his resignation'.[59] In the end Deans was not permitted to resign. Instead, he was formally dismissed — in effect sacked — from the Indian army. On 4 January 1922 the War Office cabled its decision to the commander in chief in India:

> Lieutenant S.M. Deans 16th Lancers is to be removed from the Army from first January 1921 the King having no further occasion for his services . . . Notification will appear in London Gazette of 17th January 1922 . . . Take necessary action for informing Lieutenant Deans.[60]

It was not an ideal end to a military career.

Christchurch-born and Nelson College educated, Leslie Norman Reece was a newly qualified doctor in London at the outbreak of war and about to take his final medical examination. Instead, Leslie Reece went with the British Red Cross to work in Belgium at the end of September. Back in England in July 1915 he joined the Royal Army Medical Corps Territorial Force and was initially posted to No. 2 London General Hospital. In August 1916 he was sent to Mesopotamia and worked at No. 40 British General Hospital at Basra until February 1919.[61] By then a major in the RAMC, desperate to return to the United Kingdom and finish his medical training, Reece wrote to his commanding officer, 'I wish to complete the F.R.C.S. [Fellowship of the Royal Colleges of Surgeons] as soon as possible in order to return to New Zealand to practise.'[62] However, he had one more military posting to go: the King George War Hospital at Poona in India. He was there for most of 1919, and on 15 October that year he finally sailed from Bombay bound for Southampton. He was 'demobilised with effect from 11/11/19'.[63]

Another New Zealander joined the Indian army at the end of the war and participated in several military campaigns after the Armistice was signed in November 1918. Gisborne-born Arthur John Sawyer was a wireless telegraphist and served in some most unusual places, but this may well have suited him entirely. Well before the war, Arthur Sawyer was one of several New Zealanders who were part of the 1911–14 Australian Antarctic Expedition headed by the Australian explorer Douglas Mawson. In 1912 Sawyer joined the expedition as its wireless operator and mechanic.[64] He returned to the Antarctic after the war with Ernest Shackleton's final and ill-fated *Quest* expedition of 1921, on which the explorer died from heart failure.[65]

Back in Australia in 1916, Sawyer enlisted in the AIF and served just over a year with the Rabaul Relief Force, initially posted as the wireless officer at Nauru, which had been recently captured from the Germans.[66] The Rabaul Relief Force were the garrison troops sent to occupy the parts of the German empire seized by the Australians in September 1914. (This included the town of Rabaul on East New Britain, an island some 60 kilometres to the east of New Guinea.) Nauru was a lonely post, although Sawyer spent some of his time in the Marshall Islands, which had also been seized from the Germans, and where Sawyer's task was to try to recruit the islanders to the British war effort. Sawyer did not enjoy his time with the Rabaul Relief Force and was soon bored. He wrote to a friend that '[h]e was chafing at being so far out of it all, and . . . that his most exciting experience was the capture of six German native police who did not know that the war was on'.[67]

When his enlistment time expired in May 1917, just shy of his thirty-second birthday, Sawyer rejoined the AIF and this time was posted into the Anzac Wireless Squadron for service in Mesopotamia. He spent from May to December 1917 training in Australia and must have impressed his superiors: during that time he received several promotions and rose from the rank of private to sergeant. He embarked from Australia on 19 December 1917 and arrived at Baghdad on 19 March 1918.[68]

Sawyer served with the Anzac Wireless Squadron for most of 1918 and was part of the ill-conceived Dunsterforce.[69] Officially the British Military Mission to the Caucasus, this was a secret force of around 1000 imperial soldiers commanded by Major-General Lionel C.

left Arthur John Sawyer had a very eventful war, serving in the Australian Imperial Force, in Dunsterforce, and then in the Indian army. In this last enlistment, Sawyer was an eyewitness to the infamous Amritsar massacre in April 1919. SIR GEORGE GREY SPECIAL COLLECTIONS, AUCKLAND LIBRARIES, 31-S2143

above Prior to the war Arthur Sawyer had been a member of the Australian Antarctic Expedition headed by Douglas Mawson. As the expedition's chief wireless operator he spent time on Macquarie Island, where this photograph was taken by Frank Hurley, which was the link between Mawson's Antarctic base and Australia. After the war, Sawyer returned to the Antarctic with Shackleton's last, ill-fated expedition. NATIONAL LIBRARY OF AUSTRALIA

Dunsterville. Its mission was to safeguard the large Russian oil installations at Baku from the Ottomans and the Germans. It also aimed to organise local groups of Armenians, Georgians, and anti-Bolsheviks to resist the Ottoman forces as a way of safeguarding the railways and approaches to Afghanistan and India.[70] Among the odd assortment of imperial soldiers were several from New Zealand, including Arthur Sawyer. Some of these individuals will feature in later parts of this book, but Sawyer is the focus here. He later described the 'horrors of that trek', escorting some 100,000 Armenian refugees from Anzali in northern Persia to Baquba in Mesopotamia. Sawyer estimated that as many as 40,000 Armenians perished from disease, exposure and famine on this journey.[71]

On 24 September 1918, Sawyer was discharged from the AIF at Baghdad as he had been 'Granted a Commission in [the] Indian Army'.[72] The commission was temporary; Sawyer could be discharged when his services were no longer needed. While he did not see action with the Indian army during the First World War, Sawyer participated in several military campaigns, albeit in small colonial conflicts, latterly the Indian army campaigns in Afghanistan and the North-west Frontier in 1919 and in Waziristan from 1919 to 1921. He was also in Amritsar, in the Punjab, on 13 April 1919 when Colonel Reginald Dyer gave the order to open fire on a large gathering of Indians alleged to be demonstrating against British rule. While the figures are disputed, there is little doubt that several hundreds of Indians were killed and thousands wounded. Sawyer, very much a product of his time, believed that Dyer 'took the only action possible in the circumstances' and had averted another Indian Mutiny.[73]

When he left the Indian army in 1921 after three years' service, Arthur Sawyer was awarded the Indian General Service medal with three campaign bars.[74] Life in the telegraph branch of the general post office at Wagga Wagga, and later Dubbo, New South Wales, must have seemed dull after his colourful wartime and postwar service. In February 1930 Sawyer returned to live in New Zealand. He died in Wellington on 18 January 1932 after a short illness at the relatively young age of 46.[75]

John Eric Averill, from Napier, was in the United Kingdom in 1914 on holiday and staying with his elderly uncle. To the old man's consternation, the 18-year-old Eric disappeared shortly after the outbreak of war. Subsequently he wrote to inform his uncle that he was serving on the Western Front with the Coldstream Guards. It gave the uncle 'a bit of a shock'.[76] In 1916, after being recommended for a commission, Averill attended an officers' training school at Bristol. He passed this course and joined the Cheshire Regiment on 2 November.[77] He later transferred to the Indian army as an officer in the 8th Gurkha Rifles and served with this unit on the Afghan frontier. Captain Averill died of wounds received in action in November 1921.[78]

One of the saddest cases of a New Zealander serving in India was that of Charles Stanley Lawrence Harrington, who obtained a commission in the 3rd Battalion of the Connaught Rangers. In March 1916 Harrington sailed from England bound for Mesopotamia apparently 'in sound health'. Once he arrived, however, there began a very long record of illness, to the extent that Harrington would be fit for duty for only two weeks over the next 10 months. In this time, he was hospitalised with tonsillitis, a fever (temperature 104°F), diarrhoea, typhoid, and paratyphoid A and B. After being discharged from No. 3 British Hospital at Basra, he was sent back to a hospital in India and granted two months' leave, which he spent in Ceylon, where he developed heart trouble. He was ordered back to Colombo and granted two more months of sick leave. In December the tonsillitis was back and his teeth were 'loose & sore'. Placed on light duties at the end of January 1917, Harrington underwent dental treatment that included being injected in the gums for pyorrhoea. On 10 February 1917 he was back in hospital with severe tonsillitis and a sore throat.

The detailed medical report concluded: 'His condition is undoubtedly due to a debilitated state of health following upon hardships undergone in Mesopotamia.'[79] He was sent back to the United Kingdom for six months to recuperate,[80] leaving Bombay on the New Zealand hospital ship *Marama* on 21 April 1917. During the voyage from Durban to Cape Town, the ship encountered heavy weather, and on 27 May a freak wave broke across the ship and swept two men to their deaths.[81] They were Private George Lynch Cobb of the New Zealand Medical Corps and Lieutenant Charles Harrington of the Connaught Rangers.[82]

BAB

CHAPTER FIVE

IN THE AIF

Previous pages
Christchurch-born sapper Eric Keast Burke of D Troop, 1st Australian Wireless Signal Squadron, Mesopotamian Expeditionary Force. This photograph was taken at the site of the Old Babylon Railway Station. After the war, Burke had a distinguished career as a photographer and journalist. AUSTRALIAN WAR MEMORIAL, J02028

Australia's main war effort was the creation in 1914 of the Australian Imperial Force (AIF). Whereas Canada and New Zealand designated their overseas forces as 'expeditionary', the AIF's first commander, Major-General William Throsby Bridges, chose the 'Imperial' label, 'to signify the twin nature of the Australians' duty: nation and empire'.[1] The AIF was four times larger than the NZEF. In total, 416,809 men volunteered to serve in the AIF from a population of just over four million — over half of the eligible white male population. A total of 331,781 were sent overseas before the war ended. Most served in France and Belgium on the Western Front.[2]

At least 21 per cent of the men in the AIF were born in the United Kingdom or elsewhere outside Australia. Of those born in Australia, more than half, some 55 per cent, came from the two most populous states of New South Wales and Victoria.[3] Of the 331,781 men who went overseas, the majority of those born outside of Australia came from the United Kingdom: just over 43,000.[4]

A considerable number of New Zealanders also served in the AIF. Estimates have varied widely, and the exact number may never be known.[5] Australian historian Neil C. Smith, who compiled a list of New Zealanders in the AIF based on embarkation rolls, wrote: 'The task of identifying them is formidable and could never be completed conclusively.' Some records were incomplete: many young men were reluctant to identify their birthplaces, and, according to Smith,[6] more than 15,000 AIF soldiers in the First World War used some sort of alias; furthermore, this number excludes those whose names were recorded incorrectly by the attesting officer.[7] It is estimated from the database compiled by genealogist Christine Clement that close to 5000 New Zealanders fought in the First World War wearing an Australian uniform. Clement has spent more than 20 years collating data from an extremely wide range of official and non-official sources. The Clement database, which is still accruing names, is the most accurate information we have on New Zealanders serving in the First World War.[8]

There were some critical differences between the AIF and the NZEF, starting with the uniform; the Australian outfit consisted of the slouch hat with a Rising Sun badge; a loose-fitting, roomy, four-pocket woollen service jacket with the brass buttons oxidised black so as not to reflect the sun; breeches and puttees; and tan ankle boots. This was 'quite distinctive and meant that Australians, unlike most Commonwealth armies, could easily be distinguished from British troops'.[9] The slouch hat, like the New Zealand lemon-squeezer, was soon identified as a national symbol. The Australian uniform, 'designed for the battlefield rather than the parade ground', did not encourage spit and polish and has been described as 'the most practical clobber of the war'.[10]

The next difference was that of pay. The Australian authorities made the progressive decision to make the pay of a private soldier equal to the wage of an average Australian worker. The resulting rate of six shillings a day made Australians 'the best paid soldier of the war'.[11] It was also the origin of the tag 'six bob a day tourists'. Of these six shillings, one was automatically deferred as a compulsory savings scheme and paid to the soldier on his discharge. Married men were required to allot two shillings a day to dependants until the introduction of a separation allowance in 1915. This pay rate was a shilling more than the New Zealand soldier received, while junior officers and NCOs in the AIF were much better paid than their NZEF counterparts.[12]

Military discipline was another distinguishing factor. The notion that Australian soldiers of the First World War were ill disciplined is largely a myth. An ill-disciplined force cannot be effective in combat, and the Australians were unsurpassed in their effectiveness. Nonetheless, there was a widespread perception that the AIF had serious discipline problems, especially in 1918, and this is certainly backed up by the statistics. Some 2145 New Zealand soldiers were convicted by courts martial during the war, most commonly for being absent without leave (AWL) — the reason for nearly 43 per cent of all convictions.[13] The number court-martialled was greater than other dominion forces, with some 23,000 being held for those 331,781 men on active service. The Canadian Expeditionary Force (CEF) held 18,000 courts martial for the 458,218 men who were in training camps and serving overseas.[14] Expressed as percentages, the New Zealand rate of courts martial for men on active service, at just over 2 per cent, was half that of the Canadians (3.9 per cent) and less than a third of the Australian rate (6.9 per cent).[15]

In early 1918, BEF commander Field-Marshal Sir Douglas Haig's staff officers compiled a chart that showed the numbers of men per 1000 serving sentences in British military prisons in the field since September 1914. The chart was continually updated through to December 1918. Haig was fond of showing the chart to Australian generals and visiting politicians. In March 1918 he also sent it to New Zealand to back up an attack made on Godley in the New Zealand Parliament. The chart showed that the rate of incarceration per 1000 for British soldiers had risen steeply in 1914 and early 1915 to peak at 5.1 in February of that year. After the introduction of the 'suspended sentence', the rate dropped drastically to 1.2 in June 1915 and plateaued at just less than one per 1000 for the duration of the war.

The combined rate of Canadian, New Zealand and South African forces reached one per 1000 in September 1917, climbed steadily to hit two a year later, and then fell slightly at the end of the war to 1.6. The Australian rate was the standout yet again. It climbed from the moment the AIF arrived in France, reaching five in September 1917 and then peaking at nine per 1000 in March 1918. The rate fell slightly for most of 1918, but in October it started to climb again. In December 1918 it peaked at nine per 1000 for the second time.

Haig believed the high rate for the Australians was 'greatly due the fact that the Australian [government] refuses to allow Capital punishment to be awarded to any Australian'. Excluding the Australians, Haig was pleased with what the chart revealed: 'Really the absence of crime in this Army is quite wonderful.'[16] Nonetheless, the chart clearly indicated that the dominions, and Australia in particular, had significantly more crime and criminals than the rest of the BEF. It showed that throughout 1918, and even in some months of 1917, Australian units had nine times more men incarcerated in military prisons than British units and almost six times more than the other dominion formations.[17]

New Zealanders serving in the AIF were no better behaved than their Australian comrades, as will be seen in the next chapter. They were, however, better protected from the harshest measure of military law, in that some of the crimes they committed could have attracted the death penalty in other empire armies, including that of New Zealand. The AIF certainly could impose the death penalty, but the sentence could not be enacted without the express confirmation of the Australian Governor-General. No military authority in the BEF was prepared to make the request, although in July 1917 General William Birdwood, then commanding the AIF, urged the Australian government to abolish the provision requiring the Governor-General's confirmation. The government, facing a second referendum to introduce conscription, declined to make this change, which would have been seriously damaging to the pro-conscription cause.[18] This legal sanction did not exist in the other dominion armies. Of the four men executed by the NZEF for desertion during the First World War, two were Australian-born.[19]

Another critical difference about the AIF was that it was an entirely volunteer force. Australia did not introduce conscription during the war years, unlike New Zealand and despite the two attempts to do so by referenda. It was not alone in this: Irish and South African enlistments were also voluntary. Nevertheless, this voluntary nature 'was to set it apart from other armies raised throughout the war'.[20] It would also cause serious problems: the AIF struggled to maintain its five divisions at full strength during the later years of the war as enlistment numbers plummeted. The keenest young men had already volunteered, and the brutal reality of war was all too obvious after Gallipoli. The best year for recruiting was 1915, when 165,912 men joined the ranks of the AIF. In 1916 this number had fallen but was still impressive at 124,352 voluntary enlistments. In 1917, the worst year of the war for the Allies on the Western Front, the number of men who joined the AIF was 45,101, and in 1918 it fell even further to just 28,883.[21] This was a crisis for the AIF, which in the latter half of 1917 and all through 1918 was desperately short of men. For most of 1917, battle casualties far exceeded enlistments and in 1918 'the gap between casualties and enlistments became even wider'.[22]

One of the key reasons that New Zealanders enlisted in the AIF rather than the NZEF was a direct result of this struggle to maintain numbers in the AIF. As Australian volunteers declined, the enlistment standards were lowered, too. Some of the decisions to lower the standards were official government policy, but many were the result of recruiting and medical officers ignoring age and medical conditions in order to keep numbers up.

As will be seen later in this chapter, it was much easier for under-age volunteers to join the AIF than the NZEF, and several under-age boys crossed the Tasman for this express purpose. In early 1918, with the enlistment rate at its worst, the Australian government took the extraordinary step of amending recruiting regulations to allow men under 21 years of age to enlist in the AIF without their parents' or guardians' consent.[23] Some of the men medically rejected for service in the NZEF also found that they were able to enlist in the AIF without much difficulty. Some New Zealanders joined the AIF to escape criminal convictions or family duties back home. This accounts in part for the sizable number of New Zealanders in the AIF under a false name. In addition, as occurred with New Zealanders who found themselves in the United Kingdom in August 1914, it was convenient for some New Zealanders who were travelling or studying in Australia to join the AIF. It was expected that the war would be over quickly, and these people were impatient to serve. The AIF offered an easy, lucrative and acceptable way to do this.

By far the largest number of New Zealanders who joined the AIF were those who had migrated to Australia to live. It made sense for these men and women to join the military force of their adopted country. All four New Zealanders who would be awarded the Victoria Cross (VC) while serving with the AIF are cases in point. South African War veteran Alfred Shout had moved to Sydney in 1907 seeking carpentry and joinery work. He immediately volunteered on the outbreak of war, and was one of the first Australian officers ashore on Gallipoli on 25 April 1915. Awarded the MC and mentioned in despatches as well as being awarded the VC for gallantry at Lone Pine, Alfred Shout became the most decorated AIF soldier of the Gallipoli campaign. Shout died of wounds on 11 August 1915.[24]

Like Alfred Shout, Kaikōura-born Thomas Cooke was a builder; he moved to Melbourne a few years before the war seeking work. He served with the 8th Infantry of the AIF at Pozières on the Somme, where he, too, would be awarded a posthumous VC for gallantry.[25] Napier-born Percy Valentine Storkey moved to Sydney in 1911 to work as a clerk for the Orient Steam Navigation Company. In 1912 he joined the administrative staff of the University of Sydney and the following year he enrolled at the university as a law student. Storkey joined the AIF in May 1915 and was awarded the VC for gallantry on the Somme in 1918 while serving as an officer in the 19th Infantry Battalion. He lived in Australia after the war, and eventually became a district court judge in northern New South Wales, but his connections with New Zealand remained strong. When he died in the United Kingdom in 1969, Storkey bequeathed his VC to his old school, Napier Boys' High School.[26]

Corporal Lawrence Carthage Weathers of the 43rd Infantry Battalion, AIF was awarded the VC for gallantry near Mont Saint-Quentin on 2 September 1918. Born at Te Kōpuru, near Dargaville, Weathers moved to Adelaide with his family as a child in 1897. When war was declared, he was married with two young children and working as an undertaker at Parkside, South Australia. He enlisted in the AIF in February 1916.[27] Critically wounded on 26 September 1918, Weathers died three days later, not knowing that he had been awarded the VC.[28] One of his brothers, Thomas Francis Weathers, had died of wounds on 15 June 1915 while serving on Gallipoli with the 9th Light Horse Regiment.

These men represent a broad cross-section of those New Zealanders who served with the

The most decorated Australian Imperial Force soldier of the Gallipoli campaign was Captain Alfred Shout VC, MC, MiD from Wellington. Shout died of wounds on 11 August 1915 and was buried at sea. His name is on the Lone Pine Memorial.

AUSTRALIAN WAR MEMORIAL, P05402.001

Private Thomas Cooke, of the 8th Infantry Battalion, Australian Imperial Force, was from Kaikōura, but he migrated to Australia shortly before the war and settled in Melbourne. Cooke was posthumously awarded the VC for his gallantry at Pozières on the Somme in July 1916. He was killed in action and his body was never recovered. AUSTRALIAN WAR MEMORIAL, A02649

AIF during the First World War, with a wide range of motives for enlisting with the Australians. Most of them served in infantry battalions, which made up the bulk of the AIF, but New Zealanders served in every branch and unit of this vast military organisation. Even a branch as obscure as the Australian tunnelling companies could include more than 40 tunnellers with strong New Zealand connections.[29]

As outlined, it was easier for under-age New Zealanders, some mere boys, to enlist in the AIF rather than in the NZEF. Partly this was because most people in a local recruiting community in New Zealand knew those seeking to enlist, and how old they were, but it was also because of the AIF's more lenient approach to under-age applicants.

The story of Gustav Berg, which began this book, is unusual, but it was by no means unique. In 1955 New Zealand's national radio station reported on the fortieth commemoration of the Gallipoli landing. Some 1300 veterans attended a reunion dinner held in the Wellington Town Hall. The station's reporter interviewed a veteran from Petone who gave his name as John Ellums (Allums), and said that he had enlisted in the 15th Battalion of the AIF in Tasmania at the age of 16, and had celebrated his seventeenth birthday on the shores of Gallipoli.[30]

Another under-age New Zealander was Wellingtonian Arthur Joseph Clarke, who joined the AIF at Liverpool, New South Wales, at the end of October 1914. Clarke had just turned 18 but he had completed some military training in New Zealand with the Territorial Force.[31] His father had provided him with a letter of permission stating that he 'fully agreed' that his son should enlist 'for the protection of British rights'. Richard Clarke had signed off his letter with a stirring 'God save the King'.[32]

Arthur Clarke was initially posted into the 1st Veterinary Section, and in Cairo on 20 March 1915 faced a charge of '[g]iving false name to civil police'. His punishment was '21 days Confined to Barracks and 30 Days without leave to be served concurrently'.[33] In October 1916, Clarke transferred from the 1st Veterinary Section to the 1st Infantry Battalion and was wounded in action in May 1917, with a 'GSW Head (Superficial)'.[34] During his recovery in hospital Clarke was charged with his second, highly unusual, military 'crime': 'Neglecting to comply with Depot Orders in not changing his linen and allowing himself to become verminous'. Clarke was found guilty and awarded five days confined to his room plus loss of a day's pay.[35]

Things improved for Clarke after this. In 1917 he was given two stints of leave: one in the United Kingdom and one in Paris. Five months after rejoining his unit, in May 1918 he was promoted to lance corporal. In September he was on his way back to Australia working as an NCO on board a transport ship. Arthur Clarke arrived in Melbourne at the end of November and was discharged from the AIF in January 1919.[36]

Arthur Clarke's war service ended his life just a few years later. In May 1967 his son and only living relative wrote to Australian Base Records, Melbourne, seeking to obtain Clarke's Gallipoli Star and informing the Australian military authorities that Arthur Joseph Clarke had 'died consequent to the effects of Mustard Gas at Waterfall Sanatorium, Sutherland Shire, N.S.W. on 4 April 1922'.[37] Arthur was 25 years old at the time of his death.

Not all who enlisted were young men, either. Robert Hood, aged 50, was born in Ireland and enlisted in the AIF at Rockhampton, Queensland, on 28 October 1915. He gave as his next of kin his sister Mary Jane Hood, who was then living in Christchurch.[38] Robert Hood listed his occupation as an engineer, and it is somewhat odd that he spent a year in Egypt with No. 8 Squadron of the 2nd Remount Unit. This was a unit that specialised in breaking in and training horses. It did not need a trained engineer to do this. Hood returned to Australia in mid-1916 after his unit was demobilised. He faced a charge of 'Disobedience of Orders' on the voyage back home and was discharged from the AIF in June 1916.[39]

When Wellington-born Charles Key joined the AIF in September 1915, he was three months shy of his fiftieth birthday. He had already served in three previous conflicts: seven months with the New South Wales Contingent in the Sudan in 1885; two and a half years with the New South Wales Mounted Rifles in the South African War; and in 1906 in South Africa as a gunner in Natal during the Zulu (Bambatha) rebellion.[40] Charles Key was posted into a remount unit and served in Egypt. It was to be a short stint. Key left Australia on 12 November 1915, but on 29 April 1916 he was sailing home from Suez.[41] His remount unit had been disbanded, and Key was discharged from the AIF on 16 June.[42] However, this was not the end of his war service. The day after his discharge Key, now 50 years old, rejoined the AIF in a Home Service unit. His attestation form recorded the note: 'Enlisted for service in Australia for such period as Service may be required.'[43]

When Auckland-born actor Marcus Ferdinand Fraser St John joined the AIF in August 1916 he gave his age as 44 years and 11 months. However, St John was born in 1865 so he was actually 51 in 1916. It is likely he had crossed the Tasman specifically to join the AIF after being rejected for service in New Zealand. On his attestation form St John listed his wife Margaret as his next of kin, and gave her address as Nelson, New Zealand.[44] It later emerged that St John had extensive military experience, including three years with the 16th Lancers in India, five years with the mounted police in Canada and two years' service in West Africa.[45] Serving as a private and later a lance corporal in the 13th Light Horse Regiment, St John arrived in the United Kingdom in February 1917 and spent most of that year either sick in hospital with pneumonia or malaria or working at a training depot. One of his medical reports concluded that St John was 'too old and weak to be of any use as a soldier'.[46] It must have been devastating for a man who had lived such a life of adventure. On 25 January 1918 St John was '[d]ischarged from the AIF in the UK being permanently unfit for General Service'.[47] He spent the remainder of the war working with the British YMCA.[48]

Many New Zealanders served with the AIF on Gallipoli; the exact number will never be known. Architect Charles Duke from Dunedin, who served with the 4th Battalion, AIF, made three separate landings on those distant and fatal shores. On the first, on 25 April 1915, a sprained ankle prevented him from reaching the firing line. Duke returned to Gallipoli in May and at the end of the month was shot in the face and severely wounded. After treatment in Alexandria, where a bullet was removed from his head, Duke was back on Gallipoli in August in time for the Australian attack at Lone Pine.[49] He was later commissioned from the ranks and served in France, where he was mentioned in despatches in January 1917 and awarded the

above Napier-born Captain Percy Storkey had settled in Sydney in 1911. He was awarded the VC for his gallantry in leading a platoon of the 19th Infantry Battalion in the fighting around Hangard Wood in April 1918. AUSTRALIAN WAR MEMORIAL, D00017

left Corporal Lawrence Weathers of the 43rd Infantry Battalion, Australian Imperial Force, was awarded a posthumous VC for his gallantry at Mont Saint-Quentin in September 1918. Born near Dargaville, he had moved with his family to Adelaide in 1897. A brother was killed on Gallipoli serving with the 9th Light Horse Regiment. AUSTRALIAN WAR MEMORIAL, H06789

Military Cross in July 1918. Duke returned to New Zealand with his wife Marjorie, an Australian nursing sister whom he married at Aberdeen just after the war. After unsuccessfully trying his hand at farming at Collingwood, Duke moved to Nelson to practise as an architect. In 1965 he made a fourth landing on Gallipoli as part of the fiftieth-anniversary commemorations. Charles Duke died in Nelson in May 1970, aged 81 years.[50]

William Alfred Hallahan, from Ross on the West Coast, was working as a railway engineer in Kalgoorlie when the war began. He joined the AIF in early September 1914 and was one of the first Anzacs ashore on 25 April 1915. Hallahan described the experience in one of his letters:

> When near the beach the enemy opened fire on us, the bullets from the machine guns and rifle fire buzzing all round and hitting the boat all over. If ever a man feels queer it is when under fire for the first time expecting to get a shot the Lord knows where. Anyway that feeling had to wear off quick as we had a lot of work to do. In a few minutes we were running up a very steep hill, fixing our bayonets and yelling like Hell, and, by jove, you ought to have seen those beggars run. I don't think they like the Australian language too well.[51]

Hallahan closed this letter to his family with the words: 'Now, hoping to be home soon, I will close with best love to all.' But Corporal William Hallahan never returned home. He was wounded on Gallipoli in July and was later mentioned in despatches in December 1915.[52] Six months later, on 26 June 1916, the 26-year-old was killed in action at Fleurbaix, France. He is buried at the Rue-du-Bois Military Cemetery at Fleurbaix, near Armentières.[53]

William Hallahan was one of four brothers, all born on the West Coast, to serve in the AIF during the war. Three did not return to Australia. The eldest, Wendell James Hallahan, was 28 years old when he enlisted in the AIF's 6th Battalion in December 1914. He had been born at Westport and listed his occupation as 'miner'.[54] Wounded on Gallipoli in May 1915 with a gunshot wound to his left thigh, he was sent to a hospital in the United Kingdom to recover, and rejoined his unit in Egypt in March 1916. Promoted to corporal soon after arriving in France, Wendell Hallahan served with the 6th Battalion and was again wounded on 10 June. He rejoined the battalion on 1 August, reverting to the rank of private 'at own request'. Seventeen days later Hallahan was reported 'Missing in Action', subsequently amended to 'Now reported Killed in Action'.[55] His name is recorded on the Villers-Bretonneux Australian National Memorial in the Somme region of France.

Walter Rewi Hallahan, born at Denniston, was an amalgamator. (This occupation involved extracting gold from ore using its bonding process with mercury.) Walter was 25 when he enlisted in the AIF on 18 August 1914.[56] He must have been quite a soldier: a month after joining up he was a sergeant in the 11th Battalion. He served with the battalion on Gallipoli and was wounded twice during the campaign. He suffered a gunshot wound to the nape of his neck at the end of April 1915, and in July another wound to his right hand, which necessitated the amputation of his index finger.[57] Back with the battalion in France on 20 October 1916, Hallahan was awarded the Military Medal for 'bravery in the field': this included his 'conspicuous gallantry and good work' during the Gallipoli campaign.[58] Just three months later, the now

Denniston-born Walter Rewi Hallahan was one of four New Zealand brothers who served with the Australian Imperial Force. He was decorated twice for conspicuous gallantry and received a commission in 1917. Hallahan, described as a 'most capable leader', was killed in action on 18 September 1918. Two of his brothers also lost their lives. IMPERIAL WAR MUSEUM, H109326

Captain Walter Hallahan was awarded the Military Cross: 'a reward for distinguished service in the field'.[59] This 'most capable leader' was killed in action on 18 September 1918. He is buried at the Tincourt British Cemetery near Péronne, France.[60]

The fourth and youngest brother to enlist was Robert Thomson Hallahan. Born in Denniston and listing his occupation as a chemist's assistant, Robert Hallahan was just 19 years old when he enlisted in the AIF in August 1914. He served on Gallipoli with the 11th Battalion in the rank of lance corporal and left the peninsula in September 1915 with a severe case of gastritis. After rejoining the battalion in France in 1916, Hallahan spent most of that year, 264 days in total, being treated for venereal disease, first in London and then at the base camp in Étaples.[61] He rejoined the 11th Battalion on 15 November 1916 and was promoted to full corporal at the end of January 1917. On 16 April he was reported missing in action at Lagnicourt and was later confirmed to be a prisoner of war.[62] Robert Hallahan spent the rest of the war interned at Friedrichsfeld, finally returning to Australia at the end of 1919.[63]

Civil engineer Cyril Oscar Lawrence, born in Linwood, Christchurch, enlisted in the AIF in Melbourne in December 1914. He would survive Gallipoli, serve in France, be commissioned from the ranks and win the Military Cross for gallantry.[64] His extensive diaries survived the war and were subsequently published in two separate volumes by Melbourne University Press.[65] They provide an invaluable window into the life of a military engineer on Gallipoli and the Western Front.

Of course, many New Zealanders with the AIF on Gallipoli did not survive the experience. Serving in the same battalion as Charles Duke was Edmund Robert Guthrie, a 'well-known ex-Christchurch resident' and accountant.[66] Guthrie had resigned a commission in the New Zealand Territorial Force in October 1912 to move to Australia. He enlisted as a corporal in the AIF on 25 August 1914 in rural New South Wales, took part in the landing on 25 April 1915, and was mortally wounded soon after. He died of his wounds in Alexandria on 1 May and was buried there in the Chatby War Memorial Cemetery.[67]

Robert Stone's real name was Karenema Pohatu. The Māori soldier was born at Hastings in Hawke's Bay and joined the AIF in early October 1914. He was 21 years old, listed his occupation as a shearer and had anglicised his surname: Pohatu means 'stone'. The soldier known as Robert Stone landed on Gallipoli with the 3rd Battalion, AIF on 25 April 1915 and was killed in action the following day.[68]

Only one New Zealander reached the exalted rank of general in the AIF, albeit at the one-star brigadier level. This was Alfred Joseph Bessell-Browne, who, when the war ended, was in charge of the Australian 5th Division's artillery.[69] Bessell-Browne was born in Auckland in 1877. In the mid-1880s the family moved to New South Wales and later to Perth, where he finished his schooling. In 1896 Bessell-Browne was employed as a clerk in the patents office and enlisted in the Perth Artillery Volunteers.[70]

On the outbreak of the South African War in 1899, Bessell-Browne enlisted in the 1st Western Australian Contingent of mounted infantry, which reached Cape Town in November of that year in time to be part of the Kimberley Relief Force. He served two tours in South Africa, was promoted through the ranks, and received a commission as a lieutenant in April 1900. By the end of the war he had been promoted to captain, mentioned in despatches and awarded the DSO.[71]

When war broke out in August 1914, Bessell-Browne joined the AIF with the rank of major and was given command of the 8th Field Artillery Battery. He served with distinction on Gallipoli, where he commanded, in turn, the 2nd and 3rd brigades of the Field Artillery. His final task on Gallipoli was a painful one for a gunner: supervising the destruction of the guns that could not be evacuated from Anzac Cove. For his services on the peninsula Bessell-Browne was again mentioned in despatches and was appointed a Companion of the Order of St Michael and St George (CMG).[72]

Bessell-Browne continued to serve with distinction on the Western Front, where he was involved in firing the first Australian creeping barrage at Pozières in September 1916. Placed in charge of the artillery for the 5th Division, he developed a reputation for solving difficult gunnery problems and for being able to provide effective artillery support for the infantry, no matter the obstacles. For his services in France and Flanders Bessell-Browne was awarded the American Distinguished Service Medal, was appointed a Companion of the Order of the Bath (CB) and was mentioned in despatches a further nine times.[73] Alfred Bessell-Browne served with the Australian Military Forces until his retirement in 1942. He died in August 1947, aged 70.

Another New Zealander reached the rank of brigadier general in the AIF, albeit in a temporary capacity. His case was unusual, too, in that he remained a New Zealand officer despite serving throughout the war with the AIF. William Livingstone Hatchwell Burgess had been seconded to the Australian military on 4 November 1913. He was originally meant to serve with the Australians as an exchange officer for just one year. However, with the outbreak of the war occurring towards the end of his exchange period the term was extended by another five years.[74] He joined the AIF on 17 August 1914 as a captain and was given command of the 9th Field Artillery Battery, a unit he had helped raise in Hobart, Tasmania. Burgess was promoted to major exactly a month later, and embarked with his unit from Hobart on 20 October.[75]

William Burgess served in the AIF with distinction. He commanded the 9th Artillery Battery on Gallipoli until he was evacuated sick with paratyphoid on 1 October 1915. For his performance on the peninsula he was awarded the DSO — the first of many military honours.[76] After recovering from his illness, he was promoted to lieutenant colonel and given command of the 3rd Field Artillery Brigade. He travelled with his brigade to France in April 1916 and was its commander during the Somme battle of that year. He later commanded his brigade and other attached units in 1917 in the advance to the Hindenburg Line and in the battles of Bullecourt and Messines. In August 1917 Burgess was promoted to temporary brigadier general, and he commanded the artillery of the Australian 4th Division during the various battles of Third Ypres (Passchendaele) from September to November. The casualties became so heavy in Burgess's command that it had to be pulled out of the line and its batteries temporarily reduced from six to four guns.[77]

Burgess commanded the 4th Division's artillery for the duration of the war. The situation

Brig Genl A J Bessell-Browne C.B. C.M.G. D.S.O
5th Div AIF — A.F.A —
St Gratien
July 1918

A portrait sketch of Brigadier-General Alfred Joseph Bessell-Browne, commanding officer of the 5th Division, Australian Field Artillery, seated at a desk at the division's headquarters in Saint-Gratien. Bessell-Browne was the only New Zealander to attain the rank of brigadier in the Australian Imperial Force. He was regarded as one of the AIF's best artillery commanders and was, for some weeks in October 1918, loaned to the US 30th Division's artillery, for which he would be awarded the American Distinguished Service Medal. AUSTRALIAN WAR MEMORIAL, ART02498

improved for the Allies on the Western Front from mid-1918 on, and in the pivotal battle of Hamel on 4 August Burgess had command of some 16 brigades of artillery.[78] William Burgess would finish the war as one of New Zealand's most decorated soldiers. Added to his DSO were six mentions in despatches, the Legion of Honour and the American DSM.[79] In 1919 he was invested as a CMG and a CB.[80] It must have been a slight disappointment when, on returning to New Zealand in 1919, he had to revert to the rank of lieutenant colonel.

He need not have worried as, according to distinguished historian W. David McIntyre, Burgess had been 'marked for accelerated promotion'.[81] In 1926 he changed his name to include his original family name as well as that of his stepfather: he became William Sinclair-Burgess. In 1931 he was promoted to major general and appointed general officer commanding the New Zealand military forces, while concurrently serving as Chief of the General Staff. He held both positions until 1937. William Livingstone Hatchwell Sinclair-Burgess 'was remembered as the most decorated and longest-serving head of the army, the one who held it together during the worst years of the depression'.[82] His distinguished service with the AIF during the First World War has been largely forgotten.

Another notable New Zealand-born member of the AIF was the official war artist Harold Septimus Power, who was born in Dunedin in 1879 and moved to Melbourne with his family. Power had a limited formal education and at the age of 14 ran away from home to become an artist. His first job was as a carriage painter, decorating butchers' delivery carts with animal heads.[83] By 1914 Power was a well-established artist living in London. He was particularly renowned for his skill at painting animals, which had great appeal to 'a nation of animal lovers'.[84] He tried to enlist in the BEF three times but was rejected by both the British and Australian military authorities because of a serious hearing problem. However, this was not an impediment to painting about the war, and he exhibited three of his most well-known paintings — *Anzacs, The enemy in sight* and *No. 3 Australian Advanced Dressing Station Somme Front* — before his commission as an official war artist. All three paintings are now in the national galleries of three different Australian states.[85]

On 3 September 1917 Power enlisted into the AIF with the rank of lieutenant and as one of the first two official war artists.[86] The other, George Washington Thomas Lambert, was allocated to cover the Middle East, while Power was assigned to the Western Front in France and Belgium.[87] He took his work seriously, often sketching and painting at the front line, where his deafness aided his focus. Power once related how he had been sketching some artillery horses that were becoming increasingly agitated by flying insects. It was only when a comrade grabbed him by the collar and dragged him to safety that he realised that the insects were machine-gun bullets from a diving German plane.[88] On another occasion Power was knocked over by a shell that killed a group of horses he was sketching. He suffered from gas inhalation in late 1918 and was sent back to England to recover.

Power illustrated many different aspects of the war and is particularly recognised for his paintings of horses and other animals. These works are an invaluable historical record of the First World War experience and are now part of Australia's national treasures. Recognised as a 'great Australian artist', Power died in January 1951, aged 72.[89]

A studio portrait of Honorary Lieutenant Harold Septimus Power. Born in Dunedin in 1877, Power migrated to Australia with his family when he was a young boy. He had limited formal education and, at the age of 14, ran away from home to pursue a career as an artist. During the war he was appointed an official war artist, attached to the 1st Division, Australian Imperial Force from September 1917 to March 1920, during which time he painted some iconic images of Australians at war. Power was subsequently engaged on various commissions for the Australian War Memorial until 1938, travelling frequently between Australia and England during this period. AUSTRALIAN WAR MEMORIAL, P09558.001

above This painting by war artist Harold Septimus Power shows a horse team from the 1st Australian Division Artillery, consisting of six horses (three ridden, three led), pulling a half-limber wagon and 18-pounder field gun through the mud at Flanders during the Third Battle of Ypres. AUSTRALIAN WAR MEMORIAL, ART03315

below Two horses from the 1st Australian Division Ordnance units struggle through the mud; one is being led, the other ridden, and each carries 18-pounder field gun shells in canvas holders. Harold Power painted this scene at Zonnebeke in Belgium, amid some of the most ferocious fighting of the war; his skill in depicting animals is clearly evident. AUSTRALIAN WAR MEMORIAL, ART03307

Eric Keast Burke became a well-known photographer and journalist after the First World War. He was born in Christchurch in 1896, and his family moved to Sydney when he was eight years old. When war was declared in 1914 Burke was studying for a bachelor of economics degree at the University of Sydney. After serving in the militia as a signaller for a year, he enlisted in the AIF in February 1917 just after his twenty-first birthday.[90] Because of his signalling experience, Burke was posted to the Light Motor Wireless Section and served with this unit in Mesopotamia as part of the Anzac Wireless Squadron for most of 1918.[91]

The Anzac Wireless Squadron was an unusual unit. Back in late 1915, when the campaign in Mesopotamia had bogged down, the British forces were desperately short of signalling equipment and the skilled operators needed to use it. Following from the Viceroy of India's appeal to Australia and New Zealand for wireless operators and signallers, New Zealand formed a 62-man Pack Wireless Troop. Made up primarily of men from the Post and Telegraph Department, the troop sailed on the *Willochra* on 4 March 1916 and arrived in Basra on 16 April. On 4 July the Australians arrived and the New Zealanders joined them to form the Australian and New Zealand Wireless Signal Squadron.

Eric Burke's war was relatively uneventful. Despite operating in conditions where disease was rife and temperatures could reach 132°F (55°C) in the shade,[92] he enjoyed the experience, writing of the 'grand fellowship' of army life. He later edited the unit history *With Horse and Morse in Mesopotamia* (1927), which he described as 'the memory book of our great adventure'.[93]

Burke returned to Australia at the beginning of 1920 and was discharged in Sydney at the end of January that year. In what would be the start of a distinguished career in photo-journalism, he became associate editor, under his father, of the *Australian Photo-Review*. He later edited and was a director of *Australian Popular Photography*, presented a television series for the Australian Broadcasting Commission on historical photographs, and was a consultant on photography to the National Library of Australia. Collections of his photographs are held in major Australian galleries and libraries.[94]

Taken together, these personal accounts reveal much about the relationship between Australia and New Zealand during this period. Even in the early years of the twentieth century, many New Zealanders had crossed the Tasman seeking better job opportunities and prospects. That they could do this easily, with the traffic flowing in both directions, indicated how close the two societies were. There were important, if subtle, differences. AIF soldiers enjoyed better pay and conditions of service than their NZEF equivalents, and they had protection from the British army's ultimate military punishment. The AIF also provided a much easier pathway for under-age or over-age enlistments, and New Zealanders were not slow to take advantage of this. Not all made good soldiers, though, as the next chapter will show.

CHAPTER SIX

AIF HEROES AND VILLAINS

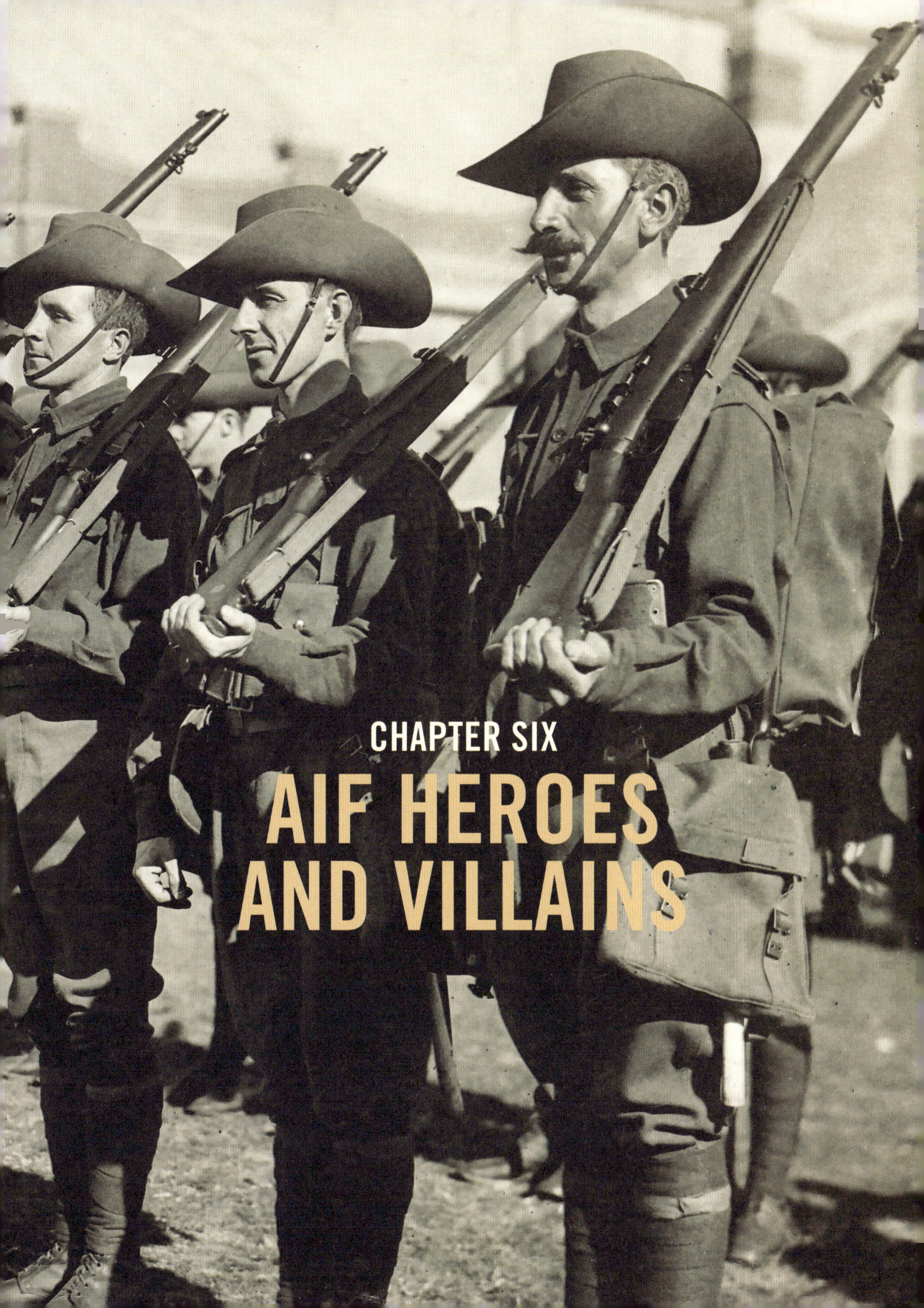

Previous pages
Soldiers of the Australian Imperial Force in their distinctive uniform. Unlike the armies of most other combatant nations (including New Zealand), members of the AIF were all volunteers. These are some of Australia's first volunteers, who were sent to Rabaul to capture the wireless station there. AUSTRALIAN WAR MEMORIAL, H19498

Not all New Zealanders who enlisted in the AIF were good soldiers or served with distinction. Some were in constant trouble with military authorities, and some were just plain bad. James Glover, who may well hold the record for the number of times one individual enlisted in the AIF, fits both categories. Glover's father, Albert Edward Glover, who was MP for Auckland Central from 1908 to 1919,[1] featured prominently in Auckland's public, business and political life. The dates, details and locations of each of James Glover's various enlistments are so numerous that they are listed here.[2]

Date of enlistment	Where enlisted	Occupation	Given age	Next of kin	Previous military service
8/6/15	Liverpool, NSW	Drover	35	Matutangi Glover (wife) c/- AE Glover Devonport	No
16/8/15	Liverpool, NSW	Horse breaker	34	Sarah Glover (mother), Wellington	No
4/5/16	Dubbo, NSW	Hairdresser	42 8/12	Jane Glover (wife), Devonport	No
1/6/16	Newcastle, NSW	Hairdresser	36 8/12	Jane Glover (wife), Devonport	No
30/11/16	Goulburn, NSW	Labourer	43 3/12	Matutangi Glover (wife), Devonport	No
27/2/17	Wodonga, Vic	Boundary rider	40 6/12	None	No
15/3/17	Wangaratta, Vic	Boundary rider	40 7/12	Matutangi Glover (wife), Devonport	Yes — 15 months South Africa
6/8/18	Brisbane, Qld	Hairdresser	45 11/12	Albert Edward Glover (father), Devonport	Yes — 6 months South Africa

Each of these eight enlistments was relatively short-lived. For example, his second, in the 1st Battalion AIF, ended in a discharge after eight months when he was discovered to have had a criminal conviction in Wellington, New Zealand.[3] His third enlistment, at Dubbo, lasted just over three weeks; his discharge note opined that he was 'not being likely to become an efficient soldier'.[4] Remarkably, four days later Glover had enlisted again, this time at Newcastle. In January 1917 he deserted from the AIF and then re-enlisted again at Wodonga a month later.[5] A letter written in July 1916 from the officer commanding the AIF Camp, Newcastle, to the

Provost Marshal indicates why James Glover would never be an effective soldier:

> This man is reported by his Company Commander to be quite unfit for embarkation. His character is bad and he is a disgrace to the uniform.
>
> He should be Court Martialled for absence without leave, for forgery of a pass and for false answer on attestation. If you will return him to this Camp after he has served his present sentence, he will be duly dealt with.[6]

Glover's military record contains a raft of charges for various military infringements and crimes. They include being absent without leave (AWL), drunkenness, refusing an order, begging, 'being in a filthy condition', providing false answers on attestation, missing parades and forging leave passes.

Glover's final stint in the AIF began well. He managed to get himself into the Rabaul Relief Force and sailed to Rabaul on 22 August 1918, where he stayed with his unit for almost a year. In March 1919, however, he was under arrest and confined to barracks for a week for being drunk and using obscene language. In May he was admonished and lost four days' pay for being AWL. In June and July 1919 James Glover spent most of his time locked up in military prison for drunkenness and 'creating a disturbance'. In early August he was taken directly from the military prison to a ship, which returned him to Australia, where he was to be immediately discharged.[7] The military authorities in Rabaul must have been relieved to watch his vessel sail from port. Moreover, despite all the troubles he had caused during his military service, James Glover still qualified for two of the standard three medals awarded to Australian soldiers: the British War Medal and the Victory Medal.[8] They were hardly well earned.

On 12 October 1944 the army secretary at Base Records in Sydney received a letter from a New Zealand law firm seeking the whereabouts of James Glover, who had been named as a beneficiary of his deceased mother's estate. According to the letter James had a wife and two children living in Auckland, but he had 'been missing since the last war' and they wanted to presume he was now deceased. The Australian military authorities told the New Zealand solicitors that Glover's discharge in December 1919 had been in Brisbane, and they provided the Brisbane address James Glover had supplied.[9] It is doubtful that James Glover or his fate were ever discovered by his New Zealand family.

Glover may have the overall AIF record for multiple enlistments, but his poor behaviour and bad character were not exceptional. New Zealander James Johnston Regna McQuillan shared these characteristics, too. Born in Waiuku, near Auckland, McQuillan enlisted in the AIF at Mackay, Queensland in early March 1915. He reached Gallipoli in August and served there less than a month before he was evacuated to No. 19 General Hospital with dysentery. McQuillan did not return to Gallipoli, and was instead transferred to the King George Hospital in London. At the end of the year he received the first of his military punishments for being AWL on two occasions. The punishment was quite mild: he was confined to barracks (CB) for 14 days and received 120 hours of detention with the military police.[10]

In early 1916 McQuillan joined the 47th Infantry Battalion and served with it in France. Barely three months later, however, he was charged with the first of many military crimes 'in the field'. He refused to board a train, and for this 'irregular conduct' McQuillan suffered Field Punishment No. 2 (hard labour in the field, usually digging trenches or making roading) for 21 days. Less than a month later, and while still under sentence for his initial crime, McQuillan was charged again, this time for being AWL while a defaulter, drunkenness, and swearing at an NCO. This time the sentence was 72 hours' Field Punishment No. 1, which meant he would be tied to a fixed object for this length of time, plus forfeiture of four days' pay.[11]

It was obviously not a deterrent, as he went AWL again in August 1916. When it happened again in November that year, he faced his first general field court martial, was found guilty and was sentenced to 30 days' Field Punishment No. 2. In March 1917 came a second court martial, for being AWL again and for abusive behaviour. This time the authorities had had enough: McQuillan was sentenced to nine months' imprisonment with hard labour.[12] Fortunately for him, the sentence was suspended at the end of the month.

McQuillan had been transferred to the AIF's 9th Battalion at the end of 1916. He rejoined the battalion in mid-1917 and was soon in trouble again. Late that year he was charged three more times and sentenced to a total of 35 days' Field Punishment No. 2, and forfeited 32 days' pay. McQuillan spent the early months of 1918 sick in hospital. He was also 'injured accidentally' on 24 June. In August he faced another charge of AWL, forfeiting eight days' pay,[13] and on 11 December, with another AWL, he received 18 days of Field Punishment No. 2 and forfeited 20 days' pay. He spent the last days of that year at the 7th Field Punishment Compound in France. It cannot have been a very happy New Year. James McQuillan returned to Australia in July 1919 and was discharged from the AIF in early October. Despite all this, McQuillan, like Glover, still qualified for his service medals.[14]

James McQuillan's life did not appear to improve after his discharge. When he wrote to the Australian army in 1949 seeking a copy of his discharge certificate from the AIF he was a patient in the NSW state hospital, being treated for bronchial asthma. He explained to the army that he needed his discharge certificate, which he had lost on his return to New Zealand after the war, in order to gain access to a repatriation hospital.[15] McQuillan died intestate at the Repatriation Veteran Home in Brisbane on 5 July 1962, in his late sixties.[16]

Wellington-born Robert Orr Miller was another who caused no end of trouble for the military authorities. He probably never fired a shot at the enemy, given that he spent most of his military service either locked up or being treated for venereal disease. Robert Miller first enlisted in the AIF in Brisbane in early February 1915, aged 26 years. He sailed from Australia at the end of June 1915 but got no further than Egypt, where he was diagnosed with a severe case of gonorrhoea, most likely contracted from one of Cairo's notorious brothels. Shipped back to Australia at the end of August, he arrived in Melbourne a month later and was discharged from the AIF.[17]

Venereal disease was a serious medical problem for the AIF. The Australian official history of its army medical services during the war admitted that the rate of infection in the AIF was among the highest of any Allied force. It stood at 158 per 1000 soldiers, four times the incidence for British soldiers.[18] Venereal disease was not just a military problem, either, and the fear and loathing of it during the war years cannot be underestimated. What must also be kept in mind is that although the symptoms could be treated, venereal disease was incurable at this time. As Mark Harrison has written in his history of military medicine during the war, in terms of preventive medicine against sexually transmitted diseases, the British army 'made little if any headway'.[19] Without the use of antibiotics, the treatment available in 1914–18 has been described as 'crude'.[20] Gonorrhoea was treated with a six-week course of urethral irrigation with potassium permanganate. It was administered twice daily and was 'painful and undignified'.[21] Syphilis patients were given intravenous injections of the arsenic compound arsphenamine (under the name Salvarsan), although mercury was still being used, and some patients received both. The course of injections was for 50 days and the side effects were severe. Some patients died during this treatment. As military medical specialist G. Dennis Shanks has written recently: 'Until antibiotics and non-punitive prevention arrived during World War 2, little progress was made with the treatment of STIs.'[22]

For obvious reasons Miller did not tell his family in New Zealand he had been returned to Australia. His worried mother, Jessie Miller, wrote to the Australian army from Wellington that all her letters to Robert in Egypt were being returned to her with the stamp 'Returned to Australia, 3/8/1915'. She was most anxious to learn what had become of her son.[23] The Australian military authorities were discreet in their reply: Robert had indeed returned to Australia in September 1915 'slightly sick' and they did not know his current whereabouts. They would make enquiries and get back to her when they knew something.[24]

Meanwhile, Robert Miller was desperate to rejoin the AIF. An attempt to re-enlist in February 1916 was refused, but a third bid later that year in Brisbane was successful. Miller sailed again from Australia on the troopship *Marathon* as a member of the AIF on 27 October 1916. The Australian military must have almost immediately regretted their decision, as he was twice in trouble during the voyage. On 11 November he had to forfeit four days' pay for being AWL. The next month he received four days' Field Punishment No. 2 for being AWL, using abusive language and being insolent to a superior officer.[25] This was just the start of a long list of military offences and punishments.

After disembarking at Plymouth on 9 January 1917, the AIF soldiers were marched into a training camp at Rollestone, on Salisbury Plain in Wiltshire. Miller was not there long. On 23 January 1917 he absconded from the camp and was finally apprehended in London on 11 March. On 24 March he was admitted to the special medical unit at Bulford for treatment for venereal disease, and underwent treatment there for 27 days.[26]

Just over a fortnight after his release from Bulford, Miller faced a district court martial at Rollestone, charged with being AWL in London and then escaping from his escort party once he had been apprehended. On 9 May Miller was sentenced to 60 days' detention. On 26 June his remaining servitude was remitted and he sailed to France that same day.

Robert Miller joined 25 Infantry Battalion of the AIF on 3 July and managed to stay out of trouble for nearly three weeks. On 23 July he was awarded 14 days' Field Punishment No. 2 for being AWL. Then a month later, he faced a field general court martial, for charges which included striking a superior officer, using insubordinate language, resisting arrest and being AWL. Miller was found guilty and sentenced to two years' imprisonment with hard labour. On 8 September he was sent to No. 1 Military Prison at Rouen.[27]

Miller did not serve much of his two-year sentence. On 20 November he was admitted to No. 1 Stationary Hospital at Rouen for further treatment for his venereal disease and other ailments, and here he stayed for the next 156 days. A medical board at the hospital held on 26 March concluded:

> This soldier is suffering from chronic gonorrhoea, arthritis of both knees with much limitation of movement and much wasting of the lower extremities. He has no urethral discharge and the V.D.G. is cured. The Board is of the opinion that it will be at least 12 months before he is fit for active service and it is quite possible he will never be fit for active service again. The Board recommends that he be discharged as permanently unfit.[28]

However, the AIF did not discharge Robert Miller. Instead, it sent him to two different hospitals in the United Kingdom. In May 1918, after his discharge from hospital, he was sent to the Lewes Detention Barracks in Sussex for his own 'safe custody'. But Miller had not changed, and in June he was sent to the military prison at Wandsworth, London. He was released at the end of November and the remaining portion of his sentence was suspended. They ought not to have bothered. In 1919, Miller was given three different awards of Field Punishment No. 2 totalling 54 days. It seems he just could not stay away from London; these punishments were all for being AWL. Robert Orr Miller was finally discharged from the AIF in Brisbane as medically unfit on 5 June 1920.[29]

Such a poor military record did not prevent Miller from applying for his service medals and replacement service badges. In May 1967 his widow, Lillian, wrote to the Australian army applying for the Anzac Commemoration Medallion.[30] One wonders if she knew the truth of her deceased husband's military service.

Walter Hill's case is a sad one. Born in Dunedin, he enlisted in the AIF at Liverpool, New South Wales, at the end of 1916 and served with the 55th Infantry Battalion. In late October 1917, after the Passchendaele battles, Hill was detached from the battalion for three weeks to serve with the local YMCA, a common route for soldiers who needed rest and a period of recovery away from the front line. In the first six months of 1918 Hill spent two months in hospital, the only recorded reason being that he was 'sick'.[31] On his return to the 55th Battalion in early June, he was arrested and charged with a 'wilfully self-inflicted' wound, 'caused by injection of petrol subentaneously [sic]'. Hill was court-martialled for this incident. He entered a 'not guilty' plea, but the medical evidence was enough to convict him and he was sentenced to a year's imprisonment with hard labour.[32] The sentence was suspended, however, and he was allowed to return to his unit. His sentence was completely remitted in February 1919.[33] The use of self-inflicted wounds as a way to escape the terrible conditions endured on the Western Front was a common court-martial offence.

William Brown, a widowed bricklayer from Christchurch, must come close to the record with the number of military offences and court martials he faced. His personal file, which is incomplete, recorded that Brown was charged with a military offence on 14 separate occasions. For these he faced four field general courts martial and one district court martial.[34] The military offences included being AWL multiple times, self-inflicted wounding (twice), using threating language to a superior, disobeying an order, selling his army kit, assaulting local civilians, and drunkenness. After the war, Brown was found guilty of three charges, including the assault of a French civilian, and was sentenced to one year's imprisonment with hard labour at Dorchester Prison in Dorset. Brown served less than four months of his sentence; on 1 July 1919 he sailed back to Australia, and was discharged from the AIF in Sydney on 17 October.[35] Both his sister and his son had written to the Australian army asking when he would be returning. They were advised:

> No. 1507 Private W.B. Brown, 4th Battalion, is returning to Australia per H.T. "Karmala", which left England on 1.7.19, and is due to arrive in Sydney about the 18th proximo. The advice also states he is being returned for disciplinary reasons, apparently to complete sentence of 1 year's imprisonment with hard labour, awarded on 6.1.19. In view of this information no railway concessions are available.[36]

It must have been a strained homecoming for William Brown, and the Australian military authorities were undoubtedly relieved to see the back of him.

It is also likely that a New Zealander held the overall AIF record for Field Punishment No. 1, with a total of 89 days over three separate occasions. Christchurch-born farrier Harry Graham joined up in early September 1915 at the age of 35, and was posted into the 15th Battery Field Artillery.[37] His many crimes ranged from stealing and selling army property and being AWL to abusing and striking a superior officer, wilful damage to civilian property, fighting, drunkenness, and refusing to obey a lawful order.[38] This resulted in five field general courts martial and included five years' penal servitude (later commuted to two years with hard labour).[39] On 1 August 1919, Harry Graham returned to Australia, where he would serve out the remainder of his sentence.

While these examples illustrate several military careers characterised by poor conduct, it was possible for a bad character to learn from his mistakes and become a good soldier. Wellington-born Hugh Elliott was a 24-year-old labourer when he joined the AIF in April 1915. Posted into A Company of the 19th Battalion, Elliott sailed from Australia for Egypt on 25 June. During the voyage, he was charged with '[c]reating a disturbance after lights out', for which he forfeited two days' pay.[40]

Elliott's next brush with military law was far more serious. On 27 October he was charged with disobeying an order 'in such a manner to shew wilful defiance of authority' and 'using insubordinate language to his superior officer'. The punishment was draconian: five years' penal servitude; this was later commuted to two years' imprisonment with hard labour,[41] but even then Elliott served only part of his sentence. In February 1916 the 604 days he had left to serve were remitted and he was transferred to the 2nd Pioneer Battalion. In August, Elliott was wounded in action in France, and a behaviour relapse soon followed. On 7 September, for being 'Drunk in the Field', the battalion commanding officer sentenced Elliott to 48 hours of Field Punishment No. 2.

Then something about Elliott seemed to change. Two months later, the same CO promoted him to corporal.[42] At the end of 1916 he was awarded the Military Medal for gallantry in the field, and a year later he was promoted to the rank of sergeant. Elliott was wounded in action again in September 1918 and at the end of the war received the Croix de Guerre.[43] It was a remarkable turnaround.

By contrast, the war also produced heroes, many of them New Zealanders. Of these, the four Victoria Cross winners mentioned earlier in this book are the most well-known examples, but there many others whose deeds have faded into obscurity. Some are discussed here.

William Henry Scott, a civil engineer born in Ōamaru in 1881, gave outstanding service in the AIF during the First World War. In 1914, he was the consulting engineer to the Borough of Wangaratta, Victoria, and had had some peacetime experience with the Victorian Mounted Rifles and the 11th Australian Light Horse dating back to 1903. Captain Scott served with the 9th Light Horse Regiment on Gallipoli, and in early 1916 he received the DSO 'for acts of gallantry and devotion to duty'.[44] He had led a small column of light horse to a distant enemy post and destroyed it, killing several of the enemy and capturing another 38, including the post's commanding officer, while losing only man and one horse. It was to be the first award of many.

For service in the Sinai–Palestine campaign, where he was wounded on four separate occasions, Scott would twice be mentioned in despatches and awarded a bar to his DSO. He was promoted to lieutenant colonel in June 1916, and early in 1918 he received a rare honour for a relatively junior field officer: he was made a CMG 'for services rendered in connexion with Military operations in the field'.[45] It was a distinguished record for any soldier. Scott died in Melbourne in September 1960.

Robert Reginald Chapman from Dunedin was awarded a Distinguished Conduct Medal (DCM) for 'conspicuous bravery and devotion to duty' during the Gallipoli campaign. Entrusted with delivering an important message to a senior officer, Chapman carried out his task despite being badly wounded and collapsing from exhaustion.[46] Having recovered from his wounds, and promoted to corporal in September 1917, the gallant soldier was killed in action near Villers-Bretonneux on 14 May 1918, aged 30.

William John Alfred Layburn, a wool buyer from Sawyer's Bay, near Dunedin, enlisted in the AIF in December 1915 and served with the 22nd Battalion in France and Belgium. He was awarded the Military Medal 'for bravery in the field' at Broodseinde on 4 October 1917.[47] Ten months later, on 28 August 1918, Lance-Corporal Layburn was killed in action. His name is commemorated on the Australian National Memorial at Villers-Bretonneux, one of the 10,885 AIF soldiers listed on that monument who were killed in France and who have no known grave.[48]

The Cranswick brothers are particularly notable.[49] Both were born in Tasmania, but the AIF embarkation rolls record their birthplace as Auckland. Both brothers listed their father, Henry Cranswick, then living in Queen Street, Auckland, as their next of kin.[50] This is somewhat odd, given that a letter from their mother to the Australian military authorities noted that Henry Walter Raleigh Cranswick 'deserted us 16 years ago' and 'it is many years since my husband contributed anything towards his children's support'.[51]

John Stewart Cranswick joined the AIF early in the war, on 24 August 1914. He listed his occupation as a surveyor and gave his age as 19 years. He was in fact considerably younger. Cranswick served on Gallipoli for just one day before being wounded on his left elbow on 25 April 1915.[52] He must have enjoyed the nightlife of Egypt on his 14 days' recovery leave; on 3 July 1915 John was returned to Australia aboard the *Ballarat* suffering from venereal disease.[53] He rejoined the 40th Battalion at the end of 1915 and was promoted to company sergeant major in May 1916. In January 2017, just one week after he received a commission, Cranswick was killed in a raid on German trenches.[54] He was buried in the Cite Bonjean Military Cemetery at Armentières. The age recorded on his headstone, and subsequently confirmed by his mother, was 20.[55] If this was correct, John could not have been 19 years old in 1914. Marion Cranswick chose for John's epitaph: 'In Life — Not death. Till we Meet again.'[56]

John's elder brother, Thurston George Cranswick, a 22-year-old bank clerk, joined the AIF's 40th Battalion in February 1916. He was promoted to corporal two months after joining and left at the end of November for France, where he was promoted to sergeant in February 1917 and commissioned four months later.[57] Just over a year later, when his officer became a casualty, Thurston led his depleted platoon to its objective, consolidating this newly won portion of the line.[58] His actions earned him a DCM for gallantry.

Another year on, during an attack on Bray, Thurston Cranswick again demonstrated outstanding courage. When his company was held up by German machine-gun nests and the officer commanding was wounded, Thurston took command, reorganised the company, outflanked the position and captured all the machine guns and the company objective.[59] This impressive performance won him the Military Cross. Just three days later, during an attack on Clery Copse, he was severely wounded. The wound slowly healed, but it would eventually prove fatal. Aged 26, Thurston George Cranswick died of tetanus in November 1920 at No. 12 Army General Hospital near Launceston, Tasmania.[60]

At least 48 New Zealand women also served in the AIF.[61] In fact, one of the most senior nurses of the Australian Army Nursing Service (AANS) was a New Zealander. Invercargill-born Evelyn Augusta Conyers had moved to Australia in her early twenties and completed her nursing training there. She joined the AIF in October 1914, aged 47 years.[62] Conyers initially served as a senior nursing sister, but on 12 January 1916 she was appointed matron-in-chief of the AIF and posted to No. 1 Australian General Hospital.[63] She would become one of the most decorated nurses of the war; in addition to being mentioned in despatches, she was awarded the Royal Red Cross decoration (First Class) and bar and the coveted Florence Nightingale Medal with Diploma, and was made a Commander of the Most Excellent Order of the British

William Henry Scott, a civil engineer from Ōamaru, in his Light Horse uniform. Scott's military service in the Australian Imperial Force was exceptional. AUSTRALIAN WAR MEMORIAL, B01131

A studio portrait of Lance-Corporal William John Alfred Layburn, 22nd Battalion, of Dunedin. Layburn was working in Melbourne as a wool buyer when war was declared, and he enlisted with the Australian Imperial Force on 1 December 1915. He served on the Western Front in France and Belgium and was awarded the Military Medal in 1917. He was killed in action on 28 August 1918, aged 30. He has no known grave but his name is recorded on the Australian Memorial at Villers-Bretonneux, France. AUSTRALIAN WAR MEMORIAL, H1885

Empire (CBE).[64] In reply to the secretary, Department of Defence about the rare award of a bar to the Royal Red Cross, she modestly wrote: 'I am proud that the work of the A.A.N.S. A.I.F. has received this recognition.'[65]

On 21 March 1915 the Australian government had cabled New Zealand asking it to supply 12 trained nurses for war service. The nurses had to be single women aged between 25 and 35, meet Australian standards for medical and surgical nursing at a 100-bed hospital, and be physically fit. In addition, they had to be ready to sail for Australia in six days' time.[66] Despite these rigid conditions, the New Zealand military authorities, under the energetic matron-in-chief Hester Maclean, had no trouble finding a dozen suitable nurses anxious to give service. They would be 'double badged' as members of both the New Zealand Army Nursing Service (NZANS) and the AANS. They would serve, however, as part of the AIF. The 12 nurses, their place of birth in New Zealand and the medical district they came from are listed below.[67]

Name	Place of birth	Medical district
Ellen Bennett Brown	Ashburton	Dunedin
Elsie May Cooke	Auckland	Auckland
Ethel Maud Dement	Christchurch	Wellington
Nora Philomena FitzGibbon	Arrowtown	Christchurch
Alice Charlotte Fraser	Auckland	Dargaville
Grace Macadam Guthrie	Palmerston North	Wellington
Dorothy Ann Rose	Dunedin	Christchurch
Winifred Merelina Scott	Onehunga	Auckland
Hilda Mary Steele	Wairoa	Auckland
Cora Evelyn Turnbull	Balclutha	Dunedin
Jessie Maud Verey	Invercargill	Dunedin
Elizabeth Jane White	Edinburgh	Dunedin

The nurses were attested in New Zealand before they sailed to Australia on 1 April 1915. On arrival, they were attested again into the AIF. In Sydney, the matron of Sydney Hospital presented them all with a Red Cross parcel. David Jones and Co., manufacturer of their Australian uniforms, gifted each nurse with a black silk umbrella. A letter published in *Kai Tiaki*, the New Zealand nursing journal, records that

> nothing could exceed the kindness of the Australian nurses, who have shown not a trace of jealousy or resentment at New Zealand being thus represented in the Commonwealth contingent — a spirit which speaks well for the women who are banded together in the same splendid common cause.[68]

The New Zealand nurses sailed from Australia on 13 April 1915 and served at No. 1 Australian General Hospital in Egypt, where they would nurse the wounded from Gallipoli. When the hospital moved to France in 1916, 11 of the New Zealand nurses went with it, and from there they were split up to serve in Australian and British hospitals, on hospital ships and trains, and at casualty clearing stations.[69] Alice Fraser, one of the 11, also spent some months nursing at a British hospital in India.[70] Like most other nurses in the military, they all had a busy, strenuous and, at times, dangerous war. Conditions were rough and the hours of work very long. As well as battling constant fatigue, the New Zealand nurses in the AIF faced debilitating illnesses including trench fever, dysentery and malaria. Two nurses were also operated on for appendicitis during their war service.[71]

The sole nurse who did not travel with the hospital to France was Dorothy Rose, who was discharged from the AIF in Egypt on 2 March 1916 upon her marriage.[72] She must have continued her nursing during the war years, but not with the AIF. Mrs Dorothy Whyte returned to Australia as a 'duty passenger' on a transport ship in January 1919.[73]

Sister Ellen Brown had a long and distinguished record of service in the AIF. Trained at the Dunedin General Hospital as a general nurse and midwife, Brown joined the AANS at the end of March 1915. Then aged 35 years, she had extensive nursing experience, which included being sister in charge of a women's surgical ward and of a gynaecological ward. She had also nursed for five years at a psychiatric hospital and spent 15 months in charge of the Pleasant Valley Sanatorium, just south of Palmerston in Otago.[74] She nursed wounded soldiers from Gallipoli at the Abbasia Hospital in Egypt and then in the United Kingdom and in France and Belgium for the next three years. At the war's end, Brown used the long delay before her return to New Zealand to complete a course at the London School of Massage. Massage at this time was the forerunner to physiotherapy and many

The New Zealand nurses recruited to join the Australian Army Nursing Service were affectionately known as the 'Twelve Apostles'. This photograph of them in their AANS uniforms was taken in April 1915, shortly before their departure for Egypt. Standing, from left: Winifred Scott, Hilda Steele, Nora FitzGibbon, Grace Guthrie, Ethel Dement, Cora Turnbull and Ellen Brown. Seated: Dorothy Rose, Elizabeth White, Alice Fraser, Elsie Cooke and Jessie Verey. HOCKEN COLLECTIONS, UARE TAOKA O HĀKENA, UNIVERSITY OF OTAGO

nurses learned it. She then set off on a tour of the Continent, beginning in Paris in October 1919.[75] Brown never lost her sense of identity as a New Zealander. At the back of her extensive diary are two poems. One, by a British officer, is titled 'The Australians' ('The Bravest thing God ever made'). The other is a tribute to 'Private Smith of the N.Z.E.F.', written by Dora Hamilton-Wilcox. In this poem a wounded and hospitalised Smith recalls his beloved homeland:

> The tussock hills, the glow
> On distant fields of snow
> Where mountain lilies blow
> Beneath Aorangi.

This soldier, 'Born of a sturdy race', dreams of his homeland, but

> Only the nurses know,
> Private Smith's dying![76]

This poem clearly meant a lot to a dedicated nurse so far from home and caring for dying soldiers every day.

On 4 December 1920, Brown sailed from the United Kingdom for Australia as the matron in charge on board the transport vessel *Bahia Castillo*. She was discharged from the AANS on 17 April 1921. During her military service she was mentioned in despatches in June 1917, and two years later received the Australian Royal Red Cross decoration (Second Class). Brown later worked as the matron of the Hanmer Springs Military Hospital in North Canterbury.

Ellen Brown's experience was not unusual for the New Zealand nurses in the AIF. Among 'the Twelve Apostles', as the nurses were sometimes called by the men in France, Elsie Cooke, Ethel Dement, Winifred Scott and Elizabeth White were awarded the Royal Red Cross, and Dement, Turnbull, White and Ellen Brown were mentioned in despatches.[77] It was an impressive record of service.

The New Zealanders were only a small component of the AIF in the war, but their contribution was significant. They were represented at all levels and in all categories. Some were recognised for their courage, dedication and heroism, while a small group were incorrigibly bad characters and bad soldiers; the bane of their commanding officers' lives. Most just served as best they could for little reward and acknowledgement. Far too many paid the ultimate price for their service, or were left physically and psychologically maimed. As author Neil Smith has observed, 'the New Zealanders were part of every major action in which the AIF were involved'.[78] Smith also notes that the service and sacrifice of the New Zealanders in the AIF has 'probably never been recognised as having contributed to the war effort of their own land'.[79] After 100 years of neglect, it is certainly time that this changed.

above Early reinforcements for the 40th Infantry Battalion of the Australian Imperial Force. This battalion was raised in Tasmania and brothers Thurston and John Cranswick both served in it. AUSTRALIAN WAR MEMORIAL, C1043375

below Members of the 9th Australian Light Horse at the foot of Walker's Ridge on Gallipoli. The New Zealander William Scott was an officer of this regiment and was awarded the DSO while serving in the Middle East. Scott was wounded four times during the war and earned a bar to his DSO and was twice mentioned in despatches. Scott ended the war as a lieutenant colonel and was also made a Companion to the Distinguished Order of St Michael and St George (CMG). It was an outstanding achievement. AUSTRALIAN WAR MEMORIAL, C1007

CHAPTER SEVEN

WITH THE FRENCH FORCES

LA DÉPÊCHE
LYON REPUBLICAIN
LE PETIT MARSEILLAIS
L'ECHO DU NORD
LES GRANDS
REGIONAUX
FIX
LE ROI
DES CINEMAS
PARISIANA
LE ROI
DES CINEMAS
PARISIANA

Previous pages
British volunteers with the French Foreign Legion march through Paris in September 1914. At least four 'British' members were New Zealanders. ALAMY, B5EWY7

A small number of New Zealanders, probably no more than 40, served with the military forces or medical services of France during the First World War. The military personnel primarily served with the French Foreign Legion, and the medical personnel with either the French Red Cross or the French Flag Nursing Corps (FFNC). As its name implied, the French Foreign Legion welcomed people of all nationalities and was relatively easy to join; the Legion was renowned for asking few questions about a person's background. Further, French medical services welcomed foreign volunteers, especially once the sheer scale of casualties became evident in the early months of 1914. In fact, the FFNC was established in 1914 as a way of obtaining the services of qualified British nurses for work in French military hospitals.[1] Initially the FFNC was under the authority of the French War Office, which partially funded the service. In April 1917, having proven its worth, the FFNC was made a department of the British Committee of the French Red Cross, which financed the service for the remainder of the war as a gift to France.[2] In all, some 30,000 women served as nurses in the French army, but three times that number served via the French Red Cross.[3]

Those New Zealanders known at the time of writing to have served with French medical services during the First World War appear below, along with their birthplace or residence.[4]

James Vere Arkle	French Red Cross	Resident of Palmerston, Otago
Ella Kate Cooke	French Flag Nursing Corps	Born Auckland
Nora Dalrymple	French Flag Nursing Corps	Born Wellington
Mary Audley Eaddy	French Flag Nursing Corps	Resident of Gisborne
Gertrude Amy Fisher	French Red Cross	Born Christchurch
Harold Delf Gillies	French Red Cross	Born Dunedin
Margaret Hitchcock	French Flag Nursing Corps	Born Dunedin
Ethelbert Petrie Hoyle	French Red Cross	Resident of Katikati
Lily Lind	French Flag Nursing Corps	Born Dunedin
Beatrice Eleanor Dormer Maunder	French Red Cross	Born lower Rangitīkei
Herbert O'Callaghan	Anglo-French Hospital Marseille	Born Auckland

Nina May Palmer	French Red Cross	Born Hokitika
Thomas James Pemberton	French Red Cross	Educated Christchurch
Beryl Rawlings	French Flag Nursing Corps	Born Timaru
Herbert William Sams	French Red Cross (driver)	Born Tasmania
Edward Percy Verity Sealy	French Red Cross	Born Timaru
Joan Sunderland	French Red Cross	Born Gisborne

At the end of February 1915 the *Feilding Star* carried an extract from the *British Journal of Nursing* about four registered New Zealand nurses working with the FFNC: sisters Lind, Hitchcock, Cooke and Eaddy. All four nurses had 'won high praise from their supervisors', the journal said, and were 'very much liked in their services'. It concluded: 'We feel sure our numerous readers in New Zealand will rejoice at their success, especially in a service so novel and difficult.'[5]

The work was indeed often difficult. One of the first New Zealand nurses to join the FFNC was Lily Lind, who left New Zealand in 1913 with her friend Margaret Hitchcock to study midwifery at a Dublin hospital. When war was declared, both Lind and Hitchcock volunteered and were recruited for the FFNC, along with four others. On reaching Rouen, they were welcomed by the French minister of war, who presented them with their badges. Lind and Hitchcock were soon at work treating the never-ending flow of wounded French soldiers. In August 1915 Lind wrote to the New Zealand nursing journal *Kai Tiaki* describing the type of work she was doing:

> It seems years since I wrote, as so many things have happened since then, the most important for us being, that we have been shelled out of Bergues where we were so happy with our little hospital. All our patients were evacuated between shells from long-range guns in the daytime, and bombs from taubes [German aircraft] at night, they are anything but safe. Then after a few weeks of a more or less exciting (but always interesting) life in cellars and so on, we went to Paris Plage, Boulogne for 2 weeks and it was a great change, sea-coast and everything so peaceful. Since then we have been working on the only two French Hospital barges transporting wounded from the Nieuport vicinity to Bourbourg. Miss Hitchcock and I are on the one barge.[6]

While nursing on the hospital barges Lind contracted pulmonary tuberculosis and was invalided back to England, where she and Hitchcock managed to obtain berths on the New Zealand hospital ship *Maheno*. However, the hoped-for tonic of the voyage back to New Zealand was not to be. Two days after leaving Colombo, on 21 November 1916, Lily Lind died aged just 34 years.[7]

Ella Cooke certainly proved to be a popular nurse, even with her German patients. She found the Germans 'really most respectful to me and very helpful in every way they can'. In return, 'Nurse Anglaise', as she was called, was often especially requested by them.[8] On New Year's Day 1916 Cooke's German patients 'made her a speech of thanks . . . and gave three rousing cheers'.[9]

Nina May Palmer, known as May, joined the French Red Cross at the end of 1914. She already had extensive experience nursing war wounded. In 1914 she had just returned to New Zealand

In 1915 Ella Kate Cooke nursed for six months with the French Flag Nursing Corps, working in hospitals at the front in France, and later in England and Egypt. She was known as the 'Nurse Anglaise' and was well liked by all her patients. She was killed in a traffic accident in Alexandria. AUCKLAND WAR MEMORIAL MUSEUM TĀMAKI PAENGA HIRA, PH-1966-3

after a long time abroad, including a stint nursing at Salonika in 1913 during the Second Balkan War. Her mother, Edith Palmer, nursed with her.[10] The conditions were poor and the wounds she encountered 'were terrible: head wounds caused by shrapnel and abdominal wounds where the intestines and bladder were riddled with bullets'.[11] Both May and Edith were decorated for their service by the Greek government.[12] May Palmer did not linger in New Zealand. By September 1914 she was on her way to Marseille, where she was immediately put to work in a 500-bed Red Cross hospital. She later became matron of an Anglo-French hospital in Menton. In August 1915, while still in France, Palmer joined Queen Alexandra's Imperial Military Nursing Service Reserve (QAIMNSR) and served on hospital ships, until treatment for breast cancer in February 1917 forced her to give this up.[13] However, the redoubtable nurse was back at work before the end of the war, and returned to New Zealand in 1919. In 1923 she was working as a matron of a hospital in the Sudan.[14]

The distinguished physician and founder of modern plastic surgery Harold Gillies began his war service working for the Red Cross in France and Belgium. Born in Dunedin and educated in medicine at Cambridge University, Gillies was a 32-year-old ear, nose and throat surgeon when the First World War broke out. He immediately offered his services to the Red Cross, and at the end of January 1915 he was called to serve in France. Gillies' first role there was as a general surgeon working with a Belgian ambulance unit near Furnes.[15]

While passing through Boulogne, Gillies met Charles Auguste Valadier, who had pioneered the treatment of facial wounds and was renowned as a skilled dentist. Valadier had studied medicine, and although he had never taken his final examinations he was permitted to perform medical operations under the supervision of a qualified surgeon. In 1915 Valadier had organised a surgical unit at No. 83 General Hospital at Wimereux for the treatment of jaw wounds. There, Valadier pioneered the technique of repairing jaw wounds with new tissue taken from parts of the body, and experimented with bone grafts. For a time Gillies worked at the hospital as Valadier's supervising surgeon. He quickly realised the value and potential of Valadier's work, and he also fully appreciated the destructive capability of modern weaponry and that these new, severe types of wound would require new and different surgical procedures.[16]

After a brief period on the staff of the Anglo-French hospital at Le Tréport, in June 1915 Gillies went on leave to Paris, where he met Hippolyte Morestin, a brilliant French surgeon who specialised in treating injuries of the face and jaw. In 1915 Morestin was 'the most celebrated practitioner of plastic surgery in western Europe'.[17] Watching Morestin work was a revelation for Gillies. He was determined to do this type of surgery, and later reflected:

> I felt a tremendous urge to do something other than the surgery of destruction. My purpose in Paris was to observe what they were doing in the way of reconstruction . . . I felt that this was the one job in the world I wanted to do.[18]

Gillies spent the rest of 1915 in France observing the treatment of facial injuries as much as he could, travelling to Boulogne, Étaples, Amiens and Paris. By year's end he had persuaded the British army medical authorities that they, too, needed a special hospital for face and

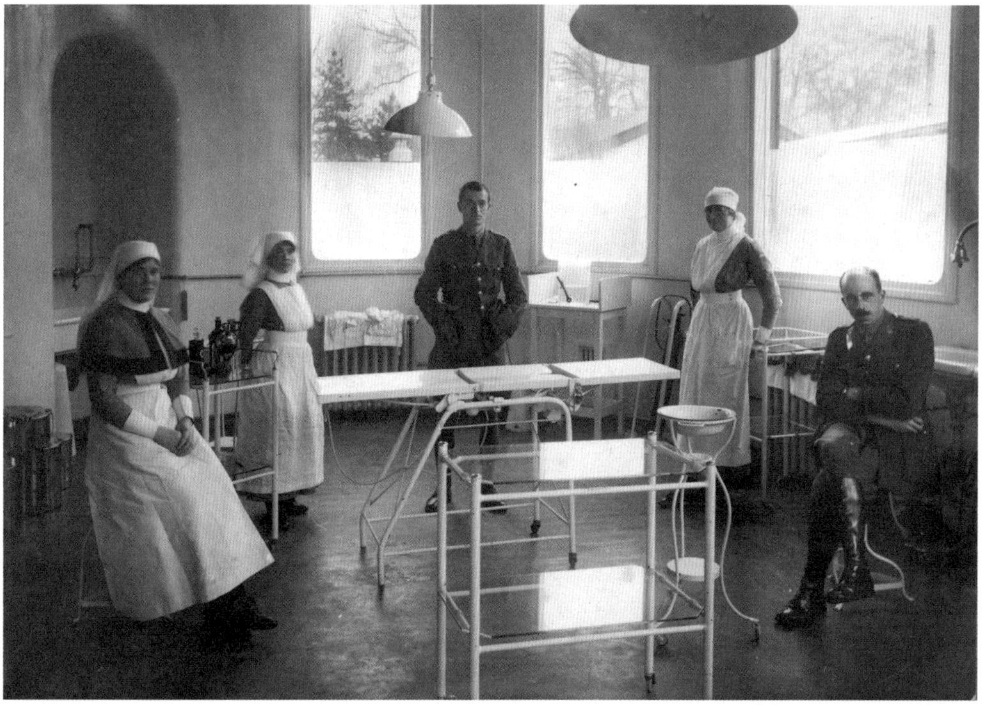

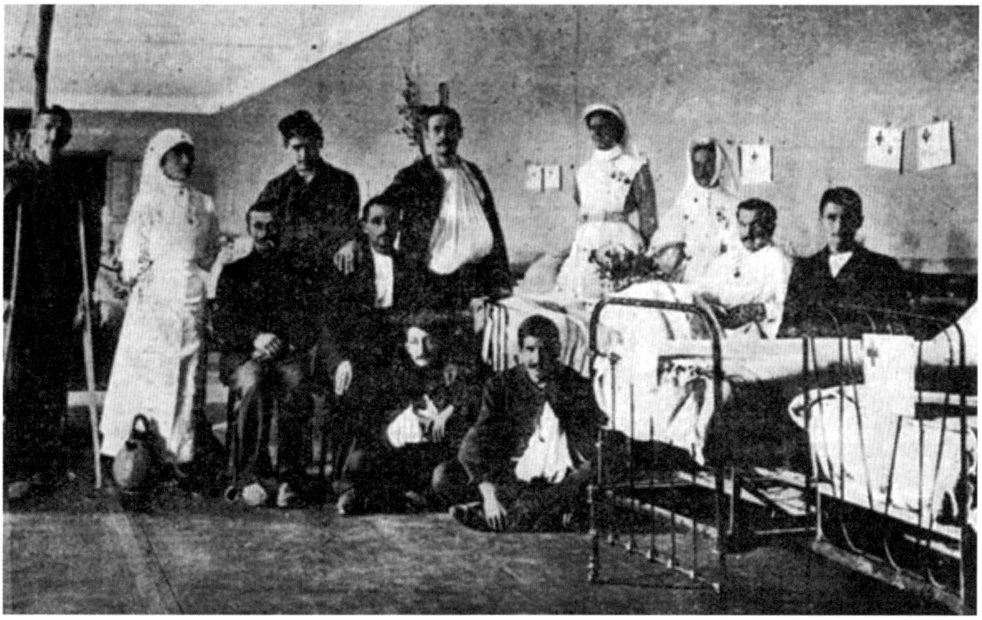

above The distinguished physician and pioneer of modern plastic surgery Harold Gillies began his war service with the French Red Cross, and in Paris was inspired to undertake facial reconstruction work. This photograph shows Gillies (seated at right) in his surgery at St Mary's Hospital in Sidcup, United Kingdom. GILLIES ARCHIVE, UK

below Nina May Palmer (standing second from right) nursed with the French Red Cross in 1914. Palmer's extensive war service included a stint as matron of an Anglo-French hospital and working on hospital ships. Despite treatment for breast cancer, she nursed throughout the war years and beyond. AUCKLAND WAR MEMORIAL MUSEUM ONLINE CENOTAPH, KINDLY DONATED BY FAMILY

jaw injuries. On 11 January 1916, Gillies received orders from the War Office to report to the Cambridge Military Hospital at Aldershot, Hampshire to set up a ward for the treatment of serious facial injuries. It was the start of a major change in the treatment of these types of injuries for British servicemen of the First World War and one that led to a new branch of war and general surgery. Harold Gillies' time in France and Belgium was critical to his development as a pioneering plastic surgeon, and by the end of the war he had treated some 11,000 patients.[19] As one historian put it, 'The art and science of modern plastic surgery, in Britain and New Zealand in particular, owe their origins to him.'[20]

One of the most notable and remarkable records of war service was that of Beatrice Eleanor Dormer Maunder. From the lower Rangitīkei, Beatrice Maunder was 47 years old in 1914 and living in the United Kingdom when war was declared. She was one of the first New Zealanders to become a British VAD, joining up on 11 September.[21] Just days later, she was on her way to Belgium to begin what would be a long period of service on the Western Front. On the eve of her departure Maunder wrote to her sister in Auckland:

> We have been working night and day, and now every detail is complete. Three of us only leave to-night, the doctor for the medical part, self for the Red Cross work, and the organiser for the base hospital, field ambulance. Relief for refugees falls to me.[22]

After her arrival in Ostend, Maunder played a leading role in the conversion of a large entertainment area on the waterfront into a hospital. She later did the same to the town's Hotel Continental. In addition to her responsibility for the Belgian refugees, in those first weeks at Ostend Maunder and the 10-person British Red Cross team, which included her niece Blanche Lucena, had to nurse hundreds of wounded British and Belgian soldiers. Maunder later recalled that in the first two weeks in Belgium she had no chance to change her clothes or go to sleep in a bed.[23]

The German occupation of Ostend forced a return to England. Maunder was not there long. The Belgian authorities had been impressed by her performance, and the inspector-general of the Belgian army, General Antonin de Selliers, invited her to a hospital for Belgian soldiers at Rouen.[24] Maunder arrived in Rouen on 26 November to find the French authorities 'enthusiastic supporters' of her work. She soon converted one of the largest public schools in the city into the King Albert Hospital. Formally opened by the Belgian minister for war exactly one month after her arrival in Rouen, the hospital could accommodate 200 soldiers, but Maunder soon expanded its capacity to 500 and, later, there would be accommodation for more than 1000 wounded soldiers.[25]

As the hospital's *directrice* Maunder was responsible for everything, including daily organisation, equipment, staffing and finance. For her work in setting up this hospital the King of Belgium awarded Beatrice the Order of Merit. New Zealand newspapers reported that the decoration was for 'Miss Maunder's courage, enterprise, and ability' and that 'this unique distinction is not only an honour to her, but to her country and her compatriots'.[26]

It was a stressful job. In May 1915 Maunder wrote to a friend in Whanganui:

> I came out to work directly war was declared, little dreaming I was ever to go on and remain as I have. Only those who have gone through such times know or can realise the cost — the terrible sufferings around, the nerve strain to meet and cope with insurmountable difficulties. There was the retreat with the Belgian army, then the bombardment, the Taubes dropping their deadly missiles, and not one day since I arrived on September 1st have I been off the strain or one moment idle. Night and day it had to be, to do one's duty and what was needed. And my staff were just as loyal, just as ready as it is possible for anyone to be. I have asked great things of them at times, and they have never failed me. This is the base surgical hospital, and is now in full swing. In all I am responsible for a thousand beds, and may have to undertake more, so great is the need.[27]

In 1916 the Belgians asked her to organise and equip another military hospital and she had readily agreed, but things were never easy, nor was danger far away. Maunder wrote to her friend:

> Heavy gales! The roof of one of the wards was blown off the other night. And so dark! When coming from the hospital at 6 o'clock the other evening, I ran into the stone balustrade over the canal. I had not seen a glimpse of it. Another six inches and I'd have gone a clean header into the liquid impurities of the canal. The same night a poor Belgian Tommy did, and was drowned, also a French soldier. It's dark as the grave here. All have to use lanterns or flash lights.[28]

In January 1917, during the coldest winter in 40 years, Maunder wrote to a friend that 'the cold is so intense it's almost beyond one's power to hold a pen'.[29] Yet, as she did so often, this strong-willed, talented woman finished the task she set herself.

Maunder had made a point of never mentioning her nationality. She explained why in another letter to a friend:

> It has been one of my principles since commencing war service never to mention the particular land of my birth. Americans have so boasted of American superiority (?) that it made one particularly reticent — allowing the work to be judged by results, and nothing else.[30]

Beatrice Maunder's war work can only be judged as exceptional and extraordinary. After the war, she continued to work on the reconstruction of Belgium and embarked on fundraising talks in the United Kingdom. In April 1920, then aged in her early fifties, she married George Knowles, a London lawyer who had been a keen supporter of her work.[31] At her wedding Maunder proudly wore her three well-earned Belgian medals. Beatrice and George Knowles visited New Zealand towards the end of 1920. On 8 June 1922 Lady Allen, the wife of the New Zealand High Commissioner, Sir James Allen, presented Beatrice at the Royal Court in London.[32] Beatrice and George Knowles later went to live in France.[33]

Another New Zealander with an extraordinary record in the French medical services was Ethelbert Petrie Hoyle. Born in Rochdale, Lancashire, Petrie Hoyle, as he was known, arrived in New Zealand on board the *Lady Jocelyn* in 1878. Aged just over 16 at the time, Hoyle was allocated 100 acres of farmland near Katikati.[34] It would seem that farming did not suit him; two years later Hoyle arrived in San Francisco on his way to Seguin, Texas. He did not stay long in Texas as he was repeatedly dogged by attacks of malaria and ague.[35]

As a boy Petrie Hoyle had been trained in homeopathy by his family's doctor in Edinburgh. He may have first practised while in New Zealand, as he recalled in later years:

> My personal experience with homeopathy dates back to 1878, as a boy of 16 and a half years, when I went to New Zealand, my mother having coached me in 'home medicine.' I went out armed with a case of 72 remedies and Edward Harris Ruddock's *The Homeopathic Vade Mecum of Modern Medicine and Surgery*. Dr Hayle . . . had also coached me in various things, including how to properly dilute any medicine which was getting low in its bottle.[36]

In San Francisco Hoyle enrolled at the Hahnemann Homeopathic Medical College of the Pacific, which had opened in 1884. He graduated in 1900 and spent many years working as a homeopath in Kittery, Maine, before retiring. He travelled a number of times between England and the United States, and in 1913, while living in Holland Park, London, he was elected as travelling secretary to the International Homeopathic Society. He was also editor of the *International Homeopathic Medical Directory*.

When the war broke out Hoyle became a volunteer in the British Mobile Hospital Service in Belgium in August 1914. In January 1915 the Anglo-French American Hospital No. 307 at Neuilly-sur-Seine (a suburb of Paris) opened in conjunction with the French Red Cross and the International Homeopathic Council. The hospital, completely homeopathic, was administered by Hoyle and served French, British, and even some German troops during the war. Homeopathic remedies were used to treat pneumonia, tuberculosis, angina pectoris, bacterial infections and a host of other illnesses. The hospital was disbanded on 15 March 1916, when many of the staff were called up for military service in the Royal Army Medical Corps.[37]

Hoyle continued his war service as *médecin en chef* at Hospital No. 50, Roubelles for one year, the Ulster Volunteer Hospital, Lyon for five months, the American Hospital (Orthopaedic) for 15 months, and Hospital No. 10, Brétigny-sur-Orge. He was awarded the Service de Santé avec Palme; the Médaille d'honneur des épidémies, première classe; and the Reconnaissance de la République Française.[38]

Hoyle retired to Mallorca, Spain with his second wife in the early 1950s and died aged 94.

A small number of New Zealanders served with French military forces during the war; those known to have served appear below. With the exception of James Waddell, very little is known about these men.

Vincent Lionel Briggs	French Foreign Legion	Resident of Ōtorohanga
Horace Bertram Cogan	French forces	Born Christchurch
Godefroy Galitzenstein	French army	Instructor in French and German, Seddon Memorial Technical College, Auckland
Geoffrey Ernest Henry Gotz	French army	Born Tauranga
Alister Christian McDonald	French Foreign Legion	Born Bulls
Pierre Marie Pascal	French army	Born Palmerston North
Joseva Lalabalavu Vanaal Sukuna	French Foreign Legion	Born Bau, Fiji; ex Wanganui Collegiate
James Waddell	French Foreign Legion	Born Dunedin

Alister McDonald from Bulls had an all-too-brief war. He left New Zealand with a consignment of horses bound for the United Kingdom; once there, for reasons unknown, he joined the French Foreign Legion. In early March 1915 McDonald was at Antwerp with an artillery battery, one of the French military units helping the Belgian army defend the great fortress city of Antwerp during its siege in September and October 1914. On 28 September the Germans began bombarding the Belgian fortifications with heavy and super-heavy artillery; McDonald's gun crew received a direct hit from a heavy German shell, and he was killed.[39] The Antwerp fortifications fell to the Germans on 9 October.

The most remarkable service record of a New Zealander in the French military during the First World War was surely that of James Waddell, who had joined the Foreign Legion well before the war began. As military historian Christopher Pugsley has written, Waddell's story 'is a tale that defies belief'.[40]

James Waddell was born in Dunedin in 1872. His father was the saddler at Cromwell, where Waddell attended primary school. He was one of the few New Zealand children in the nineteenth century to continue on to secondary schooling, attending Otago Boys' High School as a boarder. There it was observed that he was 'mad on soldiering and excelled in French'.[41] When he finished school Waddell moved to Christchurch to work as an insurance clerk, while studying for a British officer's commission at Canterbury College in the evenings. His heart was not in insurance. As he explained just before his death: 'For some time I had been restless and had a growing desire to go abroad and so applied for a military commission in the British Imperial Army.'[42] Waddell's application was successful, and at the age of 19 he received the 'momentous cable' informing him that 'Second Lieutenant James Waddell has been appointed to the Duke of Wellington's Regiment.'[43] The regiment's 2nd Battalion was stationed at Maritzburg, South Africa, and the restless youth now had his opportunity to travel.

However, if young James Waddell thought he had landed his dream job he was soon to be terribly disillusioned. Formed in 1702, the Duke of Wellington's (West Riding) Regiment was a line infantry unit with a proud record of service. While not regarded as part of an elite corps like the cavalry, the regiment was class-conscious and rigid, as many of these older regiments were. The small (just five foot three inches tall) outsider from New Zealand was not made to feel welcome; nor did he have private means or family connections to call on.[44] Enthusiasm and ability were not enough and, with the tacit approval of the commanding officer, the junior officers made Waddell's life hell over many months in an effort to get him to quit the regiment. Waddell was beaten, bound, stripped, humiliated, excluded from social events, 'his property destroyed, his reputation smeared'. At one point he was forced to draw his sword against a group of officers bent on assaulting him.[45]

It must have been a nightmare for him. When he confided in Alex C. Bailie, a retired surveyor general whom he'd met in Natal, the details were passed on to the New Zealand defence minister, Richard Seddon. In March 1897, the New Zealand representative in the United Kingdom, William Pember Reeves, made a formal complaint to the colonial secretary and the army was forced to hold a court of inquiry into Waddell's case. It found there had been 'serious misconduct' and some junior officers were censured. In July of that year, Lieutenant-Colonel Gore, the battalion's commanding officer, whom Bailie suspected of being behind Waddell's persecution, was placed on the army's retired list.[46]

These developments cannot have improved Waddell's standing in the regiment. Nonetheless, he was promoted to full lieutenant at the end of the year and went with the regiment to India. Soon after his arrival in India Waddell met Blanche Prudhomme de Foncy, who became his wife and, in his words, 'begged me to resign and apply for a commission in the French Foreign Legion'.[47] Waddell resigned from the British army in April 1898 and two years later, through Blanche's influence, was commissioned as a second lieutenant into the 2nd Infantry Regiment of the Foreign Legion.[48]

From 1900 to 1914 James Waddell served with the Legion in several of France's imperial wars or insurgencies. He initially struggled to learn French and to fit into a new military system, which was lukewarm to his arrival.[49] He completed two tours in French Indo-China and served near Tonkin during the Boxer Rebellion. He also had postings with the Legion to Morocco, the Sahara and Algeria during these years.[50] By early 1914 he had been promoted to the rank of captain, posted to the 1st Foreign Legion Regiment and awarded the Knight's Cross of the Legion of Honour for his work in Indo-China.[51] On the outbreak of war in 1914 Waddell was with the Legion in North Africa.

It must be said that Waddell's personal life was a bit of a mess in these pre-war years. In 1904 he had become a French citizen, but the following year he divorced Blanche and took their three children to New Zealand, where he arranged for them to live with relatives. In June 1914 he married Marguerite Nicole Fournier, but the couple divorced less than two years later.[52]

In April 1915 James Waddell landed on Gallipoli as a company commander in the Regiment de Marche d'Afrique. It was there that he caught the attention of his military superiors. On 4 July General Henri Gourand mentioned him in despatches for his work at Cape Helles during the landing. On 12 July, while leading his battalion, Waddell was shot through the chest and hit by shrapnel.[53] Nevertheless, despite these serious wounds, he refused to leave the field, and continued to direct the attack until an important Ottoman position had been captured. For his gallantry Waddell was promoted to major and on 27 August was awarded the Croix de Guerre.

above *Médecin en chef* E. Petrie Hoyle of the French Red Cross with his Service de Santé avec Palme. Petrie Hoyle started his career in homeopathy after immigrating to New Zealand in 1878. FREDERICK M. DEARBORN, *AMERICAN HOMEOPATHY IN THE WORLD WAR*, US INSTITUTE OF HOMEOPATHY, 1923

left Beatrice Maunder wearing the Cross of the Order of Leopold presented to her by the Belgian government for her work with their wounded. SIR GEORGE GREY SPECIAL COLLECTIONS, AUCKLAND LIBRARIES, AWNS-19150624-50-1

Waddell's wounding ended his service on Gallipoli and he spent the months from August 1915 through to March 1916 recovering in Algeria and Nice. When he was sufficiently recovered, he travelled to Paris to be decorated by the French minister of the interior.[54]

However, James Waddell's war service was far from over. On 1 April 1916 he was appointed commanding officer of the 2nd Battalion of the French Foreign Legion, then part of the Moroccan Division serving on the Western Front. Being a Legion battalion, the unit comprised many different nationalities. Waddell's sergeant major, a German called Max Mader, would become the most decorated NCO in the French army. The battalion also included the American poet and Harvard graduate Corporal Alan Seeger, whose poem 'Rendezvous' opens with these famous lines:

> I have a rendezvous with Death
> At some disputed barricade[55]

In July 1916, Waddell's battalion was involved in the early fighting on the Somme and captured the village of Belloy-en-Santerre, just to the west of Péronne. It was a costly assault as the village was heavily fortified. The Legion was ordered to take the village by bayonet point at 0600 hours. The Michelin guide to the Somme described its charge:

> Deployed in battle formation, they charged across a flat meadow 900 yards broad. When 300 yards from their objective, machine-guns hidden in the path from Estrées to Belloy were suddenly unmasked and a deadly fire mowed down the French ranks. The 9th and 11th Companies sustained particularly heavy losses, all the officers falling. One of these companies reached the objective under the command of the mess corporal. Belloy was captured and 750 Germans were taken prisoner.[56]

Some 248 legionnaires were killed in this attack and 504 were wounded. Seeger was among the fallen. Another American legionnaire, Jack Moyet, wrote of this action:

> The Legion lost many men. My battalion Chief Commandant James Waddell, a New Zealander with a fine record in the Legion, was one of the few officers to come out alive.[57]

Waddell was awarded a palm leaf to his Croix de Guerre for this attack. After the war, Seeger's grieving parents paid for the bell in the rebuilt church at Belloy. Its peal 'represented Alan Seeger's voice, still singing over the land he grew to love'.[58] For his actions on the Somme, in June 1917 Waddell was made an Officer of the Legion of Honour.[59]

After his time on the Somme, Waddell fought in some of the French army's critical battles of the war. These included the fighting on Chemin des Dames and at Verdun in 1916, the Nivelle offensive in 1917, and the German Spring Offensive in 1918. He was wounded on two more occasions and finished the war at the rank of lieutenant colonel, with seven palms added to his Croix de Guerre. James Waddell was undoubtedly one of France's most decorated soldiers

James Waddell in his French Foreign Legion uniform. Waddell, who died in Levin in February 1954, aged 81, was awarded the Légion d'honneur, the Croix de Guerre with seven palms and many campaign medals for his remarkable military service. He was also a veteran of the Gallipoli campaign. AUCKLAND WAR MEMORIAL MUSEUM ONLINE CENOTAPH, KINDLY DONATED BY FAMILY

of the First World War.[60] For a New Zealand-born soldier it was certainly a unique record of service. In 1916, after the Somme battle and while on leave in England, James Waddell had applied to serve with his countrymen in the NZEF. He wrote to Brigadier-General George Richardson, the senior New Zealand army administrator in the United Kingdom:

> Being a New Zealander having had sixteen years in the French Army and having an excellent knowledge of France as well as being a fluent French linguist, intimately familiar with the French Army Organisation in its wider scope as well as its details it might be considered that my services would be of value to the Higher Command of the New Zealand Forces at this momentous time when the New Zealand soldiers are operating so intimately with the French.[61]

Waddell's application to join the NZEF was vetoed by the New Zealand Division's commander, Major-General Sir Andrew Russell. In fact, Russell was quite heated in his response: 'No! it is out of the question from my point of view . . . we have obligations to good fellows of our own.'[62] While one New Zealand historian has seen his veto of Waddell as evidence of Russell placing 'great stock on fairness', it was an incredibly short-sighted and inflexible decision.[63] The New Zealand Division was short of officers and had ample need of 'good fellows' wherever they came from. Indeed, many of the division's officers were not New Zealanders; they included exchange officers from Australia, British army staff officers, and liaison officers from the French and Belgian armies. One more middle-ranking officer would not have made much difference.

After the war, Waddell continued to serve in the French Foreign Legion. In August 1920 he was promoted to Croix de Commander (Commander of the Legion of Honour) for his services to France. He married Aida Josephine Schmitt in September 1921 and the couple subsequently had a daughter. Waddell served in Tunisia until his retirement from the Legion in 1926. He spent the next 10 years farming in Tunisia, returned to France to live for a year, and then moved to Morocco.[64] It wasn't until 1950 that Waddell, then in his late seventies, returned to New Zealand. He spent most of his time with his daughter in Tauranga, but in 1954 travelled to Levin to stay with his son Jack, who ran a grocery store in the town. While on this visit James Waddell fell ill and died on 18 February 1954, aged 81 years.[65] The gallant and distinguished old soldier was buried in the Returned Services Association section of the Levin cemetery. As Ian McGibbon has written, Waddell has a solid claim to be 'the outstanding New Zealand soldier to have served in a foreign force'.[66]

Pierre Marie Pascal may not be as well known as James Waddell, but his war service with the French military was impressive. The Pascal family came to New Zealand in 1879 and settled at Palmerston North in the Manawatū, where his father, Claude Marie Pascal, ran a successful flaxmill business with his brother. Pierre was born in Palmerston North in 1894 and lived the first four years of his life there.

In January 1898 Claude Pascal and his wife took the family to France for an extended visit.[67] They did not return to Palmerston North, and Pierre eventually entered the military.[68] In April 1917 the *Free Lance* newspaper included a news report on the Pascal family:

> His only son, now 23 years of age, is a Brigadier in the Dragoons of Limoges, and has been in action since the first month of the war. Altogether, life over there is fairly heart-breaking, but they are brave and cheerful, never for an instant dreaming of anything else but ultimate victory, loyal to their own brave poilus, and generous in their praise of the men they call 'our splendid Allies.' There are many in the Manawatu who will remember Mr. Pascal . . . and it is good to think that both the past and the present owners of 'Beaulieu' are taking a generous hand in this dreadful conflict.[69]

Just over a year later, this newspaper reported in more detail about the notable military career of Pierre Pascal, under the headline 'Palmerston North Boy now a Brigadier General':

> Brigadier Pierre M. Pascal . . . is the only son of Mr. and Mrs. Claude Pascal, Chateau de Glergon, Angoulème, France. He was born in Palmerston North, Mr. Pascal then being the owner of the Beaulieu Estate, which he sold to the late Mr. A. McHardy. When war was declared the young soldier, who was only 20 years of age, had already served his time, having volunteered at 18 instead of waiting to be called up. In September, 1914, his regiment, the Dragoons of Limoges, were called up, and as he showed marked ability he very soon rose to the rank of Brigadier. In the French Army the soldiers get four days' leave every six months, and with the exception of this leave, Brigadier Pascal has been on service at the Front the whole time, one of the thin blue line, a soldier of France. Brigadier Pascal is a nephew, one of the very many nephews, of Mr. and Mrs. J. B. Pascal, of Palmerston North. A full-blown Brigadier at 24 is a high honour indeed.[70]

The honour was not quite so high. In the French army of the First World War, a *général de brigade* commanded a brigade, which was usually a newly promoted major general. It was a French cavalry tradition to call a corporal *brigadier*.[71]

Another New Zealander who served in the French Foreign Legion was Vincent Lionel Briggs. Briggs had been born in Barbados, but was working as an accountant in Ōtorohanga in 1914. In early 1915 he tried to join the NZEF, but failed the medical examination. He then paid his own way to Marseille, where he joined the Legion as a private soldier.[72] Briggs served with the Legion until all British-origin members were discharged so they could serve in the forces of their own countries, which were desperately short of men. (As a French citizen James Waddell was excluded from this edict.) Knowing he was unlikely to get into the NZEF, Briggs travelled to the United Kingdom and joined the British army. He served in the Queen's Own Regiment until January 1919.[73] There were probably other New Zealanders like Briggs who served with the French Foreign Legion for whom no records exist.

Other New Zealanders worked in France during the First World War. While Ethel and Hilda Stevens worked in British military hospitals in England, their youngest sister, Daisy, stayed at home to teach at primary school and nurse her ailing father, John Stevens, a former MP for Rangitīkei and former Liberal Party Senior Whip. When he died at the end of July 1916, Daisy was off to the war. She travelled to France and worked with an American woman to run the

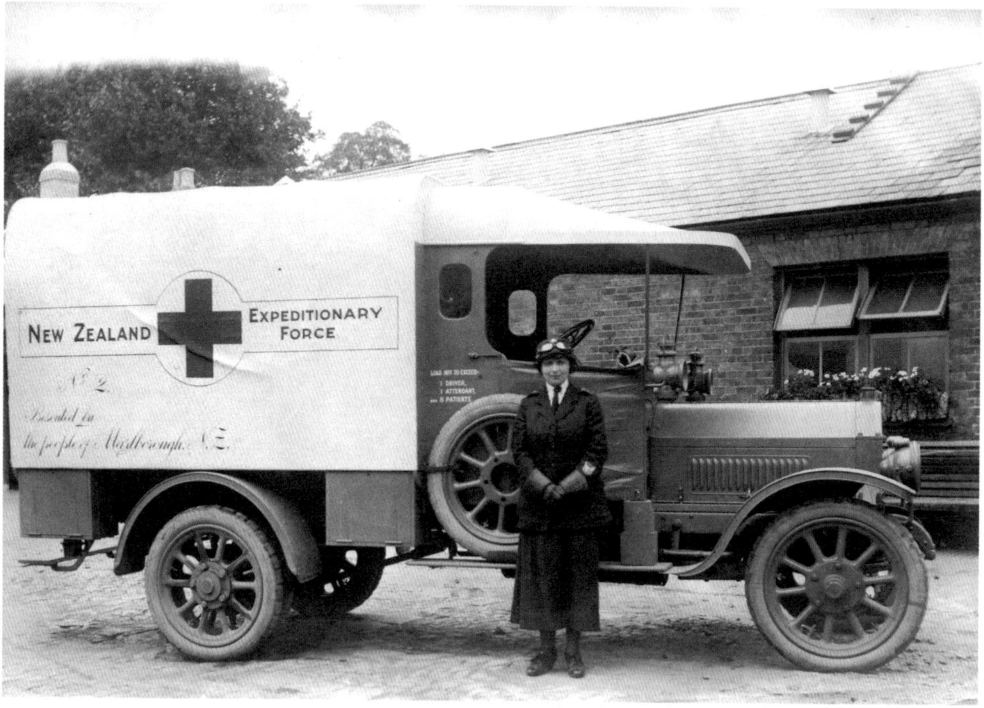

above Music-hall artist Pixie Laing secured a contract with the Folies Bergère in 1916. She later worked as a VAD and ambulance driver.
ONSLOW HISTORICAL SOCIETY

right 'Palmerston North Boy Now a French Brigadier-General' stated the caption to this photograph, which featured in the *Free Lance* on 6 June 1918. Born in Palmerston North, Pierre Marie Pascal was a brigadier in the French Dragoons at the age of 23. A brigadier in the French cavalry was the equivalent of a corporal in the New Zealand Expeditionary Force.
ALEXANDER TURNBULL LIBRARY, N-P-2024-11

Canteen de la Maison, which followed the French army during the war and served thousands of men each day.[74] When the war ended, the canteen was at Metz, which had been a German city since the Franco-Prussian War of 1870. Awarded the Croix de Guerre, Daisy Stevens went on to study in Paris and marry a British diplomat.[75]

Dunedin-born Pixie Laing's war service in France was somewhat different. Described as a 'music hall artiste' in her passport, Pixie travelled to France in 1916 to take up a contract with the Folies Bergère, the famous Paris cabaret and variety show.[76] The following year, she went to live with her sister in England, where she worked as a VAD and later an ambulance driver.[77]

Their numbers may have been small, but New Zealanders serving with the French performed some extraordinary deeds. Their service helped cement a growing engagement with France from 1914. It is noticeable, too, that they saw themselves and were regarded by others as members of a small independent nation, and not just an appendage of the United Kingdom.

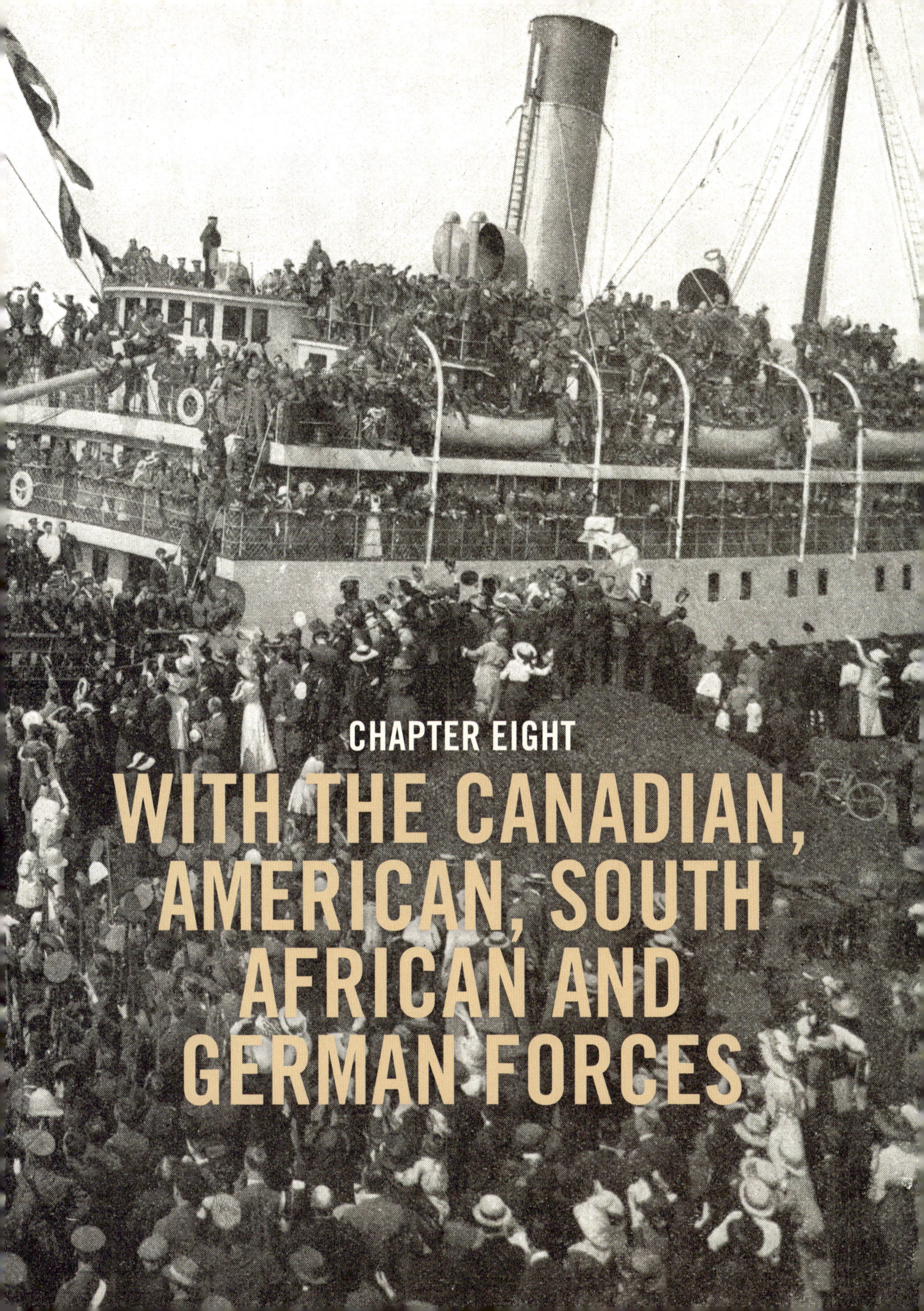

CHAPTER EIGHT

WITH THE CANADIAN, AMERICAN, SOUTH AFRICAN AND GERMAN FORCES

Previous pages
A Canadian troopship leaves Victoria, British Columbia, in 1915.
ALAMY, JW0FED

Most New Zealanders serving with other nations in the First World War did so in the military forces of the United Kingdom and Australia. The next most numerous contribution was in the Canadian Expeditionary Force (CEF). These New Zealanders were either travelling in Canada in August 1914 or had emigrated to live there. In 1914 Canada had a population of just over seven million.[1] From this number it enlisted some 630,000 personnel, of whom around 425,000 served overseas in some of the bloodiest battles of the war.[2] The CEF was the first British dominion force to serve on the Western Front, arriving just in time to take part in Second Ypres in April 1915.

The CEF was also one of the spearhead formations fighting during the hundred days in 1918 that ended the war. Being a quality force with a formidable reputation came with a heavy price: from early in the war the CEF was used often, and assigned to some of the most difficult and dangerous tasks. Canadian dead and wounded from this war eventually numbered 234,000,[3] and a considerable number of the New Zealanders in the CEF paid the ultimate price. Out of more than 400 New Zealanders who served with the CEF, over 80 died as a result of their war service.[4]

Two of those 400 were nurses.[5] Emma Constance Gill had trained at Auckland Hospital and gained her nursing certificate in 1901. In 1914 she was working in Honolulu, where she had lived for eight years. An appeal to the British Consul to enlist for the war produced no results, so Gill travelled to Europe, funded by a wealthy American family. On her arrival she joined the Canadian Army Medical Corps and worked at Basingstoke Hospital in southern England.[6] Little is known of the other New Zealand nurse, Ethel Lillian Boyer.

Some of those New Zealanders who had enlisted with the Canadians at the outbreak of war were with the CEF at Second Ypres in Belgium, a little-known battle during which chemical warfare was first used on the Western Front. On 22 April, when the wind was favourable, the Germans released chlorine gas from cylinders placed near the front line. The gas overwhelmed the French defenders. The Germans, though, were slow to exploit the advantage they had gained, and it was the 1st Canadian Division who stopped their advance. As Richard Holmes has written: 'The very gallant stand of 1st Canadian Division helped check the exploitation, and there followed a broken-backed battle as the British launched repeated, badly-coordinated counterattacks.'[7] This battle cost the Allies over 60,000 casualties, primarily in the BEF, and left the Germans on the high ground only a few kilometres from the town of Ypres. The BEF had been forced back into a narrower salient 'that barely covered the ruins of the city'.[8] Without the efforts of the CEF, Ypres would have been lost, too.

New Zealanders at that battle included Maurice Alfred Burlinson and Alan Eyre Turnbull, 'who had been in Canada when the war began and enlisted there'.[9] At least three New Zealanders were killed during Second Ypres. Private William Warren from Auckland was killed on 24 April and Lance-Corporal William Edgar Ogilvie from Auckland died the next day. Neither body was recovered, and both men are commemorated on the Menin Gate Memorial to the Missing at Ypres.[10] Private Robert Webb from Auckland, who had moved to live in Canada in 1911 to work around the Rocky Mountains district, had enlisted in the CEF's 7th Battalion, and was killed in action fighting around Hill 60 in Belgium some time between 1 and 8 May 1915.[11]

Other New Zealanders were severely wounded in the fighting around Ypres. Sergeant David Black Wilson from Waimate, South Canterbury, was probably the first New Zealander to experience a gas attack in this war. Wilson, a newspaper manager, had immigrated to Canada in October 1913 and joined the CEF in September 1914. Because of his six years with the New Zealand Territorial Force, he was immediately promoted to the rank of corporal. When he reached the front in April 1915 Wilson was promoted to sergeant.[12] At Ypres he was severely wounded, and gas inhalation led to the onset of pneumonia. He was sent to a hospital in Scotland to recover.[13] On returning to the front, Wilson was promoted to sergeant major and recommended for a commission.[14] One of his older brothers, George Wynn Wilson, also served with the CEF during the war. Corporal Maurice Alfred Burlinson, an accountant from Auckland, was 'seriously wounded in the head' at Ypres,[15] and was sent back to the United Kingdom for medical treatment.

Captain Charles Gordon Armour from Dunedin, an officer in the 24th Battalion Victoria Rifles of the CEF, arrived in the United Kingdom shortly after Second Ypres on 19 May 1915.[16] In March 1916 the *Otago Witness* featured a photograph of Private William Dorreen of Hampden, Otago, who was '[s]erving in France with the Canadian Expeditionary Force'.[17] It is likely that William Dorreen was actually D'Arcy Stuart McDonald Dorreen, given that he was the only person with this surname in the CEF.[18] William (D'Arcy) had two brothers who also served in the war. Leslie Dorreen was killed in action in Belgium in June 1917 while serving with the NZEF.[19] Leonard McCormack Dorreen was drafted into the American Expeditionary Force (AEF), and after the war became a pastor in one of the largest churches in Sioux City, Iowa. According to a contemporary news report:

> Mr Dorreen toured the country four times with a special train raising Liberty loans, besides over half a million dollars for the Red Cross. The United States presented him with a medal for services during the war.[20]

Sergeant James Gilpin from Thames, who had served with the New Zealanders in the South African War, had immigrated to Canada in 1905 and settled in Vancouver. When the war began, the veteran soldier enlisted in the 29th Infantry (Vancouver) Battalion of the CEF, nicknamed 'Tobin's Tigers' after its original commanding officer.[21] The battalion embarked from Montreal on 20 May 1915 and in September arrived in France as part of the 2nd Canadian Division.[22] At the end of that year, Gilpin was posted to London on attachment to the Canadian Record Office.[23]

Sergeant Alfred Nuttall from Picton served in France with the Canadian Field Ambulance. He was one of the earliest arrivals, too. In July 1917 the *Evening Post* informed its readers that Nuttall had spent the last 26 months 'on service in France and Belgium'.[24] In early 1918 he was sent to England to recover from an attack of enteric fever (typhoid).[25]

Many other New Zealanders, close to 100 in total, died while serving in the CEF. Charles Creagh Isdell, from Barrytown on the West Coast, was another who served in the 29th Infantry (Vancouver) Battalion; he died of wounds received during the capture of Vimy Ridge in April 1917, and was buried in the nearby Bruay Communal Cemetery Extension.[26] (His sister Helena, a nurse with the NZANS, had died in the sinking of the *Marquette* in October 1915.)[27] Lieutenant Frank Hamilton Bullock-Webster, from the Waikato, and Lieutenant Carrel W. Fidler (whose father had been the inspector of schools in Auckland) joined the CEF early in the war. Both later transferred to the Royal Flying Corps. Fidler, a balloon observer, died from wounds inflicted by an artillery shell in Belgium on 19 May 1917; Bullock-Webster was shot down on 20 September and died from his wounds on the same day.[28]

Wanganui Collegiate old boy Percy Reid had moved to Canada prior to the war to work for the Canadian Bank of Commerce. He later took an option on some land at François Lake in British Columbia.[29] When war was declared, Reid joined the CEF as a private soldier and then successfully applied for a commission in the British army. He served with his new unit, a battalion of the London Scottish Regiment, for a very short period. On 6 May 1917, two months after reaching the front, Second Lieutenant Percy Reid was killed in action.[30] His British commanding officer paid Reid a glowing tribute, which was reported back in New Zealand:

> I soon knew him for an excellent officer, beloved by his men and brother officers, and a very gallant leader. He died a glorious death, encouraging his men to the last by his noble example.[31]

Percy Reid is buried in the Tank Cemetery, Guémappe, France. Another Wanganui Collegiate old boy, Lieutenant Lancelot Edgar Ashcroft, was killed in action with the 54th Canadian Infantry Battalion when they stormed Vimy Ridge in April 1917.

Auckland-born Sydney Seymour Eyre was a cattle farmer who served in the CEF's 50th (Calgary) Battalion. Family legend has it that Eyre was rejected for service in the NZEF because of diabetes.[32] His Canadian military record does list a 'nervous debility' that may have foiled his attempt to enlist in New Zealand.[33] Determined to serve, Eyre travelled to the United States, where his sister was living, and crossed into Canada to enlist in the CEF at British Columbia some time in 1916. He fought with his battalion on the Western Front and was one of the Canadian volunteers to serve in Russia after the war. He returned to his farm at Pukekawa, in the northern Waikato, in the middle of 1920. Sydney Eyre did not long survive the war. On 24 August 1920, just a few months later, he was shot dead in his sleep by a disgruntled farm worker. Eyre left behind a wife and five children.[34]

The United States entered the war well after the main belligerent countries. It was not until 2 April 1917 that President Woodrow Wilson went to Congress and asked it to declare war on Imperial Germany; four days later, Congress sanctioned his request. In many ways, Wilson's hand had been forced both by Germany's actions and by a major shift in American public opinion. A spate of industrial sabotage carried out by German agents in the United States, the reintroduction of unrestricted submarine warfare in the eastern North Atlantic in February 1917, and the rash Zimmermann telegram, sent by the German foreign minister Arthur Zimmermann, which invited Mexico to go to war with the US as Germany's ally, were too much for a president who had done his best to keep his country out of the conflict.[35] US public opinion, meanwhile, was way ahead of its president and had turned against Germany from late 1915.[36] In the first week of April 1917 America joined the fight as a co-belligerent, but not an ally, of Britain and France.

At first the US government hoped that it could limit its involvement in the war to providing financial and material support to its co-belligerents, and limit military involvement to deploying its powerful navy. Within a month, however, Wilson realised that he would need to send troops to the Western Front and to raise a large army to do so.[37] For a president with strong pacifist tendencies — in May 1915, after the sinking of the *Lusitania*, he had declared there was

Canadian soldiers fix bayonets before 'going over the top' in a rehearsal for an attack in October 1916. The Canadians were the first Dominion troops to arrive on the Western Front, where they established a formidable reputation. ALAMY, JX4X8G

such a concept as being 'too proud to fight' — it is somewhat ironic that Wilson led what was at the time the largest war mobilisation effort in his nation's history.[38]

Conscription was introduced early in America's war and without controversy. In May 1917, Wilson signed the Selective Service Act, which required men between 21 and 35 years of age to register for the draft. Calling it 'selective service' instead of conscription, the US government

> successfully convinced the American public that the draft was an equitable, efficient and honourable way to ensure that neither the civilian economy nor the army suffered from the impulsive decisions of individuals. The promise to match the right man with the right job in either the military or civilian workplace earned the draft general acceptance as a manpower management technique suitable for the modern age.[39]

The creation of the American Expeditionary Force (AEF) was a remarkable achievement. It transformed an army of a few hundred thousand, without a single formed division, lacking heavy equipment, familiar only with small wars and border incursions, into a modern fighting force of four million men by the end of the war. Of the total number of troops raised for service in the AEF, 72 per cent had been drafted via the Selective Service Act.[40]

A very small number of New Zealanders were caught up in the creation of the AEF. They were men who were living in the US in 1917 and were most likely drafted to serve. If these New Zealanders had been desperate to volunteer for the war prior to 1917 they could have easily travelled to Canada to do so. The number of New Zealanders in the AEF is not just minuscule in comparison to the total figure for AEF soldiers; it is also minute compared to the numbers of New Zealanders who served in the British army, the AIF and even the CEF. Just over 30 New Zealanders served in the AEF during the war.[41] Moreover, very little is known about them.

One exception is David Simons Jarvis, who was born in Te Awamutu in 1895. Three years later, the Jarvis family moved to Te Puke, where his father managed the well-established Robert King's general store. Disaster struck the family in late 1901 when both parents died from tuberculosis. The three very young orphaned children, including David, were then sent back to family in Scotland.[42]

On 17 July 1914, by which time he had had four years' military service in Scotland with the Infantry Signal Corps, Jarvis migrated to the US.[43]

American soldiers march through Paris in 1917. ALAMY, CPM46R

He arrived at Ellis Island, New York on board the *Aquitania*, a sister ship to the ill-fated *Lusitania*. When the United States declared war on Germany in April 1917, Jarvis was living in Bridgeport, Connecticut. Drafted under the Selective Service Act, he enlisted at Connecticut on 27 July 1917 and was assigned to the 26th Division, known as the Yankee Division as it consisted of units from the New England area. After training, he embarked from Montreal for Liverpool, landing in France on 22 October as a private with the 102nd Field Ambulance Company. The 26th Division was the second division of the AEF to arrive on the Western Front, but it was not until April 1918, during the German Spring Offensive, that it first came under fire from the German army, in one of the first attacks on the Americans during the war. Jarvis was soon promoted to corporal, and then in July 1918 to sergeant. He also spent three periods in hospital — one in England, two in France — for reasons not noted on his records.[44]

The 26th Division experienced severe fighting in 1918 and US casualties during this period were unnecessarily high: British historian David Stevenson described them as 'extraordinary — up to 50 per cent in the units involved' and noted that by October 1918 US casualties were so high that 'they could no longer replace their losses'.[45] This was for two reasons. Not enough trained reinforcements were available to replace the huge casualty list, and, at 28,000 men apiece, US divisions were significantly larger than others on the Western Front. Initially involved in the defence of the Chemin des Dames in April through to July 1918, the 26th Division was later involved in the costly offensives of the Aisne–Marne, the reduction of the Saint-Mihiel salient and the battle of the Meuse–Argonne: actions that cost it nearly 12,000 casualties in just over seven months. With some 11,534 wounded soldiers in need of evacuation from the battlefields and follow-up intensive care, the 102nd Field Ambulance Company must have had an exceptionally strenuous war.[46]

David Jarvis survived the war and was discharged on 22 July 1919 at Bridgeport, Connecticut. He died in March 1984 in California.[47]

In 1914, the Union of South Africa was a British dominion of some 471,000 square miles and with a population of 6.5 million people.[48] It was also a comparatively young nation: only in 1910 were the separate political entities of the Cape Colony, the Transvaal, Natal and the Orange Free State united; its military, the Union Defence Force (UDF), was established two years later. The First World War

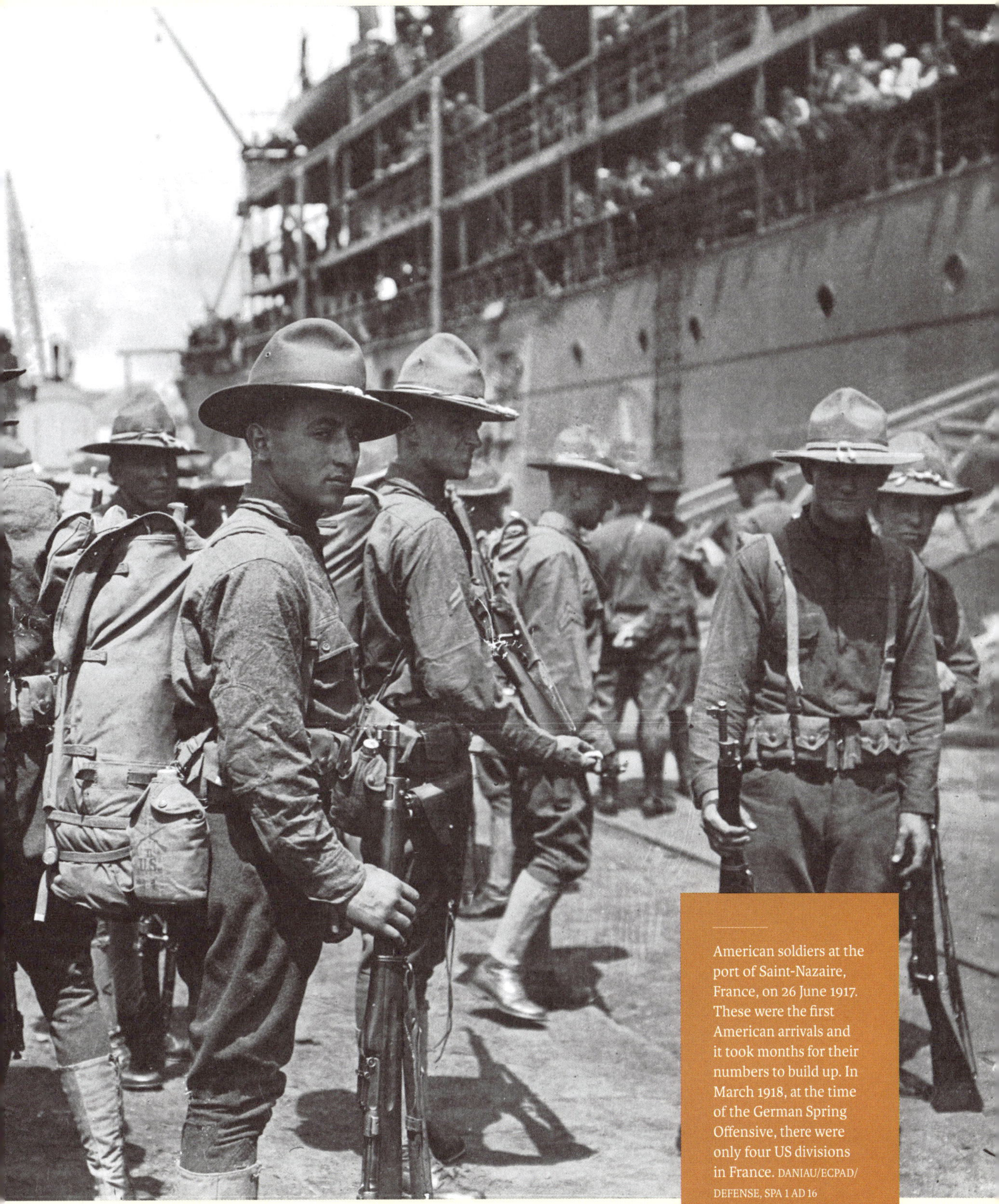

American soldiers at the port of Saint-Nazaire, France, on 26 June 1917. These were the first American arrivals and it took months for their numbers to build up. In March 1918, at the time of the German Spring Offensive, there were only four US divisions in France. DANIAU/ECPAD/DEFENSE, SPA 1 AD 16

top Troops from the South African Native Labour Corps at their camp at Dannes, France, in March 1917.
IMPERIAL WAR MUSEUM, Q4875

below South African soldiers on the Western Front. The single infantry brigade suffered devastating losses on the Somme in 1916 and 1918.
ALAMY, M99YFA

would be the country's 'first serious challenge as a unified nation'.[49]

On the outbreak of war, the Union of South Africa immediately pledged its support for the British cause, a surprising move given that the two main figures in its government, Prime Minister Louis Botha and Defence Minister Jan Smuts, had been leaders of the Boer forces against the British during the Second South African (Boer) War (1899–1902). Nonetheless, both were determined to prove the Union's loyalty to the British Empire. In August 1914 Botha informed London that not only could the 6000 imperial troops in the UDF be withdrawn to serve elsewhere, but his country would also raise a force to assist the British.

As might be anticipated, the government's decision to fully support the war efforts of its former enemy was not popular, especially with the Afrikaner or Boer community. The Union's first significant challenge came in October 1914 when 11,500 Boers, led by a former commander of the UDF, Christian Frederick Beyers, took up arms against the Union government in the Cape Colony, in the Orange Free State and in the Transvaal. This was 'a serious threat not only to South Africa's war effort but also to its very existence'.[50] It took some months and the efforts of 30,000 men before the revolt was crushed.

From January 1915 the Union of South Africa made its main military effort to the war fighting in Germany's African colonies. Botha personally led a force of 30,000 troops into German South West Africa (Namibia) in January 1915. The German colony was easily captured within six months at a cost of just over 500 Union casualties. From 1916 until the end of the war, South Africa contributed considerable numbers to the three British divisions fighting in East Africa against German and native askari (African) forces commanded by Colonel Paul von Lettow-Vorbeck. The campaign in East Africa was commanded by Jan Smuts, now a lieutenant general, who placed Afrikaners in charge of two of the three divisions under his command.[51] Despite overwhelming force — some 80,000 imperial troops against a few thousand Germans and askaris — Lettow-Vorbeck was never defeated in this campaign. He finally surrendered his force of 150 German troops, 1100 askaris and 1000 bearers on 25 November 1918 after learning that the Armistice had been signed.[52]

The Union of South Africa also sent a 6000-strong infantry brigade and some labour units to France in December 1915. As the UDF was restricted by legislation to operating in Southern Africa, these forces were designated the South African Overseas Expeditionary Force (SAOEF) and they served as part of British formations. The SAOEF brigade suffered terribly during its time on the Western Front. In the 1916 Battle of the Somme two-thirds of its strength became casualties, and in the German Spring Offensive of 1918, as they were in the front line when the Germans began their largest offensive of the war, most of the brigade became casualties or prisoners of war.[53]

Overall, the South African effort was considerable, with one in every five white males serving in the armed forces during the war. Around 25,000 served in France and a further 30,000 in East Africa, and from this total 8500 were killed in action. Non-white South Africans also served, primarily in non-combat roles. It is estimated that 6000 men of mixed race and more than 60,000 native Africans served as drivers and labourers. Of these, some 700 mixed-race and 3000 native Africans died, primarily from disease, especially from tuberculosis.[54]

South African War veteran Captain Frank Berners Knyvett in uniform as commander of the Territorial Force Unit 1st Garrison Artillery. A scandal involving unauthorised travel resulted in Knyvett being dismissed from his command and he left New Zealand in August 1911. Knyvett served in German South West Africa with the Natal Light Horse and was subsequently commissioned into the British Expeditionary Force with the Royal Field Artillery. He was wounded seven times during the war. In April 1918 Knyvett's obituary appeared in several New Zealand newspapers, but no further details were given. It is likely that these obituaries should have been for Frank's brother, Reginald Hugh Knyvett, who died of his wounds in New York in April 1918. SIR GEORGE GREY SPECIAL COLLECTIONS, AUCKLAND LIBRARIES, NZG-19091208-22-6

A small number of New Zealanders, around 40 men, served with the Union's forces in both East and South West Africa and in Europe. Some had settled in South Africa after fighting there with the New Zealand contingents in the Second Boer War, while others had immigrated to the country before the war. A few had been travelling there in 1914 when war broke out. Thirteen of them are known to have died in service.[55] Some are buried in African countries, including Namibia, Malawi, Tanzania and Mozambique. Others are buried in France and Belgium, and four are commemorated on memorials to the missing in those countries.[56] Here are some of their stories.

Ronald Tracey Matheson from Tauranga had fought in the Second Boer War with the Imperial Light Horse and he remained in South Africa when the war ended to work as a mining agent. At the outbreak of the First World War, now aged 38, Matheson rejoined the Imperial Light Horse and was commissioned as a lieutenant. He took part in the invasion of German South West Africa, where he was killed in action.[57]

Frank Berners Knyvett from Auckland had also served in the Second Boer War, but as a member of the Queensland Contingent and later with the 7th Australian Commonwealth Horse. For his gallantry at Onverwacht on 4 January 1902 Knyvett had been awarded the Distinguished Conduct Medal (DCM).[58] On the outbreak of war Knyvett joined the UDF and served with it in German South West Africa, where he was badly wounded and lost the thumb and a finger from his right hand. Discharged from the UDF and recovering from his wounds, Knyvett then applied for and received a commission with the BEF in the Royal Field Artillery. He served with the BEF on the Western Front and fought in some of its largest battles including the Somme (1916), Vimy Ridge and Messines. During his time there he was wounded a further six times, including being gassed in June 1917. He reached the rank of temporary major and in June 1917 was awarded the Distinguished Service Order (DSO) for his 'services in the prosecution of the war'.[59] It was certainly well earned.

Wellingtonian Patrick Monaghan had served as a private in the Grenadier Company of the 65th British Regiment, arriving in New Zealand with his regiment in 1845. During the New Zealand Wars he had been part of Governor Sir George Grey's personal escort. Patrick Monaghan senior died in 1898.[60] In 1918 various New Zealand newspapers reported that his grandson, Patrick Monaghan, serving as a captain in the South African forces, was missing and presumed to be a prisoner of war.[61] He was one of the many South African casualties incurred during the German Spring Offensive.

Edward Berney Bloxam from Christchurch, old boy of Christ's College, had a remarkably varied war service, all connected with South Africa. In 1914 he had taken part in the crushing of the Boer rebellion, as part of a commando force sent to fight against the forces led by Christiaan de Wet. He then fought with the South African Rifles in German South West Africa in 1915. Bloxam later transferred to the 4th South African Horse to serve with this unit in East Africa. In September 1918, by now a lieutenant, Bloxam served with the 1st Cape Corps in Palestine, where he was wounded in the leg. He spent the last months of the war recovering from his wound in a South African military hospital at Richmond in the northern Cape.[62]

Ernest Murray McIndoe of Auckland served as a sergeant with the 75th Siege Battery, South

African Heavy Artillery in France. McIndoe had joined the Cape Garrison Artillery in October 1914 and had fought against the Boers during their 1914 rebellion. He also served in German South West Africa in 1915.[63]

It is thought that at least three New Zealanders served with the German army during the First World War. Even if the number is established to be higher, it is unlikely to reach double figures. In one case there is substantial doubt whether the New Zealander assisted the German military or not. In another there are no doubts at all: the New Zealander was awarded two Iron Crosses.

The doubtful case was that of William Powell Nimot, who deserted to the German army near Armentières on 29 June 1916. As the only case of 'Deserted to Enemy' in the NZEF, Nimot's actions have received considerable attention from New Zealand historians.[64] Private William Nimot was a farm labourer from Carterton. The Nimot family had lived in the district since 1885 and his parents were both naturalised Germans.[65] Nimot enlisted in the NZEF in April 1915 and reached Egypt in September of that year. Posted into the 1st Battalion of the Wellington Regiment, he did not serve on Gallipoli but went to France with his battalion on 6 April 1916.[66] Evidence points to the fact that Nimot was a very unhappy soldier. Christopher Pugsley writes:

> From his days as a territorial soldier in New Zealand Nimot did not have a good record as a soldier. He had the reputation of not being 'a normal young man' and was erratic in his work habits. It was hoped that soldiering would be the making of him; it was not so. Nimot found army life difficult and it seems he was a loner with no close friends. Nimot's isolation was accentuated by jibes about his German background. These may have been in jest or out of frustration with a person who did not fit in as a member of the team. Whatever the reason, it prompted Nimot to desert.[67]

These jibes were both incessant and hurtful. John Towers, a fellow soldier serving in the rifle brigade, spoke in Nimot's defence and wrote of Nimot being 'subjected to many insults on account of his German origins'.[68] In a letter to the New Zealand military authorities investigating Nimot's case, Towers gave an example:

> One little incident I wish to quote to you in reference to that matter. When I was in the receiving hospital I heard one man say who I believe to belong to the same company as Nimot that Nimot was a B. [Bloody] German but we had the satisfaction of making it hot for him whilst he was here. Do you think this is keeping with the old tradition of British fair play and justice.[69]

On 21 June 1916 Nimot was awarded 14 days' Field Punishment No. 2 for being absent without leave in the field: the previous day he had been absent from his unit without permission from

9:00 a.m. to 2:25 p.m.[70] Eight days later, and just over halfway through his sentence, William Nimot deserted to the enemy.

It was later alleged that Nimot spent three weeks in the frontline trenches assisting the Germans, had informed a German officer about the New Zealanders' trenches, and had a pass that enabled him to leave the POW camp whenever he wanted.[71] An accurate bombardment of the New Zealand positions around the Mushroom position near Armentières from where Nimot had deserted 'was immediately attributed to information that he allegedly volunteered to the Germans'.[72] Although doubts later arose about just how much assistance he had given to the enemy, it is telling that the New Zealand government refused to grant Nimot an official POW status, even though he was reported as a POW by the American Embassy in Berlin.[73]

At the end of the war William Nimot worked at a cheese factory at Assenheim, near Frankfurt. He refused to be tried by court martial if New Zealand officers conducted it, and he could not be extradited.[74] He never returned to New Zealand, and died in Germany.

While Nimot may have escaped the worst consequences of his actions — he could have faced the death penalty — others paid the price for them. His desertion fuelled an already virulent anti-German feeling in New Zealand, and his family suffered the brunt of it. The Carterton district turned against the Nimots, and, as Pugsley writes, 'The desertion was a stigma the Nimots had to endure for the rest of the war and after'.[75] Others with no connection to the family also suffered. Immediately after Nimot's desertion, the New Zealand Division carried out a clumsy and insensitive purge of soldiers with German names or origins. In all, on Major-General Sir Andrew Russell's recommendation, some 96 men of German parentage were removed from frontline units and sent to the base at Étaples or to England.[76] This move produced a 'storm of protest' in the NZEF and back in New Zealand.[77] Within six months most of the men were back with their original units.[78]

Just a few months after William Nimot's desertion, reports were received that another New Zealander had joined the enemy. While opening the Red Cross rooms in Auckland, the Honourable G. W. Russell, minister of internal affairs, made an extraordinary announcement, printed the next day in the *Poverty Bay Herald*:

> . . . his son stated in a letter that among a number of German prisoners carried by the s.s. Marama from France to England was a New Zealander, trained in one of our best-known college institutions.[79]

George Russell did not name the individual, and who this person was remains a mystery.

More is known about one New Zealand-born man who served with distinction in the German army. This is primarily due to the investigative work of New Zealand historian Andrew Macdonald.[80] Leutnant-der-Reserve Emil Frederick Christoph Schroeder was born on 13 September 1885 at Tokatea, near Thames, where his father, also named Emil, was a hotelier and storekeeper. (Schroeder's German army papers spell this place-name as Tokatena.) Schroeder's mother, Margaret McKay, had married Emil Schroeder in 1884 and later that year they had a daughter, Hermina Gustave Schroeder, and then in 1885 Emil junior. Margaret Schroeder

above Officers and NCOs of Leutnant Emil Schroeder's artillery battery calculate distances for their guns. The officer seated at the base of the tripod is thought to be Schroeder. ANDREW MACDONALD COLLECTION

below Members of a German field artillery battery pose for a photograph alongside their gun. New Zealand-born Emil Schroeder served as a junior officer in a battery like this. While this gun has dead branches as camouflage, by 1918 the Allies could detect German positions using the techniques of sound ranging and flash-spotting. Their counter-battery fire took a fearful toll on the German gunners that year. ANDREW MACDONALD COLLECTION

died shortly after his birth. Soon after, his father had a stroke of good fortune: he found an 'extremely rich golden stone' in the Waikoromiko Creek near Tokatea.[81] The family left the Thames area in 1901, most likely to travel overseas.

Emil Schroeder joined the German army early in the war; he was recruited in Upper Alsace on the French-German border. In 1918 he was serving with the field artillery in No. 3 Batterie, Feldartillerie Regiment No. 15 (Ober-Elsässische), part of the 42nd Infantry Division, which was later assessed as being a 'third class' formation in 1918. The Intelligence Section of the American Expeditionary Force assessed the division as fair, noting:

> It was used as an attack division in the Lys Offensive, but thereafter was employed solely on the defensive. The division had a good composition with a large percentage of men of the younger classes.[82]

On the morning of 18 July 1918 Emil Schroeder's battery was holding a position between the villages of Dommiers and Chaudun to the south-west of Soissons, in the department of Aisne. The regimental history recorded that this day opened as a misty summer morning in peaceful silence after a night of rain and thunder. Battery positions were exceptionally muddy for the time of year.[83] Around 6:00 a.m. the silence was shattered as enemy guns opened on the German infantry and artillery positions. An attack soon developed, with infantry of the 2nd American Division and France's 1st Moroccan Division advancing with tank support behind a dense creeping barrage.

In the German trenches, infantry set off flares calling for defensive shellfire to be laid down, but many of these went unseen in the thick, acrid clouds of battle smoke. The gunners in Feldartillerie Regiment No. 15 laid down whatever blocking and destructive shellfire their guns could provide. It was soon apparent, though, that the enemy infantry had broken into the defensive position and were now approaching the gun lines. The regimental history recorded that

> [t]he battery positions, completely unsuitable for close combat, had [now] become the foremost line. In front of them the silhouettes of the enemy tanks and shock troops [in the haze of battle], protected and led by the tanks, rise up in front of them.[84]

Those artillery and infantry holding out at the gun lines realised that the fight was hopeless and their morale was poor. Batteries were being encircled one by one and overwhelmed by the enemy. In the case of No. 3 Batterie, two tanks assisted the attacking infantry to capture the position and the battery's guns. The fighting was all over by about 9:30 a.m.[85] Schroeder surrendered along with most of his battery.

The regiment's history described the action on that day as 'the beginning of the bitter fighting in the last quarter of the war'.[86] From 18 to 22 July Schroeder's regiment suffered casualties of 24 dead, 83 wounded and 188 missing. He himself was listed as 'missing', but was eventually confirmed as a prisoner of war.[87] During his war service Schroeder was awarded the Iron Cross in both first and second classes.

CHAPTER NINE

EXTRAORDINARY SERVICE

Previous pages
Officers of the Machine Gun Corps (Motors) in Baghdad in 1918. The commanding officer, Colonel J. D. Crawford, is the tall officer third from the right. Second from the right is Captain Samuel Hanna DSC, MiD, from Auckland.
NATIONAL MUSEUM OF THE ROYAL NEW ZEALAND NAVY, AUB 0017

The preceding chapters show that New Zealanders served in some unusual places and performed some incredible deeds during the war. In far too many cases, the record of much of what they did has been lost over time; but some accounts have survived, and several have only recently surfaced. A select few feature in this chapter, which is somewhat of a patchwork quilt of the varied and often surprising experiences of so many New Zealanders.

The Ceylon Planters Rifle Corps was a small part-time volunteer unit of little more than company strength, but its profile was unique, with an 'unusually selective' membership: Europeans who were tea and rubber planters, or who worked in management positions on these plantations in the country that later became Sri Lanka.[1] At the beginning of the war the Ceylon Planters Rifle Corps numbered eight officers and 229 other ranks commanded by Major John Hall-Brown. By April 1915 this number had fallen to 100 members. Being from the 'right class' and described by the ANZAC commander Lieutenant-General William Birdwood as 'such a nice lot of fellows', many members of the corps were soon offered commissions in British regiments.[2] The remaining corps members served as part of the ANZAC force on Gallipoli, where they were mainly used as Birdwood's guard; the Gallipoli campaign would be the Planters' only battle honour of the war. After December 1915, too many of its members had accepted commissions in British regiments for the unit to continue.

Among the scant records of the Ceylon Planters Rifle Corps are the details of three New Zealanders. They are Private Lancelot (Lance) Lewin, a musician from Christchurch; Gerald Ernest Overbury, from Auckland, who later transferred to the Worcestershire Regiment; and Francis Monck-Mason Troup, born in Dunedin, New Zealand, but who lived in Armadale, Victoria before heading to Ceylon. All were members of the corps in 1914, but little more is known about them. Troup obtained a commission in the Royal Fusiliers and was killed in action on 10 April 1917, aged 30.[3] He is buried in the Monchy British Cemetery near Calais.

One of the most extraordinary New Zealand wartime nursing experiences belongs to Suzanne Aubert. A French nun, Aubert had arrived in New Zealand in 1861 and founded the Home of Compassion near Wellington. Her nursing credentials were dubious. She claimed to have trained with the Sisters of Charity in France and to have nursed sick and wounded soldiers during the Crimean War, but she was probably self-taught. In 1913 the 78-year-old Aubert was in Rome to seek papal recognition for her order. When war broke out the following year, Aubert volunteered to serve in a frontline Red Cross unit, but was unsuccessful. In January 1915 a massive earthquake struck the town of Avezzano and Aubert went there to tend to the injured. Following this, wearing a New Zealand St John Ambulance medal and passing it off as the medal of a registered nurse, Aubert joined the Italian Red Cross and spent the remainder of the war nursing war wounded.[4] In August 1915 Aubert wrote to a member of her order in New Zealand describing the work she was doing:

> There are now very few of the victims of the earthquake left in hospitals, but the wounded soldiers keep on arriving. Theirs is a pitiful sight, but I think that the sight of the crushed people was worst. You see only men in the soldiers, while with the other people, there was such a number of women and children. I feel quite at home with my work, but I am forgetting English in trying to understand the different dialects of the poor sufferers. Each province, almost each district, has its own, it makes the service difficult. Fortunately we can go a long way with signs.[5]

Suzanne Aubert also worked in the slums of Rome before returning to New Zealand in January 1920. She died on 1 October 1926. In December 2016, a century after her war nursing, Pope Francis declared Suzanne Aubert to be venerable. This was a critical milestone on the path to her canonisation, a process that had begun in 1927.[6]

In 1908 Christina Annabella Hunter was the six hundred and eightieth nurse to obtain registration in New Zealand.[7] Trained in Christchurch, she left New Zealand in 1912 to broaden her nursing experience. In Hawai'i in August 1914 a wealthy benefactor, who also paid the fare of three other nurses, paid her travel expenses to the United Kingdom. There, after two initial rejections, Hunter joined the British Red Cross. She was posted to a hospital in Surrey, where she nursed Indian soldiers until the hospital was taken over by the British army. Rejecting an invitation to join the QAIMNSR, Hunter travelled to the Western Front and worked in a Belgian field hospital until early 1916, with the German artillery constantly providing a 'sinister barking'.[8] On leave later that year, and believing that the field hospital had been taken over by the Belgian army, Hunter joined the Scottish Women's Hospital and travelled with it to Corsica. She spent six months with a hospital there nursing Serbian soldiers with tuberculosis.

On her return to England, Christina Hunter joined the Anglo-Russian Hospital in Petrograd (St Petersburg), one of Lady Paget's projects. While there she witnessed the Bolshevik seizure of power and nursed some of their victims. She wrote about one haunting incident:

> I witnessed a ghastly scene the bodies of perhaps ten or more military cadets (young gentlemen) all beyond human help, were brought to us — they lay in a row, in their military coats and knee boots big men, and this is the price they paid for training to defend their country. Russia was now in a bad way.[9]

above The Anglo-Russian Hospital was housed in the Petrograd palace of a grand duke. AUCKLAND WAR MEMORIAL MUSEUM TĀMAKI PAENGA HIRA, MS 2003/107

below Medical staff of the Anglo-Russian Hospital in Petrograd pose with the Czarina and four of her daughters. Four New Zealand nurses were on the hospital staff. AUCKLAND WAR MEMORIAL MUSEUM TĀMAKI PAENGA HIRA, MS 2003/107

It was so bad, in fact, that the Anglo-Russian Hospital had to close down, and the nurses, each carrying a small food parcel, travelled back to England via Sweden, Norway and Scotland. They returned safely on 18 November 1918, when the influenza pandemic made the need for nurses desperate. Hunter was attested into the NZANS and repatriated to New Zealand in late 1919. She later received the Russian Red Cross medal for her work.[10]

Christina Hunter was not the only New Zealand nurse in Russia during the First World War. Three others, all from Whanganui, also worked there nursing wounded Russian soldiers in the field. They were Ethel Mary Strachan and Sybil Kathleen Kelly, who also nursed at Lady Paget's Anglo-Russian Hospital, and Dora Frances Dower.[11]

Dr Herbert Clifford Barclay of Waimate, commanding officer of the 2nd South Canterbury Infantry Regiment, also worked with the Russian army during the war. In August 1914, Clifford Barclay was in Japan as part of a world tour. His family received a telegram from Petrograd in September 1914: 'Volunteering England; meanwhile at Russian-Austrian front operating surgeon field hospital.'[12] It was assumed that Barclay was working with the Russian Red Cross somewhere in the Austro-Hungarian province of Galicia; in mid-November a report in *The Times* confirmed that a British officer, Colonel Barclay, was a surgeon in a large field hospital travelling from Petrograd to the southern front.[13] Just under a week later, New Zealand newspapers featured a long letter from Barclay describing his travels from Tokyo to Petrograd — 'a tiring but an absorbingly interesting journey of nearly three weeks' duration'. Barclay ended his letter with a prediction that would be partially fulfilled:

> These are spacious days in Russia, and we feel it a glorious privilege to be alive and here. Let no reader of these lines be misled. The map of Europe will be fundamentally changed as a result of this terrific conflict of nations. Of one thing we may be humanly certain — the German Empire, as such, is doomed; its days are numbered.[14]

In early 1915 Barclay's letters from Lemberg, then the capital of Galicia (and now the Ukrainian city of Lviv), described the work in the field hospital as 'pretty persistent and hard, but will no doubt grow worse'. He had received no mail from home and was able to speak only a few words of Russian. 'It seems ages since I lived amongst English people,' he wrote, 'and at times I am very lonely; but still, while I have much to do, I just put all my heart into it, and forget.'[15]

Added to Barclay's concerns was the news that the Waimate Hospital Board had refused his request for extended leave to enable him to serve with the British army. The board's decision produced a storm of outrage; one person wrote to the local paper: 'I venture to say that even the despicable German gives his citizen soldiers better treatment . . . So mean an act, at such a time, makes one wonder why.'[16] The outcry forced the Waimate Hospital Board to reverse its decision and grant Clifford Barclay extended leave.[17]

Barclay spent Christmas 1914 back at Petrograd, where there was not only snow but also no alcohol. Christmas, he wrote,

> was a terrible trial for many persons in the English colony, who had to spend an English Christmas with a scant supply of those beverages that make glad the heart of man. There is no doubt they felt it very keenly, though I think there was unanimous agreement among us all the cutting off of vodka and ardent spirits was an exceedingly good thing for the army and people under the circumstances.[18]

After Christmas, Barclay travelled to London via Finland and Sweden and offered his services to the War Office. He was immediately employed as a specialist in a large military hospital.[19]

In August 1914 Mary Jane Mander — teacher, journalist, and later author of the classic novel *The Story of a New Zealand River* — had been travelling through Belgium and Germany with two friends. They found themselves trapped in Tours, France as all essential transport was now reserved for the military. The 37-year-old Jane Mander, originally from Whangarei, took the opportunity to work with the American Red Cross at Tours.[20] In 1917, back in the United States, which by then had joined the war as a co-belligerent, Mander worked for the American Red Cross in New York. It 'gave her a feeling of doing something of real importance for the war effort'.[21] She was soon put in charge of the finances of all 560 Red Cross workrooms on Manhattan Island. At the end of 1918 Mander was involved with the work of the largest repatriation hospital in the United States and spent Christmas Day there with its 4400 returned men.[22] Jane Mander continued her work with the American Red Cross until June 1919.[23]

Esperanza (Dora or Essie) Nelson, the former deputy matron of Christchurch Hospital, spent much of the war nursing in a British military hospital in Mesopotamia.[24] In October 1916 a New Zealand newspaper featured one of her letters describing the harsh conditions in which she had to work:

> Seven new Sisters arrived yesterday, but there is little chance of relief, as nearly all go sick as soon as they come. Out of the original unit of twenty-six, only four of us have not had sick leave. We have plenty of clothing for the patients, but stores are the great things — extras, such as jelly powders, biscuits, chocolate. The bread is very bad; biscuits would be most welcome . . . tinned fruit is also very scarce.[25]

Part of Nelson's service included working on a paddle steamer that travelled up and down the Tigris River collecting sick and wounded soldiers.[26] Nelson did not return to live in New Zealand. She married a British officer serving in the Indian army and they settled in India.[27]

Mary Louisa Craig had been nursing in Gisborne before the war. She joined the Volunteer Sisterhood in 1915 and sailed directly to the United Kingdom. There she worked at the Walton-on-Thames hospital before joining the QAIMNSR and nursing in a range of locations: in London, on a hospital ship, and at a casualty clearing station in Salonika. When the war ended, Craig served on and worked at a British military hospital in Constantinople (Istanbul) until she was demobilised in 1921. By then in her early forties, Craig stayed in Constantinople to work as a matron in a girls' school. She later had a similar job in Athens. Mary Craig did not return to New Zealand until the 1930s, and died shortly after.[28]

On 14 August 1914, the New Zealand High Commissioner, Sir Thomas Mackenzie, chaired a meeting in the Westminster Palace Hotel, London. The attendees were predominantly New Zealanders who lived in the United Kingdom and the discussion focused on how they could assist the New Zealand war effort. The outcome was to establish the New Zealand War Contingent Association (NZWCA), an all-volunteer organisation whose purpose was to supplement the work of the New Zealand military headquarters by providing and extending comforts to all New Zealand soldiers when they were in the United Kingdom.[29]

The NZWCA numbered around 200 people, and its work lasted for the duration of the war. It included establishing a convalescent hospital for New Zealand soldiers at Walton-on-Thames, which opened on 31 July 1915 and was later taken over by the New Zealand military. It provided soldiers with clothing, food and cigarettes, and established clubs they could attend. New Zealanders in the United Kingdom in 1915, especially the early arrivals from Gallipoli,

> were in a truly terrible plight, possessing little, if any, clothing, and being unable to obtain authority to purchase kit was deplorable. Someone had blundered in the Dominion in not anticipating the requirements of these men, and they suffered accordingly.

The NZWCA was able to furnish these men with clothes, a little money, and a place to eat and drink in a recently opened tearoom.[30] It also set up a cheap and efficient process for sending information back to New Zealand about the condition and well-being of the men in the United Kingdom. The defence minister opposed this, fearing some political embarrassment, but his directive that the service should cease was ignored by the NZWCA.[31]

The NZWCA's eight clubs throughout the United Kingdom, all staffed by New Zealanders, were joined by a specific Soldiers' Club in Russell Square, London. The NZWCA also established a rest home for the hard-pressed nurses.[32] It assisted with the publication of *Chronicles of the NZEF*, established by Trooper Clutha Mackenzie, and published its own paper, *The New Zealander*. The NZWCA also helped establish an education scheme for limbless soldiers at Oatlands Park Hospital in Surrey.[33]

One invaluable service was deeply appreciated by the soldiers. The NZWCA arranged to meet all leave trains at London's Victoria Station, advise the men where their clubs were, and issue them with free bus tickets to get there; there was a relief fund, too, for soldiers on leave who had run out of cash. In two years, more than 4000 New Zealand soldiers used this fund, and the NZWCA never turned down a request for food or lodgings.[34] One soldier wrote back to the organisation to express his appreciation:

> It does not appear to be generally known in New Zealand that the War Contingent Association is doing the work it is. Other organisations advertise their work and this society does not. I and thousands of the boys know the benefits this Society has given to us and how its kind ladies have looked after us as if we were their brothers. Like many of the boys I have been stranded in London when on furlough from France and have had to choose between going back into the firing line with seven days of my leave still unexpired because I have had

Mary Jane Mander (known as Jane), teacher, journalist and author, worked with the American Red Cross during the war. It gave her the feeling of 'doing something of real importance'. SIR GEORGE GREY SPECIAL COLLECTIONS, AUCKLAND LIBRARIES, 7-A9827

above The humble exterior of the Kia Ora Club in the grounds of Brockenhurst, No. 1 General New Zealand Hospital, near Southampton. MTG HAWKE'S BAY

below The interior of Brockenhurst's Kia Ora Club, established by the New Zealand War Contingent Association. MTG HAWKE'S BAY

> no money and nowhere to obtain a home. Neither the High Commissioner nor the Military would advance a shilling in my pay book. I was told to go see Mr. Raymond, Chairman of the N.Z.W.C.A. He helped me to see my furlough out, as I know he has done to hundreds of others, but he made it clear that this help did not come out of any of the Society's funds, but was collected separately. I have never heard of any soldier appealing to him and being turned away if his case was deserving. I am sure the people in New Zealand cannot know the straits that we are sometimes in.[35]

This letter, written in November 1916, was sent to various New Zealand newspapers, but censorship regulations prevented its publication.[36]

When theatre manager and well-known British actress Lena Ashwell organised her first concert party to entertain soldiers on the Western Front, the response was overwhelming. The first Concert at the Front took place on 18 February 1915 at No. 15 Camp at Harfleur. In the fortnight that this first concert party toured in France it put on 38 shows and one benefit performance for the widow of a Belgian killed in a vehicle accident.[37] The soldiers' appreciation was widely reported in British newspapers. One army doctor wrote that 'the concert did wounded men more good than a month's nursing'.[38] The British government and military authorities, which had previously resisted the notion that troops on active service needed entertainment, had a sudden change of policy.

For the rest of the war Ashwell and other theatre managers like her organised hundreds of concert parties that entertained thousands of soldiers. Just four months after her first concert party had completed its tour of France, Lena Ashwell calculated that the seven tours she had organised to date had employed 250 artists who had performed over 300 events for some 300,000 soldiers.[39] By January 1918 the number of concerts performed in France had reached 4000 and another 1000 were performed elsewhere.[40] When the war ended, Ashwell had 28 concert parties performing to frontline soldiers in various theatres of war including France, Belgium, Egypt and Salonika. For this work she would be one of the first women awarded an imperial honour. On 25 August 1917 the *Daily Graphic* announced that Ashwell, along with 12 other women, including Lady Paget and Queen Mary, were the recipients of the new Order of the British Empire (OBE).[41]

In all, the Lena Ashwell Players numbered some 600 entertainers 'who, in their way, took part in the great struggle and did their "bit"'.[42] They included Auckland violinist Geraldine May (Ina) Bosworth, who received a letter from Ashwell in December 1916:

> I am so glad that you can undertake a tour on the Etaples Abbeville route for a period of from four to five weeks, leaving England on January 29th at a fee of £3 (three pounds) a week and your expenses. I should be very glad to have a formal letter from you confirming these arrangements for filing purposes.[43]

During the war the remarkable British actress and theatre manager Lena Ashwell battled the War Office to provide concert parties to soldiers on active service. The concerts were an outstanding success, and with over 5000 concerts performed, entertainers were in demand. New Zealand musician Ina Bosworth and playwright actress Rosemary Rees joined Ashwell's touring groups. NATIONAL PORTRAIT GALLERY, UK

Ina Bosworth spent most of 1917 touring the Western Front with the Femina Quartette. She did four tours that year, usually giving three concerts each day, and it was reported that 'she made a very marked success'.[44] In August 1915 Ashwell had observed that in musical performances '[t]he violin is what the men like most'.[45] Ina Bosworth's skill was particularly appreciated and she usually had to do several encores after each performance.

Conditions at the front were often hardly conducive to the performance of a string quartet. As one New Zealand newspaper reported:

> The Femina Quartette gave three concerts a day, and conditions were not made easy or pleasant by the weather. There was much rain and snow, and one day a series of mishaps ended in the car breaking down, so that the concert party had to trudge through nine inches of snow, carrying their instruments, etc. One of the concert 'halls' was a hayloft, and the stage consisted of empty bully-beef tins with the boys' blankets hung at the back and round to keep away as much of the draught as possible. It is recorded that everywhere the men appreciate good music, and the violin seems to be the favourite instrument — a favourite solo may be encored as often as seven times. The longer the war lasts the more necessary are these entertainments. It is the opinion of those in authority that the concert parties are accomplishing work of 'great military value'. The armies are enduring manifold privations, dangers, and suffering, and they ask for the happiness and inspiration that music gives them.[46]

On their return from France, the Femina Quartette performed a concert at the New Zealand military hospital at Walton-on-Thames.[47] Ina Bosworth continued to entertain in the United Kingdom, often visiting the New Zealand military hospitals and playing her violin for wounded soldiers there.[48]

Contralto Thelma Petersen was another New Zealander who went to France as an entertainer.[49] Petersen was in France in March and April 1918 during the German Spring Offensive; despite the dangers, a 'show must go on' spirit prevailed and none of the Ashwell concerts was cancelled. A New Zealand newspaper reported that, 'in spite of the difficulties and excitement of those critical days, the concerts were carried on, the performers often having to sing to the soldiers in the huts in pitch darkness'.[50]

Rosemary Frances Rees, a playwright and actress from Gisborne, was the superintendent of the NZWCA's Entertainments Committee for two years.[51] Over this period she used her influence with London theatre managers to obtain 20,000 free theatre tickets (valued at £10,000) to be used only by New Zealand soldiers.[52] When she became unwell, rather than return to New Zealand Rees accepted a job offer from Lena Ashwell to direct Plays at the Front in Rouen, France. Rees spent 14 months organising theatre performances for Allied soldiers on the Western Front.[53] She not only managed the theatre at Rouen, but also acted in some of the plays. With the signing of the Armistice in November 1918, Rosemary Rees's theatre company travelled to entertain soldiers at Douai, La Flaque and Arras.[54] After the war, Rees managed her own theatre company in New Zealand, then moved to Australia and later London, where she became a best-selling author of romance novels.[55] She returned to New Zealand in 1955 to live with a sister in Gisborne.

The remarkable Lena Ashwell reflected on her Concerts at the Front some years after the war:

> The sight of pretty, well dressed women (for we all wore our very best clothes) fresh from Home, the gay and tender songs, the magnificence of the finest music, all that the parties brought to them was a tonic to the soldiers' health, refreshment to their souls, a message of love from Home. They would go back to the firing line, pretending that they liked it, because they knew from this message that England cared for them. In the ministrations of the Padres, a remote and awful Heaven bent over them in blessing, but in the services of the concert parties was the dear and intimate human love which brought back health of mind to lonely men.[56]

Ashwell felt 'deep gratitude that, in a tiny measure, we artists were privileged to serve' those at the front.[57] Most members of her Players felt the same.

Harvey Maitland Chrystall was educated at Christ's College and the Engineering School of Canterbury College. In 1914 he was working in southern Nigeria as the chief draughtsman and assistant engineer of the Eastern Railway and River Port Scheme, based at Port Harcourt in the Niger Delta. On learning of the outbreak of war, Chrystall travelled to Egypt, where he joined the Royal Naval Division (RND), part of the Mediterranean Expeditionary Force (MEF) preparing for the landing on the Gallipoli peninsula.[58] In July 1915 he was loaned to MEF headquarters at Cape Helles to prepare accurate maps from aerial photographs and the limited survey information held by the British military. Accurate maps were critical, so Chrystall conducted his own reconnaissance and surveyed as much of the trench systems and terrain as he could. A senior staff officer wrote an assessment of Chrystall's work:

> Capt. H. M. Chrystall did most valuable work in Gallipoli throughout the operations. This consisted principally in the preparation of the large scale maps which were used by the troops in attacking the enemy's positions. These maps were of the greatest importance, and I believe them to have been the means of saving many lives.[59]

At the conclusion of the Gallipoli campaign, Chrystall was posted in January 1916 to the Topographical Section of the army headquarters in Salonika, where he worked on producing maps and helped plan defences. In May 1916 he was posted to the headquarters of the Royal Naval Air Service at Port Said to work on maps from aerial photographs and intelligence reports.[60]

In November 1917 Chrystall was transferred from the RND to the Royal Engineers (RE). He spent three months at Southampton completing the Ordnance Survey mapping course,[61] and subsequently was posted to the Depot Field Survey Battalion in France. His duties with the RE were many and varied and, once again, of considerable importance. They included undertaking

above Harvey Chrystall, an engineer, served on Gallipoli, where his skills were used to produce detailed maps of the Peninsula. He later served in Salonika, Egypt and on the Western Front. After being utilised as a map-maker in France, in October 1918 Chrystall was transferred to the Royal Engineers, where his new job was to establish watering points along the main trunk line between Lille and Brussels. AUCKLAND WAR MEMORIAL MUSEUM TĀMAKI PAENGA HIRA

left Harvey Chrystall took this photograph of temporary New Zealand graves on Gallipoli. The grave in the foreground is that of Driver Harry George Page, from Linwood, Christchurch, who was killed in action on 14 May 1915. Page is now buried at the Lancashire Landing Cemetery. AUCKLAND WAR MEMORIAL MUSEUM TĀMAKI PAENGA HIRA

trigonometrical surveys of the front line at Havrincourt and Bapaume, planning and mapping a reserve defence system in the Somme region during the German Spring Offensive, planning and installing microphones for sound ranging of artillery, working on a system to detect the height of aeroplanes, and completing a back area triangulation to connect the British sector trigonometry points with those of the Belgian and French armies on each flank.[62] The head of the Geographical Section of the British War Office wrote: 'Capt. Chrystall was distinguished for great zeal and energy, and power of initiative. I can confidently recommend him as a most capable and hard-working officer.'[63]

In October 1918 Chrystall was deemed to be surplus to the RE establishment and was posted to the 3rd Railway Survey Reconnaissance Section. As its water supply officer, his task was to organise and establish the water supply in a region of France where the retreating Germans had destroyed all water systems. In particular, Chrystall had to establish watering points along the main trunk line between Lille and Brussels. This required the construction of 30 steel 12,000-gallon tanks on towers as well as trying to repair the existing systems of water distribution. In February and March 1919 Chrystall worked on the repair of the French railway, and then supervised the construction of a rail network in the British-occupied sector of Germany around Cologne.[64] After the war he worked on engineering projects in Nigeria and British Guiana. Later, in New Zealand, Chrystall worked as a consulting and constructional civil engineer on large engineering projects, including the Lyttelton tunnel, the Arapuni hydroelectric scheme and the Kawarau River dam.[65]

Another technical specialist was Dr Edward Kidson, from a well-known Nelson and Christchurch family. He was born in Bilston, England and came to New Zealand with his family in 1885, when he was three. Kidson attended Nelson College and studied electricity and magnetism at Canterbury College.[66] In 1905 he joined the staff of the magnetic observatory in Christchurch as an assistant observer. He moved three years later to the Department of Terrestrial Magnetism at the Carnegie Institute in Washington DC, then considered the world's pre-eminent magnetic survey organisation.[67] While working for the Carnegie Institute Kidson worked on magnetic surveys in South America, Newfoundland and Australia, and also at sea.[68] The war ended this work.

In 1914 Kidson travelled to the United Kingdom, obtained a commission in the RE and was posted to its Meteorological Section. His work was invaluable. He developed a forecasting service and the application of meteorological data to gunnery techniques for the expeditionary force in Salonika.[69] For his work on how wind speed/direction and air temperature affected artillery shells in flight,[70] he was mentioned in despatches and awarded an OBE.[71]

After his military service Kidson worked in London for a short time before moving to Western Australia to become the chief observer at the Watheroo Observatory. In 1921 he was appointed supervising meteorologist at the Commonwealth Meteorological Bureau in Melbourne; he later became assistant director there. In 1927 he was appointed director of the New Zealand Meteorological Office, a position he held for 12 years. Edward Kidson is regarded as the founder of New Zealand's present-day meteorological service.[72]

In May 1915 the *Press* reported on the work of US war correspondent J. C. 'Jack' Clayton, a native of Christchurch who had been educated at Christ's College.[73] Jack Clayton had reported on several wars, including the Spanish–American War, the South African War, the Russo-Japanese War and the wars in the Balkans. In 1915 he was in France as the war correspondent for several leading New York papers.[74] When the French government restricted the activities of foreign correspondents in France, Clayton joined the British Red Cross as a voluntary driver. He was back in France in May 1915 'just in time to encounter the tremendous stream of wounded from the battles of Hill 60 and Ypres, and for four and a half days . . . they were working at top speed without time for sleep and little for food'.[75] In the five days of intensive work, the Red Cross team transported 16,500 men to various hospitals; one-third were from the Canadian Division.

Clayton was 'full of admiration' for the staff and work of the British Red Cross.[76] He was working with the Red Cross at Dunkirk when the town came under German shellfire and shrapnel hit him on the left arm, necessitating a period of recovery in London.[77]

Alfred Stewart Lindsay obtained a commission in an unusual British territorial regiment: the Fife and Forfar Yeomanry, also known as the Scottish Horse. Lindsay served with this unit on Gallipoli from June to December 1915;[78] in December he transferred to the Machine Gun Corps (Motors) and spent most of his war roving the Western Desert in Egypt in patrol cars. It was the type of war with which the next generation of New Zealand soldiers would become all too familiar. Lindsay served with the Patrol Group of the MGC (Motors) until his embarkation for the United Kingdom on 17 September 1919.[79] His service in the desert had taken its toll: on discharge Lindsay was suffering from malaria contracted at Jaghbub in July 1919, he had breathing difficulties, his eyesight was 'affected by the glare of three years in the Western Desert', and he had some deafness in his left ear.[80]

Major Frank Holmes grew up in Timaru and attended Otago Boys' High School. In 1914 he was practising as an engineer in England, but he accepted a commission in the Royal Marines. He served with the Royal Naval Division throughout the Gallipoli campaign and completed another two years' service in France. In February 1918 Holmes relinquished his commission in the Royal Marines, but retained his military rank 'in order to undertake a mission for the Foreign Office, to Abyssinia'.[81] Holmes left for Abyssinia (now Ethiopia) on 20 March 1918 to organise trade links with Great Britain. He travelled in mufti via Paris, Syracuse, Sicily, Port Said and Djibouti in French Somaliland, and then on to Addis Ababa. Holmes described Abyssinia as being 'in a very backward state', although the leading men were 'intelligent and capable'. The country was rich in export items, particularly timber, coffee and beeswax.[82] Holmes spent most of 1918 on this trade mission to Abyssinia, but was back in London at the end of the year.

In December 1920, New Zealand defence minister Sir Robert Heaton Rhodes, a former soldier who had served in the South African War, received a disturbing letter from William Bennett, a New Zealander living in Sydney. The letter described the confidence tricks of Selwyn Joyce, a former New Zealand soldier who had also served in South Africa and the First World War:

> Being a New Zealander now residing in N. S. Wales, at the above address, I take the liberty of writing to you to inform you that there is a 'gentleman?' trading around and in Sydney who goes by the name of Lieutenant Joyce. The 'gentleman?' is practicing his profession as a confidence spieler, and purports to be a son of the late Mr. Joyce, at one time member for Ashburton. 'Lieutenant Joyce' manages to meet a very large number of New Zealanders & evidently works through a pall; the pall must be either a woman or a man with a fairly good business in Sydney. A large number of New Zealanders, including myself, have been stung by him. He works in a successful and novel manner. The pall evidently finds all about where the visiting New Zealander comes from, and, later on, the worthy Lieutenant Joyce incidentally drops in, wearing the New Zealand returned soldiers badge. He soon makes visitors acquainted with him & pleads 'hard up' on account of the illness of his wife & straight out tells the visitors who his wife is and all about her family. The wife always comes from the locality in N.Z. that the visitor comes from, & as in 9 cases out of ten the visitor knows the 'alleged wife's' family well, although he may not know the 'wife'.
>
> He naturally sympathises with Joyce & 'the wife', and good naturedly lends him a few pounds; and promises to call at the address Joyce gives him. In a day or two he calls & lo! nobody ever heard of Lieutenant Joyce or Mrs Joyce.
>
> This shows how well the 'pall' pumps the visitor first, and how thoroughly Joyce is acquainted with New Zealand.
>
> Of course you will say to us: — Serve you d—d well right to be taken down by a confidence man wearing the N.Z. uniform & Returned Soldiers badge.[83]

The letter, which ran to five full pages, was of considerable concern to the defence minister. In his reply to William Bennett, Heaton Rhodes identified the conman as 'undoubtedly one Selwyn Joyce'. Rhodes informed Bennett that

> Joyce's statements as to his parentage are quite correct. He comes of a good and respected family, but is himself an out-and-out waster. His conduct in the N.Z.E.F. was so unlike that becoming an officer and a gentleman, that he was returned to New Zealand and required to resign his commission narrowly escaping being tried by Court-martial.

Rhodes advised Bennett to contact the New South Wales police about Joyce's activities and passed his letter on to the New Zealand Inspector of Police.[84] Selwyn Joyce's confidence tricks would soon catch up with him in both Australia and New Zealand.

Joyce had joined the First Contingent of New Zealanders to embark for the South African War as a private soldier. He was 22 years old in 1899 and gave his occupation as 'engineer'.[85] Joyce went on to serve in three more contingents to South Africa and was subsequently commissioned as a lieutenant. One of these transfers caused some concern to his senior officers. Joyce had requested leave from the Seventh Contingent to return to New Zealand to settle family affairs after the death of his parents. On arriving in New Zealand, however, Lieutenant Joyce 'immediately on landing' volunteered for the Eighth Contingent and sailed on the *Cornwall* as the officer in charge.[86] Joyce's South African service record hints at some scandal and an effort to protect the family's reputation. It contains a letter from Lord Kitchener, commander in chief in South Africa, to the governor of New Zealand that stated:

> I have the honour to inform you that Lieutenant S. Joyce, 7th New Zealand Mounted Rifles, has been permitted to resign his appointment. Dated 14th November, 1901.

Included with this letter was a memorandum from the minister of defence, Richard Seddon, that directed the New Zealand commandant to

> [t]ake out enclosed. I expect the resignation was owing to term of Service having expired. I have asked that in these cases the reason for resignation may be noted in General Orders. When finished with return this covering sheet.[87]

After the South African War, Joyce moved to London and worked as a reporter for the *Daily Telegraph*, and then in Toronto for the *Evening Telegram*, and New York for the *New York Times*. In August 1914, Joyce was living in Mexico, where he was a correspondent for the *Dallas Times*;[88] when war broke out, he returned to New York and offered his services at the British Consulate. His fare to London was covered, but the British War Office, which would have had a record of his military service in South Africa, offered him only a commission for garrison duty in Burma. Joyce considered this beneath his talents, so he refused it.[89] He then returned to Canada, where he obtained a commission in the 85th Highlanders, stationed at Halifax, Nova Scotia. Joyce was a member of the regiment's instructional staff, but never served with the 85th Highlanders on active service. According to a newspaper report he was one of 600 staff officers who were suddenly put on leave without pay.[90] This was most unlikely, given how desperate the Canadian Expeditionary Force was for well-qualified staff officers. And yet, for reasons unknown, Joyce was not wanted by the CEF, so he decided to try his luck back home.

Joyce successfully enlisted in the NZEF in 1917 as a second lieutenant in the Wellington Regiment. Alarm bells should have sounded early in this process: Joyce gave his occupation as 'stage director', which was then crossed out to be replaced with 'soldier', his last employer being 'United States Army'.[91] Joyce sailed with the 30th Reinforcements in mid-October 1917. He served with the NZEF for just over a year and ended his service in deep trouble. On 7 October 1918 he was placed under close arrest while his fate was considered. The decision was made not to court-martial him but rather to return him to New Zealand as quickly as possible and there discharge him from the NZEF.[92] It is most likely the issue was theft or embezzlement, but there was other poor conduct, too. While under close arrest, Joyce wrote to Miss Annie Kate Winter, who had been led to believe she was his fiancée. Joyce would leave Winter in trouble, despite his being already married to a woman back in New Zealand. The note continued his deceit:

> I am afraid they have put certain restrictions on me up here so that unless I do not hear from London today or by Monday I am going to do something desperate. I only ask you to believe in me and have faith in me unless something unforeseen turns up can you come to the Daison side gate about 8.15 tonight. I want to talk to you badly, and I am afraid I can't get out. I will explain all. Keep smiling and have confidence that all will turn out all right, and don't believe all you hear.[93]

After the war Annie Winter commenced legal proceedings against Selwyn Joyce via the NZEF. The army took up her case, writing to Joyce, then living in Dunedin, to inform him that if he denied any responsibility, proceedings against him would begin in the UK Supreme Court. The army wanted to know:

> . . . whether you admit liability, and if so, what provision you propose to make for the child and its mother, so that a reply may be cabled to N.Z.E.F. Headquarters at an early date.[94]

This same officer wrote to the New Zealand Commissioner of Police 18 months later: 'I may say that Joyce's record is a bad one. He is a waster and has absolutely no principle in regard to money matters.'[95] Joyce was again permitted to resign his commission and was gazetted out of the NZEF at the end of 1918. His poor record of service did not prevent him approaching his local member of Parliament, William Downie Stewart, seeking to have the military pay for his family's return to the United Kingdom. Downie Stewart took up his case with Sir James Allen, the minister of defence, but Allen refused the request. By then Stewart was somewhat the wiser about Joyce; he wrote to Allen: 'Since writing you re Lieut. Joyce, have heard unfavourable reports; consequently I am not much concerned whether your reply is favourable or not.'[96]

In the decade after the war, Joyce worked for the Australian Repatriation Office, and as a journalist for the *Australian Trade Journal* and a South Australian newspaper owned by his uncle. He also worked for a brief time for the United Political Party.[97] Joyce also became a well-known confidence man operating in both Australia and New Zealand, under aliases that included Samuel Joyce, John Ward, John Joyce, Selwyn Rees and the surnames Field, Foley, Kirkpatrick, Hazlett and McCorqudale. He served jail time in New South Wales and Western Australia.[98] In 1928 Joyce was sentenced to several months' jail in New Zealand, and was described by a police detective as 'a plausible imposter . . . [with] a bad record'.[99] Selwyn Joyce, conman and soldier of two countries during the First World War, died in Melbourne on 21 August 1931, just shy of his fiftieth birthday.[100]

The wartime exploits of Roger Henry Patrick Farnham Moag-Levy read like a novel, and the mystery of his ultimate fate only adds to this quality. Born Hyman Levy in Dunedin, Moag-Levy undoubtedly holds the record in the First World War for serving in the military forces of three of the five British dominions, as well as wearing the uniform of the Royal Flying Corps for a short period. He used different combinations of his name to try to avoid detection, apparently out of desperation to establish his credentials as a genuine war hero.

In June 1912, Henry Moag-Levy applied to the Union Steam Ship Company of New Zealand for a Home Trade Mate New Zealand certificate. (This maritime qualification enabled Moag-Levy to serve as an officer on Union Steam Ship vessels operating in New Zealand waters.) In evidence of his seamanship, Moag-Levy stressed his considerable work experience, which included being appointed bosun and third officer on vessels working off the Indian coast. He listed his full sea time experience 'as about six years'.[101] As Moag-Levy had just turned 22 it is doubtful he had this much sea time or had ever seen the coast of India.

In May 1915 Moag-Levy joined the Australian Imperial Force, giving his name as Roger Henry Patrick Farnham Moag. (When he had joined the shipping company in 1912, he recorded his date of birth as 1889; when he joined the AIF three years later it was 1880.)[102] He also listed extensive (but bogus) military service, including 14 years with the Royal Navy and combat action in the South African War during 1900–02, the Zululand rebellion in 1906, and the Chinese rebellion in 1911.[103] In addition, Moag-Levy claimed to have been awarded the DSO, the King Edward VII Coronation, the King George V Coronation, the Queen's and King's Boer War (1899, 1900, 1901), the Zululand Rebellion 1906, a number of Chinese medals, and the Royal Humane Society Medal 1914.[104] None of these had been awarded to Moag-Levy. The British War Office, concerned that Moag-Levy had claimed to have the DSO while serving with the AIF, launched its own enquiry in March 1916, and its findings were irrefutable. A note on the personal file of Maxwell Farnham (the alias he would later adopt in Canada) records: 'There is no officer named Moag in the Register of the D.S.O.'[105]

Moag-Levy left Australia for active service with the AIF in July 1915. After some time in Egypt he embarked for the Dardanelles on 19 October and served on Gallipoli until the evacuation. It seems he found it hard to find a home in the AIF. He was initially attached to the 1st Battalion, but was then made acting brigade machine-gun officer less than a month later. At the end of 1915 he was sent back to the 1st Battalion, but was then transferred to the 53rd Battalion after two months. Moag-Levy spent just one week with the 53rd Battalion when, on 26 February 1916, he faced a field general court martial for drunkenness. He was found guilty and sentenced 'to be dismissed from his Majesty's Service'.[106]

This sentence seems unduly harsh. He was charged with being drunk when on duty and, as a result, missed a lecture that officers in the battalion were meant to attend.[107] Perhaps the AIF wanted to make an example of him, or perhaps they were becoming wise to an imposter in their ranks. It did not help his cause that Moag-Levy pleaded not guilty and tried to lie his way out of trouble by passing off his drunken state as a bout of malaria.[108] Moag-Levy always maintained that he 'had been badly treated about the matter of "Drunkenness"'.[109] But the verdict stood, and the sentence was confirmed by both Major-General H. G. Chauvel, general officer commanding the 1st Australian Division, and General A. J. Murray, commander of the Mediterranean Expeditionary Force.

On 8 March 1916 Moag-Levy embarked from Egypt bound for Australia. On 19 March it was recorded that he had been 'struck off strength' of the AIF officers.[110] Such an ignominious end to his military career must have been torture for Moag-Levy, and it was compounded by the fact that dismissal from the AIF meant he automatically forfeited any service medals to which he was entitled.[111]

However, Moag-Levy's wartime military service was far from finished. After his discharge he went back to sea, working his passage from the United Kingdom to France, then on to the United States. On reaching New York, Moag-Levy 'jumped ship' and made his way to Canada, where he joined the CEF.[112] Using the name Maxwell Farnham, he enlisted at St Catharines, Ontario, on 26 October 1916 and served with the CEF until 12 January 1917, when he was struck off their strength, 'having been accepted as a candidate for a commission with the Imperial Army'. Moag-Levy's conduct and character during his time with the CEF was recorded as 'good'.[113]

Moag-Levy had quit the CEF for the express purpose of obtaining a commission in the RFC. At his interview, though, 'Maxwell Farnham' came unstuck. In order to increase his chances he had claimed in his application that he was an engineer, had graduated from Otago University, and had worked for the Australian government's marine department as a compass adjuster.[114] But the Canadian Military Police discovered his true identity, including his service and discharge from the AIF, and they informed the RFC recruiters.[115] When confronted with this information, he admitted that he was not Maxwell Farnham but was in fact Roger Henry Patrick Farnham Moag. The recruiters accordingly declined his application in February 1917.[116]

In desperation, Moag-Levy immediately enlisted as a private soldier in the Machine Gun Corps of the NZEF, giving his name as Roger Moag and his date of birth as 1880, and claiming, once again, to have had extensive military experience. He described his occupation as a 'master mariner', with his last employer being the China Navigation Company of Hong Kong.[117] Some alarm bells must have sounded in NZEF Headquarters, especially when Roger Moag listed his next of kin as his mother, and recorded on his attestation form that he had been court-martialled and dismissed from the AIF for drunkenness.[118] On 8 March, less than a month after enlisting, he was 'discharged for enrolling under a false name & struck off strength of N.Z.E.F.'.[119]

Moag-Levy made the New Zealand newspapers in May and June 1917, under the headings 'Broken Officer's Career' and 'Clever Man Goes Wrong'. (Even the newspapers had his name wrong, giving it as Roger Henry Moey Levy.)[120] The papers reported that the 25-year-old had been arrested and was facing trial for wearing 'a Captain's uniform of the RFC with ribbons for the DSO and a host of other decorations without authority'. When arrested, Moag-Levy declared that his one desire was 'to make good yet'. A New Zealand officer who spoke in his defence stated that Moag-Levy was 'not a coward' and wanted to serve but that his record 'is not good enough'. His ruin was caused by 'his desire to put on "swank" and fast living'. The magistrate hearing the case stated that he was 'sorry to sentence a man like the prisoner . . . and hoped he would redeem his position and go straightforwardly in the future'. Moag-Levy was nevertheless sentenced to two months' jail with hard labour.[121]

After serving his prison sentence, Roger Henry Patrick Farnham Moag-Levy's ultimate fate became somewhat of a mystery. He was either lost at sea or he faked his disappearance. At the end of January 1919 the *Evening Post* carried the news that

MAN OF MANY PARTS.

DISCHARGED FROM NEW ZEALAND FORCE.

POLICE COURT SEQUEL.

LONDON, March 27.

No. 37179 Private R. Moag, Machine-gun Corps, was discharged from the N.Z.E.F. on March 8th for enlisting under a false name.

The sequel appeared on Thursday, when at Westminster Police Court, before Mr. Horace Smith, Roger Henry Mocy Levy, 25, was charged with wearing officer's uniform and decorations without authority.

Captain Shand, N.Z. Forces, Assistant-Provost Marshal, said the prisoner had had a remarkable career, and was a man of great capacity, his military work being of a particularly high order. Originally he joined the army as a private in Australia, but very soon he obtained a commission as lieutenant and saw service in Egypt. There he was dismissed for drunkenness, and sent back to Australia in a troopship. Being qualified as a master mariner, he soon got back to England, whence he proceeded to Bordeaux as mate on a coaster. Then he joined a vessel at Havre, made his way to New York, and "skipped" to Canada. There he joined the Canada Mounted Rifles in November last, became a scout sergeant and was, with others, chosen for service in the Royal Flying Corps in England. Again over here, his abilities were so assertive that he was soon selected for a commission, but anticipating his promotion, he obtained a captain's uniform, and was found strutting about wearing the D.S.O., in addition to Zulu, Egyptian, and other decorations, to which, of course, he was not entitled. He passed in the West End as Captain Maxwell Farnham. Escaping from arrest and being dismissed the R.F.C., he enlisted in the machine-gun section of the N.Z.E.F. in the name of Moag, when his antecedents, being found out, determined his position.

Mr. Horace Smith: He seems a very clever man—too clever.

Captain Shand: Yes. And he is not a coward. I believe he wanted to get back to the fighting line, but, unfortunately, his record is not good enough. His ruin has been his desire to 'swank' and fast living. He did obtain £70 from one officer in the Royal Flying Corps—he had some friends there—but I don't think he actually obtained the money by false pretences. He had a reasonable expectation that he could repay it, when he got his commission.

Detective-Sergeant Wood stated that the defendant, on arrest, said his one desire was to "make good yet." His last enlistment was with a view of getting to France.

The magistrate said he was sorry to sentence a man like prisoner, and in the hope that he would redeem his position and go straightforwardly in the future, the term of imprisonment with hard labour was reduced to two months.

RUINED BY VANITY

"A very clever man—too clever," was the comment of Mr Horace Smith, the Magistrate at Westminster, on March 22, in sentencing to two months' hard labor a man named Roger H. Moey-Levy, who was charged with wearing officers' uniform and decorations without authority.

Captain Shand, of the New Zealand Forces, Assistant Provost-Marshal, said that prisoner, who was only 25, was a man of great capacity, his military work being of a particularly high order. Originally he joined the army in Australia as a private, but soon obtained a commission as lieutenant and saw service in Egypt. There he was dismissed for drunkenness, and sent back to Australia. Being qualified as a master mariner, he soon got back to England, and proceeded to Bordeaux as mate on a coaster. Going to Canada, he joined the Canada Mounted Rifles, became a scout sergeant, and was chosen for service in the Royal Flying Corps in England. He was soon selected for a commission, but, anticipating his promotion, he obtained a captain's uniform, and was found strutting about wearing the D.S.O., besides the Zulu, Egypt, and other decorations, to which, of course, he was not entitled. He passed in the West End as Captain Maxwell Farnham. Escaping from arrest, and being dismissed the Flying Corps, he enlisted in the New Zealand Forces. The man, Captain Shand added, was no coward. His ruin had been fast living and a desire to put on "swank."

RUINED BY "SWANK."

REMARKABLE STORY OF CLEVER SOLDIER'S ADVENTURE.

A remarkable story was told of the career of Roger H. Moey-Levy, aged 25, who was charged at Westminster on March 22 with wearing an officer's uniform and decorations without authority. Joining the Army in Australia, the accused, who was said to possess great ability, obtained a commission in Egypt, but was dismissed for drunkenness and sent back to Australia. Qualified as a master mariner, he came to England, got to New York, and "skipped" to Canada. There he joined the Mounted Rifles, became a scout sergeant and was chosen with others for service in the R.F.C. in England, Again his abilities were recognised and anticipating his promotion, he obtained a captain's uniform, and was found wearing the D.S.O., with Zulu, Egypt and other decorations to which he was not entitled, and passed as Captain Maxwell Farnham. He escaped arrest, and, dismissed from the Flying Corps, enlisted in the machine-gun section of the New Zealand Forces, where his antecedents were found out..

Captain Shand said the man's ruin had been due to his desire to put on "swank."

Mr. Horace Smith sentenced him to two months' hard labour.

The fate of conman Roger Henry Patrick Farnham Moag-Levy was widely reported in New Zealand. The headings of these newspaper articles, from the *Taranaki Herald* (26 May 1917), the *Evening Star* (11 June 1917) and the *Ohinemuri Gazette* (11 June 1917), encapsulated Moag-Levy's character. PAPERS PAST

> Mrs. A. Moag-Levy, of Wellington, has received word that her only son, Roger, was drowned through the sinking of an American transport near the Azores, in the first week of February, 1918. All hands on the vessel were lost. The late Mr. Moag-Levy was formerly a very popular officer in the Union Steam Ship Company's service.[122]

Roger Moag-Levy was supposedly working on the SS *Halifax*, which sailed from New York to Bordeaux in December 1917. Sighted leaving St Michael in the Azores on 11 December, the vessel disappeared without trace.[123] Moag-Levy could have been among those lost. However, the War Office and others were sceptical. Moag-Levy's reputation as a soldier was tarnished and his personal life was a mess. He had married four times within five years and was being pursued by the New South Wales police for deserting one of his wives and children.[124] It would have suited Moag-Levy very much to disappear and make a fresh start.

In 1926 an incident of 'a lover's trickery' was reported in the New Zealand newspapers. A man named Hyman Levy (Moag-Levy's original name) had tricked his fiancée into removing her engagement ring and had then made off with it.[125] The incident would wind up in court.[126] Was Henry Moag-Levy up to his old tricks again? It is impossible to know for sure. Whatever his fate, this unsuccessful soldier of three nations had certainly lived a most colourful life — although, with the exception of his service on Gallipoli, he had contributed very little to the Allied war effort.

Some New Zealanders served in Russia with the British Expeditionary Force at the end of 1918. Alec Noel Hawkes Whitcombe was one of eight sons of George Hawkes Whitcombe, who in 1882 founded the well-known New Zealand company Whitcombe & Tombs in Christchurch. Educated at Christ's College, Noel Whitcombe left New Zealand on 15 December 1915 for the United Kingdom, where he obtained a commission in the Royal Horse Artillery and was soon serving in France, seeing action on the Somme in 1916 and at Passchendaele the following year. He was promoted to the rank of captain during this time.[127] On the morning of 6 June 1918 Whitcombe was wounded by artillery fire. He was operated on at No. 2 Casualty Clearing Station at Rouen on 10 June, and arrived in Southampton four days later. After nearly a month in a

Armoured cars of the Royal Navy Armoured Car Division, which was attached to the Imperial Russian Army from 1915, cross a river in Romania. NATIONAL MUSEUM OF THE ROYAL NEW ZEALAND NAVY, AUB 0030

British hospital, Whitcombe was sent to Scotland on leave. On 29 July he reported for duty at the military barracks in Edinburgh and in September 'received orders for Russia'.[128]

Three weeks later Whitcombe sailed from Dundee, and arrived at Archangel 10 days later as part of the North Russian Expeditionary Force commanded by Major-General Edmund Ironside. This force was to assist the tsarist White Russians in their fight against the Bolsheviks. Whitcombe's diary entries for his time in Russia record much travelling but very little action. On 11 June he embarked for the journey back to England. His diary ended with the laconic 'Arrived England end of June. Leave until sailed Dec for NZ.'[129] Whitcombe must have done something other than travel around North Russia, as he was awarded the Military Cross for gallantry as well as the Order of St Anne of Russia for his service there.[130] The MC citation outlined Whitcombe's gallantry over two days in June 1919, and attested that '[t]his Officer's work throughout has been of the highest character and his keenness and energy have brought the artillery of the PINEGA FORCE to a high state of efficiency'.[131] On his return to New Zealand Whitcombe worked in the family business, serving as the Auckland branch manager for 20 years.

Noel Whitcombe was not the only New Zealander to serve against the Bolsheviks in Russia at the end of the First World War. At least another six did, including Lieutenant Samuel Hanna and Brigadier-General Archibald Jack. Around 150 Australians were also part of the North Russian Relief Force, as it was designated, and two, Corporal Arthur Sullivan and Sergeant Samuel Pearse, were awarded the Victoria Cross for their gallantry there.[132]

Samuel Hanna, from Auckland, had spent the early years of the war in France and Belgium with the Armoured Car Section of the Royal Naval Air Service. He commanded C Section, No. 15 Squadron, which comprised four armoured cars and eight armoured motorcycles. At the end of 1915, Hanna's unit embarked from Liverpool for Archangel, where they would be attached for service with the Imperial Russian Army.[133] No. 15 Squadron, now with the lofty name of the Royal Navy Armoured Car Division, fought with the Russian army in the Caucasus, on the Crimean peninsula, and later in Romania. For his actions during an offensive in Galicia in July 1917 Hanna was awarded the Distinguished Service Cross.[134]

Following the second and more radical Russian revolution in October 1917, what remained of the RN Armoured Car Division was transferred to the British army as part of the Motor Machine Gun Corps. Samuel Hanna was on leave in New Zealand when he learned that he was now a British army officer and was required to rejoin his unit in Basra, Mesopotamia. Hanna travelled to Basra to learn he was now the unit adjutant. It was a largely wasted journey, though, as the unit saw little action and the Ottoman Turks surrendered in October 1918, shortly after Hanna reached Basra. The following January, Hanna's unit was disbanded and he was demobilised in London two months later.[135]

Archibald Jack, born in Hokitika, attended Otago Boys' High School and in 1893 started his long career as a railway engineer in the Department of Public Works. Jack served in the Second South African War and then worked on railway projects in South Africa, China and South America.[136]

In 1917 Jack was commissioned into the Royal Engineers as a temporary lieutenant colonel, serving in Romania. In 1918 he was promoted to colonel and received command of the British Railway Mission on the Trans-Siberian Railway in Russia. War and revolution had greatly disrupted traffic along this vital rail link, and it was Jack's task to keep the railway functioning through the civil war; this would be one of the few successes of the British Mission in Russia.

When the Bolsheviks besieged the town of Yekaterinburg, Jack saved most of the trapped White Russian soldiers. He stopped a stampede of rolling stock which a few 'panic-stricken Generals' had commandeered and were using to escape, and carried out the evacuation in an orderly manner. Jack managed to get nearly everything and everyone away in train after train before the Bolsheviks captured the town. One correspondent wrote: 'It may fairly be said that the only aspect of the work of the Allies in Siberia on which it is possible to look back with any degree of satisfaction, is supplied by the activities of the Railway Mission.'[137]

Archibald Jack was promoted to the temporary rank of brigadier general in 1919. For his war services he had been mentioned in despatches three times, and he was appointed Commander of the Order of the British Empire (CBE) and CMG in 1919, followed by CB in the Siberian War Honours of January 1920.[138]

After the war, Archibald Jack worked as general manager of the United Railways of Havana, Cuba from 1920 until his retirement in 1925. Jack survived many close calls during his life: torpedoed three times during the war, he was also shot through the head by a striker in Cuba, and he survived the Sevenoaks railway disaster in the United Kingdom in 1927.[139]

AFTERWORD

In November 1916 the *Ellesmere Guardian* featured another letter from Gustav Berg of the AIF, recounting his harrowing experiences in the Somme. The enjoyment of soldiering evident in his earlier correspondence was gone, eclipsed by the brutal realities of trench fighting:

> The last couple of months we have been in and out of the trenches. It was simply 'hell' the first time, and on the second occasion we were up to our knees in mud. This is the place to see shells bursting. Where there is a bombardment you see nothing but smoke, the flash of shells and all kinds of different flares. We are at present between two artillery bombardments, and can hardly hear one another speak.[1]

That reality caught up with Berg on 18 January 1917 when he received a 'GSW Head Severe'.[2] Berg spent most of that year in the United Kingdom recovering from his wound, including months in hospitals, where he reported that the Australians got 'a great hearing' and were 'treated with the utmost kindness by the people there'.[3] Berg rejoined his unit in France on 11 October, but his service with the machine gunners was about to end. The very next day, he took another gunshot wound — this time to his left hand — and a severe gas burn to his neck, which ended his military service.[4] The burn was caused by the 'new stuff', mustard gas, and it left Berg 'covered all over with blotches' which were 'very unpleasant'.[5]

A further period of recovery in the United Kingdom followed, during which Berg had to forfeit four days' pay for overstaying a period of leave. He was declared medically unfit on 25 February 1918 and two months later was placed on a transport ship back to Australia. Gustav Berg was formally discharged from the AIF on 5 August, having served for two years and 221 days.[6] By that time he was already back home in Southbridge.[7]

In October 1918 Berg and five other returned men received a formal welcome home from the people of Southbridge. The national anthem and 'Rule, Britannia!' were sung; each returned soldier received a gold medal, and was asked to make 'a suitable reply'. The *Ellesmere Guardian* reported:

> Gunner Berg spoke interestingly of his experiences and expressed his admiration for the men of the Australian forces, whom he had found good fighters and fine comrades. He had spent a few months in Egypt before going to France, where he had been wounded three times and gassed. There had been good times as well as bad times and altogether he was glad he had been able to serve.[8]

Gustav Berg was thankful to have served, but he paid a heavy price. He married a woman he had met just before the war and together they raised a family, but his head injury 'plagued his life' and he died at the relatively young age of 57, most likely as a result of the ongoing effect of his war service.[9]

New Zealand was only a small component of the Allies' massive war effort in the First World War. But it was a significant contribution and New Zealand gave as much as a small country could. What has gone unnoticed for too long, however, is just how many New Zealanders made important contributions outside of the NZEF. The number was much higher than the authors of this book had anticipated; it is certainly much higher than has previously been recorded in histories of the war.

We now know that some 12,000 New Zealanders contributed to the Allied war effort under the flags of other countries. Of these, just over 1400 paid the ultimate price for their service. Many others were left physically and psychologically maimed by their war experiences. While the exact number may never be known, the official figures need to be amended. After 100 years of neglect, it is time to recognise all those New Zealanders who served, whatever their affiliation, in the first truly global struggle of the twentieth century.

The Thiepval (top) and Menin Gate (below) Memorials to the Missing, photographed circa 1933 and 1927 respectively. Thiepval commemorates the missing of the Somme battles and Menin Gate the missing of the three battles of Ypres. Officially there are no New Zealand names on these memorials. However, the reality is that many New Zealand names do appear on the memorials, just not as members of the New Zealand Expeditionary Force. COMMONWEALTH WAR GRAVES COMMISSION

NEW ZEALANDERS IN AN IMPERIAL WAR

RUSSIA
DIA
North Pacific Ocean
MARSHALL IS
NAURU
PAPUA NEW GUINEA
Ocean
South Pacific Ocean

APPENDIX 1
ROLL OF HONOUR

Service ID	Name	AKA	Rank	Force	Date of death	Cemetery
	ABBOTT, Victor Stephen Henry		2nd Lieutenant	RFC	15/09/1916	Upavon Cemetery, Wiltshire, England
41	ABRAHAM, Edwin	Aprahama	Private	AIF	18/01/1918	Coburg Pine Ridge Cemetery, Victoria, Australia
	ABRAHAM, Arthur Thomas (MC)		Captain	COEF	22/10/1917	Tyne Cot Memorial, West-Vlaanderen, Belgium
222	ADAIR, Robert Archibald		Private	AIF	27/05/1915	Alexandria (Chatby) Military and War Memorial Cemetery, Egypt
44	ADAMS, Francis Luke		Air Mechanic 1st Class	AFC	1/08/1916	Baghdad (North Gate) War Cemetery, Iraq
3003, 6707	ADAMS, George Alfred		Private	AIF	28/01/1917	Durrington Cemetery, Wiltshire, England
4977	ADAMS, John	John Taiuru Te Rango	Private	AIF	11/03/1919	Tidworth Military Cemetery, Wiltshire, England
	ADAMS, Robert Sefton		Captain	British Army	5/10/1917	Zantvoorde British Cemetery, West-Vlaanderen, Belgium
1027649	ADAMSON, Joseph		Sapper	COEF	12/07/1917	Bailleul Communal Cemetery Extension, Nord, France
564	ADAMSON, Henry		Private	AIF	25/07/1916	Villers-Bretonneux Memorial, Somme, France
NZE19, NZNF25, MLF25, J45382	ADLAM, Victor Louis	Victor Lewis	Able Seaman	RN	3/06/1916	Kirkee 1914–1918 Memorial, Mumbai, India
2778	AHRADSEN, Alexander		Sergeant	AIF	11/04/1917	Villers-Bretonneux Memorial, Somme, France
	AIMER, George Edmond Vernon		Lieutenant	RFC	26/06/1916	Ruislip (St Martin) Churchyard Extension, Middlesex, England
277140	AINSWORTH, Donald Roderick		Private	British Army	24/09/1918	Vis-en-Artois Memorial, Pas-de-Calais, France
	ALDERTON, Trevor Dudley Hall		2nd Lieutenant	RFC	16/06/1918	Narborough (All Saints) Churchyard, Norfolk, England
	ALDRIDGE, Douglas John		Lieutenant	RMLI	26/10/1917	Poelcapelle British Cemetery, West-Vlaanderen, Belgium
2867A	ALEXANDER, Charles	James Charles Edmond	Private	AIF	13/10/1917	Birr Cross Roads Cemetery, West-Vlaanderen, Belgium
6224	ALEXANDER, Myles	Richard Myles	Private	AIF	19/12/1916	Havelock Cemetery, Middlesex, England
	ALEXANDER, Rev. Philip George		Chaplain	RN	5/06/1916	Portsmouth Naval Memorial, Hampshire, England
5226	ALEXANDER, Charles Allan		Private	AIF	11/04/1917	Villers-Bretonneux Memorial, Somme, France
MB1839	ALEXANDER, Roy Leslie		Chief Motor Mechanic	RNVR	21/08/1918	Southend-on-Sea (Sutton Road) Cemetery, Essex, England

775	ALLAN, John Alexander		Private	SAOEF	2/04/1917	Aubigny Communal Cemetery Extension, Somme, France
	ALLAN, John Alexander McDonald	Allen	Captain	RFC	20/05/1918	Redcar Cemetery, Yorkshire, England
	ALLEN, John Hugh		Lieutenant	British Army	6/06/1915	Twelve Tree Copse Cemetery, Gallipoli, Turkey
9872	ALLEY, Alfred William		Private	AIF	20/10/1917	Bedford House Cemetery, West-Vlaanderen, Belgium
1002	ALLOM, Owen Bertram		Private	AIF	7/08/1915	Lone Pine Memorial, Gallipoli, Turkey
1886	ALLOM, Samuel Septimus		Private	AIF	9/06/1918	Villers-Bretonneux Military Cemetery, Somme, France
2779	AMODEO, Alphonsus Stephen		Private	AIF	9/08/1918	Villers-Bretonneux Memorial, Somme, France
217	ANDERSON, Andrew Fredrick		Private	AIF	26/04/1915	Lone Pine Memorial, Gallipoli, Turkey
3397	ANDERSON, Donald Clifford		Private	AIF	2/12/1918	Dunedin (Andersons Bay) Cemetery, New Zealand
1611	ANDERSON, Ernest John	Alexander Chase	Private	AIF	8/08/1918	Vignacourt British Cemetery, Somme, France
4356	ANDERSON, Frederick Kaye		Private	AIF	3/05/1917	Villers-Bretonneux Memorial, Somme, France
2	ANDERSON, Frederick Signor	Signoi	Private	AIF	24/05/1915	Lone Pine Memorial, Gallipoli, Turkey
1526	ANDERSON, Hector	Hector Harvey	Fitter	AIF	22/11/1916	Heilly Station Cemetery, Méricourt-l'Abbé, Somme, France
2366	ANDERSON, Jim		Private	AIF	5/03/1917	Villers-Bretonneux Memorial, Somme, France
	ANDREWS, Frederick George		Lieutenant	British Army	21/10/1914	Le Touret Memorial, Pas-de-Calais, France
8076	ANKETELL, Charles Edward		2nd Lieutenant	RAF	11/05/1918	Longuenesse (St Omer) Souvenir Cemetery, Pas-de-Calais, France
	ANSON, Henry Percy Richmond		Captain	British Army	25/05/1915	Potijze Chateau Lawn Cemetery, West-Vlaanderen, Belgium
	ARDEN, John Henry Morris		Lieutenant Colonel	RAF	22/07/1918	Alexandria (Hadra) War Memorial Cemetery, Egypt
1094	ARMSTRONG, John Alexander		Sergeant	AIF	9/10/1917	Menin Gate Memorial, Ypres, West-Vlaanderen, Belgium
	ARMSTRONG, Dr Walter Seymour		Captain	RAMC	31/05/1916	Le Tréport Military Cemetery, Seine-Maritime, France
MB1705	ARROWSMITH, Robert		Lieutenant	RNR	6/12/1915	Entebbe European Cemetary, Uganda

	ASHCROFT, Lancelot Edgar		Lieutenant	CEF	9/04/1917	Villers Station Cemetery, Pas-de-Calais, France
	AVERILL, John Eric		Captain	Indian Army	?/11/1921	Afghanistan
7353	BABBAGE, Herbert Ivan		Private	British Army	14/10/1916	Cardiff (Cathays) Cemetery, Glamorganshire, Wales
1297	BAILEY, Allan Richard		2nd Lieutenant	RFA	15/06/1917	Klein-Vierstraat British Cemetery, West-Vlaanderen, Belgium
660	BAIRD, David Lindsay		Private	AIF	25/04/1915	Lone Pine Memorial, Gallipoli, Turkey
	BALCOMBE-BROWN, Rainsford		Major	RFC	2/05/1918	Carnoy Military Hospital, Somme, France
	BALCOMBE-BROWN, William Edward		2nd Lieutenant	British Army	29/06/1915	Buffs Road Cemetery, West-Vlaanderen, Belgium
1568	BALSTON, Harry Love	Harry Love	Private	AIF	9/08/1915	7th Field Ambulance Cemetery, Gallipoli, Turkey
	BANNANTYNE, Walter James		Cadet	MM	19/11/1917	Tower Hill Memorial, Trinity Square, London, England
6717	BANNERMAN, Victor		Private	AIF	22/09/1917	Lijssenthoek Military Cemetery, West-Vlaanderen, Belgium
4656	BARBER, Hugh James Frederick		Sergeant	AIF	30/08/1918	Péronne Communal Cemetery Extension, Somme, France
	BARBER, Ralph Evan		2nd Lieutenant	AIF	18/11/1916	Villers-Bretonneux Memorial, Somme, France
23327	BARCLAY, James		Private	British Army	12/08/1916	Thiepval Memorial, Somme, France
1004	BARDEN, John		Sergeant	AIF	7/08/1915	Lone Pine Memorial, Gallipoli, Turkey
	BARGROVE, Robert Geoffrey		Cadet	MM	19/11/1917	Tower Hill Memorial, Trinity Square, London, England
	BARKER, Paul Studholme		Captain	RFA	26/10/1917	Solferino Farm Cemetery, West-Vlaanderen, Belgium
	BARLOW, Robin Tudor		Captain	RFC	25/04/1915	Lone Pine Memorial, Gallipoli, Turkey
292	BARNARD, Clement Aubrey John		Private	AIF	25/04/1915	Lone Pine Memorial, Gallipoli, Turkey
2342, 2342A	BARNARD, Stanley		Sergeant	AIF	26/07/1916	Bécourt Millitary Cemetery, Bécordel-Bécourt, Somme, France
	BARNES, David John		2nd Lieutenant	RFC	24/04/1917	Dover (St James's) Cemetery, Dover, England
	BARNETT, Ralph Edward Fulton		Lieutenant	British Army	6/09/1917	Tyne Cot Cemetery, West-Vlaanderen, Belgium
	BARR, Dr Hugh		Captain	RAMC	21/02/1917	Salonika (Lembet Road) Military Cemetery, Greece

6944	BARROW, Elephia Walter	Eliffe Walter Patrick Barrow	Private	AIF	27/09/1917	Menin Gate Memorial, Ypres, West-Vlaanderen, Belgium
4566	BARWELL, George		Private	AIF	6/08/1916	Sunken Road Cemetery, Contalmaison, Somme, France
2157	BASKETT, Charles		Driver	AIF	13/10/1918	Damascus Commonwealth War Cemetery, Syria
DM2, 163084	BASSETT, William Grahame		Private	RASC	2/05/1918	Baghdad (North Gate) War Cemetery, Iraq
6548	BATES, Edward Russell		Private	AIF	1/06/1918	Franvillers Communal Cemetery Extension, Somme, France
MB1914, C/1070, Z/3279	BATEY, John Foster Harbin		Chief Motor Mechanic	RNVR	12/04/1918	Dunkirk Town Cemetery, Nord, France
10386	BAXTER, Harry Neville		Gunner	AIF	3/05/1917	Villers-Bretonneux Memorial, Somme, France
819	BAXTER, Thomas Lindsay		Lance Corporal	AIF	24/08/1916	Villers-Bretonneux Memorial, Somme, France
5988	BAYLEY, Harold Bryan		Private	AIF	6/10/1917	Menin Gate Memorial, Ypres, West-Vlaanderen, Belgium
3082114	BAYNE, James Lewis		Private	COEF	10/10/1918	St Sever Cemetery Extension, Rouen, Seine-Maritime, France
	BEACALL, Henry William	Henry William Beakhall, Henry Verge	Chief Steward	MM	26/06/1918	Tower Hill Memorial, Trinity Square, London, England
229700	BEAGLEY, Bruce Sydney		Able Seaman	RN	25/09/1915	Heliopolis (Aden) Memorial, Cairo, Egypt
9058	BEATTIE, Malcolm Bartlett		Lieutenant	British Army	16/10/1917	Duisans British Cemetery, Étrun, Pas-de-Calais, France
102024/2	BEAUCHAMP, Leslie Heron		2nd Lieutenant	British Army	6/10/1915	Ploegsteert Wood Military Cemetery, Hainaut, Belgium
1314	BEAUMONT, Harold George		Private	AIF	28/04/1915	Lone Pine Memorial, Gallipoli, Turkey
190	BECKENSALL, Walter Herbert		Private	AIF	25/04/1915	Lone Pine Memorial, Gallipoli, Turkey
2582	BECKETT, Albert		Private	AIF	30/11/1916	Villers-Bretonneux Memorial, Somme, France
7148	BEDFORD, Samuel		Private	British Army	12/03/1915	Le Touret Memorial, Pas-de-Calais, France
	BEDWELL, Clifford Norman		Chief Officer	MM	27/06/1917	Tower Hill Memorial, Trinity Square, London, England
14237	BEE, James		Gunner	AIF	31/08/1918	Hem Farm Military Cemetery, Hem-Monacu, Somme, France
1707	BEHM, Benjamin		Private	AIF	7/08/1915	Lone Pine Memorial, Gallipoli, Turkey

1547	BELL, Laurence Wellington	Lawrence	Sub Lieutenant	RNR	25/01/1917	Plymouth Naval Memorial, Devon, England
	BELL, William Henry Dillon	William Henry Dillon-Bell	Lieutenant	British Army	31/07/1917	Menin Gate Memorial, Ypres, West-Vlaanderen, Belgium
419043	BELLERS, John Vernon Herbert		Lance Corporal	COEF	4/08/1916	Railway Dugouts Burial Ground, West-Vlaanderen, Belgium
5330	BENFELL, Arthur		Private	AIF	13/10/1917	Menin Gate Memorial, Ypres, West-Vlaanderen, Belgium
161351	BERGSON, Mark Bergson		Pioneer	British Army	21/10/1917	Klein-Vierstraat British Cemetery, West-Vlaanderen, Belgium
14	BERRY, Charles James		Private	AIF	13/06/1917	Mont Huon Military Cemetery, Le Tréport, Seine-Maritime, France
1622	BIGELOW, Clifford Miner		Private	AIF	18/12/1916	St Sever Cemetery Extension, Rouen, Seine-Maritime, France
51966	BISHOP, Alfred Wedderburn		2nd Lieutenant	British Army	12/05/1917	Arras Memorial, Pas-de-Calais, France
30275	BISHOP, Jack		Private	British Army	10/07/1916	Thiepval Memorial, Somme, France
1283	BISSON, William Alexander		Private	AIF	5/06/1917	Strand Military Cemetery, Hainaut, Belgium
2567	BLACK, William George		Private	AIF	28/05/1916	Cairo War Memorial Cemetery, Egypt
1109	BLACKETT, John Carruthers		Private	AIF	15/05/1915	Lone Pine Cemetery, Gallipoli, Turkey
471183	BLACKIE, Earl		Lance Sergeant	COEF	29/09/1916	Vimy Memorial, Pas-de-Calais, France
563	BLACKMORE, Alfred Penrose		Lance Corporal	AIF	18/05/1915	Beach Cemetery, Gallipoli, Turkey
	BLACKWOOD, Frederick George		Third Engineer	MM Reserve	26/03/1918	Plymouth Naval Memorial, Devon, England
4668	BLAIR, Harry		Lance Corporal	AIF	10/01/1918	Gunners Farm Military Cemetery, Comines-Warneton, Hainaut, Belgium
2384	BLANCH, John Dudley		Private	AIF	2/12/1915	Shell Green Cemetery, Gallipoli, Turkey
	BLEW, Kynnesley		2nd Lieutenant	British Army	12/04/1918	Pozières Memorial, Somme, France
	BLEWITT, Arthur		Lieutenant Colonel	British Army	4/09/1917	Longuenesse (St Omer) Souvenir Cemetery, Pas-de-Calais, France
4070	BLOCKLEY, James Joseph		Sapper	AIF	28/02/1917	Freemantle Cemetery, Western Australia
5057	BOGLE, George Stafford		2nd Lieutenant	British Army	15/10/1915	Helles Memorial, Gallipoli, Turkey
4077	BOGLE, Gordon Kennedy		Sergeant	AIF	20/09/1917	Menin Gate Memorial, Ypres, West-Vlaanderen, Belgium

1666	BOLTON, Patrick Thomas		Private	AIF	5/10/1919	Devonport (O'Neills Point) Cemetery, Auckland, New Zealand
127	BONNER, William Thomas		Private	AIF	15/11/1918	Sainte-Marie Cemetery, Le Havre, France
6230	BOOKER, William James		Private	AIF	9/04/1917	Villers-Bretonneux Memorial, Somme, France
704	BOOKLASS, John	John Hope Bookless	Lance Corporal	AIF	7/10/1917	Menin Gate Memorial, Ypres, West-Vlaanderen, Belgium
1862	BORNE, Douglas Robert		Sergeant	AIF	18/01/1917	Dartmoor Cemetery, Bécordel-Bécourt, Somme, France
1491	BOULNOIS, Edmund		Captain	British Army	23/10/1916	Thiepval Memorial, Somme, France
279	BOURNE, Albert Maurice		Private	AIF	10/10/1917	Menin Gate Memorial, Ypres, West-Vlaanderen, Belgium
565	BOURNE, Arthur Ernest Everard		Sergeant	AIF	16/07/1916	Rue-du-Bois Military Cemetery, Fleurbaix, Pas-de-Calais, France
105961	BOWDEN, John Stanley		Private	COEF	9/04/1917	Nine Elms Military Cemetery, Pas-de-Calais, France
172	BOWDEN, William		Private	AIF	8/05/1915	Helles Memorial, Gallipoli, Turkey
3244	BOWMAN, Albert Henry Claude	Albert Henry Claude Ingram	Private	AIF	4/10/1917	Passchendaele New British Cemetery, West-Vlaanderen, Belgium
1917	BOWMAN, John		Private	AIF	20/04/1916	Rue-du-Bacquerot (13th London) Graveyard, Pas-de-Calais, France
	BOYD, Stuart Wavel		Third Officer	MM	30/12/1915	Tower Hill Memorial, Trinity Square, London, England
88	BOYD, Thomas Murray		Bombardier	AIF	30/09/1917	Menin Gate Memorial, Ypres, West-Vlaanderen, Belgium
	BOYLE, The Hon. James		Captain	British Army	18/10/1914	Le Touret Memorial, Pas-de-Calais, France
3798	BRADFORD, George		Private	AIF	15/08/1916	Villers-Bretonneux Memorial, Somme, France
7359	BRADLEY, Henry		Private	AIF	19/08/1918	Sainte-Marie Cemetery, Le Havre, France
4589	BRADLEY, William Joseph		Private	AIF	6/01/1918	Boroondara General Cemetery, Victoria, Australia
2101	BRADY, Samuel		Private	AIF	7/08/1915	Beach Cemetery, Gallipoli, Turkey
17094	BRAIN, Norman Leslie		Air Mechanic 1st Class	RFC	22/10/1916	Villers Station Cemetery, Pas-de-Calais, France
	BRANDON, Edgar Thomas Colin		Lieutenant	RFC	3/04/1917	Arras Flying Services Memorial, Pas-de-Calais, France
5053	BRANLEY, John Mulkeedis		Private	AIF	16/10/1917	Menin Gate Memorial, Ypres, West-Vlaanderen, Belgium

352	BREAKSPEARE, Harry		Corporal	AIF	31/08/1918	Péronne Communal Cemetery Extension, Somme, France
1015754	BREAKWELL, Thomas John		Private	COEF	26/06/1917	Villers Station Cemetery, Pas-de-Calais, France
457	BRENTNALL, Charles Frederick Carthew		Private	AIF	5/10/1917	Nine Elms British Cemetery, West-Vlaanderen, Belgium
	BRETT, Leslie Henry		Flight-Sub-Lieutenant	RNAS	22/07/1917	East Mudros Military Cemetery, Greece
536441	BREWER, Alwyn Clarence		Private	CAMC	20/10/1918	Mont Huon Military Cemetery, Le Tréport, Seine-Maritime, France
	BRIANT, Ernest George		Greaser	MM	8/06/1917	Tower Hill Memorial, Trinity Square, London, England
1622	BRIGHT, Norman Samuel Andrew		Corporal	AIF	14/03/1917	Cite Bonjean Military Cemetery, Armentières, France
1660	BRINKWORTH, Frederick Lancelot		Sapper	AIF	8/05/1917	Grevillers British Cemetery, Pas-de-Calais, France
90	BRITTENDEN, Charles Sclater		Private	AIF	22/05/1915	Shrapnel Valley Cemetery, Gallipoli, Turkey
1894	BRITTENDEN, Fred Stephen		Private	AIF	4/08/1916	Villers-Bretonneux Memorial, Somme, France
7196	BROCKLEBANK, William Holcroft		Private	AIF	13/10/1917	Potijze Chateau Grounds Cemetery, West-Vlaanderen, Belgium
1786	BROOKE, Alfred		Private	AIF	23/06/1916	Erquinghem-Lys Churchyard, Nord, France
	BROOKES, Archie Howard		Third Officer	MM	26/06/1918	Tower Hill Memorial, Trinity Square, London, England
4574	BROOKS, Percy Neil		Private	AIF	27/03/1918	Ribemont Communal Cemetery Extension, Somme, France
5663	BROOKS, Thomas Edward		Private	AIF	7/05/1917	Grevillers British Cemetery, Pas-de-Calais, France
17250	BROUGH, John Forbes		Private	SA Army	4/05/1918	Menin Gate Memorial, Ypres, West-Vlaanderen, Belgium
	BROWN, Leslie		Fourth Engineer Officer	Australian MM	6/11/1918	Freetown (King Tom) Cemetery, Sierra Leone
6953	BROWN, Joseph Robert		Private	AIF	4/10/1917	Menin Gate Memorial, Ypres, West-Vlaanderen, Belgium
	BROWNLIE, Dr William (MC)		Captain	RAMC	25/03/1918	Heninel-Croisilles Road Cemetery, Pas-de-Calais, France
6342	BRUNING, Arthur Leslie		Private	AIF	8/05/1918	St Pierre Cemetery, Amiens, France

	BUCHANAN, Leslie		Lieutenant	AIF	5/09/1918	Mont Huon Military Cemetery, Le Tréport, Seine-Maritime, France
	BUCHANAN, William Archibald		Lieutenant	RFC	7/06/1916	Tidworth Military Cemetery, Wiltshire, England
18702	BUCKLAND, William Edward		Private	AIF	1/05/1919	Marcinelle New Communal Cemetery, Hainaut, Belgium
2621	BUCKLES, James	James Morrow	Lance Corporal	AIF	11/04/1917	Villers-Bretonneux Memorial, Somme, France
2991	BUCKLEY, Edward		Lance Corporal	AIF	28/09/1917	Menin Gate Memorial, Ypres, West-Vlaanderen, Belgium
	BULLOCK-WEBSTER, Frank Hamilton	Frank Hamilton Bullock Webster	Lieutenant	COEF/RFC	20/09/1917	Menin Road South Military Cemetery, West-Vlaanderen, Belgium
9832	BURGESS, Edward Allan		Private	AIF	3/06/1917	Strand Military Cemetery, Hainaut, Belgium
1883A	BURKE, Henry Gilbert		Private	AIF	7/06/1917	Menin Gate Memorial, Ypres, West-Vlaanderen, Belgium
17746	BURKE, John Finnken		Lance Corporal	British Army	1/07/1916	Thiepval Memorial, Somme, France
3765	BURKE, William Malcolm		Private	AIF	9/10/1917	Menin Gate Memorial, Ypres, West-Vlaanderen, Belgium
	BURN, William Wallace Allison		Lieutenant	RFC	23/08/1915	Basra Memorial, Iraq
J20524	BURNARD, Francis		Ordinary Signalman	RN	23/02/1915	Queensferry Cemetery, West Lothian, Scotland
1660	BURNET, Thomas		Private	AIF	29/11/1915	Lone Pine Cemetery, Gallipoli, Turkey
1884A	BURNS, Alexander		Private	AIF	4/08/1916	Villers-Bretonneux Memorial, Somme, France
	BURNS, Thomas Roland Roth		Flight Lieutenant	RFC	16/12/1918	Hornchurch (St Andrew) Churchyard, Essex, England
734	BURTON, Harold William	William Leonard Martin, Harold William Martin	Bugler	AIF	18/10/1915	Alexandria (Chatby) Military and War Memorial Cemetery, Egypt
128	BURTON, Ernest Wilfred		Lieutenant	AIF/AFC	4/04/1918	Montrose (Sleepyhillock) Cemetery, Angus, Scotland
50	BURTON, Lionel George Fuller		Private	AIF	25/07/1916	Puchevillers British Cemetery, Somme, France
	BUSBY, William Baldwin		2nd Lieutenant	British Army	15/02/1917	Amara War Cemetery, Iraq
4451	BUTLER, Albert Louis		Private	AIF	9/09/1916	Menin Gate Memorial, Ypres, West-Vlaanderen, Belgium

	BUTTERWORTH, Harold Winstone		2nd Lieutenant	RFC	15/07/1916	Cabaret-Rouge British Cemetery, Souchez, Pas-de-Calais, France
	BUTTERWORTH, Hugh Montagu		2nd Lieutenant	British Army	25/09/1915	Menin Gate Memorial, Ypres, West-Vlaanderen, Belgium
4469	CADOGAN, Ernest Harold		Private	AIF	25/07/1916	Villers-Bretonneux Memorial, Somme, France
1739	CALLAN, James Henry		Private	AIF	6–9/08/1915	Lone Pine Cemetery, Gallipoli, Turkey
2301	CALLENDER, George Wilfred		Captain	British Army	25/01/1917	Amara War Cemetery, Iraq
2675	CALVER, Percy Edwin		Corporal	AIF	12/11/1917	Étaples Military Cemetery, Pas-de-Calais, France
2004	CAMERON, Alexander		Driver	AIF	27/05/1916	Wimereux Communal Cemetery, Pas-de-Calais, France
573, Depot 1201	CAMERON, Alfred Ernest	John McIntyre, Alfred Ernest Cameron-McIntosh	Private	AIF	14/01/1915	Chatby Memorial, Egypt
339251	CAMERON, Andrew Perkins		Gunner	COEF	3/11/1918	Auberchicourt British Cemetery, Nord, France
4473	CAMERON, James		Lance Corporal	AIF	15/08/1916	Puchevillers British Cemetery, Somme, France
1695	CAMERON, James Alexander		Corporal	AIF	24/12/1916	AIF Burial Ground, Flers, Somme, France
316	CAMERON, John Robert William	William Ernest Cameron	Private	AIF	25/04/1915	Lone Pine Memorial, Gallipoli, Turkey
207	CAMPBELL, Augustus		Private	AIF	26/04/1915	Lone Pine Cemetery, Gallipoli, Turkey
4661	CAMPBELL, Duncan		Private	AIF	8/10/1917	Menin Gate Memorial, Ypres, West-Vlaanderen, Belgium
3008	CAMPBELL, George		Private	AIF	3/05/1917	Villers-Bretonneux Memorial, Somme, France
	CAMPBELL, Harrison McDowell		Lieutenant	AIF	23/11/1916	Heilly Station Cemetery, Méricourt-l'Abbé, Somme, France
	CAMPBELL, Ian Patrick		2nd Lieutenant	British Army	9/05/1915	Guards Cemetery, Windy Corner, Cuinchy, Pas-de-Calais, France
386	CAMPBELL, John Alexander	John Alex Campbell	Regimental Sergeant Major	AIF	16/04/1918	Villers-Bretonneux Memorial, Somme, France
8909	CAMPBELL, Robert		Private	British Army	25/05/1918	Mesnil Communal Cemetery Extension, Somme, France
	CAMPBELL, William Robinson		Major	British Army	13/05/1915	Menin Gate Memorial, Ypres, West-Vlaanderen, Belgium
428152	CAMPBELL, William Wilson		Private	COEF	9/11/1917	Menin Gate Memorial, Ypres, West-Vlaanderen, Belgium

3266	CAPPER, Alfred Metcalf		Private	AIF	25/07/1916	Bailleul Communal Cemetery Extension, Nord, France
	CARMICHAEL, D.		Able Seaman	MM	?/09/1918	
5662	CARO, Maurice Simon		Private	British Army	2/07/1916	Arras Memorial, Pas-de-Calais, France
5055A	CARR, Kenneth John		Private	AIF	29/09/1917	Menin Gate Memorial, Ypres, West-Vlaanderen, Belgium
5997	CARR, William Thomas		Private	AIF	25/04/1918	Daours Communal Cemetery Extension, Somme, France
3742	CARTER, Richard Rothwell		Sergeant	SA Army	12/04/1917	Arras Memorial, Pas-de-Calais, France
	CASTLE, Errington Edward		Lieutenant	RFC	12/08/1917	Catterick Cemetery, Yorkshire, England
	CATO, Geoffrey Maidens Walter	Geoffrey Walter Cato, Reginald Maidens Cato	Lieutenant	RFC	6/11/1917	Lijssenthoek Military Cemetery, West-Vlaanderen, Belgium
1481	CHAMBERLAIN, Cyril Percy		Private	AIF	22–27/07/1916	London Cemetery and Extension, Longueval, France
	CHAMBERS, John Harold		2nd Lieutenant	RAF	1/02/1919	Feltwell (St Nicholas) Churchyard, Norfolk, England
	CHANDLER, Henry Livingstone		Engineering Lieutenant	RNR	30/10/1917	Highgate Cemetery, London, England
	CHAPMAN, Edward Wynne		Lieutenant	British Army	17/11/1914	Ypres Town Cemetery, West-Vlaanderen, Belgium
	CHAPMAN, Dr George Martin		Captain	RAMC	13/05/1915	Potijze Chateau Grounds Cemetery, West-Vlaanderen, Belgium
2955	CHAPMAN, Percy Charles		Private	AIF	29/09/1917	Menin Gate Memorial, Ypres, West-Vlaanderen, Belgium
1124	CHAPMAN, Robert Reginald		Corporal	AIF	14/05/1918	Adelaide Cemetery, Villers-Bretonneux, France
3456	CHATWIN, Horace William		Private	AIF	2/11/1918	Purewa Public Cemetery, Auckland, New Zealand
1686	CHEESEMAN, John		Private	AIF	3/10/1918	Bellicourt British Cemetery, Aisne, France
	CHILTON, Frank		Lieutenant	British Army	4/06/1915	Helles Memorial, Gallipoli, Turkey
2193	CHISHOLM, John		Private	AIF	31/08/1916	Villers-Bretonneux Memorial, Somme, France
457	CHRISTIE, William Simpson		Private	AIF	9/07/1915	West Terrace Cemetery, Adelaide, South Australia, Australia
19650	CLAASEN, Ernest Leopold		Lance Corporal	British Army	22/04/1917	Kantara War Memorial Cemetery, Egypt
	CLACHAN, William James		Captain	British Army	6/01/1918	Mangochi Town Cemetery, Malawi

	CLAREBROUGH, Charles Alfred Walter		Lieutenant	AIF	26/08/1916	Pozières British Cemetery, Ovillers-la-Boisselle, Somme, France
61A	CLARKE, Arthur James		Private	AIF	4/04/1922	Waterfall Sanatorium, New South Wales, Australia
285574	CLARKE, Frederick William	Frederick William Clark	Stoker 1st Class	RN	17/10/1917	Chatham Naval Memorial, Kent, England
597	CLARKE, Harold Kennard		Private	AIF	3/10/1918	Templeux-le-Guérard Communal Cemetery Extension, Somme, France
	CLARKE, Nathaniel Fuhrmann		2nd Lieutenant	RFC	1/06/1917	Sutton Coldfield Cemetery, Warwickshire, England
	CLARKE, Peter		Captain	British Army	30/07/1916	Abbeville Communal Cemetery, Somme, France
1160	CLEMENTS, Ernest Arthur		Corporal	AIF	15/04/1917	Noreuil Australian Cemetery, Pas-de-Calais, France
18/458	CLEMITSON, Robert Homer		Sergeant	British Army	26/03/1919	Hexham Cemetery, Northumberland, England
3469	CLOOS, Charles Richard Edward		Private	AIF	17/08/1916	Villers-Bretonneux Memorial, Somme, France
2846	CLOUSON, Bert		Private	AIF	10/08/1918	Villers-Bretonneux Memorial, Somme, France
6981	CLYDESDALE, William Clement Shackell		Private	AIF	15/04/1917	Beaumetz Cross Roads Cemetery, Beaumetz-les-Cambrai, France
137	COADY, Edward		Sergeant	AIF	20/07/1916	V. C. Corner Australian Cemetery and Memorial, Fromelles, France
	COATES, William Henry		Lieutenant	RFC	22/07/1917	Arras Flying Services Memorial, Pas-de-Calais, France
J8194	COBB, Bernard Frank		Able Seaman	RN	8/01/1919	Plymouth Naval Memorial, Devon, England
6557	COBHAM, Francis Foster		Private	AIF	20/09/1917	Menin Gate Memorial, Ypres, West-Vlaanderen, Belgium
35	COCHRAN, Frederick John		Lieutenant	AIF	17/10/1917	Divisional Collecting Post Cemetery, West-Vlaanderen, Belgium
	COCK, John Herbert		2nd Lieutenant	RFC	14/04/1917	Beaulencourt British Cemetery, Pas-de-Calais, France
504	COFFEY, Arthur		Lance Corporal	SA Army	14/09/1919	
	COHEN, Ralph Neville	Ralph Neville Cullen	2nd Lieutenant	British Army	6/12/1915	Doiran Memorial, Greece
6967	COLE, George Edward		Private	AIF	11/04/1917	Villers-Bretonneux Memorial, Somme, France

830	COLEMAN, William Shedrach		Private	AIF	27/04/1915	Lone Pine Memorial, Gallipoli, Turkey
4444	COLES, Percival Clyde		Private	AIF	3/06/1917	Brookwood Military Cemetery, Surrey, England
6954	COLGATE, Robert Mill Park		Private	AIF	21/04/1918	Vignacourt British Cemetery, Somme, France
	COLLETT, Clive Franklyn		Captain	RFC	23/12/1917	Edinburgh (Comely Bank) Cemetery, Edinburgh, Scotland
	COLLEY, Herbert John		Master	MM	13/06/1917	Tower Hill Memorial, Trinity Square, London, England
4391	COLLINS, Francis		Private	AIF	3/05/1917	Villers-Bretonneux Memorial, Somme, France
5323	COLLINS, George		Private	AIF	2/03/1917	Wimereux Communal Cemetery, Pas-de-Calais, France
982	COLLINS, John Patrick	John Rodgers	Private	AIF	11/08/1918	Villers-Bretonneux Memorial, Somme, France
2579	COMPORT, Albert		Private	AIF	20/07/1916	Rue-du-Bois Military Cemetery, Fleurbaix, Pas-de-Calais, France
79052	CONDON, James Francis Bayntun		Lance Corporal	COEF	6/06/1916	Menin Gate Memorial, Ypres, West-Vlaanderen, Belgium
2132	CONNOLLY, Michael		Lance Corporal	AIF	29/07/1916	Courcelette British Cemetery, Somme, France
4460	CONROY, Charles William Gordon		Private	AIF	19/07/1916	V. C. Corner Australian Cemetery and Memorial, Fromelles, France
1702	CONSTABLE, Henry James		Private	AIF	27/07/1916	Pozières British Cemetery, Ovillers-la-Boisselle, Somme, France
887017	CONSTANTINE, John		Private	COEF	26/10/1917	Menin Gate Memorial, Ypres, West-Vlaanderen, Belgium
2608	COOK, Henry George	Harold Cook	Private	AIF	23/12/1916	Heilly Station Cemetery, Méricourt-l'Abbé, Somme, France
	COOKE, Ella Kate		Staff Nurse	QAIMNSR/ French Red Cross	8/09/1917	Alexandria (Hadra) War Memorial Cemetery, Egypt
3055	COOKE, Thomas (VC)		Private	AIF	24–28/07/1916	Villers-Bretonneux Memorial, Somme, France
Depot 6239	COOPER, Henry Isaiah	Harry Cooper	Private	AIF	9/08/1918	Heath Cemetery, Harbonnières, Somme, France
	COOPER, Herbert Ambrose		Captain	RFC	21/06/1916	Aubigny Communal Cemetery Extension, Somme, France
1626	COOPER, Joseph Tinsley Sutton		Private	AIF	29/07/1916	Serre Road Cemetery No. 2, Somme, France

1891	COPPELL, Robert James	Robert James Couppell	Private	AIF	28/04/1916	Ration Farm Military Cemetery, La Chapelle-Darmentières, France
1408	COPPIN, James Herdman		Sergeant	AIF	23/08/1918	Daours Communal Cemetery Extension, Somme, France
1528	CORFIELD, Seymour		Regimental Sergeant Major	AIF	26/12/1916	Bulls Road Cemetery, Flers, France
2524	CORIN, William Bennett		Private	AIF	14/06/1917	Brookwood Military Cemetery, Surrey, England
143	CORNWALL, Robert Henry Charles		Private	AIF	4/02/1917	Cite Bonjean Military Cemetery, Armentières, France
4397	CORNWELL, James Minshall		Private	AIF	8/11/1917	AIF Burial Ground, Flers, Somme, France
9946	CORRIGAN, Richard		Driver	AIF	30/08/1918	Assevillers New British Cemetery, Somme, France
3550	COSGRAVE, George Edward	George Edward Cosgrove, George Edward Wells	Sergeant	AIF	5/11/1916	Grevillers British Cemetery, Pas-de-Calais, France
903	COSGROVE, Nicholas Thomas		Sergeant	AIF	6/08/1915	Lone Pine Memorial, Gallipoli, Turkey
275	COULSON, John Herbert		Private	AIF	10/08/1915	Lone Pine Cemetery, Gallipoli, Turkey
1006	COURTNEY, John Classon		Lieutenant	AIF	7/04/1918	Arras Flying Services Memorial, Pas-de-Calais, France
1685	COUSINS, Daniel Thomas		Private	AIF	29/11/1915	Lone Pine Memorial, Gallipoli, Turkey
2619a	COWIE, Andrew Gray		Private	AIF	31/03/1917	Bapaume Australian Cemetery, Pas-de-Calais, France
	CRACROFT-WILSON, Clive Winthorpe	Clive Winthorpe Cracroft Wilson	Lieutenant	British Army	12/11/1918	Kirkee 1914–1918 Memorial, Mumbai, India
	CRAIG, Alexander Campbell		Cadet	RFC	9/02/1919	Kilmallie Old Churchyard, Invernesshire, Scotland
815	CRANSWICK, Thurston George		Lieutenant	AIF	18/11/1920	Carr Villa General Cemetery, Tasmania, Australia
814	CRANSWICK, John Stewart	Jack Cranswick	2nd Lieutenant	AIF	13/01/1917	Cite Bonjean Military Cemetery, Armentières, France
31809	CRAPP, James Arthur		Gunner	AIF	10/04/1918	Villers-Bretonneux Memorial, Somme, France
5634	CRAVEN, Thomas Reynold		Corporal	COEF	25/12/1917	Bruay Communal Cemetery Extension, Pas-de-Calais, France
1310	CREED, Harry Anthony		Private	AIF	25/12/1915	Alexandria (Chatby) Military and War Memorial Cemetery, Egypt

4942A	CREEGAN, Samuel Eric		Ordinary Seaman	RNR	13/10/1917	Port Chalmers Cemetery, Port Chalmers, Otago, New Zealand
	CRIMMIN, Florence [sic]		Lieutenant	British Army	24/04/1917	Doiran Memorial, Greece
J37896	CRISP, Arthur Edward		Able Seaman	RN	17/03/1918	New Cemetery, Gillingham, Kent, England
	CROFT, Eric		Captain	British Army	17/01/1918	Greenwich Cemetery, London, England
	CROUCH, Foster Brooke		Lieutenant	British Army	23/03/1918	Arras Memorial, Pas-de-Calais, France
	CROUCHER, Richard		Lieutenant	RAF	23/07/1919	Ismailia War Memorial Cemetery, Egypt
4464	CROZIER, Frank		Private	AIF	17/07/1916	Estaires Communal Cemetery and Extension, Nord, France
6744	CROZIER, William St Clair		Private	AIF	4/10/1917	Menin Gate Memorial, Ypres, West-Vlaanderen, Belgium
5659	CRUTCHFIELD, Charles		Private	AIF	24/02/1917	Bazentin-le-Petit Military Cemetery, Somme, France
	CULLING, Thomas Grey		Flight Lieutenant	RNAS	8/06/1917	Arras Flying Services Memorial, Pas-de-Calais, France
1126	CULPAN, Roy Gartside		Private	AIF	16/12/1914	Cairo War Memorial Cemetery, Egypt
243	CUNNINGHAM, Peter		Private	AIF	3/11/1916	Villers-Bretonneux Memorial, Somme, France
1518	DALBY, Edwin Ballard		Lieutenant	RNR	18/03/1917	Portsmouth Naval Memorial, Hampshire, England
	DALE, Allan Edward		Assistant Steward	MM	24/04/1917	Tower Hill Memorial, Trinity Square, London, England
2058	DALE, Edward Thomas		Private	AIF	10/10/1917	Menin Gate Memorial, Ypres, West-Vlaanderen, Belgium
6430	DALY, James Patrick		Sapper	AIF	26/09/1917	Menin Gate Memorial, Ypres, West-Vlaanderen, Belgium
	DANIEL, Harry Archibald		First Officer	MM	19/11/1917	Tower Hill Memorial, Trinity Square, London, England
1335	DARVILL, Joseph Alfred	Joseph Alfred Darvell	Private	AIF	28/06/1915	Shell Green Cemetery, Gallipoli, Turkey
2613	DAUE, Stanley		Sergeant	AIF	12/10/1917	Menin Gate Memorial, Ypres, West-Vlaanderen, Belgium
	DAVIDSON, Arthur Leslie		Engineer Sub-Lieutenant	RNR Patrol Yacht	6/06/1916	Pinner (Paines Lane) Cemetery, London, England
	DAVIES, Norrie		Fireman	MM Reserve	8/08/1915	Plymouth Naval Memorial, Devon, England
	DAVIES, Richard Hutton		Brigadier General	BEF	9/05/1918	Brompton Cemetery, London, England

395	DAVIS, Cecil Harold		Private	AIF	15/04/1917	Villers-Bretonneux Memorial, Somme, France
718	DAVIS, Rowland Dudley	Ronald Dudley Davis	Trooper	AIF	7/08/1915	Lone Pine Memorial, Gallipoli, Turkey
	DAWSETT, Percy John		2nd Lieutenant	AIF	4/10/1918	Prospect Hill Cemetery, Gouy, Aisne, France
143/46	DAWSON, Allan Douglas Gibb	Alex Douglas Gibb Dowton	Lieutenant	AIF	25/04/1915	Lone Pine Memorial, Gallipoli, Turkey
819	DAWSON, George William		Private	AIF	2/05/1915	Lone Pine Memorial, Gallipoli, Turkey
	DAWSON, Harold William Everard		2nd Lieutenant	RFC	4/10/1917	Bailleul Communal Cemetery Extension, Nord, France
	DAWSON, Samuel		Flight Lieutenant	RAF	17/09/1919	Koivisto Cemetery, Finland (Russia)
1668	DAWSON, William James Overend	C. W. J. Dawson	Private	British Army	27/10/1917	Bard Cottage Cemetery, West-Vlaanderen, Belgium
12498	DAYSH, Roderick Wilfred	Roderick Wilford Daysh	Private	AIF	21/10/1918	Beirut War Cemetery, Lebanon
	DE BEER, Bendix Hallenstein		2nd Lieutenant	British Army	10/07/1917	Ramscappelle Road Military Cemetery, West-Vlaanderen, Belgium
82	DE LAUTOUR, Edgar Frederick		Sergeant	AIF	23/05/1915	Shrapnel Valley Cemetery, Gallipoli, Turkey
39120	DEACON, William Henry	William Henry Deacon Price, William Henry Dacon	Bombardier	British Army	21/09/1917	Birr Cross Roads Cemetery, West-Vlaanderen, Belgium
	DEARDEN, James Ferrand		Captain	British Army	6/10/1919	Leckhampton (St Peter) Churchyard, Gloucestershire, England
3080	DEBENHAM, Harry Edward		Private	AIF	16/08/1916	Villers-Bretonneux Memorial, Somme, France
392	DEE, John Patrick		Private	AIF	6–9/08/1915	Lone Pine Memorial, Gallipoli, Turkey
654503, 235074, S8223	DEHANEY, David		Private	British Army	31/07/1917	Menin Gate Memorial, Ypres, West-Vlaanderen, Belgium
5127	DELANEY, John	Michael Murphy	Private	AIF	11/10/1917	Passchendaele New British Cemetery, West-Vlaanderen, Belgium
	DENNISTOUN, James Robert		Lieutenant	RFC	9/08/1916	Niederzwehren Cemetery, Hessen, Germany
550	DENNY, Charles Benjamin		Private	AIF	28/06/1918	Villers-Bretonneux Memorial, Somme, France
SPTS/4206	DIMANT, Roy Howard		Sergeant	British Army	27/07/1916	Thiepval Memorial, Somme, France
551	DIVE, Benjamin Francis		Private	AIF	25/10/1918	St Sever Cemetery Extension, Rouen, Seine-Maritime, France

13763	DIX, Quentin William	Quintin William Dix	Private	AIF	2/04/1918	Warloy-Baillon Communal Cemetery Extension, Somme, France
872	DIXON, George Christopher Herbert		Lance Corporal	AIF	15/04/1917	Villers-Bretonneux Memorial, Somme, France
497	DIXON, Wilfred John		Corporal	AIF	28/03/1918	Euston Road Cemetery, Colincamps, Somme, France
332	DOAK, Joseph Denver	Joseph Irvine	Sergeant	AIF	4/10/1917	Tyne Cot Cemetery, West-Vlaanderen, Belgium
	DOBSON, Robert Ambrose		Lieutenant	AIF	24/04/1918	Bonnay Communal Cemetery Extention, Somme, France
	DODWELL, Malby George Crofton		Lieutenant	AIF	13/12/1915	Lone Pine Memorial, Gallipoli, Turkey
736	DONALD, Vivian De Burgh		Lance Corporal	AIF	8/05/1915	Helles Memorial, Gallipoli, Turkey
6479	DONALDSON, Herbert Clarence		Private	AIF	20/09/1917	Menin Gate Memorial, Ypres, West-Vlaanderen, Belgium
771	DONNELLY, Arthur Harris		Corporal	AIF	20/09/1917	Menin Gate Memorial, Ypres, West-Vlaanderen, Belgium
7631	DONOVAN, Daniel William		Private	British Army	22/09/1914	Braine Communal Cemetery, Aisne, France
1965	DORAN, Loy Joseph	Lorraine Robert Joseph Doran	Trooper	AIF	26/06/1917	Beersheba War Cemetery, Israel
	DOUGHTY, Ralph Dorchel		Lieutenant	AIF	25/07/1917	Coxyde Military Cemetery, West-Vlaanderen, Belgium
J/8538	DOWDING, John		Able Seaman	RN	13/06/1916	Kirkee 1914–1918 Memorial, Mumbai, India
4773	DOWNEY, William Clarence		Private	AIF	23/09/1918	Stourbridge Cemetery, Worcestershire, England
6790	DOYLE, Frederick James		Private	AIF	10/08/1918	Terlincthun British Cemetery, Wimille, Pas-de-Calais, France
	DRAKE, Ernest Allen		Fireman	MM	20/03/1918	Southampton (Hollybrook) Cemetery, Hampshire, England
1668	DRIVER, Ernest Edward		Gunner	AIF	2/07/1915	Shell Green Cemetery, Gallipoli, Turkey
973	DRUMMOND, George Andrew		Lieutenant	RNR	19/10/1918	Dunkirk Town Cemetery, Nord, France
5339	DRUMMOND, William George		Private	AIF	4/10/1917	Menin Gate Memorial, Ypres, West-Vlaanderen, Belgium
5079	DRY, George Edward		Private	AIF	24/06/1918	Villers-Bretonneux Military Cemetery, Somme, France
	DUFF, Hugh John		Major	British Army	6/09/1918	Achiet-le-Grand Communal Cemetery Extension, Pas-de-Calais, France

	DUNBAR, Robert Mutch Masson		Third Officer	MM	10/07/1917	Fetteresso Cemetery, Stonehaven, Kincardineshire, Scotland
49	DUNDERDALE, Reginald		Private	AIF	11/04/1917	Villers-Bretonneux Memorial, Somme, France
717/881	DUNHAM, William Frederick		Private	AIF	6/08/1915	Lone Pine Memorial, Gallipoli, Turkey
6492	DUNNE, Thomas		Private	AIF	13/06/1917	Bailleul Communal Cemetery Extension, Nord, France
60	DUNPHY, George Patrick		Private	AIF	29/05/1916	Ration Farm Military Cemetery, La Chapelle-Darmentières, France
2094	DURELL, David	David Carlyon Vavasour Durell	Private	British Army	1/07/1916	Hawthorn Ridge Cemetery, No. 1 Auchonvillers, Somme, France
3076	DUTTON, Lewis James		Corporal	AIF	1/09/1918	Péronne Communal Cemetery Extension, Somme, France
	EAGER, Neale Fitzgerald	Neale Fitzgerald-Eager	2nd Lieutenant	RFC	14/06/1920	Suez War Memorial Cemetery, Egypt
J301045	EATON, William		Joiner 1st Class	RN	10/05/1921	Auckland (Waikumete) Cemetery, New Zealand, Portsmouth Naval Memorial, Plymouth, Devon, England
	ECCLES, Dr Horace Dorset		Captain	RAMC	16/08/1917	New Irish Farm Cemetery, West-Vlaanderen, Belgium
85782	EDGAR, Percy Ernest	Percival Ernest Edgar	Private	AIF	19/06/1919	Hollybrook Memorial, Southampton, England
817	EDMISTON, Stanley		Trooper	AIF	7/08/1915	Lone Pine Memorial, Gallipoli, Turkey
6252	EDMONDS, Harold		Private	AIF	13/06/1917	Trois Arbres Cemetery, Steenwerck, Nord, France
	EDWARDS, Rev. Edward		2nd Lieutenant	British Army	30/05/1917	Arras Memorial, Pas-de-Calais, France
7718	EDWARDS, Charles Thomas		Private	AIF	25/08/1918	Daours Communal Cemetery Extension, Somme, France
864	EDWARDS, Lawrence	Lawrence McCartie	Private	AIF	1/05/1915	Lone Pine Memorial, Gallipoli, Turkey
225195	EGAN, John Francis		Private	British Army	8/12/1916	Lahana Military Cemetery, Greece
422	ELLIOT, William Walker Highton		Private	AIF	26/04/1915	Lone Pine Memorial, Gallipoli, Turkey
4108	ELLIS, Ambrose Vaughan		Private	AIF	3/05/1917	Villers-Bretonneux Memorial, Somme, France
	ELLIS, John Chute		Lieutenant	British Army	6/06/1917	Lijssenthoek Military Cemetery, West-Vlaanderen, Belgium
875	ELLIS, Leicester George		Trooper	AIF	23/08/1915	Lone Pine Memorial, Gallipoli, Turkey

5363	ELLIS, Robert Alexander		Private	AIF	29/12/1916	Heilly Station Cemetery, Méricourt-l'Abbé, Somme, France
110424, SS111032	ELLISSON, Lionel George	Lionel George Ellison	Gunner, Stoker	British Army	5/04/1918	Ribemont Communal Cemetery Extension, Somme, France
4175	ELMSLY, Percy Norman		Private	AIF	5/05/1917	Grevillers British Cemetery, Pas-de-Calais, France
507	ELWOOD, Alfred Terah		Private	AIF	17/05/1915	Lone Pine Memorial, Gallipoli, Turkey
2403	ERIKSSON, Thorston Gustaf		Private	AIF	2/04/1917	Villers-Bretonneux Memorial, Somme, France
	EVANS, Dr Arthur Owen		Captain	RAMC	26/10/1919	Wandsworth (Earlsfield) Cemetery, London, England
	EVANS, Herbert Clyde		Lieutenant Commander	RND	5/06/1915	Skew Bridge Cemetery, Helles, Turkey
	EVANS, Joseph Albert		Deck Hand	MM	24/07/1915	Tower Hill Memorial, Trinity Square, London, England
	EVERETT, George Gordon		Captain	British Indian Army	1/05/1917	Delhi Memorial (India Gate), Delhi, India
1942	EWINGTON, Frederick William		Private	AIF	6/08/1915	Lone Pine Memorial, Gallipoli, Turkey
102234	FAIRNIE, William		Pioneer	COEF	4/04/1918	Vimy Memorial, Pas-de-Calais, France
	FAITHFULL, Gordon Chamberlain	Gordon Chamberlain Faithful	Lieutenant	COEF	9/04/1917	Canadian Cemetery No. 2, Neuville-St Vaast, Pas-de-Calais, France
4184	FALCONER, John		Private	AIF	30/08/1916	Villers-Bretonneux Memorial, Somme, France
623	FALCONER, Lake		Private	AIF	6/08/1915	Lone Pine Memorial, Gallipoli, Turkey
3313	FARLEY, Thomas Cecil Innes		Private	AIF	5/11/1916	Grevillers British Cemetery, Pas-de-Calais, France
11959	FARQUHAR, Norman Campion Bright		Private	AIF	16/10/1917	Nine Elms British Cemetery, West-Vlaanderen, Belgium
128360	FARR, Frederick John		Driver	British Army	26/09/1916	Thiepval Memorial, Somme, France
G/15066	FARRELL, William James Edward		Private	British Army	31/07/1917	Menin Gate Memorial, Ypres, West-Vlaanderen, Belgium
	FAWCUS, Victor Clarence Barick		Midshipman	RN	5/04/1919	Kirkee 1914–1918 Memorial, Mumbai, India
4187	FENWICK, Magnus Francis		Corporal	AIF	12/08/1916	Villers-Bretonneux Memorial, Somme, France
2141	FENWICK, Sydney		Private	AIF	20/08/1915	Lone Pine Memorial, Gallipoli, Turkey
24887	FERGUSON, Alan Ramsay		Gunner	British Army	5/04/1918	Birmingham (Lodge Hill) Cemetery, Warwickshire, England

	FERGUSON, Alexander Burns		Sub Lieutenant	RN	14/07/1920	Darwin, Northern Territory, Australia
82	FERGUSON, Archibald		Lance Corporal	AIF	8/05/1915	Redoubt Cemetery, Gallipoli, Turkey
3048	FERGUSON, John Addie		Sergeant	AIF	24/04/1918	Villers-Bretonneux Memorial, Somme, France
	FERGUSSON, Robert Arthur	Robert Arthur Ferguson, Roddy Fergusson	2nd Lieutenant	British Army	15/04/1917	Bois-Carre British Cemetery, Thélus, Pas-de-Calais, France
21067	FERNANDEZ, George Henry		Gunner	AIF	16/11/1918	Levallois-Perret Communal Cemetery, Paris, France
	FERRIER, Gilbert Colin Cunninghame		2nd Lieutenant	British Army	11/11/1914	Menin Gate Memorial, Ypres, West-Vlaanderen, Belgium
	FIDLER, Carrel Watt		2nd Lieutenant	British Army	19/05/1917	Trois Arbres Cemetery, Steenwerck, Nord, France
	FIDLER, Bertram Hay		Volunteer	YMCA	27/06/1918	Suez War Memorial Cemetery, Egypt
	FINDLAY, Ian Calcutt		Lieutenant	British Army	10/08/1915	Poperinghe New Military Cemetery, West-Vlaanderen, Belgium
3263	FINDLAY, Thomas		Private	AIF	7/06/1917	Menin Gate Memorial, Ypres, West-Vlaanderen, Belgium
	FINLAYSON, Alexander Manson Moncrieff		2nd Lieutenant	British Army	23/07/1917	Locre Hospice Cemetery, West-Vlaanderen, Belgium
2796	FIRTH, Percy Priestnall		Sapper	AIF	20/09/1917	Menin Gate Memorial, Ypres, West-Vlaanderen, Belgium
	FISHER, David		Assistant Carpenter	MM	?/9/1918	
	FITZGERALD, Roy James		Lieutenant	RAF	1/07/1918	Vignacourt British Cemetery, Somme, France
407	FITZGIBBON, James		Private	AIF	29/07/1916	Villers-Bretonneux Memorial, Somme, France
3742	FITZGIBBON, John		Private	AIF	20/08/1916	Villers-Bretonneux Memorial, Somme, France
	FITZHERBERT, Harold Lancelot		Lieutenant	British Army	30/06/1916	Cabaret-Rouge British Cemetery, Souchez, Pas-de-Calais, France
	FITZHERBERT, Wyndham Waterhouse		Captain	RFC	7/07/1917	Arras Flying Services Memorial, Pas-de-Calais, France
3794	FLEMING, Carlyle David George		Sergeant	AIF	11/08/1918	Villers-Bretonneux Memorial, Somme, France
	FLEMING, Frederick Nelson		2nd Lieutenant	British Army	22/06/1918	Niederzwehren Cemetery, Hessen, Germany

3393	FLETCHER, John Duncan		Private	AIF	12/09/1918	Harefield (St Mary) Churchyard, Middlesex, England
20726	FLETCHER, Stanley Kyrle Gordon	Stanley Kyle Gordon Fletcher	Private	British Army	26/09/1917	Tyne Cot Memorial, West-Vlaanderen, Belgium
10417	FOLLAS, Berty Albert	Bertie Albert Follas	Private	British Army	2/10/1915	Loos Memorial, Pas-de-Calais, France
SS/116258	FOLLETT, Leslie Daniel	Leslie Raymond Follett	Stoker 1st Class	RN	31/05/1916	Portsmouth Naval Memorial, Hampshire, England
310292	FOORD, James		Stoker 1st Class	RN	13/08/1915	Chatham Naval Memorial, Kent, England
K14707	FORD, Harry		Stoker 1st Class	RN	26/06/1916	Kirkee 1914–1918 Memorial, Mumbai, India
2862	FORD, Harry James	Henry Jonathan Milton Le Prou	Lance Corporal	AIF	14/04/1918	Outtersteene Communal Cemetery Extension, Bailleul, France
4303	FORREST, Harry		Private	AIF	27/09/1917	Tyne Cot Cemetery, West-Vlaanderen, Belgium
3097	FORSTER, Harry		Private	AIF	19/07/1916	V. C. Corner Australian Cemetery and Memorial, Fromelles, France
3356	FORSYTH, George Charles Stanley		Private	AIF	22–27/07/1916	Pozières British Cemetery, Ovillers-la-Boisselle, Somme, France
	FORTESCUE-PERSTON, George	George Fortescue Perston	2nd Lieutenant	British Army	12/02/1917	Karasouli Military Cemetery, Greece
481	FOSTER, Sidney Chamberlain	Sydney Chamberlain Foster	Private	AIF	30/12/1914	Cairo War Memorial Cemetery, Egypt
	FOUBISTER, John Leask		2nd Lieutenant	RFC	8/10/1917	Bandon Hill Cemetery, Surrey, England
MB1938	FOWLER, Henry		Motor Mechanic	RNVR Auxiliary Patrol	19/04/1917	Haslar Royal Naval Cemetery, Hampshire, England
5967	FOX, Justin Bede		Gunner	AIF	15/11/1917	The Huts Cemetery, West-Vlaanderen, Belgium
	FRAME, George Bruce	Garnet Frame		Admiralty Service	28/03/1915	At sea
777	FRASER, Wilfred Augustus	Wilfred Augustus Hicks	Private	AIF	26/07/1916	Sunken Road Cemetery, Contalmaison, Somme, France
143	FRASER, William Albert		Trooper	AIF	9/11/1915	Lone Pine Memorial, Gallipoli, Turkey
1945	FRAZER, Daniel	Daniel O'Donovan	Private	AIF	6/08/1915	Lone Pine Cemetery, Gallipoli, Turkey
2988	FREAR, Frederick Roland		Private	AIF	12/12/1916	Allonville Communal Cemetery, Somme, France

	FREEMAN, Douglas		Lieutenant	AIF	26/09/1917	Aeroplane Cemetery, West-Vlaanderen, Belgium
K8956	FREEMAN, Thomas Henry		Stoker 1st Class	RN	12/11/1914	Plymouth Naval Memorial, Devon, England
537	FREESTONE, Frank William Winterton		Driver	AIF	10/11/1917	Gaza War Cemetery, Israel
2192 Depot	FREETH, Lawrence Luxford		Trooper	AIF	16/06/1916	Karrakatta General Cemetery, Perth, Western Australia
	FREYBERG, Oscar		Sub Lieutenant	RND	4/06/1915	Helles Memorial, Gallipoli, Turkey
	FRY, William Mervyn		Sub Lieutenant	RNVR	29/12/1916	Chatham Naval Memorial, Kent, England
1241	FURLONG, Arthur Ernest		Trooper	AIF	23/05/1918	Fremantle Cemetery, Western Australia
622	GABITES, Eric Briggs		Private	AIF	28/06/1915	Shell Green Cemetery, Gallipoli, Turkey
553	GALE, Alfred William		Private	AIF	20/09/1917	Menin Gate Memorial, Ypres, West-Vlaanderen, Belgium
213	GALE, John Frederick Estcourt		Trooper	East African Mounted Rifles	28/01/1915	Moshi Cemetery, Tanzania
	GALITZENSTEIN, Godefroy		Private	French Army	12/01/1915	Nécropole Nationale Fauborg Pave, Meuse, France
654	GALLAHER, Douglas Wallace		Company Sergeant Major	AIF	3/06/1916	Rue-Petillon Military Cemetery, Fleurbaix, Pas-de-Calais, France
3867	GALLAHER, Henry Fletcher		Private	AIF	24/04/1918	Villers-Bretonneux Memorial, Somme, France
	GALLIE, Oscar Eugene		Lieutenant	British Army	7/12/1917	Vlamertinghe New Military Cemetery, West-Vlaanderen, Belgium
761	GALLOWAY, Donald James		Private	AIF	19/10/1917	Nine Elms British Cemetery, West-Vlaanderen, Belgium
389	GAMBLING, Alfred Astley		Private	AIF	10/06/1915	Cairo War Memorial Cemetery, Egypt
	GANE, Francis Egmont		Captain	COEF	13/05/1916	Railway Dugouts Burial Ground, West-Vlaanderen, Belgium
1071	GANNAWAY, Albert Ernest		Private	AIF	3/05/1917	Quéant Road Cemetery, Buissy, Pas-de-Calais, France
	GANNAWAY, Philip Corliss		Sub Lieutenant	RNVR Auxiliary Patrol	6/11/1918	Llandysilio Churchyard, Anglesey, Wales
	GARCIA, Oliver Dunham Melville	Oliver Dunham Melville Garsia	Lieutenant	British Army	18/09/1914	La Ferté-sous-Jouarre Memorial, Seine-et-Marne, France
	GARD, Joseph Henry		Captain	AIF	31/07/1918	Crouy British Cemetery, Crouy-sur-Somme, France

56	GARDEN, Alexander		Sapper	AIF	8/12/1915	Alexandria (Chatby) Military and War Memorial Cemetery, Egypt
	GARDINER, Francis John		2nd Lieutenant	British Indian Army	28/03/1917	Dar-es-Salaam, Dar es Salaam, Tanzania
SS/4042	GASKIN, Jabez		Able Seaman	RN	21/05/1916	Kirkee 1914–1918 Memorial, Mumbai, India
	GAVIN, Noel John Hay (MC + Bar)		Captain	RAMC	2/11/1917	Rocquigny-Equancourt Road British Cemetery, Somme, France
9642	GEDDES, Percy Mannering		Private	COEF	7/11/1915	Hollybrook Memorial, Southampton, England
	GEE, Robert Francis McLean		2nd Lieutenant	British Army	27/10/1914	Eastbourne (Ocklynge) Cemetery, Sussex, England
5104	GENET, Herbert Edward		Private	AIF	12/04/1918	St Pierre Cemetery, Amiens, France
168991	GENTRY, Raymond Clarence		Chief Petty Officer	RN	9/09/1915	Tehran War Cemetery, Iran
5536	GEORGE, James		Private	AIF	20/04/1918	Vignacourt British Cemetery, Somme, France
	GEORGE, Keith Harrison		Lieutenant	AIF	7/11/1916	Menin Gate Memorial, Ypres, West-Vlaanderen, Belgium
	GEORGE, Leslie		Lieutenant	AFC	12/05/1918	Hursley (All Saints) Church Cemetery, Hampshire, England
850	GIBBON, Harold St Aubyn		Trooper	AIF	7/08/1916	Jerusalem Memorial, Israel
87	GIBBS, Arthur Claude		Private	AIF	18/08/1918	Beacon Cemetery, Sailly-Laurette, Somme, France
1742	GIBSON, Alfred Lewis		Private	AIF	21/07/1916	Longuenesse (St Omer) Souvenir Cemetery, Pas-de-Calais, France
438	GIBSON, John		Private	AIF	26/05/1918	Adelaide Cemetery, Villers-Bretonneux, France
3222	GIBSON-SMITH, Ian	Ian Gibson Smith	Sergeant	AIF	27/09/1917	Dozinghem Military Cemetery, West-Vlaanderen, Belgium
470	GIESLER, George		Corporal	AIF	25/07/1916	Pozières British Cemetery, Ovillers-la-Boisselle, Somme, France
26377	GILBERT, Herbert Cecil		Gunner	AIF	25/10/1917	The Huts Cemetery, West-Vlaanderen, Belgium
3641	GILES, Charles Pedlar		Private	AIF	27/04/1918	St Sever Cemetery Extension, Rouen, Seine-Maritime, France
2908	GILL, George Arthur		Private	AIF	8/08/1918	Heath Cemetery, Harbonnières, Somme, France
	GILPIN, Robert Rooke		2nd Lieutenant	RAF	22/12/1918	Louvres Communal Cemetery, Val-d'Oise, France

2929A	GIVEN, Andrew Moncrief		Private	AIF	19/07/1916	V. C. Corner Australian Cemetery and Memorial, Fromelles, France
	GLANVILLE, Roland Belfield		Lieutenant	AIF	4/10/1917	Dochy Farm New British Cemetery, West-Vlaanderen, Belgium
27448	GLENNAN, John Barnard		Private	British Army	4/11/1917	Beersheba War Cemetery, Israel
1917	GOERTZ, Harold William Spencer		Private	AIF	11/04/1917	Villers-Bretonneux Memorial, Somme, France
PLY/9300	GOOD, James Alexander		Private	RMLI	4/11/1914	Rosskeen Parish Cemetery, Rosskeen, Invergordon, Ross-shire, Scotland
60	GOODFELLOW, Eric Hector		2nd Lieutenant	British Army	9/03/1916	Basra Memorial, Iraq
	GOODFELLOW, James Gordon		Major	British Army	23/03/1918	Roclincourt Military Cemetery, Pas-de-Calais, France
51	GOODISSON, Ernest John	John Edward Hutchins	Trooper	AIF	12/06/1919	Ismailia War Memorial Cemetery, Egypt
3520	GOODMAN, William John		Private	AIF	4/03/1917	Dernacourt Communal Cemetery Extension, Somme, France
8	GOODWIN, William Walter (MM)		Corporal	AIF	29/03/1917	Beugnatre Communal Cemetery, Pas-de-Calais, France
	GORDON, Albert William	Edward William Gordon	2nd Lieutenant	RFC	12/08/1917	Étaples Military Cemetery, Pas-de-Calais, France
403	GORDON, Alexander	John Kingsley	Private	AIF	18/08/1915	Norfolk Cemetery, Anzac, Gallipoli, Turkey
74332	GORMAN, Peter Joseph		Private	COEF	5/07/1915	Shorncliffe Military Cemetery, Kent, United Kingdom
	GORRIE, John William		2nd Lieutenant	British Army	19/07/1916	Pozières British Cemetery, Ovillers-la-Boisselle, Somme, France
	GOULD, George Oscar Alan		2nd Lieutenant	British Army	25/06/1916	Warlincourt Halte British Cemetery, Saulty, France
2680	GOW, Percy John		Private	AIF	27/04/1918	Villers-Bretonneux Memorial, Somme, France
	GRAHAM, Cedric Kenny Onslow		2nd Lieutenant	British Army	16/09/1916	Thiepval Memorial, Somme, France
1145	GRAHAM, Robert		Private	AIF	1–4/05/1915	Lone Pine Memorial, Gallipoli, Turkey
223	GRANT, Arthur Alexander	Alex Zimmerman	Bombardier	AIF	11/04/1917	Ecoust Military Cemetery, Pas-de-Calais, France
4502	GRANT, David Allan		Lance Corporal	AIF	14/12/1916	Caterpillar Valley Cemetery, Somme, France
2655	GRANT, Dudley		Private	AIF	7/06/1917	Menin Gate Memorial, Ypres, West-Vlaanderen, Belgium

J15258	GRANT, Frederick		Able Seaman	RN	15/09/1914	Waikumete Cemetery, Auckland, New Zealand
929	GRANT, Geoffrey Treacher		Trooper	AIF	7/08/1915	Lone Pine Memorial, Gallipoli, Turkey
	GRANT, George Muir		Lieutenant	AIF	7/08/1915	Lone Pine Memorial, Gallipoli, Turkey
102763	GRANT, Harry Osborne	Henry Osborne Grant	Sergeant	COEF	21/10/1916	Adanac Military Cemetery, Miraumont, Somme, France
383	GRANT, John		Trooper	AIF	6/08/1916	Jerusalem Memorial, Israel
	GRAVES, Geoffrey Austin Joseph		Lieutenant	COEF	18/03/1916	Menin Road South Military Cemetery, West-Vlaanderen, Belgium
512	GRAY, Clarence Brownlie		Lance Corporal	AIF	28/06/1915	Shell Green Cemetery, Gallipoli, Turkey
	GRAY, Clark Maxwell		2nd Lieutenant	AIF	19/07/1916	V. C. Corner Australian Cemetery and Memorial, Fromelles, France
7251	GRAY, Hector Victor		Private	AIF	4/12/1917	Mitchell Cemetery, Queensland, Australia
813	GRAY, James Heard	James Herd Gray	Private	AIF	5/10/1918	Ramicourt British Cemetery, Aisne, France
641	GRAY, Thomas James		Private	AIF	19/07/1918	Cairo War Memorial Cemetery, Egypt
559	GREAVES, Charles		Trooper	AIF	9/08/1915	Lone Pine Memorial, Gallipoli, Turkey
48	GREEN, George Henry		Private	AIF	10/06/1917	Menin Gate Memorial, Ypres, West-Vlaanderen, Belgium
	GREENWELL, Arthur Robert		Flight-Sub-Lieutenant	RNAS	20/10/1916	Cranwell (St Andrew) Churchyard, Lincolnshire, England
7245	GREGG, Richard Gordon Wray		Private	AIF	7/10/1917	Tyne Cot Cemetery, West-Vlaanderen, Belgium
6757	GREGOR, David Andrew		Private	AIF	7/11/1917	Menin Road South Military Cemetery, West-Vlaanderen, Belgium
	GRIBBLE, Charles Ethelbert		Captain	British Army	15/10/1918	Beaulencourt British Cemetery, Pas-de-Calais, France
627	GRINLINTON, Irwin Goodwin		Sergeant	AIF	6/11/1917	Tyne Cot Cemetery, West-Vlaanderen, Belgium
	GROUT, Henry Cranston		2nd Lieutenant	RAF	30/12/1921	St Peter's Anglican Churchyard, Christchurch, New Zealand
	GULLY, Lewis Vincent		Engineer Sub-Lieutenant	RNR	11/02/1918	Portsmouth Naval Memorial, Hampshire, England
3100	GUNN, Gordon Hugh		Private	AIF	18/02/1916	Cairo War Memorial Cemetery, Egypt
	GURR, Albert Jackson		2nd Lieutenant	AIF	14/11/1916	Villers-Bretonneux Memorial, Somme, France

17114	GUTHARDT, Henry		Gunner	AIF	15/05/1917	Grevillers British Cemetery, Pas-de-Calais, France
549	GUTHRIE, Edmund Robert		Sergeant	AIF	1/05/1915	Alexandria (Chatby) Military and War Memorial Cemetery, Egypt
	GUTTERIDGE, Richard Howard		2nd Lieutenant	British Army	2/10/1916	Thiepval Memorial, Somme, France
	HAASE, Edward George Louis		2nd Lieutenant	British Army	3/07/1916	Thiepval Memorial, Somme, France
804	HACCHE, Cecil James		Private	AIF	9/05/1915	Cairo War Memorial Cemetery, Egypt
489246	HAGAN, Bernard Joseph		Private	COEF	15/09/1916	Vimy Memorial, Pas-de-Calais, France
3840	HAGAR, Roy Alexander Morehead		Sergeant	AIF	10/08/1918	Rosières Communal Cemetery Extension, Somme, France
2764	HAGGER, Hubert Edward		Private	AIF	30/10/1918	Whitstable Cemetery, Kent, England
	HAGGERSTON, J.		Fireman	MM	8/03/1917	Tower Hill Memorial, Trinity Square, London, England
	HAIGH, William Richard		Lieutenant	AIF	26/11/1918	Brookwood Military Cemetery, Surrey, England
1361	HAILWOOD, Charles William		Private	AIF	5/06/1915	Quinn's Post Cemetery, Gallipoli, Turkey
	HALCOMBE, Norman Marshall		Major	RAF	13/02/1919	Port Said War Memorial Cemetery, Egypt
	HALL, George Foden Rooking		2nd Lieutenant	British Army	28/06/1917	Dickebusch New Military Cemetery Extension, West-Vlaanderen, Belgium
2855	HALL, Henry		Lance Corporal	AIF	31/01/1919	Melcombe Regis Cemetery, Weymouth, Dorset, England
	HALLAHAN, Walter Rewi		Captain	AIF	18/09/1918	Tincourt New British Cemetery, Somme, France
1642	HALLAHAN, Wendell James		Private	AIF	18/08/1916	Villers-Bretonneux Memorial, Somme, France
542	HALLAHAN, William Alfred		Corporal	AIF	26/06/1916	Rue-du-Bois Military Cemetery, Fleurbaix, Pas-de-Calais, France
317023	HAMILTON, Robert Hector		Gunner	COEF	8/08/1918	Vimy Memorial, Pas-de-Calais, France
34602	HAMLEY, James Hugh		Private	British Army	9/04/1917	Bailleul Road East Cemetery, St Laurent-Blangy, Pas-de-Calais, France
	HAMLIN, Herbert Bowen		Major	AIF	30/05/1919	Ismailia War Memorial Cemetery, Egypt
922	HAMMOND, Alfred Henry		Private	AIF	8/05/1915	Helles Memorial, Gallipoli, Turkey
	HAMMOND, Joseph Joel		Captain	RAF	22/09/1918	Indianapolis (Crown Hill) Cemetery, USA

9531	HANCOCK, Percy Claude Wilmot		Private	British Army	12/03/1915	Le Touret Memorial, Pas-de-Calais, France
2669	HAND, Wesley Rainsford		Private	AIF	2/09/1918	Fouquescourt British Cemetery, Somme, France
	HANDYSIDE, Thomas Fosberry		Lieutenant	British Army	29/12/1917	Jerusalem War Cemetery, Israel
1832	HANMER, John Percy		Corporal	AIF	29/03/1918	Outtersteene Communal Cemetery Extension, Bailleul, France
2701A	HARDING, Albert Ryland		Lance Corporal	AIF	10/12/1918	Brookwood Military Cemetery, Surrey, England
	HARDING, Matthew		Donkeyman	MM	28/05/1917	Tower Hill Memorial, Trinity Square, London, England
	HARPER, Owen Tannett		2nd Lieutenant	British Army	22/03/1918	Arras Memorial, Pas-de-Calais, France
3052	HARPER, Edgar Vincent		Private	AIF	13/10/1917	Menin Gate Memorial, Ypres, West-Vlaanderen, Belgium
4129	HARRIS, Arthur Edward		Private	AIF	17/02/1917	Adanac Military Cemetery, Miraumont, Somme, France
31129	HARRIS, Frank		Gunner	AIF	31/03/1917	Tidworth Military Cemetery, Wiltshire, England
	HARRIS, John George Edward		Second Engineer	MM	26/04/1918	Tower Hill Memorial, Trinity Square, London, England
23445	HARRISON, Alexander Valentine		Private	British Army	2/09/1918	Varennes Military Cemetery, Somme, France
	HARRISON, Charles Geoffrey		Lieutenant	British Army	27/11/1917	Cambrai Memorial, Louveral, Nord, France
2706	HART, Edwin		Driver	AIF	1/03/1916	Sydney (Waverley) General Cemetery, Sydney, New South Wales, Australia
	HARVEY, Alfred Wallace		Captain	RAMC	7/09/1916	Amara War Cemetery, Iraq
U2163, T1668	HATHAWAY, David		Stoker	RNR	1/01/1915	Chatham Naval Memorial, Kent, England
2234	HATRICK, Robert Ellis	Robert Glendenning Ellison Hatrick	Private	AIF	8/08/1915	Lone Pine Memorial, Gallipoli, Turkey
1336	HAUA, Andrew Charles		Corporal	AIF	11/08/1915	Lone Pine Memorial, Gallipoli, Turkey
5861	HAWKES, Samuel Gibbings		Private	AIF	7/11/1917	Bromley Cemetery, Kent, England
	HAY, Robert		2nd Lieutenant	British Army	9/10/1918	Terlincthun British Cemetery, Wimille, Pas-de-Calais, France
	HAYDEN, J.		Trimmer	MM	?/9/1918	
3838	HEAD, Joseph Arthur		Private	AIF	23/08/1916	Villers-Bretonneux Memorial, Somme, France

1040	HEALEY, Edward		Private	AIF	4/04/1915	Cairo War Memorial Cemetery, Egypt
	HEALY, Michael Darnien	Michael Pater Chance Duncan Healy	Lieutenant	AIF	20/09/1917	Menin Gate Memorial, Ypres, West-Vlaanderen, Belgium
	HEALY, William Patrick		2nd Lieutenant	AIF	14/11/1916	Warlencourt British Cemetery, Pas-de-Calais, France
223	HEBBEND, Cyril Walter		Gunner	AIF	26/03/1916	Écoivres Military Cemetery, Pas-de-Calais, France
11935	HEBERLEY, Charles	Charles Heverley	Private	British Army	25/09/1916	Thiepval Memorial, Somme, France
92	HELLIER, Stuart		Private	AIF	18/05/1915	Shrapnel Valley Cemetery, Gallipoli, Turkey
	HELMORE, Ernest Creswell		2nd Lieutenant	British Army	1/01/1917	Faubourg D'Amiens Cemetery, Arras, France
5385	HENDERSON, Alexander		Private	AIF	7/10/1917	The Huts Cemetery, West-Vlaanderen, Belgium
2618	HENDERSON, Frederick		Private	AIF	15–17/08/1916	Villers-Bretonneux Memorial, Somme, France
5810	HENDERSON, William Francis		Private	AIF	16/08/1917	Berlin South Western Cemetery, Berlin, Germany
	HENRY, Clarence		2nd Lieutenant	AIF	7/07/1916	Brisbane General (Toowong) Cemetery, Queensland, Australia
1971	HENRY, Walter		Private	AIF	14/05/1918	Rue-du-Bois Military Cemetery, Fleurbaix, Pas-de-Calais, France
637	HEPBURN, William David		Private	AIF	19/09/1915	Lone Pine Memorial, Gallipoli, Turkey
	HERBERT, Frank Thomas		Chief Steward	MM	30/12/1915	Tower Hill Memorial, Trinity Square, London, England
927	HETT, George		Private	AIF	11–20/06/1915	Beach Cemetery, Gallipoli, Turkey
447	HEWITT, Frederick Charles		Sergeant	AIF	7/08/1915	Lone Pine Memorial, Gallipoli, Turkey
6270	HEWITT, Richard		Private	AIF	6/04/1917	Morchies Australian Cemetery, Pas-de-Calais, France
3148	HIBBARD, Harold Crofton		Private	AIF	14/10/1917	Nine Elms British Cemetery, West-Vlaanderen, Belgium
5834	HICKSON, Alfred Stavely	Alfred Stanley Hickson	Private	AIF	3/05/1917	Villers-Bretonneux Memorial, Somme, France
SS114640	HIGGINS, James Thomas		Stoker 2nd Class	RN	18/08/1914	Poolewe Old Burial Ground, Ross and Cromarty, Scotland
	HIGGINSON, Thomas Cecil		Lieutenant	British Army	15/09/1916	Thiepval Memorial, Somme, France
4718	HILL, Jacob Benjamin		Private	AIF	14/11/1916	Warlencourt British Cemetery, Pas-de-Calais, France

274	HILLIER, Albert Edward	Richard Long	Private	AIF	30/04/1915	Lone Pine Memorial, Gallipoli, Turkey
	HINDLE, Harold Burn		Lieutenant	British Army	27/03/1918	Pozières Memorial, Somme, France
	HINTON, Francis Athol		2nd Lieutenant	RAF	9/11/1918	Shotwick (St Michael) Churchyard, Cheshire, England
	HOARE, Donovan O'Bryen	Donovan O'Bryan Hoare	Cadet	MM	19/11/1917	Tower Hill Memorial, Trinity Square, London, England
1110	HOBSON, Oswald		Private	AIF	8/08/1918	Villers-Bretonneux Memorial, Somme, France
	HODGES, Archibald Gordon		Lieutenant	British Army	15/09/1916	Thiepval Memorial, Somme, France
2986	HOLDSWORTH, Charles	Horace Lancelot Parker	Lance Corporal	AIF	26/07/1916	Villers-Bretonneux Memorial, Somme, France
906	HOLLOWS, James		Lance Corporal	AIF	14/07/1916	Estaires Communal Cemetery and Extension, Nord, France
1862	HOLSTED, Harold Willoughby		Private	British Army	4/02/1916	Cambrin Churchyard Extension, Pas-de-Calais, France
6615	HOLT, Frederick		Private	AIF	3/10/1917	Menin Gate Memorial, Ypres, West-Vlaanderen, Belgium
	HOMER, Charles William		2nd Lieutenant	RFC	27/10/1917	Euston (St Genevieve) Churchyard, London, England
778	HOOD, Andrew Thomas		Private	AIF	30/04/1918	Sainte-Marie Cemetery, Le Havre, France
1374	HOOPER, Francis Herbert		Private	AIF	8/05/1915	Helles Memorial, Gallipoli, Turkey
453	HOPE, Thomas Frank		Corporal	AIF	8/08/1915	Lone Pine Memorial, Gallipoli, Turkey
1728	HOPKINS, Frank William Banner		Lance Corporal	AIF	26/09/1917	Menin Gate Memorial, Ypres, West-Vlaanderen, Belgium
444	HOPKINS, Frederick William		Private	AIF	12/05/1915	Midland Junction Cemetery, Perth, Western Australia
516	HORNBY, Arthur Alexander		Private	AIF	21/11/1916	Villers-Bretonneux Memorial, Somme, France
2960	HORNE, George William		Private	AIF	28/02/1917	Bernafay Wood British Cemetery, Montauban, France
	HORNE, William John		Lieutenant	AIF	18/09/1918	Jeancourt Communal Cemetery Extension, Aisne, France
1769	HOSIE, William George		Corporal	AIF	28/10/1917	Tyne Cot Cemetery, West-Vlaanderen, Belgium
940	HOSKINS, Thomas Gregory		Private	AIF	5/06/1915	Alexandria (Chatby) Military and War Memorial Cemetery, Egypt
	HOUSTON, Frederick Neville		Captain	British Army	1/07/1916	Thiepval Memorial, Somme, France

	HOWARD, Harry Elsmore		2nd Lieutenant	British Army	8/04/1917	Roclincourt Valley Cemetery, Pas-de-Calais, France
206051	HOWE, Arthur Roderick		Leading Seaman	RN	15/11/1914	Haslar Royal Naval Cemetery, Hampshire, England
474	HOWELL, Edwin James		Private	AIF	31/07/1917	Menin Gate Memorial, Ypres, West-Vlaanderen, Belgium
10344	HUDSON, Benjamin Roy		Gunner	AIF	22/12/1916	Heilly Station Cemetery, Méricourt-l'Abbé, Somme, France
7003	HUGHES, Hughie George		Private	AIF	21/12/1916	Cape Town (Maitland) Cemetery, South Africa
K/28036	HULANCE, Joseph John		Stoker 2nd Class	RN	1/02/1916	Hullavington (St Mary) Churchyard, Wiltshire, England
161	HULL, James John		Trooper	AIF	7/11/1917	Gaza War Cemetery, Israel
5423	HULLTEN, Percy Garfield		Private	AIF	28/10/1917	Lijssenthoek Military Cemetery, West-Vlaanderen, Belgium
	HUMPHRIES, Cecil Frederick George (DSO, MC, DCM)		Lieutenant Colonel	British Army	22/08/1918	Fonquevillers Military Cemetery, Pas-de-Calais, France
3068	HUNIA, Winiata		Lance Corporal	AIF	7/07/1918	Borre British Cemetery, Nord, France
775920	HUNT, Thomas George		Private	COEF	11/11/1917	Passchendaele New British Cemetery, West-Vlaanderen, Belgium
RFC 52890	HUNTER, Cedric Alfred		Air Mechanic 2nd Class	RFC	2/01/1918	Brookwood Military Cemetery, Surrey, England
8248	HUNTER, Maurice		Driver	AIF	27/07/1917	Ypres Reservoir Cemetery, West-Vlaanderen, Belgium
20801	HUTCHINGS, Harry Bufton		Corporal	AIF	20/08/1917	Trois Arbres Cemetery, Steenwerck, Nord, France
451091	HUTCHINS, William Thomas		Rifleman	British Army	8/07/1917	Kantara War Memorial Cemetery, Egypt
	HUTTON, Lorne de Hutton		2nd Lieutenant	British Army	24/03/1918	Achiet-le-Grand Communal Cemetery Extension, Pas-de-Calais, France
4216	HUXTABLE, Harlequin Gladstone		Private	AIF	10/10/1918	Terlincthun British Cemetery, Wimille, Pas-de-Calais, France
Ply/7763	HUXTABLE, John		Private	RMLI	23/06/1917	Wellington (Karori) Cemetery, New Zealand
	HYAMS, Alec Hallenstein		Lieutenant	British Army	3/05/1915	Menin Gate Memorial, Ypres, West-Vlaanderen, Belgium
1248	HYNDMAN, Herbert Lionel		Private	AIF	13/08/1917	Reninghelst New Military Cemetery, West-Vlaanderen, Belgium
	HYSLOP, Ninian Steele	Ninian Steel Hyslop	2nd Lieutenant	RFC	30/10/1917	Basra Memorial, Iraq

	ILES, Charles Cochrane		Surgeon Lieutenant	RAMC	19/12/1914	Estaires Communal Cemetery and Extension, Nord, France
	INGLIS, P. J.		Trimmer	MM	?/9/1918	
2575	IRVINE, Harry		Private	AIF	13/12/1917	Berks Cemetery Extension, Hainaut, Belgium
4451	IRVING, Frederick Robert Roy		Private	AIF	10/11/1916	AIF Burial Ground, Flers, Somme, France
63466	IRVING, William		Lance Corporal	COEF	23/09/1915	Ploegsteert Wood Military Cemetery, Hainaut, Belgium
761027	ISDELL, Charles Creagh		Private	COEF	13/04/1917	Bruay Communal Cemetery Extension, Pas-de-Calais, France
	ISITT, Robert		Chief Carpenter	RN	10/12/1916	Islington Cemetery, Middlesex, England
1432	JACK, Alfred Lachlan		Sergeant	AIF	28/08/1915	Norfolk Trench Cemetery, Gallipoli, Turkey
58806	JACKSON, Arthur Edgar		Private	AIF	4/10/1918	Brookwood Military Cemetery, Surrey, England
1050	JACKSON, Ernest Bede		Private	AIF	9/04/1917	Hermies Hill British Cemetery, Pas-de-Calais, France
	JACKSON, Theophilus Rudolph (MC)	Theophilus Randolph Jackson	Captain	British Army	25/03/1918	Roye New British Cemetery, Somme, France
2926	JACOBSON, Enoch Andrew	Enoch Andreas Jacobson	Private	AIF	14/10/1917	Sanctuary Wood Cemetery, West-Vlaanderen, Belgium
	JAMES, Frank Harold		Third Engineer	MM	23/10/1917	Tower Hill Memorial, Trinity Square, London, England
1606	JENKINS, Thomas Oxner		Corporal	AIF	30/07/1916	Villers-Bretonneux Memorial, Somme, France
	JENNINGS, Alfred George (MC)		2nd Lieutenant	British Army	27/04/1918	Crouy British Cemetery, Crouy-sur-Somme, France
6679	JENNINGS, Denis	Dennis Jennings	Private	AIF	22/01/1918	Sydney (Waverley) General Cemetery, New South Wales, Australia
6352	JENNISON, John		Private	AIF	14/12/1916	Wareham Cemetery, Dorset, England
315	JENSEN, Francis Ernest		Lieutenant	AIF	13/09/1915	Lone Pine Memorial, Gallipoli, Turkey
2703	JEWELL, Cyril James	Cyrell James Jewell	Driver	AIF	27/09/1918	Doingt Communal Cemetery Extension, Somme, France
7027	JEWELL, Henry George		Private	AIF	29/04/1918	Caestre Military Cemetery, Nord, France
1332	JOHNSON, Alfred		Private	AIF	1/01/1917	Villers-Bretonneux Memorial, Somme, France
453	JOHNSON, Andrew Nathaniel		Private	AIF	25/04/1915	Lone Pine Memorial, Gallipoli, Turkey

1047	JOHNSON, Hector Magnus		Private	AIF	21/07/1917	Abbeville Communal Cemetery Extension, Somme, France
2711	JOHNSON, Percy Nelson		Private	AIF	5/05/1916	Brewery Orchard Cemetery, Bois-Grenier, Nord, France
	JOHNSON, William Charles Michael		Lieutenant	RNR	13/01/1915	Plymouth Naval Memorial, Devon, England
931750	JOHNSON, William Chester		Private	COEF	6/09/1917	Vimy Memorial, Pas-de-Calais, France
55987	JOHNSON, William Mauchlin		Private	British Army	24/03/1918	Arras Memorial, Pas-de-Calais, France
258	JOHNSTON, Ernest Alfred		Lance Corporal	AIF	14/11/1916	Ovillers Military Cemetery, Somme, France
	JOHNSTON, Francis Earl		Brigadier-General	British Army	7/08/1917	Bailleul Communal Cemetery Extension, Nord, France
	JOHNSTON, Octavius Ralph Featherston	Octavius Ralph Featherstone Johnston	Captain	British Army	1/07/1916	Gordon Dump Cemetery, Ovillers-la-Boisselle, Somme, France
548	JOHNSTON, William		Private	AIF	26/05/1917	Vaulx Hill Cemetery, Pas-de-Calais, France
75856	JOHNSTONE, Godfrey Gleeson		2nd Lieutenant	RFC	30/01/1918	Merville Communal Cemetery, Nord, France
	JOHNSTONE, Melville		2nd Lieutenant	RFC	16/07/1917	Longuenesse (St Omer) Souvenir Cemetery, Pas-de-Calais, France
	JONAS, Bernard		First Officer	MM	19/10/1917	Tower Hill Memorial, Trinity Square, London, England
4603	JONES, Edgar Noble		Private	British Army	22/10/1915	St Sever Cemetery, Rouen, Seine-Maritime, France
445	JONES, Fred		Trooper/Lance Corporal	British Army	13/03/1918	St Germain-au-Mont D'Or Communal Cemetery Extension, Rhône, France
2669	JONES, Frederick		Private	AIF	9/12/1915	Lone Pine Memorial, Gallipoli, Turkey
1927	JONES, Harold William Robert		Private	AIF	2/09/1918	Herbecourt British Cemetery, Somme, France
1665	JONES, Henry Lloyd	Henry Lloyd-Jones	Private	AIF	6–9/08/1915	Lone Pine Memorial, Gallipoli, Turkey
5419	JONES, John Clements		Corporal	AIF	27/08/1918	Heath Cemetery, Harbonnières, Somme, France
2263	JONES, Noel Reginald		Private	AIF	12/05/1917	Villers-Bretonneux Memorial, Somme, France
2057	JONES, Richard Maurice		Lance Corporal	AIF	11/04/1917	Villers-Bretonneux Memorial, Somme, France
377	JORDAN, Joseph		Lance Corporal	British Army	28/08/1914	Ligny-en-Cambresis, Communal Cemetery, France

	KAIN, Thomas Arthur		Wireless Operator		1/09/1917	
	KANE, Augustine Russell		Purser	MM	30/12/1915	Tower Hill Memorial, Trinity Square, London, England
3802	KAY, Francis Bertie		Captain	AIF	7/06/1917	Menin Gate Memorial, Ypres, West-Vlaanderen, Belgium
	KEAM, Frank Finley		2nd Lieutenant	AIF	27/06/1917	Kandahar Farm Cemetery, West-Vlaanderen, Belgium
6064	KEETLEY, Harry Joseph		Private	AIF	27/03/1917	Quéant Road Cemetery, Buissy, Pas-de-Calais, France
	KELL, Herbert James Graham		Master	MM	26/06/1918	Tower Hill Memorial, Trinity Square, London, England
1091	KELLAN, Arthur		Private	AIF	1/03/1917	Villers-Bretonneux Memorial, Somme, France
	KEMP, Elise Margaret		Sister	TFNS	20/10/1917	Godewaersvelde British Cemetery, Nord, France
	KENESTON, Robert Chaffey		Deck Boy	MM	10/03/1917	Tower Hill Memorial, Trinity Square, London, England
13822	KENNY, Cyril Bertram		Bombardier	COEF	31/12/1918	Vancouver (Mountain View) Cemetery, British Columbia, Canada
2593	KERR, Alfred George		Private	AIF	27/10/1917	Étaples Military Cemetery, Pas-de-Calais, France
	KERR-CLARK, Struan Robertson		Captain	British Army	25/09/1915	Loos Memorial, Pas-de-Calais, France
1	KIERNAN, Albert Arthur		Private	AIF	11/08/1915	Lone Pine Memorial, Gallipoli, Turkey
3837	KILLINGBECK, Samuel August		Private	AIF	24/07/1916	Villers-Bretonneux Memorial, Somme, France
	KILNER, Basil Hugo		Apprentice	MM	10/03/1917	Tower Hill Memorial, Trinity Square, London, England
	KINDER, Thomas Harry		Captain	British Army	3/07/1916	Thiepval Memorial, Somme, France
4816	KING, Herbert James		Private	AIF	19–20/07/1916	V. C. Corner Australian Cemetery and Memorial, Fromelles, France
602	KING, John Talbot		Lance Corporal	AIF	8/09/1915	Lone Pine Memorial, Gallipoli, Turkey
4824	KING, Leonard Charles		Private	AIF	4/02/1917	Flesquieres Hill British Cemetery, Nord, France
	KING, Thomas Inman		Able Seaman	MM	27/06/1918	Tower Hill Memorial, Trinity Square, London, England
3162	KINGSFORD, Shrewsbury Frederick		Private	AIF	19/07/1916	V. C. Corner Australian Cemetery and Memorial, Fromelles, France

3139	KIRIONA, Robert	Ruaangaanga Kiriona, Robert Tuhera	Trooper	AIF	12/09/1918	Ramleh War Cemetery, Gaza, Israel and Palestine
13693	KITSON, John		Private	British Army	27/03/1918	Arras Memorial, Pas-de-Calais, France
	KITSON, Reynolds Hamilton	Reginald Hamilton Kitson	Pilot	MM	7/06/1915	Tower Hill Memorial, Trinity Square, London, England
1404	KITTO, Francis		Private	AFC	25/11/1918	Tidworth Military Cemetery, Wiltshire, England
638	KLUGLEIN, Carl Hermann	Carl Herman Kluglein	Corporal	AIF	8/05/1915	Helles Memorial, Gallipoli, Turkey
710	KNIGHT, Wilfred Victor		Private	AIF	27–29/04/1915	Lone Pine Memorial, Gallipoli, Turkey
NZNF663	KNOWLES, William Edward		Ordinary Seaman	RN	8/02/1915	Canterbury Provincial Memorial, Christchurch, New Zealand
	KRETCHMAR, Edmund Herman	Kretschmar	Lieutenant	AIF	6/05/1915	Lone Pine Memorial, Gallipoli, Turkey
	LAIDLAW, John Ritchie Caldwell		Flight-Sub-Lieutenant	RFC	17/05/1916	Hendon Cemetery, Middlesex, England
5945	LAING, Percy Harold Hasing		Private	AIF	16/04/1918	Brighton General Cemetery, Victoria, Australia
J56927	LAING-MEASON, James Mangus	John Laving Meason	Ordinary Seaman	RN	17/03/1917	Southend-on-Sea (Sutton Road) Cemetery, Essex, England
11766	LAMBERT, Edward Over		Private	COEF	23/01/1916	Thorold (Lakeview) Cemetery, Ontario, Canada
7515	LAMPLUGH, Charles Francis Xavier		Private	AIF	12/03/1918	La Clytte Military Cemetery, West-Vlaanderen, Belgium
274	LAMPLUGH, Welby Jackson		Private	AIF	4/10/1917	Menin Gate Memorial, Ypres, West-Vlaanderen, Belgium
76197	LANCE, Charles Grenville		Private	COEF	8/05/1917	Vimy Memorial, Pas-de-Calais, France
1667	LANE, Gordon		Corporal	AIF	16/07/1917	Menin Gate Memorial, Ypres, West-Vlaanderen, Belgium
	LANE-FOX, George Henry		Lieutenant	General List	29/10/1920	Brookwood Military Cemetery, Surrey, England
5855	LANG, James Patrick		Private	AIF	27/08/1918	Terlincthun British Cemetery, Wimille, Pas-de-Calais, France
	LANG, William		Captain	AIF	13/08/1915	Lone Pine Memorial, Gallipoli, Turkey
6347	LANGDON, John		Private	AIF	22/09/1917	Étaples Military Cemetery, Pas-de-Calais, France
780	LANGRIDGE, Thomas Edward		Corporal	AIF	18/05/1917	Jerusalem Memorial, Israel
79	LANGSTONE, Arthur Ernest		Lance Corporal	AIF	31/07/1917	Menin Gate Memorial, Ypres, West-Vlaanderen, Belgium

487369	LAW, Andrew		Private	COEF	8/10/1916	Adanac Military Cemetery, Miraumont, Somme, France
3076, 1196	LAWLER, Edwin	Edward Harvey Lawler, Henry Edward Lawler	Private	AIF	19/07/1916	V. C. Corner Australian Cemetery and Memorial, Fromelles, France
	LAWRENCE, Alfred William		Captain	AIF	17/02/1918	Dunkirk Town Cemetery, Nord, France
5117	LAYBURN, William John Alfred		Lance Corporal	AIF	28/08/1918	Villers-Bretonneux Memorial, Somme, France
1007	LAYTHER, William John		Private	AIF	26/06/1915	Lone Pine Memorial, Gallipoli, Turkey
O/784	LE GRICE, Stanley Walter		Sub Conductor	British Army	18/03/1917	Nunhead (All Saints) Cemetery, London, England
1146	LEACH, William Henry		Private	AIF	1/08/1915	Shell Green Cemetery, Gallipoli, Turkey
17242	LEACOCK, Arthur Leslie		Private	COEF	24/04/1915	Menin Gate Memorial, Ypres, West-Vlaanderen, Belgium
	LEARY, Ernest Richard		2nd Lieutenant	British Army	23/07/1916	St Pierre Cemetery, Amiens, France
6786	LEDSHAM, Leicester Innes Forbes		Private	AIF	5/08/1917	Messines Ridge Cemetery, West-Vlaanderen, Belgium
2000005	LEE, Arthur Duncan		Private	COEF	1/09/1918	Vimy Memorial, Pas-de-Calais, France
116934	LEE, Horace Reginald		Private	COEF	28/01/1920	Vancouver (Mountain View) Cemetery, British Columbia, Canada
7169	LEE, Leonidis	Leonidas Lee, Leonidax Lee	Private	AIF	2/09/1918	Péronne Communal Cemetery Extension, Somme, France
3133	LEO, John		Private	AIF	22/07/1916	Villers-Bretonneux Memorial, Somme, France
	LEPPER, Harper Mervyn (MC)		Lieutenant	British Army	9/04/1916	Basra Memorial, Iraq
6762	LETT, John McLaren		Private	AIF	26/09/1917	Menin Gate Memorial, Ypres, West-Vlaanderen, Belgium
7499	LEVERTON, Richard James		Sergeant	AIF	6/06/1918	Wimereux Communal Cemetery, Pas-de-Calais, France
GS/16365	LEWIS, Gerald Sydney	Gerald Stanley Lewis	Private	British Army	7/07/1916	Thiepval Memorial, Somme, France
	LEWIS, Robert Henry		Private	British Army	20/09/1914	La Ferté-sous-Jouarre Memorial, Seine-et-Marne, France
	LIND, Lily		Sister	FFNC/French Red Cross	21/12/1916	Buried at sea
1976	LINDSAY, David		Private	AIF	17/07/1915	Lone Pine Memorial, Gallipoli, Turkey

388, 3078	LINDSAY, James Douglas McKnight		Acting Sergeant	AIF	29/09/1917	Menin Gate Memorial, Ypres, West-Vlaanderen, Belgium
	LITTLE, Arthur Howard		Third Engineer	MM	10/03/1917	Tower Hill Memorial, Trinity Square, London, England
35246	LIVINGSTONE, Frederick James		2nd Lieutenant	RFC	12/01/1918	Gainsborough General Cemetery, Lincolnshire, England
217	LOCKHART, James		Private	AIF	11/04/1916	Chatby Memorial, Egypt
528	LOGAN, George Hewish		Private	AIF	8/08/1915	Lone Pine Memorial, Gallipoli, Turkey
2423	LOGAN, John Stewart		Private	AIF	7/06/1917	Menin Gate Memorial, Ypres, West-Vlaanderen, Belgium
6111	LOMAX, Charles Mark		Private	AIF	4/10/1917	Menin Gate Memorial, Ypres, West-Vlaanderen, Belgium
	LONG, Arthur Trevor D'Arcy		Lieutenant	British Army	21/08/1915	Helles Memorial, Gallipoli, Turkey
5428	LOVEGROVE, Alfred William		Private	AIF	28/01/1917	Bazentin-le-Petit Military Cemetery, Somme, France
207	LOVELL, Ernest Rudolph	James West	Sapper	AIF	28/05/1915	Lone Pine Memorial, Gallipoli, Turkey
150, 5421	LOW, Stanley Cyril Ernest		Gunner	AIF	22/10/1917	The Huts Cemetery, West-Vlaanderen, Belgium
751	LOW, William Charles	Charles Wilson	Private	AIF	31/03/1919	Rookwood Necropolis, Sydney, New South Wales, Australia
147189	LOWE, Ernest George Strong		Private	COEF	13/05/1916	Woods Cemetery, Ypres, West-Vlaanderen, Belgium
2276	LOWES, Arthur Odell	Arthur O'Dell Lowes	Private	AIF	4/06/1919	Coburg General Cemetery, Victoria, Australia
5042	LUND, William		Private	AIF	3/01/1918	Menin Road South Military Cemetery, West-Vlaanderen, Belgium
2705	LUND, William	Wilhelm Ole Lund	Private	AIF	20/07/1916	V. C. Corner Australian Cemetery and Memorial, Fromelles, France
1584	LUSH, Philip		Private	AIF	11/05/1915	4th Battalion Parade Ground Cemetery, Gallipoli, Turkey
1954	LUSSICH, Walter Leo	Walter Leo Lussick	Private	AIF	19/01/1917	AIF Burial Ground, Flers, Somme, France
4155	LYNCH, Gladwyn Leon Earle		Private	AIF	4/08/1916	Villers-Bretonneux Memorial, Somme, France
1679	LYNCH, Thomas		Driver	AIF	5/09/1917	Brisbane General (Toowong) Cemetery, Queensland, Australia
18902	LYONS, William Holmes St John		Lieutenant	British Army	1/11/1918	Knockbreda Church of Ireland Churchyard, County Down, Northern Ireland

	MABERLEY, E.		Stewardess	MM	27/02/1916	Dover (St Mary's) Cemetery, Dover, England
	MACARTHUR-ONSLOW, Arthur William		Captain	British Army	5/11/1914	Wulverghem-Lindenhoek Road Military Cemetery, West-Vlaanderen, Belgium
	MACDONALD, Allan Cameron		Able Seaman	MM	13/02/1915	
	MACDONALD, Allan William		2nd Lieutenant	RAF	11/11/1918	Stamford Cemetery, Lincolnshire, England
	MACDONALD, Colin	Colin Boyd McDonald	Cadet	MM	19/11/1917	Tower Hill Memorial, Trinity Square, London, England
(ex NZEF)	MACDONALD, Guyon Kenneth		2nd Lieutenant	RFC	21/11/1919	St Peter's Anglican Churchyard, Christchurch, New Zealand
946	MACDONALD, John Augustine		Private	AIF	29/08/1915	Lone Pine Memorial, Gallipoli, Turkey
1248	MACDOUGALL, Allan		Captain	British Army	4/10/1916	Citadel New Military Cemetery, Fricourt, Somme, France
	MACDOUGALL, Iain		Captain	British Army	1/09/1914	Kilmhoiri (Kilvoree) Old Churchyard, Craignish, Argyllshire, Scotland
002451	MACEY, Gerald Charles		Sub Lieutenant	RNR	28/04/1916	Portsmouth Naval Memorial, Hampshire, England
77, 7096	MACK, William	John Moore, William Mack McCorquindale	Sergeant	AIF	31/08/1916	Villers-Bretonneux Memorial, Somme, France
	MACKAY, William Gordon	McKay	Engineer Sub-Lieutenant	RNR	18/10/1918	Portsmouth Naval Memorial, Hampshire, England
1877	MACKENZIE, Donald		Private	AIF	27/11/1915	Shrapnel Valley Cemetery, Gallipoli, Turkey
	MACKENZIE, Ian Kenneth	Ian Kenneth McKenzie	Officer Cadet	MM	19/11/1917	Tower Hill Memorial, Trinity Square, London, England
437	MACKIE, Charlie		Private	AIF	2/05/1915	Walker's Ridge Cemetery, Gallipoli, Turkey
	MACKIE, James		Chief Steward	MM	19/11/1917	Melcombe Regis Cemetery, Weymouth, Dorset, England
	MACKINNON, Neil Hugh		Master	MM	23/01/1918	Tower Hill Memorial, Trinity Square, London, England
818	MACMILLAN, Edward	Edward McMillan	Private	AIF	29/04/1918	Caestre Military Cemetery, Nord, France
	MADGIN, Sydney George		Private	British Army	24/05/1915	Hazebrouck Communal Cemetery, Hazebrouck, Pas-de-Calais, France
429122	MADILL, John		Private	COEF	15/08/1917	Rue-du-Bois Military Cemetery, Fleurbaix, Pas-de-Calais, France

	MAHONEY, Brian Gerald		2nd Lieutenant	RAF	3/09/1918	West Brompton Cemetery, London, England
	MAIDLOW, John Southern		Major	British Army	28/08/1914	Mons (Bergen) Communal Cemetery, Hainaut, Belgium
3137A	MAIDMENT, Horace		Private	AIF	19/07/1916	V. C. Corner Australian Cemetery and Memorial, Fromelles, France
74	MAITLAND, Frederick Albert		Sapper	AIF	19/05/1919	Dunedin North Cemetery, New Zealand
3823	MAITLAND, Harold George Musgrave		Private	AIF	16/04/1918	Villers-Bretonneux Memorial, Somme, France
2085	MANSEL, George Victor		Private	COEF	30/01/1917	Victoria (Ross Bay) Cemetery, British Columbia, Canada
6492	MANSON, William Braithwaite		Private	British Army	1/07/1916	Thiepval Memorial, Somme, France
286	MAPLESDEN, Hector		Corporal	AIF	3/12/1916	Bernafay Wood British Cemetery, Montauban, France
401	MARSH, Francis Jules		Private	AIF	25/01/1921	Karrakatta General Cemetery, Perth, Western Australia
	MARSHALL, Adam Houliston		Cadet	MM	19/11/1917	Tower Hill Memorial, Trinity Square, London, England
1506	MARSHALL, Frederick Michael	Frederick Michel Marshall	Private	AIF	24/01/1917	Rookwood Necropolis, Sydney, New South Wales, Australia
6605	MARSHALL, George		Private	AIF	24/11/1917	Étaples Military Cemetery, Pas-de-Calais, France
6600	MARSHALL, John Francis		Private	AIF	5/05/1917	Vraucourt Copse Cemetery, Vaulx-Vraucourt, France
	MARSHALL, John Willoughby Hadfield		2nd Lieutenant	British Army	21/03/1918	Arras Memorial, Pas-de-Calais, France
	MARSHALL, Robert Joseph		Cadet	MM	19/11/1917	Tower Hill Memorial, Trinity Square, London, England
164	MARSHALL, William Armitage		Corporal	AIF	17/04/1918	Villers-Bretonneux Memorial, Somme, France
	MARTIN, Dr Arthur Anderson		Lieutenant	RAMC	17/09/1916	St Pierre Cemetery, Amiens, Somme, France
654	MARTIN, Francis Aubrey Dunstan		Private	AIF	30/04/1915	Lone Pine Memorial, Gallipoli, Turkey
	MARTIN, John Anthony		Lieutenant	RNR	6/10/1919	Chatham Naval Memorial, Kent, England
1359	MARTIN, Richard		Private	AIF	28/03/1918	Villers-Bretonneux Memorial, Somme, France
	MARTIN, W. E.		Apprentice	MM	10/03/1917	Tower Hill Memorial, Trinity Square, London, England

7679	MARTYN, Bert Clayton		Driver	AIF	16/08/1916	Basra War Cemetery, Iraq
	MASEFIELD, Robert		Major	British Army	24/10/1914	Ploegstreert Memorial, Hainaut, Belgium
470	MASON, James Lowther		Private	AIF	19/07–30/10/1916	Villers-Bretonneux Memorial, Somme, France
1098	MASON, Walter		Private	AIF	30/11/1918	Hastings Cemetery, Hawke's Bay, New Zealand
	MASSEY, John Hamon		Captain	British Army	27/05/1918	Jonchery-sur-Vesle British Cemetery, Marne, France
	MASSEY, Leon Joseph		Cadet	MM	19/11/1917	Tower Hill Memorial, Trinity Square, London, England
	MASTERS, George		2nd Lieutenant	RFC	3/04/1917	Arras Memorial, Pas-de-Calais, France
2006558	MASTON, Harry Garfield		Sapper	COEF	31/08/1918	Aubigny Communal Cemetery Extension, Somme, France
306	MATHESON, Harry Mackay		Private, 2nd Lieutenant	RFC	24–26/12/1917	Gaza War Cemetery, Israel
	MATHESON, Kenneth Ronald	Kenneth Ronald Mathieson	Lieutenant	British Army	1/11/1914	Menin Gate Memorial, Ypres, West-Vlaanderen, Belgium
	MATHESON, Ronald Tracey		Lieutenant	SA Army	27/04/1915	Gibeon Station Cemetery, Namibia
701	MATHIESON, Richard James		Private	AIF	25/04/1915	Lone Pine Memorial, Gallipoli, Turkey
20022	MATHIESON, Thomas Alexander		Acting Corporal	British Army	17/04/1918	Tyne Cot Memorial, West-Vlaanderen, Belgium
1366	MATHIESON, William Douglas		Sapper	AIF	5/12/1915	Alexandria (Chatby) Military and War Memorial Cemetery, Egypt
2154	MATTHEWS, John James		Sergeant	AIF	10/12/1916	Villers-Bretonneux Memorial, Somme, France
972	MATTHEWS, Roy Marden Howard		Sergeant	AIF	23/09/1917	Menin Gate Memorial, Ypres, West-Vlaanderen, Belgium
1157	MAULE, Charles		Lance Corporal	AIF	4/05/1917	Villers-Bretonneux Memorial, Somme, France
	MAY, Charles Campbell		Captain	British Army	1/07/1916	Dantzig Alley British Cemetery, Mametz, Somme, France
4213	MAYNE, William Constantine		Corporal	AIF	14/02/1917	Hersin Communal Cemetery Extension, Pas-de-Calais, France
957	MCAHAN, James		Private	AIF	20/05/1915	Shell Green Cemetery, Gallipoli, Turkey
4284	MCANNALLEY, James Storey		Private	AIF	16/11/1916	Villers-Bretonneux Memorial, Somme, France
1360	MCARA, James Monteith		Private	AIF	8/08/1915	Lone Pine Memorial, Gallipoli, Turkey

4856	MCARDELL, Phillip Harris Oldfield		Private	AIF	15/07/1917	Mud Corner Cemetery, Comines-Warneton, Hainaut, Belgium
	MCARTHUR, James		Engineer	MM	20/10/1916	Tower Hill Memorial, Trinity Square, London, England
1362A	MCAULEY, Michael Francis		Private	AIF	1–31/07/1915	Lone Pine Memorial, Gallipoli, Turkey
	MCBARNET, Edward James		Lieutenant Commander	RNR	16/08/1915	Alexandria (Chatby) Military and War Memorial Cemetery, Egypt
2169	MCCLURE, Sidney Robert Le Messurier	Sydney Robert Le Messurier McClure	Private	AIF	7–12/08/1915	Lone Pine Memorial, Gallipoli, Turkey
3698	MCCONNELL, Ambrose Edward		Private	AIF	30/09/1918	Doingt Communal Cemetery Extension, Somme, France
464225	MCCULLOUGH, John		Private	COEF	11/11/1916	Vimy Memorial, Pas-de-Calais, France
3181	MCDERMOTT, Thomas		Private	AIF	25/04/1918	Villers-Bretonneux Memorial, Somme, France
	MCDONALD, Alister Christian			French Foreign Legion	?/03/1915	
1872	MCDONALD, David John		Lance Corporal	AIF	4/04/1918	Villers-Bretonneux Memorial, Somme, France
10196	MCDONALD, Donald James		Driver	AIF	11/02/1919	Charleroi Communal Cemetery, Hainaut, Belgium
6956	MCDOWALL, Stewart Arthur		Private	AIF	26/09/1917	Menin Gate Memorial, Ypres, West-Vlaanderen, Belgium
3560	MCFARLANE, Wallace Askew		Lance Corporal	AIF	20/09/1917	Menin Gate Memorial, Ypres, West-Vlaanderen, Belgium
630	MCGAFFIN, Robert John		Private	AIF	8/08/1915	Lone Pine Memorial, Gallipoli, Turkey
3140	MCGAHAN, Thomas Bernard		Private	AIF	11/08/1918	Daours Communal Cemetery Extension, Somme, France
4981	MCGARRIGLE, James Patrick		Driver	AIF	3/07/1916	Rue-Petillon Military Cemetery, Fleurbaix, Pas-de-Calais, France
660	MCGILL, Thomas		Lance Corporal	AIF	10/08/1915	Lone Pine Memorial, Gallipoli, Turkey
1721	MCGLASHAN, Edward		Private	AIF	14/09/1916	Railway Dugouts Burial Ground, West-Vlaanderen, Belgium
477639	MCGRATH, Charles Unsworth		Private	COEF	8/10/1916	Vimy Memorial, Pas-de-Calais, France
713	MCHOLM, Alfred		Corporal	AIF	2/05/1915	Lone Pine Memorial, Gallipoli, Turkey
6589	MCILWRAITH, George		Private	AIF	7/07/1918	Crouy British Cemetery, Crouy-sur-Somme, France

1565, 3659	MCINTOSH, Neil		Private	AIF	20/11/1918	Tidworth Military Cemetery, Wiltshire, England
	MCINTYRE, James Shattock		Second Engineer	MM	2/02/1918	Tower Hill Memorial, Trinity Square, London, England
4058	MCKAY, Alexander Patrick	Alexander Forbes McKay	Private	AIF	25/03/1917	Bapaume Australian Cemetery, Pas-de-Calais, France
	MCKAY, George		Lieutenant	AIF	6/05/1917	Grevillers British Cemetery, Pas-de-Calais, France
2474	MCKAY, Norman		Trooper	AIF	20/08/1917	Cairo War Memorial Cemetery, Egypt
6763	MCKAY, Robert		Private	SA Army	9/04/1917	Cabaret-Rouge British Cemetery, Souchez, Pas-de-Calais, France
5441	MCKAY, William John		Private	AIF	24/09/1917	Menin Road South Military Cemetery, West-Vlaanderen, Belgium
	MCKELVEY, Charles James		Engineer Sub-Lieutenant	RNR	3/08/1916	Portsmouth Naval Memorial, Hampshire, England
790307	MCKENZIE, Archibald		Private	COEF	3/03/1917	Villers Station Cemetery, Pas-de-Calais, France
6869	MCKENZIE, Colin Campbell		Lance Corporal	AIF	10/08/1918	Heath Cemetery, Harbonnières, Somme, France
620	MCKENZIE, Walter Ray	Walter Rae McKenzie	Private	AIF	12/08/1916	Warloy-Baillon Communal Cemetery Extension, Somme, France
2705	MCKINNON, Alexander		Private	AIF	11/04/1917	Villers-Bretonneux Memorial, Somme, France
1655	MCKINNON, Ian Godfrey		Bombardier	AIF	11/08/1915	Lone Pine Memorial, Gallipoli, Turkey
859394	MCKINNON, Robert Roderick		Lance Corporal	COEF	8/08/1918	Vimy Memorial, Pas-de-Calais, France
3220	MCLAREN, John Henry		Private	AIF	19/10/1917	Menin Gate Memorial, Ypres, West-Vlaanderen, Belgium
925359	MCLATCHIE, Frederick William		Private	COEF	11/11/1917	Passchendaele New British Cemetery, West-Vlaanderen, Belgium
535	MCLEAN, Donald		Trooper	AIF	29/08/1915	Lone Pine Memorial, Gallipoli, Turkey
5935	MCLEAN, John Murdock	John Murdoch McLean	Corporal	AIF	3/05/1917	Villers-Bretonneux Memorial, Somme, France
354	MCLEAN, John Raymund		Private	AIF	27/04/1915	Quinn's Post Cemetery, Gallipoli, Turkey
NZ1210	MCLEAN, Percy		Ordinary Seaman	RNR	9/03/1919	Bordeaux (Rue Judaïque) Protestant Cemetery, Gironde, France
368	MCLENNAN, Alexander		Private	AIF	29/07/1916	Villers-Bretonneux Memorial, Somme, France

301326	MCLENNAN, Murdoch		Staff Sergeant	British Army	12/05/1920	Waikaraka Park Cemetery, Auckland, New Zealand
	MCNAB, Dr Angus	Angus MacNab	Surgeon Captain	British Army	1/11/1914	Menin Gate Memorial, Ypres, West-Vlaanderen, Belgium
	MCNEILL, Alan Gordon (MID, MC)		Major	British Army	10/01/1917	Lijssenthoek Military Cemetery, West-Vlaanderen, Belgium
394	MCNEIL, James Donald George		Private	AIF	14/05/1915	Lone Pine Memorial, Gallipoli, Turkey
15567	MCNEILL, Roy Burgoyne		Gunner	AIF	13/09/1918	Hamburg Cemetery, Germany
1186	MCRAE, John David		Trooper	AIF	9/08/1916	Kantara War Memorial Cemetery, Egypt
2171	MCVEA, Jack Albert	John Albert McVea	Private	AIF	10/07/1918	Adelaide (West Terrace) Cemetery, South Australia, Australia
405	MCWHINNEY, George		Sergeant	AIF	11/04/1917	Villers-Bretonneux Memorial, Somme, France
451	MCWHIRTER, Samuel George		Sergeant Major	AIF	29/08/1915	Lone Pine Memorial, Gallipoli, Turkey
	MELLAND, Edward Guy		Lieutenant	British Army	1/07/1915	New Irish Farm Cemetery, West-Vlaanderen, Belgium
39	MELVILLE, Charles William		Private	AIF	8/05/1915	Helles Memorial, Gallipoli, Turkey
	MENZIES, Alexander Lawrence		Lieutenant	British Army	20/09/1916	St Sever Cemetery, Rouen, Seine-Maritime, France
923	MERSON, Henry Nelson	Henry Nelson	Private	AIF	29/07/1916	Villers-Bretonneux Memorial, Somme, France
10984	MERTON, Charles Henry Trischler	Charles Henry Frischler Merton	Sapper	AIF	9/06/1917	Strand Military Cemetery, Hainaut, Belgium
234	MERWIN, Stephen Francis		Private	AIF	21/06/1915	Manchester Southern Cemetery, England
	MESSENGER, Henry Frederick Roy		Lieutenant	British Army	22/08/1915	Helles Memorial, Gallipoli, Turkey
2933	MICHAEL, Ernest Augustus Mowbray		Private	AIF	31/07/1916	Keighley (Morton) Cemetery, Yorkshire, England
40019	MIDDLEDITCH, Frederick Hugh	Frederick Hugh Middelditch	Private	AIF	11/01/1918	Orbost Cemetery, Victoria, Australia
530	MILES, John William		Private	AIF	2/05/1915	Lone Pine Memorial, Gallipoli, Turkey
529	MILES, Thomas Richard		Private	AIF	2/05/1915	Lone Pine Memorial, Gallipoli, Turkey
	MILLAR, Audley Charles Hyde		Captain	British Army	15/10/1917	Menin Road South Military Cemetery, West-Vlaanderen, Belgium
	MILLAR, Charles Adolphus	Charles Adolphus Miller	First Engineer	MM	21/04/1918	Tower Hill Memorial, Trinity Square, London, England

	MILLER, Alan	Alen Miller	2nd Lieutenant	British Army	14/10/1916	Dartmoor Cemetery, Bécordel-Bécourt, Somme, France
1354	MILLER, Leonard William		Private	AIF	19/05/1915	5th Battalion Parade Ground Cemetery, Gallipoli, Turkey
14977	MILLER, Leslie Murray		Driver	AIF	5/04/1918	Warloy-Baillon Communal Cemetery Extension, Somme, France
	MILLINGTON, Robert Perrett Taipo		Wireless Operator	MM	19/11/1917	Tower Hill Memorial, Trinity Square, London, England
1969	MILLS, Jack Leslie		Gunner	AIF	26/09/1916	Railway Dugouts Burial Ground, West-Vlaanderen, Belgium
	MILLWARD, Kenneth Henry		Flight-Sub-Lieutenant	RNAS	7/07/1917	Pont-du-Hem Military Cemetery, La Gorgue, Nord, France
	MITCHELL, William George		2nd Lieutenant	RFC	23/03/1918	Bandon Hill Cemetery, Surrey, England
5894	MITCHELL, William Lyle		Private	AIF	6/10/1917	Lijssenthoek Military Cemetery, West-Vlaanderen, Belgium
507	MOFFLIN, William Harold		Corporal	AIF	16/06/1915	Ari Burnu Cemetery, Gallipoli, Turkey
4205	MONAGHAN, Walter Charles	Walter Charles Monoghan	Private	AIF	28/07/1920	Rookwood Necropolis, Sydney, New South Wales, Australia
4015	MONK, Ernest Wieland		Private	British Army	12/03/1916	Lievin Communal Cemetery Extension, France
2723	MONSEN, Johannes Christian	John Christian Monson, John Christian Monsen	Corporal	AIF	15/09/1916	Netley Military Cemetery, Netley, Hampshire, England
2497530	MONSON, Elwin Norman		Private	COEF	20/12/1918	Park Island Cemetery, Napier, New Zealand
	MONTGOMERY, Albert Barr		Captain	British Army	17/08/1917	Brandhoek New Military Cemetery No. 3, West-Vlaanderen, Belgium
2715	MOORE, Frederick William Wallace		Private	AIF	30/05/1916	Rue-du-Bois Military Cemetery, Fleurbaix, Pas-de-Calais, France
324	MOORE, Oswald Walter		Sergeant	AIF	24/05/1915	Lone Pine Memorial, Gallipoli, Turkey
1740	MOORE, Thomas Ernest Llewellyn		Gunner	AIF	15/08/1915	Lone Pine Memorial, Gallipoli, Turkey
	MOORE, William Ernest (MC)		Captain	British Army	14/11/1917	Tyne Cot Memorial, West-Vlaanderen, Belgium
826949	MORAN, Otto Tobias		Private	COEF	29/09/1918	Drummond Cemetery, Raillencourt, Nord, France
271	MORELL, Charles		Private	AIF	25–29/04/1915	Lone Pine Memorial, Gallipoli, Turkey
234721	MORETON, John Thomas		Seaman	RN	10/02/1915	Heliopolis (Aden) Memorial, Cairo, Egypt

1029	MORGAN, Charles		Sergeant	AIF	23/08/1918	Heath Cemetery, Harbonnières, Somme, France
7285	MORIARTY, John Joseph		Corporal	AIF	8/08/1918	Cerisy-Gailly Military Cemetery, Somme, France
4499	MORRIS, Harry Agnew		Private	AIF	14/11/1916	Villers-Bretonneux Memorial, Somme, France
2195	MORRIS, Henry Woodfield		Private	AIF	18/08/1916	Villers-Bretonneux Memorial, Somme, France
22877, 25465	MORRIS, Thomas Herbert		Private	British Army	2/11/1916	Thiepval Memorial, Somme, France
	MORRISON, Arnold		2nd Lieutenant	British Army	26/10/1917	Tyne Cot Memorial, West-Vlaanderen, Belgium
	MORRISON, James McGregor (MC)		2nd Lieutenant	WAFF	15/02/1919	Zaria European Cemetery, Nigeria
3691	MORRISON, Joseph		Private	AIF	2/04/1917	Lebucquière Communal Cemetery Extension, Pas-de-Calais, France
952, 1980	MORRISON, William Maver		Third Engineer, Private	MM	12/12/1917	Tower Hill Memorial, Trinity Square, London, England
1367	MORSHEAD, Herbert Edward Dillon		Private	AIF	9–10/05/1915	Lone Pine Memorial, Gallipoli, Turkey
497	MOSES, Hamilton Leslie		Lance Corporal	AIF	31/07/1917	Menin Gate Memorial, Ypres, West-Vlaanderen, Belgium
	MOSS, John		2nd Lieutenant	AIF	19/07/1918	Borre British Cemetery, Nord, France
	MOWATT, Douglas Lodder		Fourth Engineer Officer	MM	26/06/1918	Tower Hill Memorial, Trinity Square, London, England
5076, 23473	MOWBRAY, George	George Mobray	Corporal	British Army	18/11/1917	Tyne Cot Memorial, West-Vlaanderen, Belgium
2812	MOYNA, Patrick John		Private	AIF	9/04/1918	Villers-Bretonneux Memorial, Somme, France
1244	MUIR, Frederick Bailey		Private	AIF	26/06/1920	Rookwood Necropolis, Sydney, New South Wales, Australia
287	MUIR, James McLean		Trooper	British Army	10/10/1915	La Plus Douve Farm Cemetery, Hainaut, Belgium
3897	MUIR, Thomas Mintaro		Private	AIF	1/03/1918	Spoilbank Cemetery, West-Vlaanderen, Belgium
755	MULHOLLAND, John Stewart		Lance Corporal	AIF	6/08/1916	AIF Burial Ground, Flers, Somme, France
464	MULLIGAN, Leo		Private	AIF	27/04/1915	Lone Pine Memorial, Gallipoli, Turkey
995	MULLIN, Albert		Private	AIF	20/05/1915	6th Battalion Parade Ground Cemetery, Gallipoli, Turkey

825	MULLINS, Melville Ernest	Michael Mullen, Michael Mullin, Michael Gunning	Private	AIF	21/04/1918	Mont Huon Military Cemetery, Le Tréport, Seine-Maritime, France
	MULVENNA, John		Able Seaman	MM	26/06/1918	Tower Hill Memorial, Trinity Square, London, England
6291	MUMBY, John Robert George		Private	AIF	11/04/1917	Villers-Bretonneux Memorial, Somme, France
	MUNRO, Frederick John		Lieutenant	British Army	11/08/1917	Duhallow ADS Cemetery, West-Vlaanderen, Belgium
1030	MUNRO, Philip Henry		Private	AIF	22/08/1915	Lone Pine Memorial, Gallipoli, Turkey
17387, 32553	MUNSON, Job Lushanus		Private	British Army	5/05/1918	Hertfordshire County Asylum, England
1085	MUNSTER, John Thomas		Sapper	AIF	24/08/1917	Lapugnoy Military Cemetery, Pas-de-Calais, France
2843	MURDOCH, George Johnston		Private	AIF	13/10/1917	Lijssenthoek Military Cemetery, West-Vlaanderen, Belgium
	MURDOCH, James Hunter George		Second Lieutenant	British Army	3/07/1916	Norfolk Cemetery, Bécordel-Bécourt, France
	MURGATROYD, Hugh Lester		Captain	British Army	27/09/1918	Lebucquière Communal Cemetery Extension, Pas-de-Calais, France
	MURPHY, Francis George		Deck Hand	MM Reserve	23/10/1918	Haslar Royal Naval Cemetery, Hampshire, England
1653	MURPHY, James Ernest		Private	AIF	23/05/1915	Alexandria (Chatby) Military and War Memorial Cemetery, Egypt
50801	MURR, William Henry		Lieutenant	COEF	30/10/1917	Menin Gate Memorial, Ypres, West-Vlaanderen, Belgium
	MURRAY, Allan Chamberlain		Third Engineer	MM	16/06/1918	Tower Hill Memorial, Trinity Square, London, England
J82097	MURRAY, Archibald		Ordinary Seaman	RN	24/10/1919	Plymouth Naval Memorial, Devon, England
3407	MURRAY, Clarence James		Private	AIF	27/08/1917	Sainte-Marie Cemetery, Le Havre, France
77	MURRAY, Joseph Henry		Sergeant	AIF	9/01/1917	Kantara War Memorial Cemetery, Egypt
	MURRAY, Norman Cairns		Captain	British Army	30/06/1916	Hébuterne Military Cemetery, Pas-de-Calais, France
3256	NADEN, Nigel Christopher		Private	AIF	9/05/1918	Méricourt-l'Abbé Communal Cemetery Extension, Somme, France
2795A	NAGEL, John Frederick Claus		Corporal	AIF	26/03/1918	Oxford Road Cemetery, West-Vlaanderen, Belgium

	NAPPER, Albert Edward John		2nd Lieutenant	AIF	31/08/1918	Péronne Communal Cemetery Extension, Somme, France
628983	NASH, Edward		Private	COEF	6/11/1917	Menin Gate Memorial, Ypres, West-Vlaanderen, Belgium
391	NAYLOR, John Jogle	Hoani Te Okoro Wineera	Lance Corporal	AIF	11/02/1918	Trois Arbres Cemetery, Steenwerck, Nord, France
	NEALE, Richard Raymond		First Officer	MM	30/05/1918	Tower Hill Memorial, Trinity Square, London, England
1634	NEILL, John Harold		Private	AIF	19/08/1918	Heath Cemetery, Harbonnières, Somme, France
	NEILL, Lyonel Clare Fyans		Air Mechanic 3rd Class	RFC	30/10/1917	Brookwood 1914–1918 Memorial, Surrey, England
	NEILSEN, Peter	Peter Neilson	Lieutenant	RAF	18/06/1918	Heath Cemetery, Harbonnières, Somme, France
	NELSON, Beresford Joseph	Beresford Nohally Nelson	2nd Lieutenant	AIF	19/07/1916	V. C. Corner Australian Cemetery and Memorial, Fromelles, France
728	NELSON, Henry Oscar		Private	AIF	20/07/1916	V. C. Corner Australian Cemetery and Memorial, Fromelles, France
2753	NEWMAN, Henry		Private	AIF	10/05/1917	Grevillers British Cemetery, Pas-de-Calais, France
	NEWMAN, Reuben McCarthy		2nd Lieutenant	Indian Army	23/11/1918	Karachi 1914–1918 War Memorial, Sindh, Pakistan
EA2082	NEWSHAM, Richmond Harold		Engineer Lieutenant	RNR	28/09/1918	Hartlepool (Stranton) Cemetery, Durham, England
	NICCOL, George McLaughlan	Tally Niccol	Trooper/ Captain	British Army	30/10/1918	Wandsworth (Putney Vale) Cemetery and Crematorium, London, England
	NICHOL, Alexander John		Chief Officer	MM	26/06/1918	Tower Hill Memorial, Trinity Square, London, England
	NICHOLS, Cyril Robert		Lieutenant	British Army	23/09/1918	Ruyaulcourt Military Cemetery, Pas-de-Calais, France
	NICHOLS, Walter Harry		Major	British Army	15/10/1915	Niederzwehren Cemetery, Hessen, Germany
	NICOL, Hector		Lieutenant	AFC	16/10/1918	Stratford-sub-Castle (St Lawrence) Churchyard, Wiltshire, England
2394	NICOL, John Littlejohn		Private	AIF	23/10/1917	Lijssenthoek Military Cemetery, West-Vlaanderen, Belgium
1397, 1308	NOLAN, James Bernard		Private	AIF	25/07/1916	Villers-Bretonneux Memorial, Somme, France

951	NORRIS, John		Sergeant	AIF	10/06/1918	Villers-Bretonneux Memorial, Somme, France
154161	NORTH, John Henry		Private	COEF	1/03/1916	Shorncliffe Military Cemetery, Kent, United Kingdom
5414	NORTON, Wilfred		Private	AIF	10/06/1918	Villers-Bretonneux Memorial, Somme, France
5069, 352104	NUGENT, Francis Joseph		Corporal	British Army	2/12/1917	St Sever Cemetery Extension, Rouen, Seine-Maritime, France
1467	NUTTALL, Frank (MC, DFC)		Captain	RAF	18/09/1920	Tehran War Cemetery, Iran
15876	O'BRIEN, Hezekiah Gordon		Corporal	British Army	23/03/1918	Mont Huon Military Cemetery, Le Tréport, Seine-Maritime, France
975	O'CONNOR, Roderick		Corporal	AIF	15/04/1917	Villers-Bretonneux Memorial, Somme, France
2217	O'CONNOR, Thomas		Private	AIF	8/01/1917	Bulls Road Cemetery, Flers, France
5389	O'CONNOR, Thomas		Private	AIF	8/06/1918	Méricourt-l'Abbé Communal Cemetery Extension, Somme, France
2487	O'DONOGHUE, Henry Patrick		Private	AIF	28/08/1918	Villers-Bretonneux Memorial, Somme, France
1803	O'DONOGHUE, James Maurice		Private	AIF	4/09/1915	East Mudros Military Cemetery, Greece
13370	OGILVIE, William Edgar		Lance Corporal	COEF	25/04/1915	Menin Gate Memorial, Ypres, West-Vlaanderen, Belgium
	OGILVIE-GRANT, James (11th Earl of Seafield)	James Ogilvie Grant Seafield	Captain	British Army	12/11/1915	Lijssenthoek Military Cemetery, West-Vlaanderen, Belgium
54211	O'GRADY, Thomas		Stoker	RNR	3/03/1915	Queensferry Cemetery, West Lothian, Scotland
1260	O'HARA, William Henry		Sergeant	AIF	4/10/1918	Tincourt New British Cemetery, Somme, France
3888	OLDFIELD, Arthur William		Private	AIF	10/08/1918	Villers-Bretonneux Memorial, Somme, France
1154	O'LEARY, Daniel Cornelius		Sergeant	AIF	10/07/1917	Strand Military Cemetery, Hainaut, Belgium
945	O'LEARY, John		Trooper	AIF	11/11/1915	Embarkation Pier Cemetery, Gallipoli, Turkey
1397, 6179	OLIVER, Alfred Arthur		Private	AIF	20/09/1917	Birr Cross Roads Cemetery, West-Vlaanderen, Belgium
4190	OLLIVER, Oswald Thomas		Private	AIF	20/09/1917	Menin Gate Memorial, Ypres, West-Vlaanderen, Belgium
932	O'NEILL, Herbert Frank		Sergeant	AIF	21/09/1917	Menin Gate Memorial, Ypres, West-Vlaanderen, Belgium

	ORBELL, Ivan Douglas Scott		2nd Lieutenant	British Army	25/10/1914	Le Touret Memorial, Pas-de-Calais, France
667	O'REILLY, Fleming Pinkston		Captain	COEF	27/09/1918	Bucquoy Road Cemetery, Ficheux, Pas-de-Calais, France
	ORMOND, Alexander		2nd Lieutenant	British Army	30/09/1916	Thiepval Memorial, Somme, France
	O'RORKE, Dennis Clifford		Captain	British Army	24/03/1918	Pozières Memorial, Somme, France
2200	ORR, Alfred Charles		Private	AIF	9/12/1919	Brighton General Cemetery, Victoria, Australia
164	PAGE, James Delahunty		Sapper	AIF	21/09/1916	Railway Dugouts Burial Ground, West-Vlaanderen, Belgium
	PARK, Robert		Captain	AIF	26/09/1917	Menin Gate Memorial, Ypres, West-Vlaanderen, Belgium
	PARKER, Cyril Edmund		Lieutenant	British Army	1/01/1915	Le Touret Memorial, Pas-de-Calais, France
877	PARKER, Harry Kelvin		Private	AIF	7/06/1917	Menin Gate Memorial, Ypres, West-Vlaanderen, Belgium
	PARKER, Jeffery Wimpris (MRCS, LRCP, DPH)		Lieutenant	British Army	7/08/1915	Helles Memorial, Gallipoli, Turkey
6080	PARKES, William George		Private	AIF	13/08/1918	Vignacourt British Cemetery, Somme, France
	PARSONS, Forrest Gale		2nd Lieutenant	RFC	16/10/1916	Arras Flying Services Memorial, Pas-de-Calais, France
290	PARTRIDGE, Edwin	Edward Plummer	Private	AIF	29/04/1915	Lone Pine Memorial, Gallipoli, Turkey
1511	PASCO, Merlin Owen		Sapper	AIF	6/08/1918	La Neuvelle British Cemetery, Corbie, Somme, France
16564	PATCHETT, Albert George	Alfred George Patchett	Private	British Army	15/04/1917	Mikra Memorial, Greece
	PATTERSON, Nolan Tweedale		Lieutenant	COEF	1/06/1916	Lijssenthoek Military Cemetery, West-Vlaanderen, Belgium
	PAUL, Carrick Stewart		Lieutenant	AFC	22/01/1919	Chatby Memorial, Egypt
6830	PAYNE, James		Private	AIF	21/09/1917	Menin Gate Memorial, Ypres, West-Vlaanderen, Belgium
MB984, 31/281	PEACOCK, James Ernest		Chief Motor Mechanic	RNVR Auxiliary Patrol	22/02/1920	Waipukurau Cemetery, Hawke's Bay, New Zealand
	PEARCE, Nathaniel Arthur	Neil Pearce	Lieutenant	British Army	25/11/1917	Trescault Communal Cemetery, Pas-de-Calais, France
6849	PEARSALL, Arthur McBain		Private	AIF	30/09/1917	Huts Cemetery, Ypres, West-Vlaanderen, Belgium
954	PEED, William Arthur		Sergeant	AIF	29/03/1918	Damascus Commonwealth War Cemetery, Syria

1996	PELVIN, Bruce Fawthrope		Corporal	AIF	4/09/1916	Villers-Bretonneux Memorial, Somme, France
	PEMBER-REEVES, Fabian	Fabian Pember Reeves	Flight Lieutenant	RNAS	6/06/1917	Arras Flying Services Memorial, Pas-de-Calais, France
4345	PERCIVAL, Darcy		Private	AIF	22/08/1916	Villers-Bretonneux Memorial, Somme, France
6336	PERRY, John		Private	AIF	19/06/1917	Hamburg Cemetery, Hamburg, Germany
	PETERSEN, Frederick		Fireman and Trimmer	MM	7/02/1917	Tower Hill Memorial, Trinity Square, London, England
182785	PHILLIPS, George		Chief Petty Officer	RN	25/09/1915	Heliopolis (Aden) Memorial, Cairo, Egypt
	PHILLIPS, Henry		Ship's Baker	MM	?/9/1918	
11594	PHILLIPS, Samuel		Gunner	AIF	26/02/1917	Dernacourt Communal Cemetery Extension, Somme, France
727	PICKUP, William John		Private	AIF	19/05/1915	Shrapnel Valley Cemetery, Gallipoli, Turkey
	PILKINGTON, Stanley Howard		Lieutenant	AFC	24/10/1917	Brookwood Military Cemetery, Surrey, England
2972	PILKINGTON, Frederick		Private	AIF	26/09/1917	Menin Gate Memorial, Ypres, West-Vlaanderen, Belgium
	PINCKNEY, John William	Jack Pinckney	Trooper/ Lieutenant	British Army	11/04/1918	Bailleul Road East Cemetery, St Laurent-Blangy, Pas-de-Calais, France
3857	PINEAHA, Paturoa		Private	AIF	5/05/1916	Brewery Orchard Cemetery, Bois-Grenier, Nord, France
2176	POHATU, Karenema	Robert Stone	Private	AIF	26/04/1915	Quinn's Post Cemetery, Gallipoli, Turkey
812113	POLLOCK, Robert Scott		Greaser	MM Reserve	19/03/1918	Plymouth Naval Memorial, Devon, England
3113	POOLE, Albert Robert		Private	AIF	25/04/1918	Adelaide Cemetery, Villers-Bretonneux, France
	POOLE, William James Sturgiss Grove		Lieutenant	AIF	9/08/1918	Heath Cemetery, Harbonnières, Somme, France
1445	POPPLEWELL, Cecil		Private	AIF	19/05/1915	Lone Pine Cemetery, Gallipoli, Turkey
	PORTER, George Basil Lee (MC)		Lieutenant	British Army	8/10/1918	Honnechy British Cemetery, Nord, France
2765	PORTER, Herbert Bishop		Lance Corporal	AIF	14/08/1916	Villers-Bretonneux Memorial, Somme, France
6316	PORTER, William Alexander		Private	AIF	25/02/1917	AIF Burial Ground, Flers, Somme, France
5614	POTTER, Peter Stedmand	Peter Johnson	Private	AIF	26/03/1917	Villers-Bretonneux Memorial, Somme, France

3886	POUNDS, Harold John		Private	AIF	24/12/1916	Villers-Bretonneux Memorial, Somme, France
882	POUPARD, Leonard Bryant		Private	AIF	6/11/1917	Menin Gate Memorial, Ypres, West-Vlaanderen, Belgium
	POWELL, George Aubyn		2nd Lieutenant	RFC	7/12/1916	Bishop's Hatfield (St Luke) Churchyard, Hertfordshire, England
	POWELL, William Oliver		Stoker Petty Officer	RN	26/11/1914	Portsmouth Naval Memorial, Hampshire, England
	PRATT, Albert Ernest		2nd Lieutenant	AIF	19/07/1916	Fromelles (Pheasant Wood) Military Cemetery, Nord, France
836, 319	PRICE, Arthur Albert		Private	AIF	27/04/1917	Sydney (Waverley) General Cemetery, New South Wales, Australia
487535	PRICE, John		Private	COEF	5/01/1917	Écoivres Military Cemetery, Pas-de-Calais, France
	PROUDFOOT, David		Greaser	MM	31/07/1915	Tower Hill Memorial, Trinity Square, London, England
	PROUDFOOT, John Frederick		Cadet	MM	19/11/1917	Tower Hill Memorial, Trinity Square, London, England
	PULLING, Edward Laston		Flight Lieutenant	RNAS	2/03/1917	Great Yarmouth (Caister) Cemetery, Norfolk, England
3087	PYBUS, Arthur Coventry Leroux		Private	AIF	19–20/07/1916	V. C. Corner Australian Cemetery and Memorial, Fromelles, France
3616	PYE, William Leslie		Private	AIF	21/10/1917	Menin Gate Memorial, Ypres, West-Vlaanderen, Belgium
1372	QUINN, John	Patrick Joseph Quinn	Private	AIF	14/04/1918	Villers-Bretonneux Memorial, Somme, France
2791	QUINN, Joseph	Joseph Thomson	Private	AIF	7/06/1917	Menin Gate Memorial, Ypres, West-Vlaanderen, Belgium
938	RAEBURN, Thomas Walter Henry		Private	AIF	27/04/1915	Lone Pine Memorial, Gallipoli, Turkey
23270	RALSTON, Guy Walter		Gunner	AIF	4/10/1917	Lijssenthoek Military Cemetery, West-Vlaanderen, Belgium
	RAMSAY, Alex McKinley	Alexander McKinlay Ramsay	Cadet	MM	19/11/1917	Tower Hill Memorial, Trinity Square, London, England
	RAMSAY, Stuart (DSO)		Captain	British Army	2/06/1917	St Quentin Cabaret Military Cemetery, West-Vlaanderen, Belgium
582	RASMUSSEN, Allen Christian		Private	AIF	4/09/1915	Cairo War Memorial Cemetery, Egypt
2674	RASMUSSEN, Charles James Francis		Private	AIF	24/07/1916	Puchevillers British Cemetery, Somme, France

1028	RAWLINS, Glenrowan Edward Champion		Corporal	British Army	11/12/1914	Kandahar Farm Cemetery, West-Vlaanderen, Belgium
	RAWSON, Henry		Pilot 1st Class	MM	28/12/1917	Tower Hill Memorial, Trinity Square, London, England
6575	RAY, Reuben Napier Heath		Private	AIF	19/09/1918	Doingt Communal Cemetery Extension, Somme, France
	RAYMOND, Wynne Dudley		2nd Lieutenant	British Army	26/10/1918	Beirut War Cemetery, Lebanon
L/16894	REA, Jack	John Rea, Jack Reeve	Private	British Army	7/07/1916	Thiepval Memorial, Somme, France
	READ, Lawrence William	Laurence William Read	Lieutenant	British Army	9/12/1916	Thiepval Memorial, Somme, France
3637, 2241	REARDON, Bartholomew John		Trooper	AIF	19/06/1918	Ramleh War Cemetery, Gaza, Israel and Palestine
7474	REARDON, John		Able Seaman	RAN	14/09/1914	Plymouth Naval Memorial, Devon, England
	REED, Percival Francis		Lieutenant	AIF	24/04/1918	Meteren Military Cemetery, Nord, France
266790	REES, Stanley Joseph Lloyd		Private	British Army	31/07/1917	Menin Gate Memorial, Ypres, West-Vlaanderen, Belgium
1409	REES, William Goldney		Private	AIF	4/05/1915	Beach Cemetery, Gallipoli, Turkey
	REEVE, Stanley Thornton Seymour		Lieutenant	COEF	22/08/1917	Aix-Noulette Communal Cemetery Extension, Pas-de-Calais, France
154	REID, Alexander		2nd Lieutenant	AIF	28/02/1917	Villers-Bretonneux Memorial, Somme, France
872	REID, David John		Private	AIF	2/11/1916	Bernafay Wood British Cemetery, Montauban, France
	REID, John Laurie		Lieutenant	RFC	16/07/1916	Couin British Cemetery, Pas-de-Calais, France
	REID, Percy Cargill		2nd Lieutenant	British Army	6/05/1917	Tank Cemetery, Guémappe, Pas-de-Calais, France
	REID, Dr William Douglas		Captain	British Army	5/10/1917	Menin Road South Military Cemetery, West-Vlaanderen, Belgium
	RENDLE, Anthony Darley Russell		2nd Lieutenant	British Army	10/10/1917	Hooge Crater Cemetery, West-Vlaanderen, Belgium
2343	RESTON, Victor Septimus		Private	AIF	22/11/1915	Chatby Memorial, Egypt
3126	REYCRAFT, William Calver		Corporal	AIF	9/08/1918	Villers-Bretonneux Military Cemetery, Somme, France
191	REYNOLDS, Frederick Ralph Austin	Fred Reynolds	Sapper	AIF	25/04/1918	Shrapnel Valley Cemetery, Gallipoli, Turkey
369	RHODES, James	James Percy Wederell, James Percy Wederill	Lance Corporal	AIF	7–12/08/1915	Lone Pine Memorial, Gallipoli, Turkey

	RHODES-MOORHOUSE, William Barnard (VC)		Lieutenant	RFC	27/04/1915	Parnham Private Cemetery, Beaminster, Dorset, England
3794	RICE, John William		Private	AIF	8/09/1919	Brighton General Cemetery, Victoria, Australia
213	RICHARDS, Charles		Driver	AIF	29/07/1916	Delville Wood Cemetery, Longueval, Somme, France
214	RICHARDS, Edward Sydney		Private	AIF	7/11/1915	Embarkation Pier Cemetery, Gallipoli, Turkey
	RICHARDS, Henry Stokes		2nd Lieutenant	RAF	1/08/1918	Shorncliffe Military Cemetery, Kent, United Kingdom
2676	RICHARDSON, Victor Albert		Private	AIF	6/04/1917	Villers-Bretonneux Memorial, Somme, France
19106	RICKARD, Frederick George		Lance Corporal	British Army	21/04/1917	Thiepval Memorial, Somme, France
3515, 203423	RICKETTS, John Mark Walter		Private	British Army	6/05/1917	Alexandria (Hadra) War Memorial Cemetery, Egypt
2960	RIGBY, Thomas		Private	AIF	18/10/1917	Tyne Cot Cemetery, West-Vlaanderen, Belgium
1154	RILEY, John		Private	AIF	20/04/1917	Villers-Bretonneux Memorial, Somme, France
	RITCHIE, John Nevill		2nd Lieutenant	British Army	21/04/1916	Basra Memorial, Iraq
968	ROBERTS, John Meyrick		Private	AIF	19/05/1915	7th Battalion Parade Ground Cemetery, Gallipoli, Turkey
	ROBERTSON, W. H.		Fireman	MM	19/02/1918	Tower Hill Memorial, Trinity Square, London, England
	ROBINSON, Claude Gladstone		2nd Lieutenant	British Army	20/10/1915	Assevillers New British Cemetery, Somme, France
8300	ROBINSON, William Albert	Walter Albert Simmons	Sergeant	British Army	11/07/1917	Boulogne Eastern Cemetery, Pas-de-Calais, France
	ROBSON, William Friend		2nd Lieutenant	British Army	3/05/1917	Jeancourt Communal Cemetery Extension, Aisne, France
474A	ROCKSTROW, Augustus Isidor		Private	AIF	25/09/1917	Lijssenthoek Military Cemetery, West-Vlaanderen, Belgium
5895	RODERIQUE, Nelson Francis Skinner	Nelson Francis Skinner	Private	AIF	20/09/1917	Hooge Crater Cemetery, West-Vlaanderen, Belgium
6601	ROEBUCK, Charles Clement		Sergeant	AIF	2/09/1917	Brookwood Military Cemetery, Surrey, England
10906	ROGERS, F.		Private	SA Army	5/03/1918	Etretat Churchyard Extension, Seine-Maritime, France

13461	ROGERS, Francis Henry		Private	SA Army	7/05/1918	Péronne Communal Cemetery Extension, Somme, France
	ROGERSON, Thomas		Chief Engineer	MM	19/11/1917	Tower Hill Memorial, Trinity Square, London, England
2173	ROLLINS, Edgar		Private	AIF	5/03/1917	AIF Burial Ground, Flers, Somme, France
5761	ROSS, Frank Colin		Private	AIF	25/02/1917	Warlencourt British Cemetery, Pas-de-Calais, France
2865	ROSS, Henry Hassal		Private	AIF	17/07/1917	Trois Arbres Cemetery, Steenwerck, Nord, France
	ROUT, William Owen Nelson		Lieutenant	British Army	25/09/1915	Cambrin Churchyard Extension, Pas-de-Calais, France
695	ROWE, George Thornton		Private	AIF	11/08/1920	Karrakatta General Cemetery, Perth, Western Australia
3627	ROWE, Percy		Private	AIF	15/08/1916	Villers-Bretonneux Memorial, Somme, France
	RUSSELL, Francis Gerald		2nd Lieutenant	RFC	28/01/1917	AIF Burial Ground, Flers, Somme, France
	RUSSELL, Lawrence Dobree		2nd Lieutenant	RFC	2/09/1916	Heilly Station Cemetery, Méricourt-l'Abbé, Somme, France
23090	RUSSELL, Richard (DFC, Croix de Guerre)		Captain	RFC	11/11/1920	New Plymouth, New Zealand
	RUSSELL, Walter Russell		Captain	British Army	23/10/1914	Menin Gate Memorial, Ypres, West-Vlaanderen, Belgium
	RUTLEDGE, George Robert		Engineer-Lieut-Commander	RNR	25/01/1917	Plymouth Naval Memorial, Devon, England
4293	RUTLEDGE, Joseph Ward		Lieutenant	British Army	31/07/1917	Menin Gate Memorial, Ypres, West-Vlaanderen, Belgium
3137	RYAN, James		Private	AIF	25/12/1916	Villers-Bretonneux Memorial, Somme, France
2255	RYAN, William Henry		Private	AIF	15/05/1917	Villers-Bretonneux Memorial, Somme, France
1505	SADLER, Edgar Harold		Private	AIF	31/01/1917	Cite Bonjean Military Cemetery, Armentières, France
4203	SAMSON, Arthur Ronald		Private	AIF	5/11/1916	Warlencourt British Cemetery, Pas-de-Calais, France
267058	SAMUEL, James Elder Adams		Private	British Army	20/09/1917	Tyne Cot Memorial, West-Vlaanderen, Belgium
176987	SANDALLS, Frederick		Chief Petty Officer	RN	16/12/1917	Wellington (Karori) Cemetery, New Zealand
1261	SANDERS, William Edward (VC)		Lieutenant Commander	RNR	14/08/1917	Plymouth Naval Memorial, Devon, England

3666	SANDERSON, Benjamin		Private	AIF	23/10/1917	Aeroplane Cemetery, West-Vlaanderen, Belgium
	SANKEY, Thomas		2nd Lieutenant	British Army	13/12/1917	Longuenesse (St Omer) Souvenir Cemetery, Pas-de-Calais, France
719	SANSON, David		Sergeant	AIF	31/07/1916	Étaples Military Cemetery, Pas-de-Calais, France
1339	SAUNDERS, Fred Edward Richard		Lance Corporal	AIF	24/07/1916	Puchevillers British Cemetery, Somme, France
370	SAVAGE, Samuel	Haami Savage	Lance Corporal	AIF	4/10/1917	Menin Gate Memorial, Ypres, West-Vlaanderen, Belgium
	SAYLE, George Randall Fysh		Lieutenant	British Army	9/05/1915	Sailly-sur-la-Lyes Canadian Cemetery, Pas-de-Calais, France
1007	SCANLAN, Daniel		Corporal	AIF	23/02/1917	Bailleul Communal Cemetery Extension, Nord, France
	SCHIFF, Alfred Sydney Borlase		2nd Lieutenant	British Army	9/04/1917	Brown's Copse Cemetery, Roeux, Pas-de-Calais, France
253	SCHMIDT, William Alexander		Private	AIF	8/05/1915	Helles Memorial, Gallipoli, Turkey
3938	SCHONFELDER, Andrew William		Private	AIF	16/08/1916	Villers-Bretonneux Memorial, Somme, France
	SCOLLARD, William Patrick		Assistant Steward	MM Reserve	11/03/1915	Plymouth Naval Memorial, Devon, England
427632	SCOTT, Alexander	Aleck Scott	Private	COEF	17/03/1916	Galashiels (Ladhope) Cemetery, Selkirkshire, Scotland
	SCOTT, Leonard Randall		Private	British Army	30/07/1916	Bapaume Post Military Cemetery, Albert, Somme, France
7061	SCOTT, William John		Private	AIF	9/07/1918	Villers-Bretonneux Memorial, Somme, France
	SCRIVENER, Ernest	Ernest William Scrivener	Greaser	MM	19/09/1916	Suez War Memorial Cemetery, Egypt
	SCULLY, Albert Edward William		Engine Room Artificer 3rd Class	MM	9/11/1917	Tower Hill Memorial, Trinity Square, London, England
19452	SEABROOK, Arthur Melville		Private	British Army	8/10/1915	Loos Memorial, Pas-de-Calais, France
375430, 483298	SEARS, Guy Douglas Hackett		Private	British Army	8/05/1919	Walton-on-Thames Cemetery, Walton-on-Thames, Surrey, England
	SELBY, William Gilhome		Captain	AIF	8/09/1916	Lucknow Cantonment Military Cemetery, India
242	SELLGREN, Claude John	Claud John Laurence Sellgren	Sergeant	AIF	5/08/1916	Serre Road Cemetery No. 2, Somme, France

301	SEXTON, James		Private	AIF	20/07/1916	New Irish Farm Cemetery, West-Vlaanderen, Belgium
28021	SEYMOUR, Guy Blundell		Private	British Army	18/12/1917	Birmingham (Lodge Hill), Cemetery, Warwickshire, England
	SHARLAND, Frederick James	Frederic James Sharland	2nd Lieutenant	RFC	24/10/1917	Arras Flying Services Memorial, Pas-de-Calais, France
2044	SHARPE, Charles Frederick		Corporal	AIF	22/08/1917	Reninghelst New Military Cemetery, West-Vlaanderen, Belgium
	SHATTOCK, Ernest Arthur		Chief Officer	MM	20/03/1918	Tower Hill Memorial, Trinity Square, London, England
84	SHAW, Bertram George		Sergeant	AIF	4/10/1917	Menin Gate Memorial, Ypres, West-Vlaanderen, Belgium
	SHAW, William		Cadet	MM	19/11/1917	Tower Hill Memorial, Trinity Square, London, England
986	SHEED, William		Private	AIF	1–4/05/1915	Lone Pine Memorial, Gallipoli, Turkey
512	SHIELDS, William Dorey		Lance Corporal	AIF	3/06/1917	Strand Military Cemetery, Hainaut, Belgium
	SHOUT, Alfred John (VC)		Captain	AIF	11/08/1915	Lone Pine Memorial, Gallipoli, Turkey
748	SIBBALD, Hugh Elmar		Private	AIF	25/04/1918	Étaples Military Cemetery, Pas-de-Calais, France
1776	SIMMERS, Frank		Sergeant	AIF	27/03/1917	Aveluy Communal Cemetery Extension, Somme, France
10351	SIMMONS, Edward Marshall Michael	Marshall Edward Simmons	Lance Corporal	AIF	7/06/1917	Strand Military Cemetery, Hainaut, Belgium
580	SIMON, Faulkner Charles Roy		Private	AIF	27/04/1915	Lone Pine Memorial, Gallipoli, Turkey
193590/5	SIMPSON, George (MC)		2nd Lieutenant	British Army	12/09/1918	Gouzeaucourt New British Cemetery, Nord, France
	SIMPSON, Hector Joseph		Lieutanant	Rhodesian Army	29/01/1917	Iringa Cemetery, Tanzania
680	SIMPSON, Nevill Wynn	Neville Wynn Simpson, Neville Wyan Simpson	Corporal	AIF	29/07/1916	Puchevillers British Cemetery, Somme, France
2684	SIMS, Samuel		Private	AIF	26/07/1916	Y Farm Military Cemetery, Bois-Grenier, Nord, France
	SIMSON, Herbert Cyrus	Herbert Waipu Simson	Lieutenant	RFC	12/01/1918	Hollybrook Memorial, Southampton, England
	SINCLAIR-THOMSON, George Alastair	George Alastair Sinclair Thomson	Captain	British Army	21/07/1916	Corbie Communal Cemetery Extension, Somme, France

1433	SKINNER, Arthur		Private	AIF	22–25/07/1916	Villers-Bretonneux Memorial, Somme, France
2895	SLOAN, Robert Douglas		Private	AIF	19/07/1916	V. C. Corner Australian Cemetery and Memorial, Fromelles, France
	SLOSS, James Duncan		2nd Lieutenant	RFC	23/11/1918	Terlincthun British Cemetery, Wimille, Pas-de-Calais, France
502884	SMAILL, William Charles		Sapper	COEF	27/06/1918	Vimy Memorial, Pas-de-Calais, France
1937B	SMITH, Albert Charles		Private	AIF	18/03/1917	Cite Bonjean Military Cemetery, Armentières, France
	SMITH, Alexander Bisset (VC)		Master	MM	10/03/1917	Tower Hill Memorial, Trinity Square, London, England
1103	SMITH, Charles Walter	Charles Wakdrick Smith, Charles Walduck Smith	Private	AIF	13/06/1916	Mazargues War Cemetery, Marseilles, France
514	SMITH, Clarence Sydney		Corporal	AIF	10/05/1917	Stratford-sub-Castle (St Lawrence) Churchyard, Wiltshire, England
205769	SMITH, David Prowse		Lance Corporal	British Army	1/09/1918	Vis-en-Artois Memorial, Pas-de-Calais, France
PLY/3885	SMITH, Edwin		Private	RMLI	9/07/1915	Dalmeny Parish Cemetery, South Queensferry, Linlithgowshire, Scotland
	SMITH, Harold Andrew		2nd Lieutenant	British Army	21/03/1918	Arras Memorial, Pas-de-Calais, France
	SMITH, John Gordon		Cadet	MM	19/11/1917	Tower Hill Memorial, Trinity Square, London, England
S/40905	SMITH, Leonard Francis		Private	British Army	12/04/1917	Aubigny Communal Cemetery Extension, Somme, France
5413	SMITH, Ralph Wilson		Private	AIF	25/03/1917	Villers-Bretonneux Memorial, Somme, France
	SMITH, Reginald Frank		2nd Lieutenant	British Army	12/02/1919	Taita Cemetery, Lower Hutt, New Zealand
918	SMITH, Sidney O'Carroll		Lieutenant	British Army	25/08/1916	Dernacourt Communal Cemetery Extension, Somme, France
	SOLOMON, Hubert Philip		2nd Lieutenant	RFC	20/10/1917	Gainsborough General Cemetery, Lincolnshire, England
50674	SOLVANDER, Edward Harrison		Private	COEF	24/03/1917	Écoivres Military Cemetery, Pas-de-Calais, France
	SOUTH, Edward Marshall		Lance Corporal	British Army	5/08/1917	Derry House Cemetery No. 2, West-Vlaanderen, Belgium

	SOUTH, Harold		Captain	AIF	9/09/1919	Sutton Veny (St John) Churchyard, Sutton Veny, Wiltshire, England
1184	SPARROW, John Archibald Dick		Private	AIF	22/12/1914	Coburg Pine Ridge Cemetery, Victoria, Australia
5623	SPENCE, William Joseph		Sapper	AIF	1/10/1917	Menin Gate Memorial, Ypres, West-Vlaanderen, Belgium
2488, 5462	SPINLEY, Frederick Thomas		Corporal	AIF	15/04/1917	Villers-Bretonneux Memorial, Somme, France
	SPRAGG, Wesley Neal		Lieutenant	RFC	1/01/1918	Cairo War Memorial Cemetery, Egypt
20096	SPRAGUE, Arthur Thomas		Corporal	AIF	28/06/1919	Sydney (Waverley) General Cemetery, New South Wales, Australia
5473	SPRATLEY, William Nelson		Sergeant	AIF	25/06/1918	St Pierre Cemetery, Amiens, France
	SPROTT, Maurice William Campbell		Captain	British Army	21/03/1918	Arras Memorial, Pas-de-Calais, France
10548	SQUIRRELL, Thomas Walter		Sapper	AIF	5/08/1917	Adinkerke Military Cemetery, West-Vlaanderen, Belgium
	ST HILL, Collis George Herbert		Lieutenant Colonel	British Army	8/07/1917	Neuville-Bourjonval British Cemetery, Pas-de-Calais, France
J9099	STANLEY, George Thomas		Signalman	RN	29/06/1919	Somes Island Cemetery, Wellington, New Zealand
6166	STANTON, James		Lance Corporal	AIF	4/10/1917	Menin Gate Memorial, Ypres, West-Vlaanderen, Belgium
	STARKY, James Bayntun	James Baynton Starky	2nd Lieutenant	British Army	6/07/1916	Thiepval Memorial, Somme, France
	STEELE, Thomas Lancaster (MC)		2nd Lieutenant	RFC	10/04/1918	Jerusalem Memorial, Israel
	STEELE, Oliver		Captain	British Army	25/10/1914	Menin Gate Memorial, Ypres, West-Vlaanderen, Belgium
	STEERS, Arthur		Second Engineer	MM	5/06/1918	Tower Hill Memorial, Trinity Square, London, England
16	STEPHENS, Robert		Corporal	AIF	2/05/1915	Lone Pine Memorial, Gallipoli, Turkey
3982	STEVENSON, George		Stoker	RAN	21/05/1918	Exeter Higher Cemetery, Exeter, Devon, England
1625	STEWART, George Blakeney		Private	COEF	8/05/1915	Menin Gate Memorial, Ypres, West-Vlaanderen, Belgium
	STEWART, Hugh Duncan		Major	British Army	12/10/1918	Wellington Cemetery, Rieuxen-en-Cambrésis, Nord, France
2403	STEWART, Walter		Private	AIF	12/06/1916	Estaires Communal Cemetery and Extension, Nord, France
	STEWART-RICHARDSON, Sir Edward Austin		Captain	British Army	28/11/1914	St Madoe's Parish Churchyard, Perthshire, Scotland

4289	STONE, Jack Fairburn	John Fairburn Stone	Lance Corporal	AIF	23/12/1916	Bernafay Wood British Cemetery, Montauban, France
60	STONE, John Edward	Harry Edwin Taylor, Harry Edward Taylor	Lieutenant	AIF	3/08/1916	Pozières British Cemetery, Ovillers-la-Boisselle, Somme, France
2659, 958	STOREY, Francis		Private	AIF	5/08/1917	Menin Gate Memorial, Ypres, West-Vlaanderen, Belgium
198, 1797	STOREY, Frank		Private	AIF	26/04/1915	Quinn's Post Cemetery, Gallipoli, Turkey
1294	STRACHEY, Claude Otto		Private	AIF	2/05/1915	Lone Pine Memorial, Gallipoli, Turkey
	STRANGMAN, John Gerald		2nd Lieutenant	AIF	19/07/1916	V. C. Corner Australian Cemetery and Memorial, Fromelles, France
21502	STREET, Alfred Cecil		Private	AIF	10/06/1917	Menin Gate Memorial, Ypres, West-Vlaanderen, Belgium
3351	STREETER, William Sendall	William Lendall Streeter	Lance Corporal	AIF	29/09/1918	Bellicourt British Cemetery, Aisne, France
7306	STUART, Albert William		Private	AIF	14/04/1918	Villers-Bretonneux Memorial, Somme, France
2402	STUBBS, George Dilworth		Private	AIF	27/05/1918	Aubigny British Cemetery, Somme, France
3282	STUBBS, Robert Maurice		Private	AIF	2/04/1918	Doullens Communal Cemetery Extension No. 1, Somme, France
4891	STURMAN, William Henry		Private	AIF	31/08/1918	Suzanne Communal Cemetery Extension, Somme, France
5137	SULLIVAN, Jack	John Ormsby Sullivan	Private	AIF	9/10/1916	Croix-du-Bac British Cemetery, Steenwerck, Belgium
509	SUNDERLAND, Geoffrey		Captain	British Army	24/09/1918	Berthaucourt Communal Cemetery, Pontru, Aisne, France
995	SUTTON, John Briggs		Private	AIF	2/11/1915	Embarkation Pier Cemetery, Gallipoli, Turkey
1501	SYME, Noel Herbert		Sergeant	AIF	10/05/1917	Grevillers British Cemetery, Pas-de-Calais, France
	TAIT, Robert		Second Engineer	MM	8/02/1917	Tower Hill Memorial, Trinity Square, London, England
	TALBERT, William Caithness	William Caithness Talbot	Lieutenant	RAF	20/07/1918	Upavon Cemetery, Wiltshire, England
	TALBOT, Arthur Sydney		Lieutenant	RFC	27/09/1917	Rochford (St Andrew) Churchyard, Essex, England
	TALL, John		Assistant Steward	MM	14/10/1916	Greenwich Cemetery, London, England

214734	TALMAY, George Richard		Leading Seaman	RN	25/09/1915	Heliopolis (Aden) Memorial, Cairo, Egypt
J35268	TAMBLING, Leonard John		Able Seaman	RN	6/05/1921	Auckland (Waikumete) Cemetery, New Zealand
	TANNER, Charles Cyril Pontin		Captain	British Army	5/10/1918	Baghdad (North Gate) War Cemetery, Iraq
	TANNER, Samuel		Fourth Engineer Officer	MM	11/06/1917	Tower Hill Memorial, Trinity Square, London, England
688	TANSLEY, Eric John		Private	AIF	27/04/1915	Lone Pine Memorial, Gallipoli, Turkey
	TAYLER, Eric Hardwick		Lieutenant	British Army	9/02/1915	Hazebrouck Communal Cemetery, Nord, France
5924	TAYLOR, George Edward		Private	AIF	29/10/1917	Menin Gate Memorial, Ypres, West-Vlaanderen, Belgium
718	TAYLOR, Robert Douglas		Private	AIF	19/04/1917	Villers-Bretonneux Memorial, Somme, France
2139	TAYLOR, Walter Leslie		Private	AIF	26/02/1917	Trois Arbres Cemetery, Steenwerck, Nord, France
SP/3063	TAYLOR, Walter Prince		Lance Sergeant	British Army	29/04/1917	Arras Memorial, Pas-de-Calais, France
1806A	TAYLOR, William Henry		Gunner	AIF	21/08/1918	Villers-Bretonneux Memorial, Somme, France
	TAYLOR, William Jack Macdonald		2nd Lieutenant	British Army	19/12/1915	Lancashire Landing Cemetery, Turkey
58804	TE WAHIA, Tare	Charles Woods	Sapper	British Army	26/09/1918	Karitane Cemetery, Dunedin, New Zealand
570	TEMPLER, Francis Darvall		Trooper	AIF	22/10/1915	Lone Pine Memorial, Gallipoli, Turkey
	TENNANT, Charles		Fourth Engineer	MM	5/09/1918	
	TENNENT, Bernard Charles (MC + Bar)		Major	British Army	22/08/1918	Bellacourt Military Cemetery, Pas-de-Calais, France
1972	THOMAS, Walter Geoffrey		Private	AIF	22/08/1916	Villers-Bretonneux Memorial, Somme, France
NZNF1216	THOMPSON, Alfred		Stoker	RN Fleet Auxiliary	26/03/1918	Plymouth Naval Memorial, Devon, England
464	THOMPSON, Frederick John		Private	AIF	25/04/1915	Lone Pine Memorial, Gallipoli, Turkey
K11573	THOMPSON, George		Acting Leading Stoker	RN	6/05/1920	Lincoln (St Swithin's) Cemetery, Lincolnshire, England
279735	THOMPSON, George David		Stoker 1st Class	RNR	5/01/1918	Southampton Old Cemetery, Hampshire, England
673	THOMPSON, John Alfred		Private	AIF	29/04/1915	Lone Pine Memorial, Gallipoli, Turkey
1098	THOMPSON, William		Private	AIF	10–14/05/1915	Shrapnel Valley Cemetery, Gallipoli, Turkey

VR/465	THOMSON, Frederick Twiss		Assistant Paymaster	RN	31/03/1918	Ottawa (Beechwood) Cemetery, Ontario, Canada
	THOMSON, Kenneth Sinclair		Lieutenant	British Indian Army	3/03/1915	Basra War Cemetery, Iraq
1623	THOMSON, William Dennis	William Denis Thomson	Private	AIF	8/12/1915	Pieta Military Cemetery, Malta
216932	THORNE, Sydney Robert		Regulating PO	RN	19/01/1920	Laperouse Cemetery, Port of Spain, Trinidad
4267	THORPE, Daniel		Private	AIF	13/07/1918	Brookwood Military Cemetery, Surrey, England
3512	THOW, David Cornelius		Private	AIF	9/08/1918	Vignacourt British Cemetery, Somme, France
	TIBBS, Bernard Edmund		Lieutenant	British Army	9/01/1918	Basra Memorial, Iraq
	TISDALL, Arthur Walderne St Clair (VC)		Sub Lieutenant	RNVR	6/05/1915	Helles Memorial, Gallipoli, Turkey
	TISDALL, John Theodore St Clair		2nd Lieutenant	British Army	8/08/1916	Thiepval Memorial, Somme, France
351	TOBIN, Arthur		Private	AIF	30/07/1920	Wellington (Karori) Cemetery, New Zealand
3261	TODD, Robert Henry		Private	AIF	24/07/1916	Villers-Bretonneux Memorial, Somme, France
	TODD, Thomas John		Lieutenant Colonel	AIF	23/01/1919	Cairo War Memorial Cemetery, Egypt
	TODD, Willliam			Imperial Forces	19/01/1915	
	TOMLINSON, David Mitchell (MID)		Major	British Army	13/05/1916	Béthune Town Cemetery, Pas-de-Calais, France
1712	TORR, Ernest McKain		Private	AIF	29/07/1916	Villers-Bretonneux Memorial, Somme, France
1458	TORRENS, Walter Edward		Private	AIF	25/06/1917	Ration Farm (La Plus Douve) Annexe, Hainaut, Belgium
4350	TREASURE, Wyndham		Private	AIF	15/08/1916	Villers-Bretonneux Memorial, Somme, France
3427	TRELOAR, John Henry		Private	AIF	28/08/1918	Suzanne Military Cemetery No. 3, Somme, France
13296	TREPO, Thomas	Thomas Vucasivitch, Trepo Vucasivitch	Private	SA Army	18/10/1917	Menin Gate Memorial, Ypres, West-Vlaanderen, Belgium
5784	TRESTON, Richard Patrick		Private	AIF	5/04/1917	Dernacourt Communal Cemetery Extension, Somme, France
4600	TREWBY, Percy		Lance Corporal	AIF	19/04/1918	Ebblinghem Military Cemetery, Nord, France
492	TREWHELLA, William Hector	William George Trewheela	Sergeant	AIF	11/04/1917	Noreuil Australian Cemetery, Pas-de-Calais, France

	TROUP, Francis Monk-Mason	Francis Monck-Mason Troup	Lieutenant	British Army	10/10/1917	Monchy British Cemetery, Monchy-le-Preux, Pas-de-Calais, France
3915	TRUDGEON, James Jacob		Private	AIF	2/05/1918	Crucifix Corner Cemetery, Villers-Bretonneux, Somme, France
2605	TURK, Charles William		Private	AIF	10/07/1918	Dunkirk Town Cemetery, Nord, France
7059	TURNBULL, George Dowling	Gordon Dowling Turnbull	Private	AIF	4/10/1917	Menin Gate Memorial, Ypres, West-Vlaanderen, Belgium
	TURNER, John Lancelot Harcourt		Captain	British Army	14/07/1916	Cite Bonjean Military Cemetery, Armentières, France
51124	TURNER, Henry	Harry Turner	Sapper	British Army	10/02/1916	Menin Gate Memorial, Ypres, West-Vlaanderen, Belgium
426516	TURTILL, Hubert Sydney		Sergeant	British Army	9/04/1918	Brown's Road Military Cemetery, Festubert, Pas-de-Calais, France
	TYLEE, Errol Tom		Engineer Sub-Lieutenant	RN	26/01/1919	Edinburgh (Morningside) Cemetery, Edinburgh, Scotland
	UREN, Philip		2nd Lieutenant	British Army	18/05/1916	Miraumont Communal Cemetery, Somme, France
	VAVASOUR, Rudolph Dunstan	Rollo Dunstan Vavasour	2nd Lieutenant	RFC	16/01/1917	Fulham (St Thomas of Canterbury) Roman Catholic Churchyard, London, England
	VEALE, Allan Adolphus	Allan Adolphus Veal	2nd Lieutenant	RFC	22/01/1918	Bailleul Communal Cemetery Extension, Nord, France
92	VENN, Alfred		Private	AIF	14/10/1917	Hooge Crater Cemetery, West-Vlaanderen, Belgium
2058	VICARY, Henry Walter		Private	AIF	6–9/08/1915	Johnston's Jolly Cemetery, Gallipoli, Turkey
508	VINCENT, Robert		Corporal	AIF	9/05/1915	Beach Cemetery, Gallipoli, Turkey
544	VINCENT, Thomas		Private	AIF	19/02/1917	Tidworth Military Cemetery, Wiltshire, England
118	VIVIAN, George Alfred		Sapper	AIF	30/05/1915	Alexandria (Chatby) Military and War Memorial Cemetery, Egypt
	VOYCE, Henry Eugene	Harry Yoyce	2nd Lieutenant	British Army	6/08/1915	Twelve Tree Copse Cemetery, Gallipoli, Turkey
1387D	WADE, Charles Robert		Ordinary Seaman	RN	11/10/1915	East London Cemetery, Plaistow, London, England
1021	WADE, William (DCM)		Sergeant	AIF	21/10/1917	Menin Road South Military Cemetery, West-Vlaanderen, Belgium

7112	WADSWORTH, Arthur		Driver	AIF	6/11/1918	Middleton Junction (St Gabriel) Churchyard, Lancashire, England
798	WAGSTAFF, Arthur		Private	AIF	29/04/1915	Lone Pine Memorial, Gallipoli, Turkey
S/3275, A6058	WAGSTAFF, Thomas Reginald		Private	British Army	25/09/1915	Loos Memorial, Pas-de-Calais, France
	WAKEFIELD, Oliver		Second Lieutenant	British Army	12/10/1917	Tyne Cot Cemetery, West-Vlaanderen, Belgium
7608	WALINCK, John	John Malinck	Private	British Army	10/03/1915	Le Touret Memorial, Pas-de-Calais, France
	WALKER, Henry John Innes		Captain	British Army	25/04/1915	New Irish Farm Cemetery, West-Vlaanderen, Belgium
2548	WALKER, William James		Lance Corporal	AIF	27/09/1917	Menin Gate Memorial, Ypres, West-Vlaanderen, Belgium
468	WALLACE, Donal Wally	Donald Wally Wallace	Private	AIF	25/11/1915	Walker's Ridge Cemetery, Gallipoli, Turkey
3962	WALLACE, Robert		Private	AIF	29/07/1916	Warloy-Baillon Communal Cemetery Extension, Somme, France
	WALLIS, Henry Digby		Lieutenant	British Army	21/10/1914	Menin Gate Memorial, Ypres, West-Vlaanderen, Belgium
359	WALLS, Stuart		Private	AIF	27/08/1915	Lone Pine Memorial, Gallipoli, Turkey
2020288	WALMSLEY, Guy Harold		Private	COEF	3/06/1918	Bellacourt Military Cemetery, Pas-de-Calais, France
942	WALSH, Andrew William		Private	AIF	23/08/1915	Embarkation Pier Cemetery, Gallipoli, Turkey
8201	WAND, Philip Courtenay	Philip Courtenay Waud, J. C. Wand	Air Mechanic 1st Class	RFC	31/12/1917	Chatby Memorial, Egypt
	WANKLYN, John Endell		Lieutenant	British Army	29/05/1918	Lilliers Communal Cemetery Extension, Pas-de-Calais, France
R/15255	WARING, Hugh George		Rifleman	British Army	9/05/1916	Bruay Communal Cemetery Extension, Pas-de-Calais, France
3964	WARLE, Edward		Private	AIF	22/09/1916	Bedford House Cemetery, West-Vlaanderen, Belgium
27766	WARREN, William Albert	William Thomas Warren	Private	COEF	24/04/1915	Menin Gate Memorial, Ypres, West-Vlaanderen, Belgium
7111	WARRING, Albert Richard		Private	AIF	20/09/1917	Brookwood Military Cemetery, Surrey, England
4005	WASTNEY, Nolan Dyson		Private	AIF	9/04/1917	Villers-Bretonneux Memorial, Somme, France

2707	WATERS, William John Henry		Lance Corporal	AIF	4/10/1917	Tyne Cot Cemetery, West-Vlaanderen, Belgium
1191	WATSON, Alfred Godfrey		Corporal	AIF	27/04/1915	Beach Cemetery, Gallipoli, Turkey
3241	WATSON, Andrew James		Private	AIF	5/08/1916	Villers-Bretonneux Memorial, Somme, France
1052	WATSON, Basil Percy		Lance Corporal	AIF	29/04/1916	Rue-David Military Cemetery, Fleurbaix, Pas-de-Calais, France
515	WATSON, Charles		Private	AIF	17/10/1917	Lijssenthoek Military Cemetery, West-Vlaanderen, Belgium
357	WATSON, Richard Victor		Private	AIF	5/05/1916	City of London and Tower Hamlets Cemetery, London, England
4934	WATSON, Sherwood Alexander		Private	AIF	20/08/1916	Warloy-Baillon Communal Cemetery Extension, Somme, France
1647	WATSON, William Young		Private	AIF	20/09/1918	Doingt Communal Cemetery Extension, Somme, France
684	WATT, Donald Washington		Private	AIF	10/02/1918	Menin Gate Memorial, Ypres, West-Vlaanderen, Belgium
3197	WATT, George James		Private	AIF	2/04/1917	Noreuil Australian Cemetery, Pas-de-Calais, France
1457	WATT, Joseph William		Private	AIF	17/05/1915	Lone Pine Memorial, Gallipoli, Turkey
	WATTS, Charles Harold Reynell		Captain	British Army	25/12/1914	Le Touret Memorial, Pas-de-Calais, France
1153	WEATHERS, Lawrence Carthage		Lance Corporal	AIF	29/09/1918	Unicorn Cemetery, Vendhuile, Aisne, France
204	WEATHERS, Thomas Francis		Private	AIF	15/06/1915	Ari Burnu Cemetery, Gallipoli, Turkey
1146	WEBBER, Gerard Kingsley		Private	British Army	2/02/1917	Manchester Southern Cemetery, Manchester, England
115	WEIR, Frank Percy		Private	AIF	10/08/1915	9th Field Ambulance Cemetery, Gallipoli, Turkey
999	WEIR, John Hay		Private	AIF	1/08/1917	Menin Gate Memorial, Ypres, West-Vlaanderen, Belgium
4518	WEIR, Michael John Watt		Lieutenant	AIF	18/08/1918	Daours Communal Cemetery Extension, Somme, France
784	WELCH, William Bradley		Trooper	AIF	7/08/1915	Lone Pine Memorial, Gallipoli, Turkey
1531	WELLS, Percy Warner		Driver	AIF	30/10/1917	The Huts Cemetery, West-Vlaanderen, Belgium
742849	WELLS, William David		Private	COEF	6/11/1917	Menin Gate Memorial, Ypres, West-Vlaanderen, Belgium

TS6399	WEST, Gilbert		Trimmer	RNR	12/11/1918	Hull Northern Cemetery, Yorkshire, England
	WESTON, Henry Gerald		Regimental Sergeant Major	British Army	17/11/1915	Voormezeele Enclosures No. 1 and No. 2, West-Vlaanderen, Belgium
831	WESTRUPP, Walter		Private	AIF	25/04/1915	Lone Pine Memorial, Gallipoli, Turkey
1430	WHELAN, Patrick Conrad		Corporal	AIF	6/10/1917	Menin Gate Memorial, Ypres, West-Vlaanderen, Belgium
3472	WHITCOMBE, Aubrey Cresswell		Private	AIF	12/10/1917	Passchendaele New British Cemetery, West-Vlaanderen, Belgium
3663	WHITE, Charles		Private	AIF	29/07/1916	Villers-Bretonneux Memorial, Somme, France
1450	WHITE, Edmund John		Private	AIF	19/11/1918	Auckland (Waikumete) Cemetery, New Zealand
	WHITE, Gerald John Davis		2nd Lieutenant	British Army	5/07/1916	Thiepval Memorial, Somme, France
	WHITE, Hill Wilson		Captain	British Army	12/04/1918	Ploegsteert Memorial, Hainuit, Belgium
489	WHITE, John Joseph		Trooper	AIF	19/04/1917	Jerusalem Memorial, Israel
	WHITE, Melville Arthur		2nd Lieutenant	RFC	23/04/1917	Jeancourt Communal Cemetery Extension, Aisne, France
J13518	WHITECHURCH, Arthur Frank		Able Seaman	RN	17/11/1917	Plymouth Naval Memorial, Devon, England
	WHITEMAN, John		Lieutenant Colonel	British Army	25/04/1917	Aubigny Communal Cemetery Extension, Somme, France
695	WHITEMAN, Reuben George Keefe	Ruben George Whiteman	Private	AIF	10/10/1915	Shrapnel Valley Cemetery, Gallipoli, Turkey
	WHYTE, William Bruce		Sub-Lieutenant/ Engineer	MM	10/01/1920	English Channel
454	WIGGINS, Ernest Alfred		Private	AIF	31/05/1915	Beach Cemetery, Gallipoli, Turkey
	WIGLEY, Arthur James (MC)		Lieutenant	Indian Army	11/07/1923	Haifa Cemetery, Palestine
	WILDING, Anthony Frederick		Captain	RM	9/09/1915	Rue-des-Berceaux Military Cemetery, Richebourg-l'Avoué, France
6111	WILDMAN, Nugent Robert		Private	AIF	8/05/1917	Villers-Bretonneux Memorial, Somme, France
4924	WILKES, William Henry		Private	AIF	3–4/05/1917	Villers-Bretonneux Memorial, Somme, France
	WILKINSON, Charles Harold		Lieutenant	British Army	13/10/1918	West Norwood Cemetery and Crematorium, London, England
2196	WILKINSON, James Harvey		Private	AIF	16/07/1915	Beach Cemetery, Gallipoli, Turkey

R/10182	WILLIAMS, Cecil Horatio Childe		Lance Corporal	British Army	26/04/1915	Menin Gate Memorial, Ypres, West-Vlaanderen, Belgium
3227	WILLIAMS, Edward Willis		Private	AIF	13/10/1917	Menin Gate Memorial, Ypres, West-Vlaanderen, Belgium
	WILLIAMS, Erl Temple		Lieutenant	RFC	14/07/1918	
3131	WILLIAMS, Frank Hill		Lieutenant	AIF	10/07/1918	Longuenesse (St Omer) Souvenir Cemetery, Pas-de-Calais, France
	WILLIAMS, Harold Sutton		Major	British Army	21/03/1915	Boulogne Eastern Cemetery, Pas-de-Calais, France
5514	WILLIAMS, Henry William		Driver	AIF	5/11/1916	Villers-Bretonneux Memorial, Somme, France
	WILLIAMS, Selwyn Coldham		Lieutenant	British Army	18/01/1917	Klein-Vierstraat British Cemetery, West-Vlaanderen, Belgium
3024	WILLIAMS, Thomas Edward		Private	AIF	23/12/1917	Outtersteene Communal Cemetery Extension, Bailleul, France
	WILLIAMS, William Harry		Cadet	MM	19/11/1917	Tower Hill Memorial, Trinity Square, London, England
	WILLIAMSON, Charles Geddes		Seaman	RN	10/11/1918	Auckland Hospital, New Zealand
7794	WILLIAMSON, Henry Alexander		Private	AIF	2/05/1918	Daours Communal Cemetery Extension, Somme, France
1594	WILLIAMSON, Henry James		Private	AIF	23/07/1915	Lone Pine Memorial, Gallipoli, Turkey
77	WILLIS, Arthur Joseph		Private	AIF	29/04/1915	Lone Pine Memorial, Gallipoli, Turkey
	WILLIS, H. J.		Steward	MM	10/03/1917	Tower Hill Memorial, Trinity Square, London, England
3248	WILLOUGHBY, Alfred Seymour Bolton		Private	AIF	27/09/1917	Menin Gate Memorial, Ypres, West-Vlaanderen, Belgium
1634	WILLS, Ralph		Private	AIF	30/06/1917	Bailleul Communal Cemetery Extension, Nord, France
W/399	WILSON, Alexander		Company Sergeant Major	British Army	7/07/1916	Thiepval Memorial, Somme, France
61	WILSON, Allan Elwood		Corporal	AIF	2/09/1915	Helles Memorial, Gallipoli, Turkey
110	WILSON, George Henry		Sapper	AIF	20/04/1918	Hazebrouck Communal Cemetery, Nord, France
7746	WILSON, Jacob		Private	AIF	28/04/1916	Rookwood Necropolis, Sydney, New South Wales, Australia
8117	WILSON, John		Private	AIF	22/07/1917	Trois Arbres Cemetery, Steenwerck, Nord, France
76	WILSON, Thomas Clark	Thomas Clarke Wilson	Lance Corporal	AIF	24/04–24/05/1915	Lone Pine Memorial, Gallipoli, Turkey

1019	WILSON, Thomas Walter		Private	AIF	10/05/1916	Merville Communal Cemetery, Nord, France
	WILSON, Robert Alexander		Lieutenant	British Army	2/05/1917	Thiepval Memorial, Somme, France
1956	WISHART, Charles		Lance Corporal	AIF	24/06/1918	Kandahar Farm Cemetery, West-Vlaanderen, Belgium
2153	WITHY, Samuel		Private	AIF	10/04/1918	St Sever Cemetery Extension, Rouen, Seine-Maritime, France
	WOOD, Frederick S.		Yeoman of Signals	RN	8/09/1915	Tehran War Cemetery, Iran
1025	WOOD, Robert		Corporal	AIF	29/12/1917	Kandahar Farm Cemetery, West-Vlaanderen, Belgium
569	WOODNORTH, William Nicholson		Sergeant	AIF	23/08/1918	Heath Cemetery, Harbonnières, Somme, France
4560	WOODRUFFE, Arthur		Private	AIF	14/11/1916	Villers-Bretonneux Memorial, Somme, France
595	WOODS, Edward		Private	AIF	12/10/1917	Tyne Cot Cemetery, West-Vlaanderen, Belgium
1851	WOOLLEY, James Nathaniel		Private	AIF	6/08/1915	Lone Pine Cemetery, Gallipoli, Turkey
6155	WORTH, Hector Clayton		Private	AIF	3/05/1917	Villers-Bretonneux Memorial, Somme, France
	WRIGGLESWORTH, Alfred Gunn		2nd Lieutenant	British Army	4/09/1916	Thiepval Memorial, Somme, France
384	WRIGHT, Reginald Clarke		Private	AIF	21/08/1915	Cairo War Memorial Cemetery, Egypt
S5813	WRIGHT, Richard Robinson		Stoker	RNR	30/12/1915	Chatham Naval Memorial, Kent, England
760	WRIGHT, Robert Young		Private	AIF	8/10/1915	Pieta Military Cemetery, Malta
3596	WRIGHT, Walter William		Lance Corporal	British Army	13/07/1919	Dunedin (Andersons Bay) Cemetery, New Zealand
216	YELLS, Cyril Alfred		Private	AIF	11/04/1917	Villers-Bretonneux Memorial, Somme, France
	YOUNG, Edward Charles Roi		Engineer Lieutenant	RNR	19/12/1918	Haslar Royal Naval Cemetery, Hampshire, England
1596	YOUNG, Horace James		Private	AIF	7–12/08/1915	Lone Pine Memorial, Gallipoli, Turkey
926	YOUNG, John Buchanan		Lance Corporal	AIF	6–11/06/1917	Menin Gate Memorial, Ypres, West-Vlaanderen, Belgium
7458	YOUNGHUSBAND, Allan Wadham		Gunner	AIF	3/05/1917	Quéant Road Cemetery, Buissy, Pas-de-Calais, France

A note on burial places: the burial places of some servicemen are unknown, and some died in the years after the war from their wounds or from other effects of war, and are therefore buried outside Europe.

APPENDIX 2
MENIN GATE MEMORIAL ROLL

Service ID	Name	AKA	Rank	Force	Date of death	Panel reference
1094	ARMSTRONG, John Alexander		Sergeant	AIF	9/10/1917	Panel 31
6944	BARROW, Elephia Walter	Eliffe Walter Patrick Barrow	Private	AIF	27/09/1917	Panel 7 - 17 - 23 - 25 - 27 - 29 - 31
5988	BAYLEY, Harold Bryan		Private	AIF	6/10/1917	Panel 7 - 17 - 23 - 25 - 27 - 29 - 31
	BELL, William Henry Dillon	William Henry Dillon-Bell	Lieutenant	British Army	31/07/1917	Panel 42 and 44
5330	BENFELL, Arthur		Private	AIF	13/10/1917	Panel 7 - 17 - 23 - 25 - 27 - 29 - 31
4077	BOGLE, Gordon Kennedy		Sergeant	AIF	20/09/1917	Panel 7 - 17 - 23 - 25 - 27 - 29 - 31
704	BOOKLASS, John	John Hope Bookless	Lance Corporal	AIF	7/10/1917	Panel 7 - 17 - 23 - 25 - 27 - 29 - 31
279	BOURNE, Albert Maurice		Private	AIF	10/10/1917	Panel 7 - 17 - 23 - 25 - 27 - 29 - 31
88	BOYD, Thomas Murray		Bombardier	AIF	30/09/1917	Panel 7
5053	BRANLEY, John Mulkeedis		Private	AIF	16/10/1917	Panel 7 - 17 - 23 - 25 - 27 - 29 - 31
17250	BROUGH, John Forbes		Private	SA Army	4/05/1918	Panel 15 - 16 and 16A
6953	BROWN, Joseph Robert		Private	AIF	4/10/1917	Panel 7 - 17 - 23 - 25 - 27 - 29 - 31
2991	BUCKLEY, Edward		Lance Corporal	AIF	28/09/1917	Panel 7 - 17 - 23 - 25 - 27 - 29 - 31
1883A	BURKE, Henry Gilbert		Private	AIF	7/06/1917	Panel 7 - 17 - 23 - 25 - 27 - 29 - 31
3765	BURKE, William Malcolm		Private	AIF	9/10/1917	Panel 7 - 17 - 23 - 25 - 27 - 29 - 31
4451	BUTLER, Albert Louis		Private	AIF	9/09/1916	Panel 7 - 17 - 23 - 25 - 27 - 29 - 31
	BUTTERWORTH, Hugh Montagu		2nd Lieutenant	British Army	25/09/1915	Panel 46 - 48 and 50
4661	CAMPBELL, Duncan		Private	AIF	8/10/1917	Panel 7 - 17 - 23 - 25 - 27 - 29 - 31
	CAMPBELL, William Robinson		Major	British Army	13/05/1915	Panel 5
428152	CAMPBELL, William Wilson		Private	COEF	9/11/1917	Panel 18 - 28 - 30
5055A	CARR, Kenneth John		Private	AIF	29/09/1917	Panel 7 - 17 - 23 - 25 - 27 - 29 - 31
2955	CHAPMAN, Percy Charles		Private	AIF	29/09/1917	Panel 31
6557	COBHAM, Francis Foster		Private	AIF	20/09/1917	Panel 7 - 17 - 23 - 25 - 27 - 29 - 31
79052	CONDON, James Francis Bayntun		Lance Corporal	COEF	6/06/1916	Panel 24 - 28 - 30
887017	CONSTANTINE, John		Private	COEF	26/10/1917	Panel 18 - 26 - 28
6744	CROZIER, William St Clair		Private	AIF	4/10/1917	Panel 7 - 17 - 23 - 25 - 27 - 29 - 31
2058	DALE, Edward Thomas		Private	AIF	10/10/1917	Panel 7 - 17 - 23 - 25 - 27 - 29 - 31

6430	DALY, James Patrick		Sapper	AIF	26/09/1917	Panel 7
2613	DAUE, Stanley		Sergeant	AIF	12/10/1917	Panel 7 - 17 - 23 - 25 - 27 - 29 - 31
654503, 235074, S8223	DEHANEY, David			British Army	31/07/1917	Panel 21
6479	DONALDSON, Herbert Clarence		Private	AIF	20/09/1917	Panel 7 - 17 - 23 - 25 - 27 - 29 - 31
771	DONNELLY, Arthur Harris		Corporal	AIF	20/09/1917	Panel 7 - 17 - 23 - 25 - 27 - 29 - 31
5339	DRUMMOND, William George		Private	AIF	4/10/1917	Panel 7 - 17 - 23 - 25 - 27 - 29 - 31
G/15066	FARRELL, William James Edward		Private	British Army	31/07/1917	Panel 45 and 47
	FERRIER, Gilbert Colin Cunninghame		2nd Lieutenant	British Army	11/11/1914	Panel 6 and 8
3263	FINDLAY, Thomas		Private	AIF	7/06/1917	Panel 7 - 17 - 23 - 25 - 27 - 29 - 31
2796	FIRTH, Percy Priestnall		Sapper	AIF	20/09/1917	Panel 7
553	GALE, Alfred William		Private	AIF	20/09/1917	Panel 31
	GEORGE, Keith Harrison		Lieutenant	AIF	7/11/1916	Panel 7
2655	GRANT, Dudley		Private	AIF	7/06/1917	Panel 7 - 17 - 23 - 25 - 27 - 29 - 31
48	GREEN, George Henry		Private	AIF	10/06/1917	Panel 7 - 17 - 23 - 25 - 27 - 29 - 31
3052	HARPER, Edgar Vincent		Private	AIF	13/10/1917	Panel 7 - 17 - 23 - 25 - 27 - 29 - 31
	HEALY, Michael Darnien	Michael Pater Chance Duncan Healy	Lieutenant	AIF	20/09/1917	Panel 7 - 17 - 23 - 25 - 27 - 29 - 31
6615	HOLT, Frederick		Private	AIF	3/10/1917	Panel 7 - 17 - 23 - 25 - 27 - 29 - 31
1728	HOPKINS, Frank William Banner		Lance Corporal	AIF	26/09/1917	Panel 7 - 17 - 23 - 25 - 27 - 29 - 31
474	HOWELL, Edwin James		Private	AIF	31/07/1917	Panel 31
	HYAMS, Alec Hallenstein		Lieutenant	British Army	3/05/1915	Panel 6 and 8
3802	KAY, Francis Bertie	Francis Bert Kay	Captain	AIF	7/06/1917	Panel 7 - 17 - 23 - 25 - 27 - 29 - 31
274	LAMPLUGH, Welby Jackson		Private	AIF	4/10/1917	Panel 7 - 17 - 23 - 25 - 27 - 29 - 31
1667	LANE, Gordon		Corporal	AIF	16/07/1917	Panel 31
79	LANGSTONE, Arthur Ernest		Lance Corporal	AIF	31/07/1917	Panel 31
17242	LEACOCK, Arthur Leslie		Private	COEF	24/04/1915	Panel 18 - 28 - 30
6762	LETT, John McLaren		Private	AIF	26/09/1917	Panel 7 - 17 - 23 - 25 - 27 - 29 - 31
388, 3078	LINDSAY, James Douglas McKnight		Acting Sergeant	AIF	29/09/1917	Panel 7 - 17 - 23 - 25 - 27 - 29 - 31

2423	LOGAN, John Stewart		Private	AIF	7/06/1917	Panel 7 - 17 - 23 - 25 - 27 - 29 - 31
6111	LOMAX, Charles Mark		Private	AIF	4/10/1917	Panel 7 - 17 - 23 - 25 - 27 - 29 - 31
	MATHESON, Kenneth Ronald	Kenneth Ronald Mathieson	Lieutenant	British Army	1/11/1914	Panel 11
972	MATTHEWS, Roy Marden Howard		Sergeant	AIF	23/09/1917	Panel 7 - 17 - 23 - 25 - 27 - 29 - 31
1838	MCCOOK, Arthur Tiverton Archibald		Private	AIF	7/06/1917	Panel 7 - 17 - 23 - 25 - 27 - 29 - 31
6956	MCDOWALL, Stewart Arthur		Private	AIF	26/09/1917	Panel 7 - 17 - 23 - 25 - 27 - 29 - 31
3560	MCFARLANE, Wallace Askew		Lance Corporal	AIF	20/09/1917	Panel 7 - 17 - 23 - 25 - 27 - 29 - 31
3220	MCLAREN, John Henry		Private	AIF	19/10/1917	Panel 7 - 17 - 23 - 25 - 27 - 29 - 31
	MCNAB, Dr Angus	Angus MacNab	Surgeon Captain	British Army	1/11/1914	Panel 56
497	MOSES, Hamilton Leslie		Lance Corporal	AIF	31/07/1917	Panel 7 - 17 - 23 - 25 - 27 - 29 - 31
50801	MURR, William Henry		Lieutenant	COEF	30/10/1917	Panel 26 - 30
628983	NASH, Edward		Private	COEF	6/11/1917	Panel 18 - 28 - 30
13370	OGILVIE, William Edgar		Lance Corporal	COEF	25/04/1915	Panel 18 - 26 - 28
4190	OLLIVER, Oswald Thomas		Private	AIF	20/09/1917	Panel 7 - 17 - 23 - 25 - 27 - 29 - 31
932	O'NEILL, Herbert Frank		Sergeant	AIF	21/09/1917	Panel 7 - 17 - 23 - 25 - 27 - 29 - 31
	PARK, Robert		Captain	AIF	26/09/1917	Panel 7
877	PARKER, Harry Kelvin		Private	AIF	7/06/1917	Panel 7 - 17 - 23 - 25 - 27 - 29 - 31
6830	PAYNE, James		Private	AIF	21/09/1917	Panel 7 - 17 - 23 - 25 - 27 - 29 - 31
2972	PILKINGTON, Frederick		Private	AIF	26/09/1917	Panel 7 - 17 - 23 - 25 - 27 - 29 - 31
882	POUPARD, Leonard Bryant		Private	AIF	6/11/1917	Panel 7 - 17 - 23 - 25 - 27 - 29 - 31
3616	PYE, William Leslie		Private	AIF	21/10/1917	Panel 7 - 17 - 23 - 25 - 27 - 29 - 31
2791	QUINN, Joseph	Joseph Thomson	Private	AIF	7/06/1917	Panel 7 - 17 - 23 - 25 - 27 - 29 - 31
266790	REES, Stanley Joseph Lloyd		Private	British Army	31/07/1917	Panel 4 and 6
	RUSSELL, Walter Russell		Captain	British Army	23/10/1914	Panel 43 and 45
4293	RUTLEDGE, Joseph Ward		Lieutenant	British Army	31/07/1917	Panel 5 and 9
370	SAVAGE, Samuel	Haami Savage	Lance Corporal	AIF	4/10/1917	Panel 7 - 17 - 23 - 25 - 27 - 29 - 31
84	SHAW, Bertram George		Sergeant	AIF	4/10/1917	Panel 7 - 17 - 23 - 25 - 27 - 29 - 31
5623	SPENCE, William Joseph		Sapper	AIF	1/10/1917	Panel 7

6166	STANTON, James		Lance Corporal	AIF	4/10/1917	Panel 7 - 17 - 23 - 25 - 27 - 29 - 31
	STEELE, Oliver		Captain	British Army	25/10/1914	Panel 45
1625	STEWART, George Blakeney		Private	COEF	8/05/1915	Panel 10
2659, 958	STOREY, Francis		Private	AIF	5/08/1917	Panel 7 - 17 - 23 - 25 - 27 - 29 - 31
21502	STREET, Alfred Cecil		Private	AIF	10/06/1917	Panel 7 - 17 - 23 - 25 - 27 - 29 - 31
5924	TAYLOR, George Edward		Private	AIF	29/10/1917	Panel 7 - 17 - 23 - 25 - 27 - 29 - 31
13296	TREPO, Thomas	Thomas Vucasivitch, Trepo Vucasivitch	Private	SA Army	18/10/1917	Panel 16 - 16 and 16A
7059	TURNBULL, George Dowling	Gordon Dowling Turnbull	Private	AIF	4/10/1917	Panel 7 - 17 - 23 - 25 - 27 - 29 - 31
51124	TURNER, Henry	Harry Turner	Sapper	British Army	10/02/1916	Panel 9
2548	WALKER, William James		Lance Corporal	AIF	27/09/1917	Panel 7 - 17 - 23 - 25 - 27 - 29 - 31
58	WALLACE, James		Corporal	British Army	31/10/1914	Panel 38
	WALLIS, Henry Digby		Lieutenant	British Army	21/10/1914	Panel 11
27766	WARREN, William Albert	William Thomas Warren	Private	COEF	24/04/1915	Panel 18 - 24 - 26 - 30
684	WATT, Donald Washington		Private	AIF	10/02/1918	Panel 7 - 17 - 23 - 25 - 27 - 29 - 31
999	WEIR, John Hay		Private	AIF	1/08/1917	Panel 7 - 17 - 23 - 25 - 27 - 29 - 31
742849	WELLS, William David		Private	COEF	6/11/1917	Panel 26 - 28
1430	WHELAN, Patrick Conrad		Corporal	AIF	6/10/1917	Panel 7 - 17 - 23 - 25 - 27 - 29 - 31
387	WHITWORTH, James		Private	AIF	30/10/1917	Panel 31
R/10182	WILLIAMS, Cecil Horatio Childe		Lance Corporal	British Army	26/04/1915	Panel 51 and 53
3227	WILLIAMS, Edward Willis		Private	AIF	13/10/1917	Panel 7 - 17 - 23 - 25 - 27 - 29 - 31
3248	WILLOUGHBY, Alfred Seymour Bolton		Private	AIF	27/09/1917	Panel 7 - 17 - 23 - 25 - 27 - 29 - 31
2782	WOODS, William Potter		Private	AIF	26/09/1917	Panel 7 - 17 - 23 - 25 - 27 - 29 - 31
926	YOUNG, John Buchanan		Lance Corporal	AIF	6/06/1917	Panel 7 - 17 - 23 - 25 - 27 - 29 - 31

ABBREVIATIONS, NOTES, BIBLIOGRAPHY, ACKNOWLEDGEMENTS, ABOUT THE AUTHORS, INDEX

ABBREVIATIONS

AANS	Australian Army Nursing Service
ADC	aide-de-camp (personal assistant)
Adjt	adjutant
AEF	American Expeditionary Force
AFC	Australian Flying Corps
AIF	Australian Imperial Force
ANZAC	Australian and New Zealand Army Corps
AWL	absent without leave
AWM	Australian War Memorial
BEF	British Expeditionary Force
BNG	British New Guinea
CAMC	Canadian Army Medical Corps
CB	Companion of the Order of the Bath; confined to barracks
CBE	Commander of the British Empire
CEF	Canadian Expeditionary Force
CMG	Companion of the Order of St Michael and St George
CO	commanding officer
COEF	Canadian Overseas Expeditionary Force
Coy	company
DSO	Distinguished Service Order
DCM	Distinguished Conduct Medal
DCLI	Duke of Cornwall's Light Infantry
FFNC	French Flag Nursing Corps
GOC	general officer commanding
GSW	gunshot wound
HM	His Majesty's
HLI	Highland Light Infantry
2/Lt or 2/Lieut.	second lieutenant
Lieut.	lieutenant
MBE	Member of the British Empire
MC	Military Cross
MEF	Mediterranean Expeditionary Force
MGC	Machine Gun Corps
MiD	mentioned in despatches
MM	Mercantile Marine
MP	member of Parliament; military police
NCO	non-commissioned officer
NZANS	New Zealand Army Nursing Service

NZEF	New Zealand Expeditionary Force
NZVAD	New Zealand Voluntary Aid Detachment
NZWCA	New Zealand War Contingent Association
OBE	Order of the British Empire
PTSI	post-traumatic stress injury
QAIMNSR	Queen Alexandra's Imperial Military Nursing Service Reserve
QC	Queen's Council
RAF	Royal Air Force
RAMC	Royal Army Medical Corps
RAN	Royal Australian Navy
RASC	Royal Army Service Corps
RE	Royal Engineers
Regt	regiment
RFA	Royal Field Artillery
RFC	Royal Flying Corps
RHA	Royal Horse Artillery
RMLI	Royal Marine Light Infantry
RN	Royal Navy
RNAS	Royal Naval Air Service
RND	Royal Naval Division
RNR	Royal Navy Reserve
RNVR	Royal Naval Volunteer Reserve
RRC	Royal Red Cross
SAOEF	South African Overseas Expeditionary Force
Sergt	sergeant
TFNS	Territorial Force Nursing Service
UDF	Union Defence Force
VAD	Volunteer Aid Detachment
VD	volunteers decoration; venereal disease
VDG	venereal disease gonorrhoea
VC	Victoria Cross
WAFF	Royal West African Frontier Force
WO	War Office

NOTES

ABBREVIATIONS

ANZ	Archives New Zealand Te Rua Mahara o te Kāwanatanga
ATL	Alexander Turnbull Library, Wellington
AWMM	Auckland War Memorial Museum Tāmaki Paenga Hira
NAA	National Archives of Australia, Canberra
NAM	National Army Museum, Waiouru
TNA	The National Archives of the United Kingdom

INTRODUCTION: LARGELY FORGOTTEN

1 https://www3.stats.govt.nz/historic_publications/1916 census/Report%20on%20Results%20of%20 Census%201916/1916-report-results census%20.html#idchapter_1_2204 (accessed 14 June 2018). After the war, because of strong anti-German feeling in New Zealand, Gustav added an H to his surname, as he believed Bergh looked less of a German name. His Australian army records, including the attestation papers, and all accounts in New Zealand newspapers record the surname as Berg, and I have used this earlier version of the surname throughout this book.

2 'In an Australian Camp', *Ellesmere Guardian*, 26 January 1916.

3 Ibid.

4 G. V. Berg, B2455, NAA.

5 'In an Australian Camp', *Ellesmere Guardian*, 18 March 1916.

6 'News of the Day', *Ellesmere Guardian*, 22 July 1916.

7 G. V. Berg, B2455, NAA.

8 'Letters from the Trenches', *Ellesmere Guardian*, 9 September 1916.

9 J. L. Sleeman, 'The Supply of Reinforcements During the War', in H. T. B. Drew (ed.), *The War Effort of New Zealand* (Auckland: Whitcombe & Tombs, 1923), 13.

10 The figure is usually given as 100,444. It includes 250 New Zealanders who embarked from the United Kingdom. From John Studholme, *New Zealand Expeditionary Force: Record of personal services during the war of officers, nurses, and first-class warrant officers; and other facts relating to the N.Z.E.F. Unofficial, but based on official records* (Wellington: Government Printer, 1928). These numbers also feature in the *New Zealand Official Year-Book 1919* (Wellington: Government of New Zealand, 1920), 255–58.

11 *New Zealand Year Official Year-Book 1919* (Wellington: Government of New Zealand, 1920), 821. The New Zealand government paid the difference between imperial rates of pay, allowances and gratuities and the New Zealand rates for equivalent ranks.

12 Ian McGibbon, *New Zealand's Western Front Campaign* (Auckland: David Bateman Ltd, 2016), 15.

13 The figure of 850 New Zealanders in the RFC/RAF is from Adam Claasen, *Fearless: The extraordinary untold story of New Zealand's Great War airmen* (Auckland: Massey University Press, 2017), 8. The Australian numbers are examined in detail later in the book.

CHAPTER ONE: WITH THE OLD CONTEMPTIBLES

1 BEF Routine Orders, 24 September 1914, WO 123/199, TNA.

2 http://blog.helion.co.uk/spencer-jones-was-the-kaisers-old-contemptibles-telegram-a-fabrication/ (accessed 20 January 2016).

3 A. Corbett-Smith, *The Marne — And After* (London: Cassell & Company, 1917), 297.

4 Richard Holmes, *Soldiers: Army lives and loyalties from redcoats to dusty warriors* (London: HarperPress, 2012), 183.

5 Max Hastings, *Catastrophe: Europe goes to war 1914* (London: William Collins, 2013), 201.

6 Lyn MacDonald, *1914* (London: Guild Publishing, 1987), xi.

7 Hastings, *Catastrophe*, 206; Spencer Jones (ed.), *Stemming the Tide: Officers and leadership in the British Expeditionary Force 1914* (Solihull, West Midlands: Helion & Company, 2013), 17.

8 Jones, *Stemming the Tide*, 18.

9 Corbett-Smith, *The Marne*, 295.

10 MacDonald, *1914*, 425.

11 Ibid., 421.

12 Richard Holmes, *Tommy: The British soldier on the Western Front 1914–1918* (London: HarperCollins, 2004), 33.

13 Part of the first and third verses of 'Tipperary Days', Robert W. Service, *Rhymes of a Red Cross Man* (London: T. Fisher Unwin Ltd, 1916), 43, 44. This book of rhymes was dedicated to Service's brother Albert, who was killed in action in France in August 1916.

14 John Crawford, 'Andrew, Brigadier-General Albert William', in Ian McGibbon (ed.), *The Oxford Companion to New Zealand Military History* (Auckland: Oxford University Press, 2000), 17.

15 'On Service: New Zealanders and the war', *Otago Witness*, 21 April 1915.

16 'Another New Zealander Killed in Action in France', *Evening Post*, 3 November 1914.

17 Harmer Steele, letter to the War Office, 4 November 1914, and the War Office's reply to Mr Steele on 11 November 1914. Also Mrs Florence Steele to The Secretary, War Office, November 1914, WO 374/65059 Oliver Steele, TNA.

18 Ian McGibbon, *New Zealand's Western Front Campaign* (Auckland: David Bateman Ltd, 2016), 19.

19 'A Palmerstonian in Belgium', *Manawatu Standard*, 2 July 1915.

20 Ibid.

21 'With the British Forces: New Zealand casualties', *Auckland Star*, 28 October 1916.

22 Garry Clayton, 'Davies, Richard Hutton 1861–1918', *Dictionary of New Zealand Biography Te Ara — The Encyclopedia of New Zealand* (accessed 24 February 2017).

23 McGibbon, *New Zealand's Western Front Campaign*, 15.

24 Clayton, 'Davies, Richard Hutton'.

25 Minute Sheet, Record of Service, WO 339/50002 Richard Hutton Davies, TNA. The handwritten minute was made in 1915.

26 Richard Davies, letter to Sir James Allen, 16 January 1915, AD 1 873, 38/1 Personnel: Transfers and promotions — Miscellaneous correspondence — General R. H. Davies, ANZ.

27 Ibid.

28 McGibbon, *New Zealand Military History*, 134.

29 Lord Cavan, Secret and Confidential Memorandum, 2 March 1916, WO 339/50002 Richard Hutton Davies, TNA.

30 D. Haig, letter to The Secretary, War Office, 5 March 1916, WO 339/50002 Richard Hutton Davies, TNA.

31 Richard Davies, letter to Sir James Allen, 24 September 1916, AD 1 873, 38/1 Personnel: Transfers and promotions — Miscellaneous correspondence — General R. H. Davies, ANZ.

32 Alexander Godley, letter to Louisa Godley, 23 December 1916, in Godley Papers, WA 252 Item 12 Letters of General Alexander Godley and Lady Godley, ANZ.

33 Alexander Godley, letter to James Allen, 10 December 1916, in Godley Papers, WA 252 Item 3 Correspondence between General Sir Alexander Godley and Colonel Hon Sir James Allen, 4 January–29 December 1916, ANZ.

34 Richard Davies, letter to Sir James Allen, 12 February 1917, AD 1 873, 38/1 Personnel: Transfers and

promotions — Miscellaneous correspondence — General R. H. Davies, ANZ.

35 James Allen, letter to Alexander Godley, 27 January 1917, in Godley Papers, WA 252 Item 4 Correspondence between General Sir Alexander Godley and Colonel Hon Sir James Allen, 6 January–28 December 1917, ANZ.

36 Report on the death of Major General R. H. Davies, 10 May 1918, WO 339/50002 Richard Hutton Davies, TNA.

37 Ibid. See also Clayton, 'Davies, Richard Hutton'.

38 The Secretary, War Office, memo to Headquarters, London District, 13 May 1918, Report on the death of Major General R. H. Davies, 10 May 1918, WO 339/50002 Richard Hutton Davies, TNA.

39 War Office to The Under Secretary of State, Colonial Office, 30 August 1914, in Henry Arthur Davies, Personal File, ANZ.

40 Personal Files of Rayner Barrington Smythe, Robert Oswald Chesney, Murray Menzies Gard'ner and Charles William Melvill, ANZ.

41 McGibbon, *New Zealand Military History*, 316.

42 Charles Melvill, letter to The Secretary, War Office, 27 November 1919, WO 374/47296 Charles W. Melvill, TNA.

43 Ibid.

44 John Lancelot Harcourt Turner, Personal File, ANZ.

45 Henry Arthur Davies, Personal File, ANZ.

46 Secretary of State for Colonies to New Zealand Government, 15 January 1914, G1/181, quoted in Richard G. H. Kay, 'In Pursuit of Victory: British–New Zealand relations during the First World War', PhD thesis, University of Otago, Dunedin, October 2001, 26.

47 'British Reservists', *Evening Post*, 26 August 1914.

48 'News in Brief', *Sun*, 6 May 1915.

49 Board of Trade: Commercial and Statistical Department and successors: Inward Passengers Lists, Series BT26/595/, TNA.

50 'Shooting: Imperial Reservists v. Manawatu Club', *Manawatu Standard*, 21 September 1914.

51 'Transport State', *Evening Post*, 18 September 1914.

52 Board of Trade: Commercial and Statistical Department and successors: Inward Passengers Lists, Series BT26/594/76, TNA.

53 'Three Reservists Killed', *Poverty Bay Herald*, 19 January 1915.

54 *Maoriland Worker*, 3 February 1915.

55 Everard Wyrall, *The 17th (S.) Battalion Royal Fusiliers, 1914–1919* (London: Methuen & Company, 1930), 2.

56 Frederick Miles, letter to The Secretary, War Office, 30 November 1920, WO 339/1046 Frederick Fisher Miles, TNA.

57 Proceedings of a Medical Board, WO 339/1046 Frederick Fisher Miles, TNA.

58 Frederick Miles, letter to The Secretary, War Office, 30 November 1920, WO 339/1046 Frederick Fisher Miles, TNA.

59 The War Office, letter to F. F. Miles Esq, 26 January 1921, Frederick Miles, letter to The Secretary, War Office, 30 November 1920, WO 339/1046 Frederick Fisher Miles, TNA.

60 Rainsford Balcombe-Brown, letter to The Secretary, War Office, London, 7 September 1915, WO 339/11481 William Edward Balcombe-Brown, TNA.

61 Adam Claasen, *Fearless: The extraordinary untold story of New Zealand's Great War airmen* (Auckland: Massey University Press, 2017), 195, 337.

62 Death Notice, Rainsford Balcombe-Brown, WO 339/31372, TNA.

63 Claasen, *Fearless*, 359.

64 'New Zealander Abroad', *Southland Times*, 27 November 1914.

65 'John Hugh Allen: A memoir', *Press*, 26 December 1919.

66 High Commissioner of New Zealand, letter to The Secretary, War Office, 25 June 1915, WO 339/25763 John Hugh Allen, TNA. The High Commissioner had written on 22 June seeking this information.

67 The Secretary, War Office, letter to High Commissioner of New Zealand, 27 June 1915, WO 339/25763 John Hugh Allen, TNA.

68 McGibbon, *New Zealand's Western Front Campaign*, 17.

69 'The First Wounded', *Poverty Bay Herald*, 22 October 1914.

70 'New Zealander Abroad', *Southland Times*, 27 November 1914.

71 Minute Sheet and Attestation Form, WO 339/34855 Joseph Ward Rutledge, TNA.

72 Statement of Service, WO 339/11953 Edmund Boulnois, TNA.

73 War Office, Telegram to Miss Boulnois, 26 October 1916, WO 339/11953 Edmund Boulnois, TNA.

74 The Treasury, Wellington, letter to The Secretary, War Office 22 May 1920, WO 339/11953 Edmund Boulnois, TNA.

75 Schedule of Motor Cycle belonging to Claude Gladstone Robinson 30254, WO 339/25873 Claude Gladstone Robinson, TNA.

76 War Office, Telegram to Robinson, 28 October 1915, WO 339/25873 Claude Gladstone Robinson, TNA.

77 'A Very Brave Man', *Taranaki Daily News*, 15 May 1920.

78 Conduct Sheet, WO 339/4177 Cecil F. G. Humphries, TNA. The date of the action for which the DCM was awarded was 21 December 1914.

79 'A Wonderful Escape', *Wanganui Chronicle*, 17 March 1915.

80 'A New Zealand Hero', *Wanganui Chronicle*, 27 December 1917.

81 War Diary 1 Battalion Norfolk Regiment, 22 August 1918, WO 95/1573/2, TNA.

82 'A Very Brave Man'.

83 'Lieut-Col. Humphries. The Bravest Man. A Striking Tribute', *Star*, 3 September 1918.

84 Michael King, *The Penguin History of New Zealand* (Auckland: Penguin, 2003), 398.

85 'Returning Maoris', *Manawatu Times*, 23 May 1913.

86 June Northcroft-Grant, 'Papakura, Makereti', *Dictionary of New Zealand Biography Te Ara — The Encyclopedia of New Zealand* (accessed 9 March 2017).

87 'Local and General News', *New Zealand Herald*, 1 May 1918.

88 'Trooper J. D. Mossman', *The Press*, 12 June 1915.

89 Anon, *The Great War, 1914–1918: New Zealand Expeditionary Force roll of honour* (Wellington: Government Printer, 1924), 212.

90 'Trooper J. D. Mossman'.

91 'Local and General', *Star*, 25 August 1914.

92 Stevan Eldred-Grigg, *The Great Wrong War: New Zealand society in WWI* (Auckland: Random House, 2010), 77.

93 Tripp and Rolleston, Timaru, letter to The War Office, London, 29 July 1919, WO 339/27809 John William Pinckney, TNA.

94 The Army Council, letter to Tripp and Rolleston, 30 September 1919, WO 339/27809 John William Pinckney, TNA.

95 'King Edward's Horse. A Record of Service. The King's Oversea Dominions', *Evening Post*, 10 May 1919.

96 'On Service: Personal notes about New Zealanders', *Press*, 9 May 1919.

97 Application for a Temporary Commission, WO 339/46311, T. A. Izard, TNA.

98 The Secretary, War Office, letter to the Colonial Office, 7 March 1919, WO 339/46311, T. A. Izard, TNA.

99 Assistant Private Secretary, The Colonial Office letter to The Secretary, War Office, 14 February 1919, WO 339/46311, T. A. Izard, TNA.

100 Protection Certificate, WO 339/72145 Frederick Allan Hellaby, TNA.

101 Casualty Form–Active Service, WO 339/72145 Frederick Allan Hellaby, TNA.

102 Paul Freyberg, *Bernard Freyberg, VC: Soldier of two nations* (London: Hodder & Stoughton, 1991), 36.

103 Ibid., 37.

104 Ibid., 66.

105 General Freyberg's Farewell Speech, 5 January 1940, http://www.ngataonga.org.nz/collections/catalogue/catalogue-item?record_id=218438

106 Marcus Riske, interview with Jack Shallcrass, *Looking Back*, 23 January 1981, http://www.ngataonga.org.nz/collections/catalogue/catalogue-item?record_id=216175

107 'Battlefield Panorama', *Northern Advocate*, 20 February 1915.

108 Ibid.

109 'Mr Albert A. Corrigan, The Genial Skipper of the D.I.C., Wellington', *New Zealand Free Lance*, 29 May 1909.

110 'Battlefield Panorama'.

111 Bernard Freyberg ADM 337/117/245, TNA; Freyberg, *Bernard Freyberg*, 41.

112 The words are Major-General Sir Henry Beauvoir de Lisle's, quoted in Glyn Harper and Colin Richardson, *Acts of Valour: The history of the Victoria Cross and New Zealand* (Auckland: HarperCollins, 2016), 129.

113 Bernard Freyberg ADM 337/117/245, TNA.

114 Matthew Wright, *Freyberg's War: The man, the legend, the reality* (Auckland: Penguin, 2005), 238–39.

115 'War Jottings', *The Press*, 17 December 1914.

116 Eldred-Grigg, *The Great Wrong War*, 97.

117 Anthony Wilding, letter to Julia Wilding, 24 September 1914, quoted in Len and Shelley Richardson, *Anthony Wilding: A sporting life* (Christchurch: Canterbury University Press, 2005), 353.

118 Anthony Wilding, letters to Julia Wilding, 22 October and 1 December 1914, February 1915, quoted in Richardson, *Anthony Wilding*, 357, 359.

119 Anthony Wilding, letter to Julia Wilding, 15 March 1915, quoted in Richardson, *Anthony Wilding*, 361.

120 Richardson, *Anthony Wilding*, 374.

121 'The First in France', *Press*, 22 May 1915.

122 Arthur Anderson Martin, *A Surgeon in Khaki: Through France and Flanders in World War I* (Lincoln, NA: University of Nebraska Press, 2011), vi.

123 Ibid., 230.

124 Ibid., 123.

125 Glyn Harper, 'Introduction', in ibid., ix.

126 Ibid., xii.

127 A. D. Carbery, *The New Zealand Medical Service in the Great War 1914–1918* (Auckland: Whitcombe & Tombs, 1924), 212.

128 Ibid., 212.

129 McGibbon, *New Zealand's Western Front Campaign*, 19.

130 Dr William Johnston, letter to his parents, 23 September 1914, in *Star*, 14 November 1914.

131 The McNab surname is spelt differently in some other books and documents. It appears variously as McNabb, MacNab and MacNabb. His file at National Archives spells the surname as MacNab, but in it the doctor has signed his name as McNab. I am assuming he knew best. WO 374/45175 Angus MacNab, TNA.

132 Anna Rogers, *While You're Away: New Zealand nurses at war 1899–1948* (Auckland: Auckland University Press, 2003), 155.

133 'On Service: New Zealanders and the war'.

134 Ibid.

135 'Captain Eric Croft, MC', *Otago Witness*, 20 March 1918.

136 War Office, cable to Defence Wellington, 4 November 1917, WO 339/42429 Eric Croft, TNA.

137 War Office, cable to Defence Wellington, 22 January 1918, WO 339/42429 Eric Croft, TNA.

138 'Captain Eric Croft, MC', *Otago Witness*, 20 March 1918.

139 Quoted in Sherayl McNabb, *100 Years. New Zealand Military Nursing. New Zealand Army Nursing Service — Royal New Zealand Nursing Corps, 1915–2015* (Wairoa, Hawke's Bay: Sherayl McNabb, 2015), 214.

140 Ibid., 204.

141 Quoted in R. E. Rawstron, *A Unique Nursing Group: New Zealand Army nurse anaesthetists of WWI* (Christchurch: Rawstron Publishing Company, 2005), 20.

142 Ibid., 21.

143 'On Service: New Zealanders and the war'.

144 'Dominion Doctors: Nest together at Hull', *Dominion*, 13 January 1915.

145 Hastings, *Catastrophe*, 358.

146 Ibid., 548.

147 'The First Wounded', *Poverty Bay Herald*, 22 October 1914.

148 'Interesting Letter From a Wounded New Zealander', *Dunstan Times*, 16 November 1914.

149 'War Jottings', *Press*, 17 December 1914.

150 Thomas Edmund Sotheron-Estcourt, Statement to the Army Council, 30 January 1919, WO 339/5919 Thomas Edmund Sotheron-Estcourt, TNA.

151 War Office, Minute to Thomas Edmund Sotheron-Estcourt, 26 March 1919, WO 339/5919 Thomas Edmund Sotheron-Estcourt, TNA.

152 Thomas Edmund Sotheron-Estcourt, letter to the Military Secretary, 30 May 1919, WO 339/5919 Thomas Edmund Sotheron-Estcourt, TNA.

153 'Jottings', *Press*, 7 November 1914.

154 Telegram, War Office to Captain C. Garsia, n.d., WO 339/6181 Oliver Durham Melville Garsia, TNA.

155 Oliver Garsia, memorandum to OC, Base Details 1/DCLI, 19 August 1914, WO 339/6181 Oliver Durham Melville Garsia, TNA.

156 McGibbon, *New Zealand's Western Front Campaign*, 20.

157 Certificate of Death, WO 339/19469 Frederick George Andrews, TNA.

158 Laura Andrews, letter to The Secretary, War Office, 1 February 1915, WO 339/19469 Frederick George Andrews, TNA.

159 WO 339/15920 Ivan Scott Orbell, TNA.

160 Ruth Orbell, letter to Captain Staunton, 15 February 1915, WO 339/15920 Ivan Scott Orbell, TNA.

161 High Commissioner for New Zealand, letter to The Secretary, War Office, 10 December 1914, WO 339/15920 Ivan Scott Orbell, TNA.

162 The Secretary, War Office, letter to High Commissioner for New Zealand, 19 December 1914, WO 339/15920 Ivan Scott Orbell, TNA.

163 High Commissioner for New Zealand, letter to The Secretary, War Office, 15 February 1915, WO 339/15920 Ivan Scott Orbell, TNA.

164 Ruth Orbell, letter to Captain Staunton, 12 August 1915, WO 339/15920 Ivan Scott Orbell, TNA.

165 The Secretary, War Office, letter to Mrs Orbell, 4 October 1915, WO 339/15920 Ivan Scott Orbell, TNA.

166 Telegrams, War Office to Miss M. A. Buckley, 30 October 1914 and 22 August 1915, WO 339/8625 Frederick Neville Houston, TNA.

167 Officer's Statement, n.d., WO 339/8625 Frederick Neville Houston, TNA.

168 Mrs E. M. Houston, letters to War Office, 22 July and 7 August 1916, WO 339/8625 Frederick Neville Houston, TNA.

169 Mrs F. N. Houston, letter to War Office 31 August 1916, War Office reply 2 September 1916, Frederick Neville Houston, TNA.

170 War Office, letter to Messrs Cockburn, Gestling and Cockburn, 23 February 1917, WO 339/8625 Frederick Neville Houston, TNA.

171 Telegram, War Office to G. T. Gee, 21 October 1914; Telegram, Royal Victoria Hospital, Netley to War Office, 20 October 1914; Telegram, War Office to G. T. Gee, 28 October 1914, WO 339/10685 Robert Francis McLean Gee, TNA.

172 G. F. Gee, letters to the War Office, 30 January and 6 October 1915, WO 339/10685 Robert Francis McLean Gee, TNA.

173 Minute Sheet, WO 339/7663 Edward Wynne Chapman, TNA.

174 'Clergyman and Soldier', *Hawera & Normanby Star*, 8 March 1915.

175 'On Service: Appointments and promotions', *Evening Post*, 6 September 1918.

176 Mark Brewer, 'New Zealand and the Légion d'honneur: The Great War', in *The Volunteers: The Journal of the New Zealand Military Historical Society (Inc)*, vol. 37, no. 3 (November 2008), 172.

177 'Lieutenant Findlay', *Otago Witness*, 17 November 1915.

178 Brewer, 'New Zealand and the Légion d'honneur', 172.

179 Ibid.

180 'Lieutenant Findlay'.

181 Hastings, *Catastrophe*, 495.

182 Ian Kershaw, *Hitler, 1889–1936: Hubris* (London: Penguin, 1998), 90.

183 Director General, Army Medical Services, letter to High Commissioner of New Zealand, 6 January 1915, WO 339/11054 Charles Cochrane Iles, TNA.

184 Field Service Record, WO 339/6409 Charles Harold Reynell Watts, TNA.

185 'Personal Matters', *Evening Post*, 18 February 1915; *Otago Daily Times*, 11 June 1915.

186 Application for a Commission in the RAMC, WO 374/45175 Angus MacNab, TNA.

187 'A New Zealander Killed', *Waikato Argus*, 10 November 1914.

188 Declaration of Birth, WO 374/45175 Angus MacNab, TNA.

189 Richard Holmes, *Fatal Avenue: A traveller's history of the battlefields of Northern France and Flanders 1346–1945* (London: Vintage, 2008), 161.

190 Casualty list, War Diary 1/14 Battalion London Regiment (London Scottish), 6 November 1914, WO 95/1266/2, TNA.

191 Mark Lloyd, *The London Scottish in the Great War* (London: Pen & Sword, 2001), 43.

192 War Diary 1/14 Battalion London Regiment (London Scottish), 1 November 1914, WO 95/1266/2, TNA.

193 Quoted in Lloyd, *The London Scottish in the Great War*, 44.

194 'Killing of Captain McNab', *The Times*, 12 November 1914.

195 *The Times*, 12 November 1914, 5.

196 Paul Chapman, *Menin Gate South: In memory and mourning* (Barnsley: Pen & Sword Military, 2016), 387.

197 https://ww100.govt.nz/the-menin-gate-last-post-ceremony-an-enduring-tradition (accessed 9 May 2018).

198 Information provided by the Last Post Association, 3 May 2018, and Paul Foster, 5 May 2018. The names of the New Zealanders recorded on the Menin Gate are in Appendix 2 of this book.

199 *Otago Daily Times*, 24 February 1915.

200 'Clasp to 14 Star', *Evening Post*, 18 February 1915; *Otago Daily Times*, 2 January 1920.

CHAPTER TWO: WITH THE BRITISH ARMY AND MEDICAL ORGANISATIONS

1 'Imperial Commissions', *North Otago Times*, 14 July 1916.

2 The air war volume is Adam Claasen, *Fearless: The extraordinary untold story of New Zealand's Great War airmen* (Auckland: Massey University Press, 2017). The war at sea volume, written by Peter Dennerly, is forthcoming at the time of writing.

3 See Glyn Harper, *Johnny Enzed: The New Zealand soldier in the First World War 1914–1918* (Auckland: Exisle, 2015), 51–52.

4 Stevan Eldred-Grigg, *The Great Wrong War: New Zealand society in WWI* (Auckland: Random House, 2010), 77.

5 Ibid., 307.

6 Thomas Mackenzie, letter To Whom It May Concern, 11 February 1915, WO 339/35941 Leslie Heron Beauchamp, TNA.

7 Application for a Temporary Commission, WO 339/75661 Ernest Cyril Branson, TNA.

8 The Commandant, No. 1 R.F.A. Officer Cadet School, memorandum to The Secretary, The War office, 24 July 1917, WO 339/75661 Ernest Cyril Branson, TNA.

9 Minute for The Gazette, WO 339/75661 Ernest Cyril Branson, TNA.

10 Trevor Noel Holmden, Unpublished autobiography, 9–10, Trevor Noel Holmden, MS-Papers-2223, ATL.

11 Ibid., 11.

12 Ibid.

13 Ibid., chapter IV, 6.

14 Harper, *Johnny Enzed*, 155.

15 'Personal Notes from London', *Otago Daily Times*, 30 July 1919.

16 Ibid.

17 Colonel, Commanding Grenadier Guards, letter to The Secretary, War Office, 1 November 1915, WO 339/47745 Daniel Henry Strother Riddiford, TNA.

18 Medical Report on a Disabled Officer, 11 May 1918, WO 339/47745 Daniel Henry Strother Riddiford, TNA.

19 Application for Appointment to a Temporary Commission in the British Regular Army, WO 339/32475 Percy Ashton Elworthy, TNA.

20 Medical Board Report on a Disabled Officer, WO 339/32475 Percy Ashton Elworthy, TNA.

21 'Personal', *Star*, 9 June 1915.

22 'Personal Items', *Timaru Herald*, 24 November 1915.

23 Military Secretary, letter to Lieut. P. A. Elworthy, 21 April 1917, WO 339/32475 Percy Ashton Elworthy, TNA.

24 Officer Commanding, Reserve Regiment First Life Guards, letter to The General Officer Commanding, London District, 5 June 1917, WO 339/32475 Percy Ashton Elworthy, TNA.

25 Officer Commanding, Reserve Regiment First Life Guards, letter to The Secretary, War Office, 24 April 1918, WO 339/32475 Percy Ashton Elworthy, TNA.

26 Harper, *Johnny Enzed*, 98–99.

27 Frederick Holford Personal File, WWI 10/349, ANZ.

28 'On Service', *Evening Post*, 8 June 1918.

29 Robert Heaton Livingstone, Personal File, WWI 6/86, ANZ.

30 Medical Board Report on a Disabled Officer, 7 March 1918, WO 339/67846 Robert Heaton Livingstone, TNA. Livingstone's disability in the report is described as 'neurasthenia' and its origin listed as 'Gallipoli, 1915'.

31 Proceedings of a Medical Board, 12 June 1917, WO 339/67846 Robert Heaton Livingstone, TNA.

32 Medical Board Report on a Disabled Officer, 7 March 1918, WO 339/67846 Robert Heaton Livingstone, TNA.

33 Air Board Office, Minute 1, March 1918, WO 339/67846 Robert Heaton Livingstone, TNA.

34 Military Secretary, War Office, minute to Director of Air Organisation, 3 April 1918, WO 339/67846 Robert Heaton Livingstone, TNA.

35 Active Service Record, WO 339/67846 Robert Heaton Livingstone, TNA.

36 Record of Service, WA II 806716 Robert Heaton Livingstone, ANZ.

37 'An Adventurous Experience', *Poverty Bay Herald*, 1 May 1916.

38 Hugh Ludlow, ADM 188/1101, TNA.

39 'An Adventurous Experience'.

40 'Letters from the Front. Private Ludlow's Experiences', *Bruce Herald*, 19 October 1916.

41 Ibid.

42 Hugh Ludlow, Medal Card, WO 372/12/159478, TNA.

43 'Clutha News Items', *Bruce Herald*, 8 February 1917.

44 H. Ludlow, Court Martial Book 1916, WO 213/11, TNA.

45 Hugh Ludlow, ADM 188/1101, TNA.

46 Territorial Force Attestation Form, WO 339/94219 Reginald Victor Deacon, TNA.

47 Reginald Deacon, letter to the War Office, 5 November 1918, WO 339/94219 Reginald Victor Deacon, TNA.

48 Minute Sheet 1, Notes, WO 339/94219 Reginald Victor Deacon, TNA.

49 Reginald Deacon, letter to the War Office, 5 November 1918, WO 339/94219 Reginald Victor Deacon, TNA.

50 Reginald Deacon, letter to the War Office, 16 October 1918, WO 339/94219 Reginald Victor Deacon, TNA.

51 L. P. Leary, *Not Entirely Legal: An autobiography* (Christchurch: Whitcoulls, 1977), 13, 14.

52 Ibid., 48.

53 Leonard Poulter Leary, interview with Jack Perkins, 1982, Ngā Taonga Sound & Vision Archive, http://www.ngataonga.org.nz/collections/catalogue/catalogue-item?record_id=177152

54 Harper, *Johnny Enzed*, 42.

55 Busby, William Baldwin — WW1 1/284 — Army, ANZ.

56 War Office, Telegram to Mrs Busby, 22 February 1917, WO 339/36812 William Baldwin Busby, TNA.

57 Casualty Form May 1916, WO 339/33753 Leonard Poulter Leary, TNA.

58 Ernest Leary, letter to Dear Len, 28 June 1916, WO 339/36752 Ernest Richard Leary, TNA.

59 New Zealand Stationary Hospital, Telegram to War Office, 21 July 1916, WO 339/36752 Ernest Richard Leary, TNA.

60 Leary, *Not Entirely Legal*, 50.

61 Ibid., 52.

62 Leary, interview with Jack Perkins, Ngā Taonga Sound & Vision Archive.

63 Leary, *Not Entirely Legal*, 59.

64 Ibid., 74.

65 Ibid., 189, 190.

66 Katherine Mansfield to Sylvia Payne, letter, 4 March 1908, in Vincent O'Sullivan (ed.), *Katherine Mansfield: Selected letters* (New York: Oxford University Press, 1989), 11.

67 Katherine Mansfield to Leslie Beauchamp, letter, 25 August 1915, in ibid., 36–37.

68 Leslie Beauchamp to Katherine Mansfield, letter, 5 October 1915, https://nzhistory.govt.nz/media/video/leslie-beauchamp-great-war-story (accessed 20 August 2017).

69 The Secretary, War Office, Telegram to Beauchamp c/o Bank of New Zealand, WO 339/35941 Leslie Heron Beauchamp, TNA.

70 In Leslie's personal file at The National Archives there are two letters from the New Zealand High Commission and one from the Bank of New Zealand seeking further information on Leslie's death. WO 339/35941 Leslie Heron Beauchamp, TNA.

71 A. G. A. Lang, Report to Headquarters 75th Brigade, WO 339/35941 Leslie Heron Beauchamp, TNA.

72 James Allen, letter to Alexander Godley, 11 July 1916, in Godley Papers, WA 252 Item 3 Correspondence between General Sir Alexander Godley and Colonel Hon Sir James Allen, 4 January–29 December 1916, ANZ.

73 Quoted in Gerri Kimber, 'Katherine Mansfield's Literary Response to the Great War', in Nathalie Philippe (ed.), *The Great Adventure Ends: New Zealand and France on the Western Front* (Christchurch: John Douglas Publishing Ltd, 2013), 242.

74 Ibid.

75 C. A. Hankin, *Katherine Mansfield and her Confessional Stories* (London: Macmillan, 1983), 235.

76 Ibid.

77 Katherine Mansfield to My dearest Father, letter, 31 December 1922, in O'Sullivan, *Katherine Mansfield*, 284.

78 'The Roll of Honour', *Otago Daily Times*, 8 February 1918.

79 Ibid.

80 Application for Appointment to the Special Reserve of Officers, WO 339/38277 John Nevill Ritchie, TNA.

81 Obituary, *Chronicles of the N.Z.E.F.*, 30 August 1916.

82 David Stevenson, *1914–1918: The history of the First World War* (London: Penguin, 2004), 121.

83 Obituary, *Chronicles of the N.Z.E.F.*, 30 August 1916.

84 Casualty Form — Active Service, WO 339/38277 John Nevill Ritchie, TNA.

85 War Office, telegram to Mrs Ritchie, 27 April 1916, WO 339/38277 John Nevill Ritchie, TNA.

86 High Commissioner's Office, London, letter to The Secretary, War Office, 5 June 1917, War Office reply 7 June 1917, WO 339/38277 John Nevill Ritchie, TNA.

87 Army Council, letter to Mrs Ritchie, 7 November 1917, WO 339/38277 John Nevill Ritchie, TNA.

88 Mrs Eviene M. Ritchie, letter to Army Council, 12 November 1917, WO 339/38277 John Nevill Ritchie, TNA.

89 Army Council, letter to Mssrs Corbould, Rigby & Company, 17 December 1917, WO 339/38277 John Nevill Ritchie, TNA.

90 Hannah Clark, 'Sisters in a Distant Land: The exploration of identity and travel through three New Zealand nurses: Diaries from the Great War', *Women's Studies Journal*, vol. 30, no. 1 (July 2016), 24.

91 Anna Rogers, *While You're Away: New Zealand nurses at war 1899–1948* (Auckland: Auckland University Press, 2003), 153.

92 Sherayl McNabb, *100 Years. New Zealand Military Nursing. New Zealand Army Nursing Service — Royal New Zealand Nursing Corps, 1915–2015* (Wairoa, Hawke's Bay: Sherayl McNabb, 2015), 403–6.

93 http://www.qaranc.co.uk/voluntary-aid-detachment.php (accessed 26 June 2018).

94 McNabb, *100 Years*, 406.

95 Jane Tolerton, *Make Her Praises Heard Afar: New Zealand women overseas in World War One* (Wellington: Book Lovers Books, 2017), 116, 114.

96 'A Unique Record', unnamed newspaper article, in MS-1535, George Ernest and Harriet Simeon, Papers, 1894–1963, AWMM.

97 Lieut. S. Scheratter, Alexandria Egypt, 6 May 1916, MS-1535, George Ernest and Harriet Simeon, Papers, 1894–1963, AWMM.

98 'A Unique Record'.

99 Tolerton, *Make Her Praises Heard Afar*, 164–65.

100 Quoted in ibid., 200.

101 Ibid., 214.

102 Ibid., 239.

103 Quoted in ibid., 334.

104 Jean Garner, 'Grigg, Mary Victoria Cracroft', *Dictionary of New Zealand Biography Te Ara — The Encyclopedia of New Zealand*, https://teara.govt.nz/en/biographies/5g22/grigg-mary-victoria-cracroft (accessed 7 February 2018).

105 Tolerton, *Make Her Praises Heard Afar*, 356.

106 'Fighting Families', *New Zealand Herald*, 12 April 1917.

107 'Nurses Examination', *New Zealand Herald* and *New Zealand Times*, 30 June 1915.

108 E. H. Beecher, Matron-in-Chief QAIMNSR, letter to Miss Nancy Robertson, 6 November 1916, MS-85-128, Nancy Marion Page, Documents relating to service in World War I, AWMM.

109 Report on S/Nurse Robertson, Nancy Marion, Nancy Marion Robertson, WO 399/7117, TNA.

110 Record of Service (File J 147), Laura James, WO 399/4234, TNA.

111 Quoted in Rogers, *While You're Away*, 156.

112 Record of Service (File J 147), Laura James, WO 399/4234, TNA.

113 Rogers, *While You're Away*, 157.

114 Casualty Form — Active Service, Laura James, WO 399/4234, TNA.

115 'A Much Decorated Nurse', *Star*, 30 September 1919.

116 Record of Service (File J 147), Laura James, WO 399/4234, TNA.

117 'A Nurse's Letter', *Hastings Standard*, 8 November 1916.

118 Louisa Higginson, diary entry, 9 May 1915, Louisa Higginson Diaries, MS-Papers 2477-1, ATL.

119 Ibid., 17 May 1915.

120 Ibid., 13 June 1915.

121 Ibid., 16 June 1915.

122 Ibid., 25 June 1915.

123 Quoted in Rogers, *While You're Away*, 162.

124 Mary Collins, letter to Miss Beacher, 10 January 1917, Mary M. Collins, WO 399/1637, TNA.

125 M. Thurston, letter to Miss Becher [sic], 30 January 1917, Louisa Higginson, WO 399/3813, TNA.

126 Quoted in Clark, 'Sisters in a Distant Land', 19.

127 Louisa Higginson, diary entry, 24 November 1916, Louisa Higginson Diaries, MS-Papers 2477-2, ATL.

128 Ibid., 7 March 1917.

129 Ibid., 6 June 1917.

130 See Rogers, *While You're Away*, 130–32.

131 Louisa Higginson, diary entry, 15 June 1917, Louisa Higginson Diaries, MS-Papers 2477-2, ATL.

132 'Personal Notes from London', *Evening Post*, 14 September 1918.

133 'Personal', *Waikato Times*, 18 March 1919.

134 Louisa Higginson, letter to Matron-in-Chief, QAIMNS, 3 March 1919, Louisa Higginson, WO 399/3813, TNA.

135 Louisa Higginson, diary entry, 24 August 1919, Louisa Higginson Diaries, MS-Papers 2477-3, ATL.

136 Ibid., 25 August 1919.

137 Rogers, *While You're Away*, 180.

138 'Women's Corner', *The Press*, 28 June 1917.

139 'On Active Service', *New Zealand Herald*, 1 June 1915.

140 'Women in Print', *Evening Post*, 2 August 1920.

141 Rogers, *While You're Away*, 158–59.

142 Cooke, letter to Florrie Williams, 23 July 1915, quoted in ibid., 160.

143 Rogers, *While You're Away*, 160.

144 Summary of Accident Report with eyewitness statements, Ella Cooke, WO 399/1701, TNA.

145 'The Roll of Honour', *Otago Daily Times*, 8 February 1918.

146 Rogers, *While You're Away*, 161.

147 'Nurse in Flanders', *New Zealand Herald*, 28 July 1915.

148 Rogers, *While You're Away*, 161.

149 'New Zealand Nurses at the Front', *Dominion*, 9 February 1915.

150 Alan Wakefield and Simon Moody, *Under the Devil's Eye: Britain's forgotten army at Salonika 1915–1918* (Barnsley, South Yorkshire: Pen & Sword Military, 2017), 165.

151 Rogers, *While You're Away*, 167.

152 'Lady Paget Home Again', *Evening Post*, 20 May 1916.

153 'Personal Notes From London', *Evening Post*, 17 April 1919.

154 Rogers, *While You're Away*, 167–68.

155 'News of Nurse Lewis', *Manawatu Standard*, 15 March 1916.

156 Rogers, *While You're Away*, 168. Grant Tobin in 'Staff Nurse Ethel Mary Lewis 22/444. The gallant little nurse', in *The Volunteers: The Journal of the New Zealand Military Historical Society (Inc)*, vol. 39, no. 2 (November 2013), 80–93, provides an illustration of Ethel Lewis at Walton-on-Thames with her arm in a cast. She had previously broken it in Ōtaki in 1912.

157 'Gallant Sister's Career', *Feilding Star*, 4 June 1919.

158 Tobin, 'Staff Nurse Ethel Mary Lewis', 92.

159 Mark Brewer, email to author, 13 June 2018. Mark has a letter from the Grande Chancellerie de la Légion d'honneur dated 7 August 2014 confirming it has no record of Ethel Lewis receiving the award.

160 Rogers, *While You're Away*, 173.

161 Agnes Kerr, Annual Confidential Report, 3 February 1918, Agnes Kerr, WO 399/12558, TNA.

162 Ibid., 11 January 1919.

163 Principal Matron, TANS, 1st Southern General Hospital letter to The Matron-in-Chief, TANS regarding Agnes Kerr's resignation, 19 February 1930, Agnes Kerr, WO 399/12558, TNA.

164 Rogers, *While You're Away*, 170.

165 Ibid.

166 Anna Rogers, *With Them Through Hell: New Zealand medical services in the First World War* (Auckland: Massey University Press, 2018).

167 McNabb, *100 Years*, 207.

168 Tolerton, *Make Her Praises Heard Afar*, 3.

169 Ibid., 157.

170 Ibid., 139.

171 Ibid., 63.

172 Part of Redpath's diary of his war experience is held by the National Army Museum in Waiouru. See 2012.420.1, Diary. Lieutenant George Redpath — France WWI, NAM.

173 Mrs R. W. Wilkinson, letter to Brigadier General McGavin, 22 February 1920, AABK 18805 3/2950 George Redpath, ANZ.

174 R. M. Gunn, M.D., letter to the Director General Medical Services, 2 February 1920, AABK 18805 3/2950 George Redpath, ANZ.

175 John Craig, interview with Thomas Remi Morrison, 9 February 1967, Ngā Taonga Sound & Vision Archive, http://www.ngataonga.org.nz/collections/catalogue/catalogue-item?record_id=224987

176 'Alexander Ormond', Last Post Stories Project, Ministry for Culture and Heritage, http://www.nzhistory.net.nz/keyword/last-post-stories (accessed 2 May 2017).

177 Territorial Force Attestation Form, WO 339/60593 Alexander Ormond, TNA.

178 'Alexander Ormond'.

179 Handwritten note, WO 339/96866 Charles Edward Anketell, TNA.

180 'New Zealander's Part', *New Zealand Herald*, 6 April 1915.

181 'New Zealanders Abroad', *Sun*, 23 February 1915; Handwritten note, WO 339/96866 Charles Edward Anketell, TNA.

182 *Evening Post*, 20 July 1918.

183 Casualty Form — Active Service, WO 339/96866 Charles Edward Anketell, TNA.

184 Medical Board Report on a Disabled Officer, WO 339/96866 Charles Edward Anketell, TNA.

185 'Statement of Capture', WO 339/44693 Henry Norman Spence, TNA.

186 Secretary of the War Office, letter to 2nd Lieutenant H. N. Spence, 14 June 1919, WO 339/44693 Henry Norman Spence, TNA.

187 'On Service. New Zealanders Abroad: Appointments and promotions', *Evening Post*, 27 August 1917 and 27 December 1917.

188 *Evening Post*, 24 July 1918.

CHAPTER THREE: TRANSFERS TO THE BRITISH MILITARY

1 John Studholme, *New Zealand Expeditionary Force: Record of personal services during the war of officers, nurses, and first-class warrant officers; and other facts relating to the N.Z.E.F. Unofficial, but based on official records* (Wellington: Government Printer, 1928), 365.

2 Ibid., 366–72.

3 Alexander Godley, letter to Sir James Allen, 8 July 1915, WA 252 (2) Godley Correspondence 2 April–18 December 1915, ANZ.

4 Ibid.

5 Sir James Allen, letter to Alexander Godley, 20 September 1915, WA 252 (2) Godley Correspondence 2 April–18 December 1915, ANZ.

6 Alexander Godley, letter to Sir James Allen, 4 March 1916, WA 252 (3) Godley Correspondence 1916, ANZ. Andrew Russell was general officer commanding (GOC), New Zealand Division.

7 Lieutenant-General Alexander Godley, letter to Sir Thomas Mackenzie, 3 March 1916, WA 95, Box 1, Item 2b, ANZ.

8 Alexander Godley, letter to Sir James Allen, 29 November 1916, WA 252 (3) Godley Correspondence 1916, ANZ.

9 Sir James Allen, letter to Alexander Godley, 11 July 1916, WA 252 (3) Godley Correspondence 1916, ANZ.

10 Alexander Godley, letter to Sir James Allen, 8 September 1916, WA 252 (3) Godley Correspondence 1916, ANZ.

11 Ibid., 4 March 1916.

12 Alexander Godley, letter to Sir James Allen, 27 January 1917, WA 252 (4) Godley Correspondence 1917, ANZ; Studholme, *New Zealand Expeditionary Force*, 366–72.

13 Territorial Force Attestation Form, WO 339/60593 Alexander Ormond, TNA.

14 David Stevenson, *With Our Backs to the Wall: Victory and defeat in 1918* (London: Allen Lane, 2011), 255. The exact number in March 1918 was 3,808,990, but 4.4 million men from the UK enlisted during the war.

15 Ibid.

16 Alexander Godley, letter to Sir James Allen, 24 October 1918, WA 252 (5) Godley Correspondence 6 January–20 January 1920, ANZ.

17 'All Sorts of People', *New Zealand Free Lance*, 29 October 1919.

18 George Dacre Hamilton, Personal File, WWI 11/1640, ANZ.

19 'All Sorts of People'.

20 Studholme, *New Zealand Expeditionary Force*, 371.

21 Service and Casualty Form, WO 339/64809 Geoffrey Gordon Rich, TNA.

22 G. G. Rich MC, letter to The Secretary, War Office, 10 December 1918, WO 339/64809 Geoffrey Gordon Rich, TNA.

23 'Obituary Mr E. De C. Drury', *Press*, 19 October 1935.

24 Studholme, *New Zealand Expeditionary Force*, 371; Medical Board Report, WO 339/82185 George Gordon de Courcy Drury, TNA. Note that the New Zealand record has de Courcy spelt as de Coursey.

25 Handwritten note, page 1, WO 339/82185 George Gordon de Courcy Drury, TNA.

26 'Obituary Mr E. De C. Drury'.

27 Richard Holmes, *Tommy: The British soldier on the Western Front 1914–1918* (London: HarperCollins, 2004), 626.

28 The Secretary, War Office, Telegram to J. W. Marshall, 2 April 1918, WO 339/80928 John Willoughby Hadfield Marshall, TNA.

29 Rev. J. L. Dove, Letter to Enquiries, War Office, 29 May 1918, WO 339/80928 John Willoughby Hadfield Marshall, TNA.

30 The Secretary, War Office, letter to Rev. J. L. Dove, 2 June 1918, WO 339/80928 John Willoughby Hadfield Marshall, TNA.

31 Captain J. W. Vick, letter to Lieutenant-Colonel N. Fitz-Herbert, N.Z. Records, London, 30 August 1918; Lieutenant-Colonel N. Fitz-Herbert, OIC NZ Records Section London, letter to The Secretary, War Office, 6 September 1918, WO 339/80928 John Willoughby Hadfield Marshall, TNA.

32 Cpl S. Bradford 31104, Statement, 16 October 1918, WO 339/80928 John Willoughby Hadfield Marshall, TNA.

33 The Secretary, War Office, letter to John W. Marshall, 18 September 1918, WO 339/80928 John Willoughby Hadfield Marshall, TNA.

34 Assistant Secretary, New Zealand High Commission, letter to The Secretary, War Office, 8 July 1919, WO 339/80928 John Willoughby Hadfield Marshall, TNA.

35 Controller of Officers Casualties Department, Military Secretary's Office, letter to High Commissioner of New Zealand, 10 July 1919, WO 339/80928 John Willoughby Hadfield Marshall, TNA.

36 Studholme, *New Zealand Expeditionary Force*, 370.

37 Casualty Form — Active Service, WO 339/3137 Henry Frederick Roy Messenger, TNA.

38 Mrs E. S. Harris and Lt.-Col. N. Fitz-Herbert, NZ Records, London, letters to the War Office, 29 August and 28 July 1916, War Office reply 3 September 1916, WO 339/3137 Henry Frederick Roy Messenger, TNA.

39 Mrs E. S. Harris, letter to the Officer Commanding 6th Yorkshires, 29 August 1916, War Office, WO 339/3137 Henry Frederick Roy Messenger, TNA.

40 Army Council, letter to New Zealand High Commission, London, 19 June 1918, WO 339/3137 Henry Frederick Roy Messenger, TNA.

41 The Treasury, Wellington, letter to The Secretary, War Office, 14 May 1920, WO 339/3137 Henry Frederick Roy Messenger, TNA.

42 Studholme, *New Zealand Expeditionary Force*, 372.

43 Application for Appointment to a Temporary Commission in the Regular Army, WO 339/3083 Henry Eugene Voyce, TNA.

44 The Secretary, War Office, Telegram to Mrs Voyce, Christchurch, New Zealand, 13 August 1915, WO 339/3083 Henry Eugene Voyce, TNA.

45 Mrs Eugene L. Francis, letter to The Secretary, War Office, 21 October 1915, WO 339/3083 Henry Eugene Voyce, TNA.

46 The Secretary, War Office, letter to Mrs Eugene L. Francis, 3 November 1915, WO 339/3083 Henry Eugene Voyce, TNA.

47 Studholme, *New Zealand Expeditionary Force*, 371.

48 The Secretary, War Office, Telegram to Lt.-Col. Rendle, Apia, Samoa, 21 October 1917, WO 339/76376 Anthony Darley Russell Rendle, TNA.

49 Secretary to the Department, New Zealand High Commission, letter to The Secretary, War Office, 26 March 1918, War Office reply 6 April 1918, WO 339/76376 Anthony Darley Russell Rendle, TNA.

50 The Treasury, Wellington, letter to The Secretary, War Office, 14 May 1920, WO 339/76376 Anthony Darley Russell Rendle, TNA.

51 Studholme, *New Zealand Expeditionary Force*, 372.

52 Minute Sheet 2, WO 339/35039 William Caithness Talbot, TNA.

53 On the prevalence of malaria at Salonika, see Alan Wakefield and Simon Moody, *Under the Devil's Eye: Britain's forgotten army at Salonika 1915–1918* (Barnsley, South Yorkshire: Pen & Sword Military, 2017), 52, 168.

54 Medical Board Report on a Disabled Officer, 21 January 1918, WO 339/35039 William Caithness Talbot, TNA. It should be noted that William's surname was actually Talbert, but all his military records have it as Talbot.

55 'Roll of Honour', *Timaru Herald*, 27 July 1918.

56 Studholme, *New Zealand Expeditionary Force*, 370.

57 Application for Appointment to a Temporary Commission in the Regular Army, Minute Sheet 1, WO 339/112369 Brian Gerald Mahoney, TNA.

58 Minute Sheet 1, WO 339/112369 Brian Gerald Mahoney, TNA.

59 'Latest Hospital Reports', *Bruce Herald*, 21 October 1918.

60 Ibid.

61 Record of Service, Frank George Massey, WW I 24/1268, ANZ.

62 Alexander Godley, letter to Sir James Allen, 6 January 1917, WA 252 (4) Godley Correspondence 1917, ANZ.

63 Record of Service, Frank George Massey, WW I 24/1268, ANZ.

64 Ibid.

65 Ibid. 'GSW' is short for 'gunshot wound'.

66 'Major Massey, D.S.O. Award for Gallantry', *Auckland Star*, 6 September 1918.

67 Record of Service, Frank George Massey, WW I 24/1268, ANZ.

68 Richard Stowers, *Heroes of Gallipoli: The gallantry of New Zealanders on Gallipoli* (Christchurch: John Douglas Publishing, 2015), 379; Arthur Tahu Gravenor Rhodes, WW1 15/3, ANZ.

69 Quoted in Stowers, *Heroes of Gallipoli*, 379.

70 Arthur Tahu Gravenor Rhodes, WW1 15/3, ANZ.

71 Ibid.

72 'Weddings at Home', *Press*, 16 March 1916.

73 http://www.aucklandmuseum.com/war-memorial/online-cenotaph/record/C53857 (accessed 27 June 2018).

CHAPTER FOUR: IN THE INDIAN ARMY

1 Richard Holmes, *Sahib: The British soldier in India* (London: Harper Perennial, 2006), xxv.

2 Ibid.

3 Ibid., 293.

4 For an explanation of the rank system for sepoys, see Alan Jeffreys, *Approach to Battle: Training the Indian Army during the Second World War* (Solihull: Helion & Company Limited, 2016), xviii.

5 Stephen Badsey, *The British Army in Battle and Its Image 1914–18* (London: Continuum UK, 2009), 4.

6 Jeffreys, *Approach to Battle*, 30–31.

7 Vedica Kant, *'If I Die Here, Who Will Remember Me?' India and the First World War* (New Delhi: Roli Books, 2014), 15.

8 Ibid.

9 Jeffreys, *Approach to Battle*, 29.

10 Ibid., 27–30.

11 Laura J. Hutton, 'India Army', in Spencer C. Tucker (ed.), *World War I. The Definitive Encyclopedia and Document Collection, vol. 2: D–J* (Santa Barbara: ABC-CLIO, 2014), 794.

12 L. C. Dunsterville, *Stalky's Adventures* (London: Jonathan Cape, 1941), 11.

13 Ibid., 51–52.

14 Ibid., 57–59.

15 John Crawford, 'Andrew, Brigadier-General Albert William', in Ian McGibbon (ed.), *The Oxford Companion to New Zealand Military History* (Auckland: Oxford University Press, 2000), 17.

16 'Selby, William Gilhome', in J. Bryant Haigh and Alan J. Polaschek (compilers), *New Zealand and the Distinguished Service Order. Being a record of New Zealanders and those associated with New Zealand, appointed as Companions of the Distinguished Service Order* (Christchurch: J. Bryant Haigh and Alan J. Polaschek, 1993), 444.

17 https://www.cwgc.org/find/find-war-dead/results?firstName=William&lastName=Selby%2B&country=India (accessed 27 June 2018).

18 'Kenneth Sinclair Thomson', http://www.aucklandmuseum.com/war-memorial/online-cenotaph/record/C35204 (accessed 9 May 2018).

19 Ibid.

20 'Sinclair-Thomson, Kenneth', https://museum.timaru.govt.nz/explore/whats-on/ww100/scroll/profile?id=2233 (accessed 9 May 2018).

21 'Colonel Hardwicke Holderness', in John O'Reilly (compiler), 'New Zealanders in the Indian Army 1900–1947', PowerPoint presentation, copy in author's possession.

22 Ibid.

23 'A Fine Record', *Colonist*, 19 April 1916.

24 'Personal Notes', *Greymouth Evening Star*, 15 November 1917.

25 'Lieutenant-Colonel A. F. Hamilton', in O'Reilly, 'New Zealanders in the Indian Army'.

26 'Lieutenant Frank James Medley', in O'Reilly, 'New Zealanders in the Indian Army'.

27 'Captain S. N. Ziman', *Auckland Star*, 6 February 1918.

28 'On Service', *Press*, 9 May 1919.

29 Statement of Service, AABK 18805 WWI 51587 Louis Isaac Ziman, ANZ.

30 'Late Mr Gordon Cunningham', *Press*, 8 March 1932.

31 Ibid.

32 'Personal Items', *Press*, 11 April 1917.

33 'Late Mr Gordon Cunningham'.

34 'Obituary: Mr Gordon Cunningham', *Press*, 18 February 1932.

35 'The War', *Otago Daily Times*, 10 December 1915.

36 Reuben McCarthy Newman, Personal File, WWI 8/3817, ANZ.

37 L. W. Shakespear, *History of King Edward's Own Goorkhas, The Sirmoor Rifle Regiment, vol. 2, 1911–21* (Aldershot: Gale & Polden, 1924), 193.

38 Reuben McCarthy Newman, Personal File, WWI 8/3817, ANZ.

39 'Roll of Honour', *Dominion*, 10 December 1918.

40 John Studholme, *New Zealand Expeditionary Force: Record of personal services during the war of officers, nurses, and first-class warrant officers; and other facts relating to the N.Z.E.F. Unofficial, but based on*

official records (Wellington: Government Printer, 1928), 365.

41 Ibid., 366–72.

42 H.Q.N.Z.E.F. in Egypt, memo to A.M.S., G.H.Q. E.E.F., 1 October 1917, WA 1/3 XFE 730, Re-Commissions in Indian Army and Indian Navy, 11 September–21 November 1917, ANZ.

43 MS Circular No. 6, WA 1/3 XFE 730, Re-Commissions in Indian Army and Indian Navy, 11 September–21 November 1917, ANZ.

44 Studholme, *New Zealand Expeditionary Force*, 365.

45 QMS J. Robertson, letter to OC, N.Z.E.F. Headquarters Cairo, 22 December 1917, WA 1/3 XFE 730, Re. Commissions in Indian Army and Indian Navy, 11 September–21 November 1917, ANZ.

46 Statement of Service of Lieut. W. H. Gibb, WO 339/30955 William Henderson Gibb, TNA.

47 Proceedings of a Medical Board, 8 January 1916, WO 339/30955 William Henderson Gibb, TNA.

48 Casualty Form — Active Service, WO 339/30955 William Henderson Gibb, TNA.

49 Casualty Report, Lt. A. D. D. Maclean, WO 339/8321 Algernon Donald Douglas McLean, TNA.

50 Commanding Officer, 3rd Battalion, Cameron Highlanders, letter to the War Office, 11 May 1915, WO 339/8321 Algernon Donald Douglas McLean, TNA.

51 Medical Statement, Captain A. D. D. McLean, WO 339/8321 Algernon Donald Douglas McLean, TNA.

52 Arrival Report, War Office, WO 339/8321 Algernon Donald Douglas McLean, TNA.

53 Travellers' Club, Pall Mall, Note to War Office, WO 339/8321 Algernon Donald Douglas McLean, TNA.

54 Charge Sheet, 2nd Lieutenant F. M. Jenkins, 17 May 1918, WO 339/30486 Frederick Adrian Maunsell Jenkins, TNA.

55 Proceedings of Court Martial, 12 February 1920, WO 339/30486 Frederick Adrian Maunsell Jenkins, TNA.

56 Memorandum on the case of Lieutenant Stuart Maxwell Deans, 16th Lancers, n.d., WO 339/78208 Stuart Maxwell Deans, TNA.

57 Lieut S. M. Deans, letter to GOC N.Z. Military Forces 12 July 1921, WO 339/78208 Stuart Maxwell Deans, TNA.

58 Minute Sheet No. 1, 6 December 1921, WO 339/78208 Stuart Maxwell Deans, TNA.

59 Government of India, letter to Governor-General of New Zealand, 30 April 1921, WO 339/78208 Stuart Maxwell Deans, TNA.

60 War Office, cable to C-in-C India, 4 January 1922, WO 339/78208 Stuart Maxwell Deans, TNA.

61 Major L. N. Reece, letter to OC, No. 40 British General Hospital, 21 February 1919, WO 374/56607 Leslie Norman Reece, TNA.

62 Ibid.

63 A.M.D.1, WO 374/56607 Leslie Norman Reece, TNA.

64 http://www.antarctica.gov.au/about-antarctica/history/exploration-and-expeditions/australasian-antarctic-expedition/staff-and-crew-of-the-aae (accessed 11 May 2018); 'Personal', *Dubbo Liberal and Macquaries Advocate*, 22 November 1927.

65 'Twenty Years of Adventure. Radio Operator and Soldier', *Dominion*, 26 February 1930; MS-Papers-8335-5, Sawyer, Arthur John, Papers, ATL.

66 Ibid.

67 'Local and General', *Dominion*, 10 January 1917.

68 Statement of Service, Arthur John Sawyer, B2455, NAA.

69 P. J. Kelleher, War Graves Division Wellington, letter to OIC Base Records Australia, 26 February 1932, Arthur John Sawyer, B2455, NAA.

70 Timothy C. Winegard, 'Dunsterforce', https://encyclopedia.1914-1918-online.net/article/dunsterforce (accessed 27 June 2018).

71 'Twenty Years of Adventure'.

72 Statement of Service, Arthur John Sawyer, B2455, NAA.

73 'Obituary: Mr Arthur Sawyer, Jun', *Poverty Bay Herald*, 19 January 1932; MS-Papers-8335-5, Sawyer, Arthur John, Papers, ATL.

74 Medal Page, Personal File, Base Records, Statement of Service, Arthur John Sawyer, B2455, NAA.

75 P. J. Kelleher, War Graves Division Wellington, letter to OIC Base Records Australia, 26 February 1932, Arthur John Sawyer, B2455, NAA.

76 Edward (Ted) Piddocke Averill and Shirley Averill, Interview, Knowledge Bank, Hawke's Bay Digital Archive Trust, provided by Christine Clement.

77 Supplement to the *London Gazette*, 2 November 1916, 10630.

78 'Obituary', *Press*, 24 November 1921.

79 Medical Report, Lieut. C. S. Harrington, WO 339/48282 Charles Stanley Lawrence Harrington, TNA.

80 Proceedings of a Board of Medical Officers, 3 April 1917, WO 339/48282 Charles Stanley Lawrence Harrington, TNA.

81 Gavin McLean, *The White Ships: New Zealand's First World War hospital ships* (Wellington: New Zealand Ship & Marine Society, 2013), 142.

82 New Zealand Military Forces, Court of Inquiry, 28 May 1917, WO 339/48282 Charles Stanley Lawrence Harrington, TNA.

CHAPTER FIVE: IN THE AIF

1 Peter Dennis, Jeffrey Grey, Ewan Morris and Robin Prior, with Jean Bou, *The Oxford Companion to Australian Military History*, 2nd edn (Melbourne: Oxford University Press, 2008), 62.

2 Jeffrey Grey, *A Military History of Australia* (Cambridge, UK: Cambridge University Press, 1999), 115.

3 Ibid., 85.

4 Peter Dennis and Jeffrey Grey, 'New Zealanders in the AIF: An introduction to the AIF Database Project', in John Crawford and Ian McGibbon (eds), *New Zealand's Great War: New Zealand, the Allies and the First World War* (Auckland: Exisle, 2007), 399.

5 In 'New Zealanders in the AIF', Dennis and Grey give two different figures of 2213 and 2533 men (pages 400 and 401). In *New Zealand's Western Front Campaign* (Auckland: David Bateman Ltd, 2016), Ian McGibbon records it as a vague 'several thousand' (page 164).

6 Neil C. Smith, 'New Zealanders in the First Imperial Force, 1914–1919, 2, F940.40993S655, AWM.

7 Neil C. Smith, 'What's in a Name: Aliases of the Australian Military Forces 1914–1919', SLT 940.394 SM5W, State Library of Victoria.

8 The number identified by Christine Clement 31 January 2018 was 4886 New Zealanders enlisting in the AIF. The task of identifying this number was made harder by the men who were discharged for a variety of reasons, including being 'claimed by wife', as well as 83-odd who deserted before embarkation. In addition, some 700 New Zealanders enlisted under an alias. Also, many New Zealanders gave an Australian place of birth, making them harder to find. As Neil Smith writes, the exact number will never be known.

9 Dennis, Grey, et al., *Australian Military History*, 539.

10 Peter Pedersen, *The Anzacs: Gallipoli to the Western Front* (Melbourne: Penguin, 2007), 23.

11 Grey, *A Military History of Australia*, 85.

12 Glyn Harper, *Johnny Enzed: The New Zealand soldier in the First World War 1914–1918* (Auckland: Exisle, 2015), 16.

13 Ibid., 592–93.

14 Christopher Pugsley, *On the Fringe of Hell: New Zealanders and military discipline in the First World War* (Auckland: Hodder & Stoughton, 1991), 298.

15 Ibid., 300, 332.

16 Haig, diary entry, 21 March 1918, Haig Papers No. 124, vol. 26, March 1918, Haig Papers, NLS. The completed table is attached to the back of this month's diary.

17 Ashley Ekins, 'Fighting to Exhaustion: Morale, discipline and combat effectiveness in the armies of 1918', in Ashley Ekins (ed.), *1918 Year of Victory: The end of the Great War and the shaping of history* (Wollombi, NSW: Exisle, 2010), 112.

18 Dennis, Grey, et al., *Australian Military History*, 176.

19 They were Private John King, executed in August 1917, and Private John Joseph Sweeny from Tasmania, shot at dawn on 2 October 1916. A fifth NZEF soldier, Lance Corporal John Braithwaite, was executed by the British military authorities for mutiny. See Pugsley, *On the Fringe of Hell*, chapters 8, 9 and 13.

20 Joan Beaumont, *Australian Defence: Sources and statistics* (Melbourne: Oxford University Press, 2001), 105.

21 Ibid., Table 3.2, 108–9.

22 Joan Beaumont, *Broken Nation: Australians in the Great War* (Sydney: Allen & Unwin, 2013), 422.

23 Ibid., 421.

24 Glyn Harper and Colin Richardson, *Acts of Valour: The history of the Victoria Cross and New Zealand* (Auckland: HarperCollins, 2016), 112–14.

25 Ibid., 128.

26 Warren Derkenne, 'Storkey, Percy Valentine (1893–1969)', *Australian Dictionary of Biography*, National Centre of Biography, Australian National University, http://adb.anu.edu.au/biography/storkey-percy-valentine-8687/text15197 (accessed 15 November 2017), first published in 1990.

27 John Ritchie, 'Weathers, Lawrence Carthage (1890–1918)', *Australian Dictionary of Biography*, National Centre of Biography, Australian National University, http://adb.anu.edu.au/biography/weathers-lawrence-carthage-9021/text15867 (accessed 15 November 2017), first published in 1990.

28 Harper and Richardson, *Acts of Valour*, 169.

29 Nominal Roll — Tunnellers with NZ connections, provided by Ross Thomas, Townsville, Australia.

30 https://www.ngataonga.org.nz/collections/catalogue/catalogue-item?record_id=198024, Ngā Taonga Sound & Vision Archive.

31 Attestation Paper, Arthur Joseph Clarke, B2455, NAA.

32 Richard F. Clarke, letter to The Commandant of Expeditionary Forces, 25 October 1914, Arthur Joseph Clarke, B2455, NAA.

33 Statement of Service, Arthur Joseph Clarke, B2455, NAA.

34 Medical Report, Arthur Joseph Clarke, B2455, NAA.

35 Statement of Service, Arthur Joseph Clarke, B2455, NAA.

36 Ibid.

37 William Joseph Clarke, letter to C.B.R.O. St Kilda Barracks, Melbourne, 18 May 1967, Arthur Joseph Clarke, B2455, NAA.

38 Robert Hood, B2455, NAA.

39 Statement of Service and Charge Sheet, Robert Hood, B2455, NAA.

40 Attestation Form, Charles Key, B2455, NAA. See also the Attestation Form in Key/Charles MT1486/1, NAA.

41 War Gratuity Schedule, Charles Key, B2455, NAA.

42 Statement of Service, Charles Key, B2455, NAA.

43 Attestation Form in Key/Charles, MT1486/1, NAA.

44 Attestation Paper, Marcus Fraser St John, B2455, NAA.

45 Headquarters Melbourne, memo to AAG, 3rd MD Victoria Barracks, 4 August 1916, Marcus Fraser St John, B2455, NAA.

46 Medical Report on an Invalid, 26/11/17, Marcus Fraser St John, B2455, NAA.

47 Statement of Service, Marcus Fraser St John, B2455, NAA.

48 Administrative Headquarters AIF UK, memo to The Secretary, Department of Defence, Australia, 25 January 1918, Marcus Fraser St John, B2455, NAA.

49 Charles Duke, http://www.ngataonga.org.nz/collections/catalogue/catalogue-item?record_id=194839, http://anzacsightsound.org/audios/every-one-of-those-lads-was-lying-dead, Ngā Taonga Sound & Vision Archive. See also C. R. Duke, B2455, NAA.

50 Duke, Charles Robert, http://ww100.nelsonmuseum.co.nz/character?profileID=12

51 William Hallahan, letter to Dear Dad and Girls, 15 May 1915, 1 DRL 329, Cpl W. A. Hallahan, 51 Bn AIF, AWM.

52 Statement of Service, W. A. Hallahan, B2455, NAA.

53 Ibid.

54 Attestation Paper, W. J. Hallahan, B2455, NAA.

55 Statement of Service, W. J. Hallahan, B2455, NAA.

56 Attestation Paper, Walter Rewi Hallahan, B2455, NAA.

57 Statement of Service, Walter Rewi Hallahan, B2455, NAA.

58 Military Medal citation, Walter Rewi Hallahan, B2455, NAA.

59 Military Cross citation, Walter Rewi Hallahan, B2455, NAA.

60 Burial details, Walter Rewi Hallahan, B2455, NAA.

61 Statement of Service, R. T. Hallahan, B2455, NAA.

62 Ibid.

63 Ibid.

64 Cyril Lawrence, B2455, NAA.

65 Ronald East (ed.), *The Gallipoli Diary of Sergeant Lawrence of the Australian Engineers — 1st A.I.F. 1915* (Melbourne: Melbourne University Press, 1981); Peter Yule (ed.), *Sergeant Lawrence Goes to France* (Melbourne: Melbourne University Press, 1987).

66 'Sergeant Guthrie', *Star*, 3 May 1915.

67 John H. Gray, *The Canterbury Officers' Club (Inc) Biographical Essays on Members on the Roll of Honour of the Great War* (Christchurch: The Canterbury Officers' Club, 2015), 69.

68 Robert Stone, B2455, NAA.

69 Smith, 'New Zealanders in the First Imperial Force, 1914–1919', 4.

70 Merrilyn Lincoln, 'Bessell-Browne, Alfred Joseph (1877–1947)', *Australian Dictionary of Biography*, Australian National University, http://adb.anu.edu.au/biography/bessell-browne-alfred-joseph-5223/text8789 (accessed 23 January 2018), first published in 1979.

71 Ibid.

72 Ibid.

73 Ibid.

74 https://www.aif.adfa.edu.au/OrderOfBattle/Generals/burgess.html (accessed 4 July 2018).

75 Statement of Service, W. L. H. Burgess, B2455, NAA.

76 Casualty Form, Active Service, W. L. H. Burgess, B2455, NAA.

77 https://www.aif.adfa.edu.au/OrderOfBattle/Generals/burgess.html (accessed 4 July 2018).

78 Ibid.

79 Statement of Service, W. L. H. Burgess, B2455, NAA.

80 W. David McIntyre, 'Sinclair-Burgess, William Livingston Hatchwell', *Dictionary of New Zealand Biography Te Ara — The Encyclopedia of New Zealand*, https://teara.govt.nz/en/biographies/4s26/sinclair-burgess-william-livingston-hatchwell (accessed 4 July 2018), first published in 1998.

81 Ibid.

82 Ibid.

83 Max Middleton, 'Introduction', in Harold Septimus Power, *The Art of Septimus Power* (Melbourne: Rigby Limited, 1974), 2.

84 Ibid., 3.

85 Katherine Kovacic, 'Artists at War', *Wartime*, issue 57 (Summer 2012), 51.

86 Attestation Papers, Power, Harold Septimus, B2455, NAA.

87 Middleton, 'Introduction', 4.

88 Kovacic, 'Artists at War', 53.

89 Middleton, 'Introduction', 12.

90 Attestation Paper, K. Burke, B2455, NAA.

91 Statement of Service, K. Burke, B2455, NAA.

92 See Harper, *Johnny Enzed*, 515–21.

93 Kimberley Webber, 'Burke, Eric Keast (1896–1974)', *Australian Dictionary of Biography*, Australian National University, http://adb.anu.edu.au/biography/burke-eric-keast-9628/text16981 (accessed 11 December 2017), first published in 1993.

94 Ibid.

CHAPTER SIX: AIF HEROES AND VILLAINS

1 'Death at 92: Mr A. E. Glover', *New Zealand Herald*, 12 September 1941.

2 Compiled from James Glover's 152-page Personal File, J. Glover, B2455, NAA.

3 Statement of Service, J. Glover, B2455, NAA.

4 Ibid.

5 Ibid.

6 OC, AIF Camp, Newcastle to The Provost Marshal, 2nd Military District, 18 July 1916, J. Glover, B2455, NAA.

7 Casualty Form — Active Service, J. Glover, B2455, NAA.

8 War History Index, J. Glover, B2455, NAA.

9 Earl Kent Stanton Massey North and Palmer, letter to The Army Secretary, Base Records, Sydney, 12 October 1944, Base Records reply 23 October 1944, J. Glover, B2455, NAA.

10 War Gratuity Schedule, J. J. R. McQuillan, B2455, NAA.

11 Statement of Service, J. J. R. McQuillan, B2455, NAA.

12 Ibid.

13 Ibid.

14 War History Index, J. J. R. McQuillan, B2455, NAA.

15 James McQuillan, letter to Officer in Charge, Central Army Records, 22 August 1949, J. J. R. McQuillan, B2455, NAA.

16 Public Curator Office, letter to The Officer in Charge, Central Army Records, 25 February 1963, J. J. R. McQuillan, B2455, NAA.

17 Attestation Papers and Particulars of Service, R. O. Miller, B2455, NAA.

18 Glyn Harper, *Johnny Enzed: The New Zealand soldier in the First World War 1914–1918* (Auckland: Exisle, 2015), 158. This was the same rate as Canadian soldiers, with the New Zealand rate being around 130 per 1000 soldiers. In 1914–15, while billeted on Salisbury Plain, Canadian soldiers had the highest rate of infection at 222 per 1000 soldiers.

19 Mark Harrison, *The Medical War: British military medicine in the First World War* (Oxford: Oxford University Press, 2010), 152–53.

20 G. Dennis Shanks, 'Legacy of the 1914–18 War: How World War I changed global attitudes to war and

infectious diseases', *The Lancet*, vol. 384 (8 November 2014), 1703.

21 Harrison, *The Medical War*, 157.

22 Shanks, 'Legacy of the 1914–18 War', 1704.

23 Jessie Miller, letter to The Secretary, Records Office, 27 January 1916, R. O. Miller, B2455, NAA.

24 Officer i/c Base Records, letter to Mrs J. Miller, 5 February 1916, R. O. Miller, B2455, NAA.

25 Statement of Service, R. O. Miller, B2455, NAA.

26 Ibid.

27 Ibid.

28 Medical Board Proceedings held at No. 1 Staty Hosp, R. O. Miller, B2455, NAA.

29 Statement of Service, R. O. Miller, B2455, NAA.

30 Mrs Lillian Miller, letter to The Officer in Charge, 9 May 1967, R. O. Miller, B2455, NAA.

31 Statement of Service, W. Hill, B2455, NAA.

32 Statement of Service and Proceedings of a Field General Court Martial on Active Service, W. Hill, B2455, NAA.

33 Service and Casualty Form, W. Hill, B2455, NAA.

34 W. B. Brown, B2455, NAA.

35 Ibid.

36 Officer-in-Charge Base Records, confidential letter to Master William Brown, 31 July 1919, W. B. Brown, B2455, NAA.

37 Particulars of Forfeitures, H. Graham, B2455, NAA.

38 Ibid.

39 Ibid.

40 Statement of Service, H. Elliott, B2455, NAA.

41 Ibid.

42 Ibid.

43 Ibid.

44 Record of Service in the Field, W. H. Scott, B2455, NAA.

45 Base Records, letter to Mrs R. M. Scott, 3 May 1918, W. H. Scott, B2455, NAA.

46 R. R. Chapman, B2455, NAA.

47 Medal citation, William John Alfred Layburn, B2455, NAA.

48 William John Alfred Layburn, Biographical information sheets from the AIF Project (UNSW/ADFA), AWM.

49 Neil C. Smith, 'New Zealanders in the First Imperial Force, 1914–1919', 5, F940.40993S655, AWM.

50 J. S. Cranswick and T. G. Cranswick, B2455, NAA; Smith, 'New Zealanders in the First Imperial Force', 5, 12.

51 Marion Cranswick, letter to Major Hearn, 9 July 1920, J. S. Cranswick, B2455, NAA.

52 Medical Report of an Invalid, J. S. Cranswick, B2455, NAA.

53 Statement of Service, J. S. Cranswick, B2455, NAA.

54 Casualty Form — Active Service, J. S. Cranswick, B2455, NAA.

55 Order Form and letter, OIC Base Records to Mrs Marion Cranswick, 6 March 1922, J. S. Cranswick, B2455, NAA.

56 Epitaph, 20 March 1922, J. S. Cranswick, B2455, NAA.

57 Statement of Service, T. G. Cranswick, B2455, NAA.

58 Ibid.

59 Thurston George Cranswick, Biographical information sheets from the AIF Project (UNSW/ADFA), AWM.

60 Statement of Service, T. G. Cranswick, B2455, NAA.

61 Christine Clement, 'New Zealanders in the AIF', 31 January 2018.

62 Attestation Paper, Evelyn Augusta Conyers, B2455, NAA; Jane Tolerton, *Make Her Praises Heard Afar: New Zealand women overseas in World War One* (Wellington: Book Lovers Books, 2017), 46.

63 Statement of Service, Evelyn Augusta Conyers, B2455, NAA.

64 Ibid.

65 E. A. Conyers, letter to Secretary, Department of Defence, 13 April, 1920, Evelyn Augusta Conyers, B2455, NAA.

66 Sherayl McNabb, *100 Years. New Zealand Military Nursing. New Zealand Army Nursing Service — Royal New Zealand Nursing Corps, 1915–2015* (Wairoa, Hawke's Bay: Sherayl McNabb, 2015), 53.

67 Ibid., 53. The place of birth has been taken from the nurses' AIF personal files.

68 *Kai Tiaki*, April 1915, quoted in ibid., 55.

69 McNabb, *100 Years*, 55.

70 Casualty Form — Active Service, Alice Charlotte Fraser, B2455, NAA.

71 These were Grace Guthrie and Hilda Steele. For the debilitating effects of malaria, see the personal files of Elizabeth Jane White, G. M. Guthrie, Hilda Mary Steele, E. J. White, NAA B2455.

72 Statement of Service, Dorothy Ann Rose, B2455, NAA.

73 War History Index, Dorothy Ann Rose, B2455, NAA.

74 Record Sheet, First Australian General Hospital, Brown E B, B2455, NAA.

75 Statement of Service, Brown E B, B2455, NAA. For a detailed description of her continental tour, see Ellen's diary at the Auckland War Memorial Museum, MS 826 Papers of Ellen Manson.

76 Ellen Manson, diary, MS 826 Papers of Ellen Manson, AWMM.

77 McNabb, *100 Years*, 60.

78 Smith, 'New Zealanders in the First Imperial Force', 5, 8.

79 Ibid., 8.

CHAPTER SEVEN: WITH THE FRENCH FORCES

1 Sherayl McNabb, *100 Years. New Zealand Military Nursing. New Zealand Army Nursing Service — Royal New Zealand Nursing Corps, 1915–2015* (Wairoa, Hawke's Bay: Sherayl McNabb, 2015), 205; Anna Rogers, *While You're Away: New Zealand nurses at war 1899–1948* (Auckland: Auckland University Press, 2003), 157.

2 http://www.scarletfinders.co.uk/167.html (accessed 8 February 2018).

3 David Stevenson, *With Our Backs to the Wall: Victory and defeat in 1918* (London: Allen Lane, 2011), 440.

4 List compiled by Christine Clement, 31 January 2018.

5 'Concerning Cancer', *Feilding Star*, 27 February 1915.

6 Quoted in McNabb, *100 Years*, 205.

7 Rogers, *While You're Away*, 158.

8 Ibid., 130.

9 Ibid.

10 Jane Tolerton, *Make Her Praises Heard Afar: New Zealand women overseas in World War One* (Wellington: Book Lovers Books, 2017), 38.

11 McNabb, *100 Years*, 206.

12 Tolerton, *Make Her Praises Heard Afar*, 38.

13 McNabb, *100 Years*, 206.

14 Ibid.

15 Reginald Pound, *Gillies: Surgeon extraordinary* (London: Michael Joseph Ltd, 1964), 22.

16 Ibid., 22–23.

17 Ibid., 24.

18 Quoted in ibid., 24.

19 Rex Wright-St Clair, 'Gillies, Harold Delf', *Dictionary of New Zealand Biography Te Ara — The Encyclopedia of New Zealand*, https://teara.govt.nz/en/biographies/3g9/gillies-harold-delf (accessed 14 February 2018), first published in 1996.

20 Ibid.

21 Tolerton, *Make Her Praises Heard Afar*, 34.

22 'Red Cross in Belgium: New Zealanders at work', *New Zealand Herald*, 30 October 1914.

23 Tolerton, *Make Her Praises Heard Afar*, 34.

24 'Honour for New Zealand', *Auckland Star*, 20 March 1914.

25 Ibid.

26 Ibid.

27 'A Noble Daughter of the Rangitikei', *Manawatu Standard*, 16 July 1915.

28 'In a Belgian Hospital: A New Zealand nurse's work', *Wanganui Herald*, 28 March 1916.

29 Quoted in Tolerton, *Make Her Praises Heard Afar*, 224.

30 'War Work', *Wanganui Chronicle*, 26 April 1917.

31 Tolerton, *Make Her Praises Heard Afar*, 345.

32 'New Zealanders Abroad', *Auckland Star*, 10 July 1922.

33 Tolerton, *Make Her Praises Heard Afar*, 346.

34 Christine Clement and Ellen McCormack, *The Pioneers, Settlers and Families of Katikati and District* (Te Puke: Christine Clement, 2012), 130.

35 Ibid.

36 Quoted in *Homeopathic Recorder*, August 1942, http://sueyounghistories.com/archives/2009/03/28/ethelbert-petrie-hoyle-1861-1955/ (accessed 10 May 2018).

37 Clement and McCormack, *The Pioneers*, 131.

38 Ibid., 132.

39 'Personal', *Manawatu Times*, 6 March 1915.

40 Christopher Pugsley, *The Camera in the Crowd: Filming New Zealand in peace and war, 1895–1920* (Auckland: Oratia Books in association with Ngā Taonga Sound & Vision, 2017), 229.

41 David Johnston, 'Lt Colonel James Waddell, Commander Legion of Honour Croix de Guerre with 7 Palms + other awards — Time Line and Key Dates', copy in author's possession.

42 Enoch Coppin, *Victory Forever: 'Waddell of Gallipoli'. Amazing true story of New Zealand-born hero of the Foreign Legion* (Levin: K. B. H. Print, 1957), 5.

43 Ibid.

44 Paul Chapman, 'Gallipoli Hero Survived Bullying, Sexual Assault', *New Zealand Herald*, 24 April 2015.

45 Ibid.

46 Johnston, 'Lt Colonel James Waddell'.

47 Coppin, *Victory Forever*, 5.

48 Johnston, 'Lt Colonel James Waddell'.

49 Pugsley, *The Camera in the Crowd*, 229.

50 Coppin, *Victory Forever*, 5. See also Johnston, 'Lt Colonel James Waddell'.

51 Johnston, 'Lt Colonel James Waddell'.

52 Ibid.

53 Coppin, *Victory Forever*, 6.

54 Ibid., 6.

55 Johnston, 'Lt Colonel James Waddell'; A. P. Wavell, *Other Men's Flowers: An anthology of poetry compiled by A. P. Wavell (Field-Marshal Earl Wavell)* (London: Pimlico, 1992), 88.

56 Quoted in Tonie and Valmai Holt, *Major and Mrs Holt's Battlefield Guide to the Somme* (Barnsley: Pen & Sword Military, 2008), 219–20.

57 Quoted in Johnston, 'Lt Colonel James Waddell'.

58 Holt and Holt, *Battlefield Guide to the Somme*, 220.

59 Mark Brewer, 'New Zealand and the Légion d'honneur: The Great War', in *The Volunteers: The Journal of the New Zealand Military Historical Society (Inc)*, vol. 37, no. 3 (March 2012), 173.

60 Johnston, 'Lt Colonel James Waddell'.

61 Waddell, letter to Richardson, 16 October 1916, quoted in Ian McGibbon, *New Zealand's Western Front Campaign* (Auckland: David Bateman Ltd, 2016), 185.

62 Russell, letter to Major John Studholme, 22 October 1916, quoted in McGibbon, *New Zealand's Western Front Campaign*, 185.

63 Ibid.

64 Quoted in Johnston, 'Lt Colonel James Waddell'.

65 Chapman, 'Gallipoli Hero'.

66 Ian McGibbon (ed.), *The Oxford Companion to New Zealand Military History* (Auckland: Oxford University Press, 2000), 572.

67 *Manawatu Herald*, 25 January 1898.

68 *Manawatu Times*, 6 January 1905.

69 Reported in *New Zealand Free Lance*, 5 April 1917. A *poilu*, literally 'hairy one', was a slang reference to a French soldier. It was a term the French soldiers disliked.

70 Reported in *New Zealand Free Lance*, 6 June 1918.

71 https://www.overthefront.com/resources/military-ranks/french-ranks and https://foreignlegion.info/ranks/ (accessed 4 July 2018).

72 Garnet Arrowsmith, letter to OIC NZEF War Account Records, 12 March 1921, Vincent Briggs — French Foreign Legion and Imperial Forces (R22423259), AABK, 22525, ANZ.

73 Ibid.

74 Tolerton, *Make Her Praises Heard Afar*, 312–13.

75 Ibid., 313.

76 Ibid., 274.

77 Ibid.

CHAPTER EIGHT: WITH THE CANADIAN, AMERICAN, SOUTH AFRICAN AND GERMAN FORCES

1 https://www65.statcan.gc.ca/acyb07/acyb07_0007-eng.htm (accessed 28 February 2018). The figure recorded in the official census of 1911 was 7.2 million.

2 http://www.thecanadianencyclopedia.ca/en/article/canadian-expeditionary-force (accessed 28 February 2018).

3 Ibid.

4 Christine Clement database, 31 January 2018.

5 The number identified by Christine Clement at 31 January 2018 was 408. As with those in the AIF, the exact number will never be known.

6 'On Active Service', *New Zealand Herald*, 10 July 1918.

7 Richard Holmes, *Tommy: The British soldier on the Western Front 1914–1918* (London: HarperCollins, 2004), 35.

8 David Stevenson, *1914–1918: The history of the First World War* (London: Penguin, 2004), 154.

9 Ian McGibbon, *New Zealand's Western Front Campaign* (Auckland: David Bateman Ltd, 2016), 25.

10 NZL-CEF-CWGC, table provided by Nicholas Clarke, Canadian War Museum, 10 January 2017.

11 'Killed in Action', *New Zealand Herald*, 22 June 1915.

12 'Careers of the Fallen', *Auckland Star*, 4 April 1916.

13 *Auckland Weekly News*, 26 August 1915; 'Careers of the Fallen'.

14 'Careers of the Fallen'.

15 'Personal', *Feilding Star*, 27 April 1915.

16 'New Zealanders Abroad', *Dominion*, 28 July 1915.

17 'Private William Dorreen of Hampton, Otago', *Otago Witness*, 8 March 1916.

18 Christine Clement database, 31 January 2018.

19 Christine Clement, email to author, 8 May 2018. Also https://www.cwgc.org/find-war-dead/casualty/165097/dorreen,-leslie/

20 'Doreen [sic] Mission', *Evening Star*, 10 May 1920.

21 'On Service', *Otago Witness*, 15 December 1915.

22 https://archive.org/details/CEF_29thBn_1915 (accessed 28 February 2018).

23 'On Service'.

24 'On Service: New Zealanders abroad', *Evening Post*, 4 July 1917.

25 'On Service: New Zealanders abroad', *Evening Post*, 21 January 1918.

26 NZL-CEF-CWGC, table provided by Nicholas Clarke, Canadian War Museum, 10 January 2017.

27 Ian McGibbon, *New Zealand's Western Front Campaign* (Auckland: David Bateman Ltd, 2016), 103.

28 'Personal', *Feilding Star*, 29 September 1917. See also Te Ara https://nzhistory.govt.nz/media/photo/british-kite-balloon; http://warmemscot.s4.bizhat.com/warmemscot-ftopic234-0-asc-60.html

29 'On Service: New Zealanders abroad', *Evening Post*, 29 August 1917.

30 Ibid.

31 Quoted in ibid.

32 Liz West, email to Glyn Harper, 13 July 2018. The authors are grateful to Liz West for alerting us to Sydney Eyre's story.

33 Attestation Paper, Eyre, Sydney Seymour, www.bac-lac.gc.ca/eng/discover/military-heritage/first-world-war/personnel-records/Pages/item.aspx?IdNumber=383945 (accessed 13 July 2018).

34 'Midnight Murder', *New Zealand Herald*, 26 August 1920.

35 Michael S. Neiberg, *The Path to War: How the First World War created modern America* (New York: Oxford University Press, 2016), 215–29.

36 Ibid., 84–94.

37 Jennifer D. Keene, 'Americans at War: Assessing the significance of American participation in the Great War', in John Crawford and Ian McGibbon (eds), *New Zealand's Great War: New Zealand, the Allies and the First World War* (Auckland: Exisle, 2007), 106–7.

38 What Wilson actually said was: 'The example of America must be a special example. The example of America must be the example not merely of peace because it will not fight, but of peace because peace is the healing and elevating influence of the world and strife is not. There is such a thing as a nation being so right it does not need to convince others by force that it is right.' Wilson made the speech on 10 May 1915 at a citizen naturalisation ceremony in Philadelphia, Pennsylvania. It is known as the 'Too proud to fight' speech. http://www.rmslusitania.info/primary-docs/too-proud-to-fight (accessed 1 March 1918).

39 Keene, 'Americans at War', 107.

40 Ibid.

41 The number in Christine Clement's database at 31 January 1918 was 31.

42 Board of Trade: Commercial and Statistical Department and successors: Inwards Passenger Lists; Class: BT26; Piece: 199; Item: 68, TNA.

43 Ancestry.com, 'World War I Selective Service System Draft Registration Cards, 1917–1918' (online database) (Provo, UT: Ancestry.com Operations Inc., 2005).

44 Ancestry.com, 'Connecticut WWI Military Questionnaires, 1919–1920, Connecticut State Library, Hartford, Connecticut' (online database) (Provo, UT: Ancestry.com Operations Inc., 2013).

45 David Stevenson, *With Our Backs to the Wall: Victory and defeat in 1918* (London: Allen Lane, 2011), 251, 164.

46 http://www.hampton.lib.nh.us/hampton/history/military/26thDivisionYD/26thDivisionHistory1919.htm (accessed 11 May 2018).

47 Ancestry.com, 'California Death Index, 1940–1997, Sacramento, CA' (online database) (Provo, UT: Ancestry.com Operations Inc., 2000).

48 Dierk Walter, 'Union of South Africa', in Spencer C. Tucker (ed.), *World War I. The Definitive Encyclopedia and Document Collection, vol. 4: ER–Z* (Santa Barbara: ABC-CLIO, 2014), 1593.

49 Ibid.

50 Ibid.

51 Ibid.

52 https://encyclopedia.1914-1918-online.net/article/lettow-vorbeck_paul_von (accessed 6 March 2018).

53 Walter, 'Union of South Africa', 1593–94.

54 Ibid., 1594.

55 Christine Clement database, 31 January 2018.

56 Ibid.

57 'Killed and Wounded', *New Zealand Herald*, 7 May 1915. See also 'New Zealander Killed in German S.W. Africa', *Wanganui Chronicle*, 6 May 1915.

58 J. Bryant Haigh and Alan J. Polaschek (compilers), *New Zealand and the Distinguished Service Order. Being a record of New Zealanders and those associated with New Zealand, appointed as Companions of the Distinguished Service Order* (Christchurch: J. Bryant Haigh and Alan J. Polaschek, 1993), 428.

59 Ibid., 428.

60 'Obituary: Major Patrick Monaghan', *Evening Post*, 17 January 1898.

61 'Roll of Honour', *Press*, 15 April 1918.

62 'On Service', *Press*, 9 May 1919.

63 'On Service: New Zealanders abroad', *Evening Post*, 27 August 1917.

64 See Christopher Pugsley, *On the Fringe of Hell: New Zealanders and military discipline in the First World War* (Auckland: Hodder & Stoughton, 1991), 77–90, and McGibbon, *New Zealand's Western Front Campaign*, 51, 192. The phrase 'deserted to enemy' is used repeatedly in Nimot's personal file at Archives New Zealand, AABK 18805 W5549 0086716 William Powell Nimot, ANZ.

65 Pugsley, *On the Fringe of Hell*, 80; McGibbon, *New Zealand's Western Front Campaign*, 192.

66 Casualty Form — Active Service, AABK 18805 W5549 0086716 William Powell Nimot, ANZ.

67 Pugsley, *On the Fringe of Hell*, 78.

68 John Towers, letter to the Editor of 'The Press', 20 July 1917, in AABK 18805 W5549 0086716 William Powell Nimot, ANZ.

69 John Towers, letter to Dear Sir (NZ military), 18 August 1917, in AABK 18805 W5549 0086716 William Powell Nimot, ANZ.

70 Conduct Sheet and Casualty Form — Active Service, AABK 18805 W5549 0086716 William Powell Nimot, ANZ.

71 Statement of Private William Rowe, quoted in McGibbon, *New Zealand's Western Front Campaign*, 193.

72 Pugsley, *On the Fringe of Hell*, 77.

73 Extract from Order Paper, House of Representatives, 4 July 1917, in AABK 18805 W5549 0086716 William Powell Nimot, ANZ.

74 Pugsley, *On the Fringe of Hell*, 81.

75 Ibid.

76 Godley, letter to Allen, 29 July 1916, WA 252 Items 1-5, Godley correspondence, letters to Sir James Allen, ANZ.

77 Pugsley, *On the Fringe of Hell*, 84.

78 McGibbon, *New Zealand's Western Front Campaign*, 193.

79 'New Zealand German Prisoner of War', *Poverty Bay Herald*, 19 October 1916.

80 Andrew Macdonald has provided all of the information on Emil Schroeder here.

81 *Thames Advertiser*, 20 November 1885.

82 Intelligence Section, American Expeditionary Forces, 'Histories of 251 Divisions of the German Army Which Participated in the War 1914–1918' (Washington: Government Printing Office, 1920), 451. Information provided by Andrew Macdonald.

83 Wagner (Oberstleutnant) and Scheffel (Oberst), Das 1. *Ober-Elsässische Feldartilerie-Regiment Nr. 15 im grossen Kriege 1914–1918* (Berlin: Verlag der Offizier-Vereinigung, 1930), 269.

84 Ibid.

85 Ibid.

86 Ibid.

87 Ibid.

CHAPTER NINE: EXTRAORDINARY SERVICE

1 Neil C. Smith, 'Empire's Other Anzacs: The Ceylon Planters Rifle Corps World War One: An outline history and biographical study of those who served with the Australian and New Zealand Army Corps', 1.

2 Ibid., 2.

3 Ibid., 'Nominal Roll'.

4 Anna Rogers, *While You're Away: New Zealand nurses at war 1899–1948* (Auckland: Auckland University Press, 2003), 174.

5 Suzanne Aubert, letter to My Dear Sister Angela, 10 August 1915, in Jessie Munro (ed.), *Letters on the Go: The correspondence of Suzanne Aubert* (Wellington: Bridget Williams Books, 2009), 373.

6 suzanneaubert.co.nz/home/journey-to-sainthood/ (accessed 16 March 2018).

7 Sherayl McNabb, *100 Years. New Zealand Military Nursing. New Zealand Army Nursing Service — Royal New Zealand Nursing Corps, 1915–2015* (Wairoa, Hawke's Bay: Sherayl McNabb, 2015), 209.

8 Ibid., 213.

9 Quoted in ibid.

10 Rogers, *While You're Away*, 169.

11 McNabb, *100 Years*, 214.

12 'Waimate Man at the Front', *Waimate Daily Advertiser*, 12 September 1914.

13 'Waimate Doctor at the Front', *Waimate Daily Advertiser*, 17 November 1914.

14 'Across Siberia and Russia', *Waimate Daily Advertiser*, 24 November 1914.

15 'With the Russian Red Cross', *Waimate Daily Advertiser*, 15 January 1915.

16 'Hospital Committee and British Soldier', *Waimate Daily Advertiser*, 25 February 1915.

17 'The Surgeon Gets Extended Leave', *Waimate Daily Advertiser*, 3 March 1915.

18 'From Petrograd to London', *Waimate Daily Advertiser*, 3 May 1915.

19 'Dr Barclay's Experiences', *Waimate Daily Advertiser*, 5 February 1915.

20 Jane Tolerton, *Make Her Praises Heard Afar: New Zealand women overseas in World War One* (Wellington: Book Lovers Books, 2017), 16–17.

21 Rae McGregor, *The Story of a New Zealand Writer: Jane Mander* (Dunedin: Otago University Press, 1998), 68.

22 Ibid., 70–71.

23 Ibid., 73.

24 Tolerton, *Make Her Praises Heard Afar*, 229–30.

25 'Red Cross News', *Star*, 14 October 1916.

26 Tolerton, *Make Her Praises Heard Afar*, 230.

27 Ibid., 231.

28 Ibid., 350–51.

29 I. W. Raymond, *New Zealanders in Mufti 1914–1918* (London: Argus Printing Co., 1924), 5.

30 Ibid., 17–18.

31 Ibid., 21.

32 Ibid., 24.

33 Ibid., 27.

34 Ibid., 34.

35 Quoted in ibid., 54.

36 Ibid.

37 Margaret Leask, *Lena Ashwell: Actress, patriot, pioneer* (Hertfordshire: University of Hertfordshire Press, 2012), 117.

38 Quoted in ibid., 119.

39 Ibid., 120. Ashwell made this statement to the *Bristol Times and Mirror* on 15 June 1915.

40 Ibid., 131, 141.

41 Ibid., 144.

42 Lena Ashwell, *Myself a Player* (London: Michael Joseph Ltd, 1936), 194.

43 Lena Ashwell, letter to Miss Bosworth, 28 December 1916, MS-696, Papers relating to the career of musician Ina Bosworth, 1915–1918, AWMM.

44 'Concerts at the Front', *Evening Post*, 2 June 1917.

45 Quoted in Leask, *Lena Ashwell*, 123.

46 'Concerts at the Front'.

47 'Personal Notes from London', *Evening Post*, 17 April 1918.

48 Tolerton, *Make Her Praises Heard Afar*, 242.

49 Ibid., 242, 297.

50 'Personal Notes from London', *Otago Daily Times*, 25 June 1919.

51 'Musical and Dramatic', *New Zealand Herald*, 20 April 1918.

52 'Entertaining the Soldiers: Miss Rees' interesting experiences', *Poverty Bay Herald*, 9 December 1919.

53 Nancy Swarbrick, 'Rees, Rosemary Frances', *Dictionary of New Zealand Biography Te Ara — The Encyclopedia of New Zealand*, https://teara.govt.nz/en/biographies/4r11/rees-rosemary-frances (accessed 20 March 2018), first published in 2010.

54 'Entertaining the Soldiers'.

55 Swarbrick, 'Rees, Rosemary Frances'.

56 Ashwell, *Myself*, 198–99.

57 Ibid., 223.

58 Particulars of Training and Experience, H. M. Chrystall, R. E., MS-532, Harvey Maitland Chrystall. Papers, 1913–1964, AWMM.

59 V. W. Nugent, Lt. Col., General Staff, Statement on Particulars of War Service Capt. H. M. Chrystall, R. E., MS-532, Harvey Maitland Chrystall. Papers, 1913–1964, AWMM.

60 Particulars of War Service Capt. H. M. Chrystall, R. E., MS-532, Harvey Maitland Chrystall. Papers, 1913–1964, AWMM.

61 Established in 1791, Ordnance Survey was the United Kingdom's national mapping agency; during the First World War it produced detailed maps of France and Belgium.

62 Ibid.

63 N. M. Jack, Lt. Col., Statement on Particulars of War Service Capt. H. M. Chrystall, R. E., MS-532, Harvey Maitland Chrystall. Papers, 1913–1964, AWMM.

64 Statement on Particulars of War Service Capt. H. M. Chrystall, R. E., MS-532, Harvey Maitland Chrystall. Papers, 1913–1964, AWMM.

65 Biographical Notes, MS-532, Harvey Maitland Chrystall. Papers, 1913–1964, AWMM.

66 James W. Brodie, 'Kidson, Edward', *Dictionary of New Zealand Biography Te Ara — The Encyclopedia of New Zealand*, https://teara.govt.nz/en/biographies/4k12/kidson-edward (accessed 21 March 2018), first published in 2010.

67 Ibid.

68 'Meteorological Office: New director's arrival', *New Zealand Herald*, 11 August 1927.

69 Ibid.

70 Brodie, 'Kidson, Edward'.

71 'Meteorological Office'.

72 Brodie, 'Kidson, Edward'.

73 'Personal Notes from London', *Press*, 19 May 1915.

74 Ibid.

75 'On Service', *Press*, 23 June 1915.

76 Ibid.

77 Ibid.

78 Statement of Service, WO 374/42204 Alfred Stewart Lindsay, TNA.

79 Arrival Report, WO 374/42204 Alfred Stewart Lindsay, TNA.

80 'Statement by a Soldier Concerning His Own Case', WO 374/42204 Alfred Stewart Lindsay, TNA.

81 'In Abyssinia; New Zealander's Interesting Experiences', *Evening Post*, 3 January 1919.

82 Ibid.

83 William Bennett, letter to the Hon R. Heaton Rhodes, 23 December 1920, AABK 18805 W5573 0356326 Selwyn Joyce, ANZ.

84 R. Heaton Rhodes, letter to William Bennett, 13 January 1921, AABK 18805 W5573 0356326 Selwyn Joyce, ANZ.

85 'First Contingent for Service in South Africa Attestation Form', AABK 18805 W5573 0356326 Selwyn Joyce, ANZ.

86 Memorandum, Lieut Joyce, 7th Contingent, 18 February 1902, AABK 18805 W5573 0356326 Selwyn Joyce, ANZ.

87 Lord Kitchener, letter to His Excellency, The Governor of New Zealand, 29 November 1901, Memorandum, Minister of Defence, R. J. S., 30 January 1902, AABK 18805 W5573 0356326 Selwyn Joyce, ANZ.

88 'How He Nipped', *New Zealand Truth*, 13 December 1928.

89 'Plausible Imposter', *New Zealand Herald*, 6 December 1928.

90 'How He Nipped'.

91 History Sheet, AABK 18805 W5515 0006377 Selwyn Joyce, ANZ.

92 Conduct Sheet, AABK 18805 W5515 0006377 Selwyn Joyce, ANZ.

93 S. Joyce, letter to My Darling, undated, AABK 18805 W5515 0006377 Selwyn Joyce, ANZ.

94 C. E. Andrews, GOC Administration, Confidential Letter to Selwyn Joyce, 21 June 1919, AABK 18805 W5515 0006377 Selwyn Joyce, ANZ.

95 C. E. Andrews, GOC Administration, Letter to The Commissioner of Police, 10 January 1921, AABK 18805 W5515 0006377 Selwyn Joyce, ANZ.

96 William Downie Stewart, letter to Sir James Allen, 22 January 1919, AABK 18805 W5515 0006377 Selwyn Joyce, ANZ. Downie Stewart's request had been made by letter on 15 January 1919 and Allen had replied on 24 January.

97 'How He Nipped'.

98 Ibid.

99 'Plausible Imposter'.

100 Handwritten note, AABK 18805 W5515 0006377 Selwyn Joyce, ANZ.

101 Application Form, Union Steam Ship Company of New Zealand, Masters and Officers, AC110982, Union Steam Ship Company Archives, Wellington City Council Archives.

102 Application for a Commission in the Australian Imperial Force, Roger Henry Patrick Farnham Moag, B2455, NAA.

103 Record of Service and Application for a Commission in the Australian Imperial Force, Roger Henry Patrick Farnham Moag, B2455, NAA.

104 Record of Service, Roger Henry Patrick Farnham Moag, B2455, NAA.

105 Handwritten note, 30 March 1916, WO 339/83370 Maxwell Farnham, TNA.

106 Casualty Form — Active Service, Roger Henry Patrick Farnham Moag, B2455, NAA.

107 Charge Sheet, Roger Henry Patrick Farnham Moag, B2455, NAA.

108 Evidence of the Accused, Roger Henry Patrick Farnham Moag, B2455, NAA.

109 Handwritten note on file, WO 339/83370 Maxwell Farnham, TNA.

110 Casualty Form — Active Service, Roger Henry Patrick Farnham Moag, B2455, NAA.

111 Precis of Service of Lieut R. H. P. F. Moag, 1/Battalion, Casualty Form — Active Service, Roger Henry Patrick Farnham Moag, B2455, NAA.

112 'Broken Officer's Career', *Thames Star*, 30 May 1917.

113 High Commissioner of New Zealand, letter to the Air Ministry, 27 May 1927, WO 339/83370 Maxwell Farnham, TNA.

114 Application for Appointment to a Temporary Commission in the Regular Army for the Period of the War, WO 339/83370 Maxwell Farnham, TNA.

115 Assistant Provost Marshal — Canadian Troops, Confidential Memorandum Maxwell Farnham, 25 January 1917, WO 339/83370 Maxwell Farnham, TNA.

116 Minute Sheet, WO 339/83370 Maxwell Farnham, TNA.

117 Attestation Form, Roger Moag, AABK 18805 W5549 0081912, ANZ.

118 Ibid.

119 Casualty Form — Active Service, Roger Moag, AABK 18805 W5549 0081912, ANZ.

120 'Broken Officer's Career'; '"Broken" Officer: Clever man "goes wrong"', *Nelson Evening Mail*, 28 June 1917; 'Man of Many Parts', *Hastings Standard*, 25 May 1917.

121 Ibid.

122 'Personal Matters', *Evening Post*, 27 January 1919.

123 https://sailstrait.wordpress.com/tag/s-s-halifax/ (accessed 27 March 1918).

124 Information supplied by Christine Clement. See 'Married Twice: Ex-officer's Wives', *Sydney Sun*, 25 March 1920.

125 'A Lover's Trickery: Ring obtained by ruse', *New Zealand Herald*, 12 August 1926.

126 'Who Owns the Ring?', *Auckland Star*, 11 September 1926.

127 Obituary, Mr A. N. H. Whitcombe, MS-2004-56, Papers relating to war service of Captain Alec Noel Hawkes Whitcombe, 2002, AWMM.

128 Undated diary entries, Alec Noel Whitcombe, MS-2004-56, Papers relating to war service of Captain Alec Noel Hawkes Whitcombe, 2002, AWMM.

129 Ibid.

130 Obituary, Mr A. N. H. Whitcombe, MS-2004-56, Papers relating to war service of Captain Alec Noel Hawkes Whitcombe, 2002, AWMM.

131 Military Cross Citation: Captain Noel Whitcombe, MS-2004-56, Papers relating to war service of Captain Alec Noel Hawkes Whitcombe, 2002, AWMM. White Russian forces, bolstered by Allied troops of the AEF, clashed with Bolsheviks at the Pinega River Front in North Russia from late 1918 onward.

132 https://www.awm.gov.au/articles/encyclopedia/north_russia (accessed 5 July 2018).

133 http://navymuseum.co.nz/lieutenant-samuel-hanna-dsc/ (accessed 5 July 2018).

134 Ibid.

135 Ibid.

136 https://www.revolvy.com/main/index.php?s=Archibald+Jack&item_type=topic (accessed 5 July 2018).

137 Information provided by Mark Brewer. From https://www.dnw.co.uk/auction-archive/past-catalogues/lot.php?auction_id=94&lot_id=131419 (accessed 11 July 2018).

138 https://www.revolvy.com/main/index.php?s=Archibald+Jack&item_type=topic (accessed 5 July 2018).

139 Ibid.

AFTERWORD

1 'A Gunner in Action', *Ellesmere Guardian*, 18 November 1918.

2 G. V. Berg, B2455, NAA.

3 'News of the Day', *Ellesmere Guardian*, 23 May 1917.

4 Casualty Form — Active Service, G. V. Berg, B2455, NAA.

5 'A Gunner's Experience', *Ellesmere Guardian*, 2 January 1918.

6 Casualty Form — Active Service, G. V. Berg, B2455, NAA.

7 'News of the Day', *Ellesmere Guardian*, 31 August 1918.

8 'Welcome Home at Southbridge', *Ellesmere Guardian*, 5 October 1918.

9 Liz Remmerswaal, email to Glyn Harper, 13 March 2017. Liz Remmerswaal is Gustav Berg's granddaughter, and we are grateful to her for sharing Gustav's story.

BIBLIOGRAPHY

UNPUBLISHED SOURCES

Australia

Australian War Memorial

Robert Henry Catlin papers, PRO 3991.

Sergeant Alfred Fisher papers, 3 DRL 5021.

William Alfred Hallahan letters, 1 DRL 329.

Lieutenant Clarence Henry letters, 1 DRL 346.

Biographical information sheets from the AIF Project (UNSW/ADFA)

David Crotters Barker

Alfred Joseph Bessell-Browne

Robert Henry Catlin

Robert Reginald Chapman

Jack Stuart Cranswick

Thurston George Cranswick

Alfred Fisher

William Alfred Hallahan

Clarence Henry

William Alfred Layburn

H. Septimus Power

James Fraser Scott

Percival Lascelles Smith

Lawrence Weathers

(Neil C. Smith, 'New Zealanders in the First Imperial Force, 1914–1919', F940.40993S655)

Mitchell Library (State Library of New South Wales)

May Ellen Dodson Moore WWI papers 1915–1955 MLMSS 2590/1-2.

Liddle diary and notebook June 1915–December 1918 MLMSS 1987/1-2.

Tennent War Narrative 30 September 1916–1 October 1919.

John Albert Giles papers 1914–1919 MLMSS 1842/1-4.

Noel Glendenning Linton MLMSS 1096/1-2.

Eric Keast Burke papers 1838–1974 MLMSS 1611.

National Archives of Australia, Canberra (NAA)

B2455 series

Gustav Victor Berg

William B. Brown

William Livingstone Hatchwell Burgess

K. Burke

Robert Reginald Chapman
Arthur Joseph Clarke
Arthur Thomas Clarke
Evelyn Augusta Conyers
Elsie May Cooke
John Stewart Cranswick
Thurston George Cranswick
Ethel Maud Dement
Charles Robert Duke
Hugh Elliott
Nora Philomena FitzGibbon
Alice Charlotte Fraser
Michael George
James Glover
Edmund Robert Guthrie
Grace Macadam Guthrie
Robert Thomson Hallahan
William Alfred Hallahan
Wendell James Hallahan
Walter Rewi Hallahan
Clarence Henry
Walter Hill
Robert Hood
Charles Key
Benjamin Jonas
Cyril Lawrence
William John Alfred Layburn
Leonard Francis McCartie
Hori McGregor
Alexander Patrick McKay
James Johnston Regna McQuillan
Eric Mason
James Lowther Mason
Herbert William Maxwell
George Robert Miller
Lewis Miller
Robert Orr Miller
Roger Henry Patrick Farnham Moag
John Peck
Harold Septimus Power
Bernard Percival Revenall
Dorothy Ann Rose

Arthur John Sawyer

William Henry Scott

Percival Lascelles Smith

Hilda Mary Steele

Marcus Fraser St John

Robert Stone [aka Karenema Pohatu]

Cora Evelyn Turnbull

Jessie Maud Verey

Elizabeth Jane White

MT1486/1

Charles Key

State Library of Victoria

John McGrath diary 1915–1917 MS Box 3133/8.

Faye Guthrie, 'Index to New Zealanders in other forces', ISBN 095894 1580.

Hunter Family papers 1908–1919 MS Box 4420/1.

Robyn Siers, 'Ancestry: Stories of multicultural Australians'.

Neil C. Smith, 'Empire's Other Anzacs: The Ceylon Planters Rifle Corps World War One: An outline history and biographical study of those who served with the Australian and New Zealand Army Corps'.

———, 'Kiwi Connection: Australians in the New Zealand Expeditionary Forces 1914–1919'.

———, 'Under Friendly Flags: Australians who served in the land, sea, and air forces of allied nations in World War One'.

———, 'What's in a Name: Aliases of the Australian Military Forces 1914–1919'.

New Zealand

Auckland War Memorial Museum (AWMM)

MS-696, Papers relating to the career of musician Ina Bosworth, 1915–18.

MS-532, Harvey Maitland Chrystall, Papers, 1913–64.

MS-89-120, Willen Crock, Documents relating to service in World War I, 1916.

MS-826, Ellen Bennett Manson, Papers, 1915–21.

MS-95-1, Hugh St Clair Miller, Documents relating to service in World Wars I and II, 1915–20.

MS-85-128, Nancy Marion Page, Documents relating to service in World War I.

MS-1561, W. F. Sampson, A soldier's diary, 1917.

MS-92-19, John Seabrook, Papers, 1936–70.

MS-1535, George Ernest and Harriet Simeon, Papers, 1894–1963.

MS-2004-56, Noel Whitcombe, Papers relating to war service of Captain Alec Noel Hawkes Whitcombe, 2002.

MS-2004-11, John H. Winder, John Yates; Service with the Quaker Ambulance Unit, Italy, 1916–18.

Alexander Turnbull Library (ATL)

Trevor Noel Holmden, MS-Papers-2223.

Johnston Family, Letters and papers, MS-Papers-9592.

Louisa Higginson 1885–1978, Diaries transcribed by Mrs R. L. Wilson, MS-Papers-2477-1 -3.

Arthur John Sawyer, MS-Group-1402.

Archives New Zealand (ANZ)

AABK 18805 W5549 0086716 William Powell Nimot.

AABK 22525 (Item R22423259), Vincent Briggs — French Foreign Legion and Imperial Force.

AABK 18805 W5515 0006377 Selwyn Joyce.

AABK 18805 W5573 0356326 Selwyn Joyce.

AABK 18805 W5549 0081912 Roger Moag.

AABK 18805 3/2950 George Redpath.

AABK 18805 WWI 51587 Louis Isaac Ziman.

AABK 18805 B WW1 1/284 William Baldwin Busby.

AABK 18805 WW1 15/3 Arthur Tahu Gravenor Rhodes.

R21380116 WW18/3817 Reuben McCarthy Newman.

AD1 Box 728, record 10/234, Territorial Force — Nominal Roll — New Zealanders serving in units other than NZEF.

AD 1 873, 38/1 Personnel: Transfers and promotions — Miscellaneous correspondence — General R. H. Davies.

WA 1/3 XFE 730, Re-Commissions in Indian Army and Indian Navy, 11 September–21 November 1917.

WA 2/1 item 23/94, Officers struck off Expeditionary Force strength.

WA 2/1 item 11/1, Indian Army and reserve of Officers.

WA 95, Box 1, Item 2b, Commissions in Imperial Forces.

WA 252 Items 1-5, Godley correspondence, letters to Sir James Allen.

WA 252 Item 12, Letters of General Alexander Godley and Lady Godley.

Personal Records of First World War Soldiers.

Kippenberger Military Archive, National Army Museum (NAM)

2012.420.1, Diary. Lieutenant George Redpath — France WWI.

Newspapers and periodicals

Papers Past (PP): New Zealand newspapers 1914–20.

Chronicles of the N.Z.E.F., 1916–19.

Ngā Taonga Sound & Vision Archive

Recordings

John Ellims:

https://www.ngataonga.org.nz/collections/catalogue/catalogue-item?record_id=198024

Charles Duke:

http://www.ngataonga.org.nz/collections/catalogue/catalogue-item?record_id=194839

http://anzacsightsound.org/audios/every-one-of-those-lads-was-lying-dead

Bernard Freyberg:

http://www.ngataonga.org.nz/collections/catalogue/catalogue-item?record_id=218438

http://www.ngataonga.org.nz/collections/catalogue/catalogue-item?record_id=216654

http://www.ngataonga.org.nz/collections/catalogue/catalogue-item?record_id=216175

Leonard Poulter Leary — Samoa Exp. Force but then Royal Horse Artillery:

http://www.ngataonga.org.nz/collections/catalogue/catalogue-item?record_id=177152

http://anzacsightsound.org/audios/steeds-and-shellfire-on-the-western-front

http://www.ngataonga.org.nz/collections/catalogue/catalogue-item?record_id=157501

Sonny Breeze [Brees?] of Rotorua

John Craig, interview with Thomas Remi Morrison, 9 February 1967:

http://www.ngataonga.org.nz/collections/catalogue/catalogue-item?record_id=224987

Charles Bathgate of Hawera, served in Dunsterforce — combined Allied unit raised for service in Persia in 1917 (no links attached).

Isaac Giles Sykes [known as Captain Ike Sykes]. Born 18 Jan 1892 at Masterton, died 6 May 1970 also at Masterton. He sailed on the *Rona* 1907–11 and served in the Australian Army during the war including on Gallipoli. We have an interview about his career on sail and steam vessels, but no mention of his war service in it.

Wellington City Council Archives

Union Steam Ship Company Archives: Masters and Officers, AC110982.

Hawke's Bay Digital Archive Trust

Edward (Ted) Piddocke Averill & Shirley Averill. Interview. https://knowledgebank.org.nz/1590/40507

Christine Clement: Database of New Zealanders who served in other nations' military during the First World War. Prepared by Christine Clement of Te Puke, 31 January 2018.

The United Kingdom

British Library

456/111, Asian Collection — Payments to New Zealand Nurses.

National Library of Scotland, Edinburgh

Papers of Field Marshal Sir Douglas Haig, Accession numbers 3137, 3155, 3678, 7706, 8008, 8676, 10638, 11838.

The National Archives (TNA), Kew Gardens, London

Admiralty files

ADM, 188/1101, Hugh Ludlow.

ADM, 196/100/3, D'Arcy Chaytor.

ADM, 337/117/245, Bernard Freyberg.

Board of Trade

Series BT26 — Commercial and Statistical Department and successors: Inward Passengers Lists.

Cabinet files

CAB, 45/208, Bernard Freyberg ('A Linesman in Picardy').

War Office files

WO76/419	Record of Special Reserve Officers' services
WO76/419/71	Ernest Cresswell Hellmore
WO84/12	Court martial charge book 1916
WO84/14	Court martial charge book 1917
WO213/11	Court martial charge book 1916
WO213/14	Court martial book 1917
WO95/1266/2	War Diary 1/14 Battalion London Regiment (London Scottish) 1914
WO95/1573/2	War Diary 1 Battalion Norfolk Regiment 1918
WO123/199	BEF Routine Orders August–September 1914
WO339/1046	Frederick Fisher Miles
WO339/3083	Henry Eugene Voyce

WO339/3137	Henry Frederick Roy Messenger
WO339/4177	Cecil F. G. Humphries
WO339/5919	Thomas Edmund Sotheron-Estcourt
WO339/6181	Oliver Durham Melville Garsia
WO339/6409	Charles Harold Reynell Watts
WO339/7663	Edward Wynne Chapman
WO339/8321	Algernon Donald Douglas McLean
WO339/8625	Frederick Neville Houston
WO339/10685	Robert Francis McLean Gee
WO339/11054	Charles Cochrane Iles
WO339/11481	William Edward Balcombe-Brown
WO339/11953	Edmund Boulnois
WO339/14074	William James Clachan
WO339/14548	Edward Rhodes Moorhouse
WO339/15920	Ivan Scott Orbell
WO339/17727	Archibald Gordon Hodges
WO339/19469	Frederick George Andrews
WO339/21819	Charles Colin Kinloch Campbell
WO339/22886	Montagu Robert McGregor-Turnbull
WO339/25763	John Hugh Allen
WO339/25873	Claude Gladstone Robinson
WO339/27809	John William Pinckney
WO339/29036	Theophilus Rudolph Jackson
WO339/30486	Frederick Adrian Maunsell Jenkins
WO339/30955	William Henderson Gibb
WO339/31372	Rainsford Balcombe-Brown
WO339/31847	James Bayntun Starky
WO339/32271	William George Thornton
WO339/32475	Percy Ashton Elworthy
WO339/33753	Leonard Poulter Leary
WO339/34855	Joseph Ward Rutledge
WO339/34917	Harold Salmon
WO339/35039	William Caithness Talbot
WO339/35941	Leslie Heron Beauchamp
WO339/36752	Ernest Richard Leary
WO339/36812	William Baldwin Busby
WO339/37410	Audley Charles Hyde Millar
WO339/37746	B. Arthur
WO339/38277	John Nevill Ritchie
WO339/38338	Eric Wright Nairn
WO339/39854	John Hutton Grigg
WO339/42429	Eric Croft

WO339/44693	Henry Norman Spence
WO339/46311	Theodore Arthur Izard
WO339/47745	Daniel Henry Strother Riddiford
WO339/48282	Charles Stanley Lawrence Harrington
WO339/50002	Richard Hutton Davies
WO339/57275	William Averill Humphreys
WO339/59213	Charles Ethelbert Gribble
WO339/59725	William Walker
WO339/60593	Alexander Ormond
WO339/62568	Nathaniel Arthur Pearce
WO339/64469	Alex Noel Hawkes Whitcombe
WO339/64809	Geoffrey Gordon Rich
WO339/67846	Robert Heaton Livingstone
WO339/70716	Guy Campbell Russell
WO339/71333	Lorne de Hutton Hutton
WO339/72145	Frederick Allan Hellaby
WO339/75661	Ernest Cyril Branson
WO339/76376	Anthony Darley Russell Rendle
WO339/78208	Stuart Maxwell Deans
WO339/80319	Matthew Roland Farrer
WO339/80928	John Willoughby Hadfield Marshall
WO339/82185	George Gordon de Courcy Drury
WO339/83370	Maxwell Farnham (aka Roger Henry Patrick Farnham Moag and Roger Henry Moag-Levy)
WO339/94150	George Alexander Pearson
WO339/94219	Reginald Victor Deacon
WO339/96672	Geoffrey William Douglas Mulgan
WO339/96866	Charles Edward Anketell
WO339/100568	Ernest Andrew Mahoney
WO339/102700	Cuthbert Trelawder MacLean
WO339/112369	Brian Gerald Mahoney
WO339/114520	William Henry Coates
WO339/116786	Humphrey Gilbert Machell
WO374/20401	George Robert Poynter Douglas
WO374/26945	Charles Monk Gibbon
WO374/37889	William Johnston
WO374/42204	Alfred Stewart Lindsay
WO374/45175	Angus MacNab
WO374/47296	Charles W. Melvill
WO374/56607	Leslie Norman Reece
WO374/58117	Noel Francis Edward Robertshawe
WO374/65059	Oliver Steele
WO374/65514	Mervyn James Stewart

WO374/68152	George Alfred Thompson
WO374/71380	Michael Norman Wallace
WO398/136	Ethel Lewis
WO399/1637	Mary Collins
WO399/1701	Ella Kate Cooke
WO399/2619	Edith Fairchild
WO399/3813	Louisa Higginson
WO399/4234	Laura James
WO399/6913	Mildred Rees
WO399/7117	Nancy Marion Robertson
WO399/12558	Agnes Kerr
WO372/12/159478	Medal Card Hugh Ludlow Gloucester Regiment

The National Army Museum UK (NAMUK)

1994-01-238	WRAC papers of Miss G. J. Baxter
2006-11-39	An extract from an autobiography by Charles Edward Cullen

THESIS

Richard G. H. Kay, 'In Pursuit of Victory: British–New Zealand relations during the First World War', PhD thesis, University of Otago, Dunedin, October 2001.

PUBLISHED SOURCES

Anon. *The Great War, 1914—1918. New Zealand Expeditionary Force Roll of Honour*. Wellington: Government Printer, 1924.

Ashwell, Lena. *Myself a Player*. London: Michael Joseph Ltd, 1936.

Badsey, Stephen. *The British Army in Battle and Its Image 1914–18*. London: Continuum UK, 2009.

Barrie, John Charles. *Memoirs of an Anzac: A first-hand account by an AIF officer in the First World War*. Sydney: Scribe Publications, 2015.

Bean, C. E. W. *Anzac to Amiens*. Ringwood, Vic: Penguin, 1946.

———. *The Australian Imperial Force in France 1917*. St Lucia: University of Queensland Press, 1982.

Beaumont, Joan. *Australian Defence: Sources and statistics*. Melbourne: Oxford University Press, 2001.

———. *Broken Nation: Australians in the Great War*. Sydney: Allen & Unwin, 2013.

Belich, James. *Paradise Reforged: A history of the New Zealanders from the 1880s to the year 2000*. Auckland: Penguin, 2001.

Bou, Jean (ed.). *The AIF in Battle: How the Australian Imperial Force fought 1914–1918*. Melbourne: Melbourne University Press, 2016.

Carbery, A. D. *The New Zealand Medical Service in the Great War 1914–1918*. Auckland: Whitcombe & Tombs, 1924.

Chapman, Paul. *Menin Gate South: In memory and mourning*. Barnsley: Pen & Sword Military, 2016.

Claasen, Adam. *Fearless: The extraordinary untold story of New Zealand's Great War airmen*. Auckland: Massey University Press, 2017.

Clarke, Stephen. *After the War: The RSA in New Zealand*. Auckland: Penguin, 2016.

Clement, Christine, and Ellen McCormack. *The Pioneers, Settlers and Families of Katikati and District.* Te Puke: Christine Clement, 2012.

Corbett-Smith, A. *The Marne — And After*. London: Cassell & Company, 1917.

Crawford, John and Ian McGibbon (eds). *New Zealand's Great War: New Zealand, the Allies and the First World War.* Auckland: Exisle, 2007.

Dennis, Peter, Jeffrey Grey, Ewan Morris and Robin Prior, with Jean Bou. *The Oxford Companion to Australian Military History,* 2nd edn. Melbourne: Oxford University Press, 2008.

Drew, H. T. B. (ed.). *The War Effort of New Zealand.* Auckland: Whitcombe & Tombs, 1923.

Dunsterville, L. C. *Stalky's Adventures.* London: Jonathan Cape, 1941.

Ekins, Ashley (ed.). *1918 Year of Victory: The end of the Great War and the shaping of history.* Wollombi, NSW: Exisle, 2010.

East, Ronald (ed.). *The Gallipoli Diary of Sergeant Lawrence of the Australian Engineers — 1st A.I.F. 1915.* Melbourne: Melbourne University Press, 1981.

Eldred-Grigg, Stevan. *The Great Wrong War: New Zealand society in WWI.* Auckland: Random House, 2010.

Fell, Alison S. and Christine E. Hallett (eds). *First World War Nursing: New perspectives.* New York: Routledge, 2013.

Ferguson, Niall. *The Pity of War.* London: Penguin, 1998.

Freyberg, Paul. *Bernard Freyberg, VC: Soldier of two nations.* London: Hodder & Stoughton, 1991.

Grey, Jeffrey. *A Military History of Australia.* Cambridge, UK: Cambridge University Press, 1999.

Haigh, J. Bryant and Alan J. Polaschek (compilers). *New Zealand and the Distinguished Service Order. Being a record of New Zealanders and those associated with New Zealand, appointed as Companions of the Distinguished Service Order.* Christchurch: J. Bryant Haigh and Alan J. Polaschek, 1993.

Hamilton, Robert. *Victoria Cross Heroes of World War 1: 628 extraordinary stories of valour.* Croxley Green, Hertfordshire: Atlantic Publishing, 2015.

Hankins, C. A. *Katherine Mansfield and her Confessional Stories.* London: Macmillan, 1983.

——— (ed.). *The Letters of John Middleton Murry to Katherine Mansfield.* Auckland: Hutchinson Group, 1983.

Harper, Glyn. *Johnny Enzed: The New Zealand soldier in the First World War 1914–1918.* Auckland: Exisle, 2015.

Harper, Glyn and Colin Richardson. *Acts of Valour: The history of the Victoria Cross and New Zealand.* Auckland: HarperCollins, 2016.

Harrison, Mark. *The Medical War: British military medicine in the First World War.* Oxford: Oxford University Press, 2010.

Hastings, Max. *Catastrophe: Europe goes to war 1914.* London: William Collins, 2013.

Hay, Ian. *The First Hundred Thousand.* Edinburgh and London: William Blackwood & Sons, 1916.

Haythornthwaite, Philip J. *The World War One Source Book.* London: BCA, 1992.

Holmes, Richard. *Tommy: The British soldier on the Western Front 1914–1918.* London: HarperCollins, 2004.

———. *Sahib: The British soldier in India.* London: Harper Perennial, 2006.

———. *Fatal Avenue: A traveller's history of the battlefields of Northern France and Flanders 1346–1945.* London: Vintage, 2008.

———. *Soldiers: Army lives and loyalties from redcoats to dusty warriors.* London: HarperPress, 2012.

Holt, Tonie and Valmai. *Major & Mrs Holt's Battlefield Guide to the Somme.* Barnsley: Pen & Sword Military, 2008.

Jeffreys, Alan. *Approach to Battle: Training the Indian Army during the Second World War.* Solihull: Helion & Company, 2016.

Jones, Heather. *Violence Against Prisoners of War in the First World War: Britain, France and Germany, 1914–1920.* New York: Cambridge University Press, 2011.

Jones, Spencer (ed.). *Stemming the Tide: Officers and leadership in the British Expeditionary Force 1914.* Solihull, West Midlands: Helion & Company, 2013.

Kant, Vedica. *'If I Die Here, Who Will Remember Me?': India and the First World War.* New Delhi: Roli Books, 2014.

Kershaw, Ian. *Hitler, 1889–1936: Hubris.* London: Penguin, 1998.

King, Michael. *The Penguin History of New Zealand.* Auckland: Penguin, 2003.

Leary, L. P. *Not Entirely Legal: An autobiography.* Christchurch: Whitcoulls, 1977.

Leask, Margaret. *Lena Ashwell: Actress, patriot, pioneer.* Hertfordshire: University of Hertfordshire Press, 2012.

Lindsay, J. H. (ed.). *The London Scottish in the Great War.* London: The Naval & Military Press, 1926.

Lloyd, Mark. *The London Scottish in the Great War.* London: Pen & Sword, 2001.

Lloyd, Nick. *Passchendaele: A new history.* London: Penguin, 2017.

Macdonald, Lyn. *1914.* London: Guild Publishing, 1987.

McGibbon, Ian (ed.). *The Oxford Companion to New Zealand Military History.* Auckland: Oxford University Press, 2000.

——— *New Zealand's Western Front Campaign.* Auckland: David Bateman, 2016.

McGregor, Rae. *The Story of a New Zealand Writer: Jane Mander.* Dunedin: Otago University Press, 1998.

McLean, Gavin. *The White Ships: New Zealand's First World War hospital ships.* Wellington: New Zealand Ship & Marine Society, 2013.

McNabb, Sherayl. *100 Years. New Zealand Military Nursing. New Zealand Army Nursing Service — Royal New Zealand Nursing Corps, 1915–2015.* Wairoa, Hawke's Bay: Sherayl McNabb, 2015.

Martin, Arthur Anderson. *A Surgeon in Khaki: Through France and Flanders in World War I.* Lincoln, NA: University of Nebraska Press, 2011.

Munro, Jessie. *The Story of Suzanne Aubert.* Wellington: Bridget Williams Books, 1998.

——— (ed.). *Letters on the Go: The correspondence of Suzanne Aubert.* Wellington: Bridget Williams Books, 2009.

Neiberg, Michael S. *The Path to War: How the First World War created modern America.* New York: Oxford University Press, 2016.

New Zealand Year Official Year-Book, 1919. Wellington: Government of New Zealand, 1920.

Nicholson, J. B. R. *The Ghurka Rifles.* Reading, Berkshire: Osprey Publishing, 1974.

O'Neill, H. C. *The Royal Fusiliers in the Great War.* Heathfield, East Sussex: The Naval & Military Press, n.d.

O'Sullivan, Vincent (ed.). *Katherine Mansfield: Selected letters.* New York: Oxford University Press, 1989.

O'Sullivan, Vincent, with Margaret Scott (eds). *The Collected Letters of Katherine Mansfield: Volume 2 1918–1919.* New York: Oxford University Press, 1987.

Palmer, Alan. *The Gardeners of Salonika.* London: André Deutsch, 1965.

Pedersen, Peter. *The Anzacs: Gallipoli to the Western Front.* Melbourne: Penguin, 2007.

Philippe, Nathalie (ed.). *The Great Adventure Ends: New Zealand and France on the Western Front.* Christchurch: John Douglas Publishing, 2013.

Pound, Reginald. *Gillies: Surgeon extraordinary.* London: Michael Joseph, 1964.

Power, Harold Septimus. *The Art of Septimus Power.* Melbourne: Rigby Limited, 1974.

Pugsley, Christopher. *On the Fringe of Hell: New Zealanders and military discipline in the First World War*. Auckland: Hodder & Stoughton, 1991.

———. *The Camera in the Crowd: Filming New Zealand in peace and war, 1895–1920*. Auckland: Oratia Books in association with Ngā Taonga Sound & Vision, 2017.

Rawstron, R. E. *A Unique Nursing Group: New Zealand Army nurse anaesthetists of WWI*. Christchurch: Rawstron Publishing Company, 2005.

Raymond, I. W. *New Zealanders in Mufti 1914–1918*. London: Argus Printing Co., 1924.

Rees, Peter. *Anzac Girls: The extraordinary story of our World War I nurses*. Sydney: Allen & Unwin, 2014.

Richardson, Len and Shelley. *Anthony Wilding: A sporting life*. Christchurch: Canterbury University Press, 2005.

Roberts, Priscilla (ed.). *World War I: The definitive encyclopedia and document collection*. Santa Barbara, CA: ABC-CLIO, LLC, 2014.

Rogers, Anna. *While You're Away: New Zealand nurses at war 1899–1948*. Auckland: Auckland University Press, 2003.

Service, Robert W. *Rhymes of a Red Cross Man*. London: T. Fisher Unwin, 1916.

Shakespear, L. W. *History of King Edward's Own Goorkhas, The Sirmoor Rifle Regiment, vol. 2: 1911–21*. Aldershot: Gale & Polden, 1924.

Stanley, Peter. *Die in Battle: Do not despair*. Solihull, West Midlands: Helion & Co., 2015.

Stevenson, David. *1914–1918: The history of the First World War*. London: Penguin, 2004.

———. *With Our Backs to the Wall: Victory and defeat in 1918*. London: Allen Lane, 2011.

Stowers, Richard. *Heroes of Gallipoli: The gallantry of New Zealanders on Gallipoli*. Christchurch: John Douglas Publishing, 2015.

Studholme, John. *New Zealand Expeditionary Force: Record of personal services during the war of officers, nurses, and first-class warrant officers; and other facts relating to the N.Z.E.F. Unofficial, but based on official records*. Wellington: Government Printer, 1928.

Tolerton, Jane. *Make Her Praises Heard Afar: New Zealand women overseas in World War One*. Wellington: Book Lovers Books, 2017.

Tucker, Spencer C. (ed.). *World War I: The definitive encyclopedia and document collection, vol. 4: ER–Z*. Santa Barbara, CA: ABC-CLIO, 2014.

Wagner (Oberstleutnant) and Scheffel (Oberst), *Das 1. Ober-Elsässische Feldartilerie-Regiment Nr. 15 im grossen Kriege 1914–1918*. Berlin: Verlag der Offizier-Vereinigung, 1930.

Wakefield, Alan and Simon Moody. *Under the Devil's Eye: Britain's forgotten army at Salonika 1915–1918*. Barnsley, South Yorkshire: Pen & Sword Military, 2017.

Wavell, A. P. *Other Men's Flowers: An anthology of poetry compiled by A. P. Wavell (Field-Marshal Earl Wavell)*. London: Pimlico, 1992.

Wyrall, Everard. *The 17th (S.) Battalion Royal Fusiliers, 1914–1919*. London: Methuen & Co., 1930.

Wright, Matthew. *Freyberg's War: The man, the legend, the reality*. Auckland: Penguin, 2005.

Yule, Peter (ed.). *Sergeant Lawrence Goes to France*. Melbourne: Melbourne University Press, 1987.

Articles

Guildford Anzacs, Bessell-Browne, Alfred Joseph, http://www.guildfordanzacs.org.au/anzac/49 (accessed 23 January 2018).

Brewer, Mark. 'Greek Orders, Decorations and Medals, Awarded to New Zealanders at War', *The Volunteers: The Journal of the New Zealand Military Historical Society (Inc)*, vol. 26, no. 2 (November 2000), 110–19.

———. 'New Zealand and the Légion d'honneur: The Great War', *The Volunteers: The Journal of the New Zealand Military Historical Society (Inc)*, vol. 34, no. 2 (November 2008), 79–87.

———. 'Serbian Awards to NZ Women: Medical personnel in WWI recognised', *The Volunteers: The Journal of the New Zealand Military Historical Society (Inc)*, vol. 37, no. 2 (November 2011), 111–25.

———. 'New Zealand and the Légion d'honneur: The Great War', *The Volunteers: The Journal of the New Zealand Military Historical Society (Inc)*, vol. 37, no. 3 (March 2012), 171–80.

Clark, Hannah. 'Sisters in a Distant Land: The exploration of identity and travel through three New Zealand nurses: diaries from the Great War', *Women's Studies Journal*, vol. 30, no. 1 (July 2016), 17–29.

Cook, Tim. 'The Politics of Surrender: Canadian soldiers and the killing of prisoners in the Great War', *The Journal of Military History*, vol. 78, no. 1 (January 2014), 37–71.

Holden, Robert. 'Power, Harold Septimus (1877–1951)', *Australian Dictionary of Biography*, Australian National University, http://adb.anu.edu.au/biography/power-harold-septimus-8089/text14117 (accessed 11 December 2017). First published in 1988.

Kovacic, Katherine. 'Artists at War', *Wartime*, issue 57 (Summer 2012), 50–54.

Leask, Margaret. 'Lena Ashwell's Modern Troubadours — Entertaining the Troops, 1915–1919', *Popular Entertainment Studies*, vol. 5, no. 1, 2014, 8–27.

Lincoln, Merrilyn. 'Bessell-Browne, Alfred Joseph (1877–1947)'. *Australian Dictionary of Biography*, Australian National University, http://adb.anu.edu.au/biography/bessell-browne-alfred-joseph-5223/text8789 (accessed 23 January 2018). First published in 1979.

Shanks, G. Dennis. 'Legacy of the 1914–18 War: How World War I changed global attitudes to war and infectious diseases', *The Lancet*, vol. 384 (8 November 2014), 1699–1707.

Tobin, Grant. 'Staff Nurse Ethel Mary Lewis 22/444. The gallant little nurse', *The Volunteers: The Journal of the New Zealand Military Historical Society (Inc)*, vol. 39, no. 2 (November 2013), 80–93.

Webber, Kimberley. 'Burke, Eric Keast (1896–1974)'. *Australian Dictionary of Biography*, Australian National University, http://adb.anu.edu.au/biography/burke-eric-keast-9628/text16981 (accessed 11 December 2017). First published in 1993.

PRIVATE PUBLICATION

Gray, John H. *The Canterbury Officers' Club (Inc) Biographical Essays on Members on the Roll of Honour of the Great War*. Christchurch, 2015.

WEBSITES

https://www.londonscottishregt.org/index.php/en/

http://ww100.nelsonmuseum.co.nz/character?profileID=12

https://nzhistory.govt.nz/media/video/leslie-beauchamp-great-war-story

http://blog.helion.co.uk/spencer-jones-was-the-kaisers-old-contemptibles-telegram-a-fabrication/

Garry Clayton. 'Davies, Richard Hutton 1861–1918'. *Dictionary of New Zealand Biography Te Ara — The Encyclopedia of New Zealand*. http://www.TeAra.govt.nz/en/biographies/3d3/davies-richard-hutton (accessed 24 February 2017).

June Northcroft-Grant. 'Papakura, Makereti', *Dictionary of New Zealand Biography Te Ara — The Encyclopedia of New Zealand*. http://www.TeAra.govt.nz/en/biographies/3p5/papakura-makereti (accessed 9 March 2017).

'Alexander Ormond'. Last Post Stories Project, Ministry for Culture and Heritage. http://www.nzhistory.net.nz/keyword/last-post-stories (accessed 2 May 2017).

Warren Derkenne. 'Storkey, Percy Valentine (1893–1969)'. *Australian Dictionary of Biography*, National Centre of Biography, Australian National University, http://adb.anu.edu.au/biography/storkey-percy-valentine-8687/text15197 (accessed 15 November 2017). First published in 1990.

Jean Garner. 'Grigg, Mary Victoria Cracroft', *Dictionary of New Zealand Biography Te Ara — The Encyclopedia of New Zealand*. https://teara.govt.nz/en/biographies/5g22/grigg-mary-victoria-cracroft (accessed 7 February 2018). First published in 2000.

John Ritchie. 'Weathers, Lawrence Carthage (1890–1918)', *Australian Dictionary of Biography*, National Centre of Biography, Australian National University, http://adb.anu.edu.au/biography/weathers-lawrence-carthage-9021/text15867 (accessed 15 November 2017). First published in 1990.

http://www.scarletfinders.co.uk/167.html (accessed on 8 February 2018).

Rex Wright-St Clair. 'Gillies, Harold Delf'. *Dictionary of New Zealand Biography Te Ara — The Encyclopedia of New Zealand*. https://teara.govt.nz/en/biographies/3g9/gillies-harold-delf (accessed 14 February 2018). First published in 1996.

https://www.armymuseum.co.nz/blog/a-kiwi-one-of-the-finest-within-the-french-foreign-legion.html

https://www65.statcan.gc.ca/acyb07/acyb07_0007-eng.htm (accessed 28 February 2018).

http://www.thecanadianencyclopedia.ca/en/article/canadian-expeditionary-force (accessed 28 February 2018).

https://archive.org/details/CEF_29thBn_1915 (accessed 28 February 2018).

http://www.rmslusitania.info/primary-docs/too-proud-to-fight (accessed 1 March 1918).

https://encyclopedia.1914-1918-online.net/article/lettow-vorbeck_paul_von (accessed 6 March 2018).

suzanneaubert.co.nz\home\journey-to-sainthood\ (accessed 16 March 2018).

Nancy Swarbrick, 'Rees, Rosemary Frances', *Dictionary of New Zealand Biography Te Ara — The Encyclopedia of New Zealand*. https://teara.govt.nz/en/biographies/4r11/rees-rosemary-frances (accessed 20 March 2018). First published in 2010.

James W. Brodie. 'Kidson, Edward', *Dictionary of New Zealand Biography Te Ara — The Encyclopedia of New Zealand*. https://teara.govt.nz/en/biographies/4k12/kidson-edward (accessed 21 March 2018). First published in 2010.

https://sailstrait.wordpress.com/tag/s-s-halifax/ (accessed 27 March 2018).

https://ww100.govt.nz/the-menin-gate-last-post-ceremony-an-enduring-tradition (accessed 9 May 2018).

Kenneth Sinclair Thomson, http://www.aucklandmuseum.com/war-memorial/online-cenotaph/record/C35204 (accessed 9 May 2018).

Sinclair-Thomson Kenneth, https://museum.timaru.govt.nz/explore/whats-on/ww100/scroll/profile?id=2233 (accessed 9 May 2018).

http://sueyounghistories.com/archives/2009/03/28/ethelbert-petrie-hoyle-1861-1955/ (accessed 10 May 2018).

http://www.antarctica.gov.au/about-antarctica/history/exploration-and-expeditions/australasian-antarctic-expedition/staff-and-crew-of-the-aae (accessed 11 May 2018).

http://www.hampton.lib.nh.us/hampton/history/military/26thDivisionYD/26thDivisionHistory1919.htm (accessed 11 May 2018).

https://www3.stats.govt.nz/historic_publications/1916-census/Report%20on%20Results%20of%20Census%201916/1916-report-results-census%20.html (accessed 14 June 2018).

http://www.qaranc.co.uk/voluntary-aid-detachment.php (accessed 26 June 2018).

http://www.aucklandmuseum.com/war-memorial/online-cenotaph/record/C53857 (accessed 27 June 2018).

Timothy C. Winegard, 'Dunsterforce', https://encyclopedia.1914-1918-online.net/article/dunsterforce (accessed 27 June 2018).

https://www.cwgc.org/find/find-war-dead/results?firstName=William&lastName=Selby%2B&country=India (accessed 27 June 2018).

https://www.aif.adfa.edu.au/OrderOfBattle/Generals/burgess.html (accessed 4 July 2018).

W. David McIntyre. 'Sinclair-Burgess, William Livingston Hatchwell', *Dictionary of New Zealand Biography Te Ara — The Encyclopedia of New Zealand*. https://teara.govt.nz/en/biographies/4s26/sinclair-burgess-william-livingston-hatchwell (accessed 4 July 2018). First published in 1998.

https://www.overthefront.com/resources/military-ranks/french-ranks (accessed 4 July 2018).

https://foreignlegion.info/ranks/ (accessed 4 July 2018).

https://www.awm.gov.au/articles/encyclopedia/north_russia (accessed 5 July 2018).

http://navymuseum.co.nz/lieutenant-samuel-hanna-dsc/ (accessed 5 July 2018).

https://www.revolvy.com/main/index.php?s=Archibald+Jack&item_type=topic (accessed 5 July 2018).

https://www.dnw.co.uk/auction-archive/past-catalogues/lot.php?auction_id=94&lot_id=131419 (accessed 11 July 2018).

www.bac-lac.gc.ca/eng/discover/military-heritage/first-world-war/personnel-records/Pages/item.aspx?IdNumber=383945 (accessed 13 July 2018).

ACKNOWLEDGEMENTS

This book would not have been possible without the input and support of so many people, and it would not have been written without the backing of the organisations that make up the partnership of the Centenary History Project and the individuals who are members of the Governance Group. These organisations are the New Zealand Defence Force, the Ministry for Culture and Heritage, and Massey University. We would like to thank Professor Giselle Byrnes and Gerald Hensley, co-chairs of the Governance Group of the Centenary History Project. Not only have Gerald and Giselle steered the Governance Group with skill and dedication, they also both agreed to contribute the fitting foreword to this volume of the Centenary History.

The generosity of those who are so willing to share family history in the form of letters, diaries and photographs never fails to amaze and touch us; this book is much stronger for their contribution. We would like to thank the following people for their assistance in providing material and images: Michael Wynd at the National Museum of the Royal New Zealand Navy, Zoe Richardson and Shaun Higgins at the Auckland War Memorial Museum, Sue Madden-Grey at Otago Boys' High School, Jane Teal at Christ's College, Ian Connerty of the Last Post Association in Ieper, David Robertson at Nelson College, Julian Holderness, Phil Beattie, Mark Brewer, Liz Remmerswaal Hughes and Corrie Hughes, John O'Reilly and Shaun Fogarty.

We thank and acknowledge all the research institutions in Australia, New Zealand and the United Kingdom where many of the documents and photographs were obtained. The main institutions we accessed were: the national archives of the United Kingdom, Australia and New Zealand; the Australian War Memorial; the Auckland War Memorial Museum; and the state libraries of New South Wales and Victoria. We also made extensive use of the New Zealand National Library's Papers Past, the Commonwealth War Graves Commission website and ancestry.com.au.

John Crawford, Mark Brewer and Nicola Legat read an earlier draft of the manuscript and made many helpful suggestions.

We would like to thank Massey University Press and, in particular, Nicola Legat, who decided that the outline of the book had enough merit to warrant publishing. Nicola and the Massey University Press team have been encouraging and supportive throughout the publishing process. In particular, we would like to acknowledge Anna Bowbyes; the indexer, Peter Cooke; and the book's editor, Matt Turner. Needless to say, we are very happy with the way the book has turned out.

We would like to acknowledge and thank past and present members of the New Zealand Society of Genealogists. These people are throughout New Zealand and their collections have been invaluable.

Glyn's wife, Susan, has lived with this book and the Centenary History for many years. She has helped with the research for it, read several versions, and has contributed in many ways. Susan believes it is about time Glyn moved on from the First World War.

ABOUT THE AUTHORS

Glyn Harper is Professor of War Studies at Massey University, where he has worked since 2001. A former teacher, Glyn joined the Australian Army in 1988 and after eight years transferred to the New Zealand Army, rising to the rank of lieutenant colonel. Glyn is Massey's project manager for the Centenary History of New Zealand and the First World War. He is the author of more than 30 books on military history, including several bestsellers, and books for children. His other book published as part of the Centenary History of New Zealand and the First World War is *Johnny Enzed: The New Zealand soldier in the First World War 1914–1918* (Auckland: Exisle, 2015).

Christine Clement has been a family and local historian for over half her life and has a major interest in the First World War. She is the author of numerous databases, articles, books and a website, and is the New Zealand consultant for ancestry.com.au, as well as the researcher for the over 900 men and women of the Salute Wairoa World War One project. Christine was responsible for a new First World War memorial in Te Puke, where she is chair of the War Memorial Hall Society and secretary of the Anzac Day Commemoration Group. Her other interests include New Zealand disasters and tragedies, and the historical migration schemes and periods of New Zealand's history.

Rebecca Johns is a researcher and administrator for the Centenary History of New Zealand and the First World War. Rebecca graduated from Massey University with an MA, and has a strong interest in military history.

INDEX

Items in **bold** refer to illustrations
The appendices have not been indexed

OTHER BOOKS IN THE CENTENARY HISTORY PROGRAMME PUBLISHED BY MASSEY UNIVERSITY PRESS

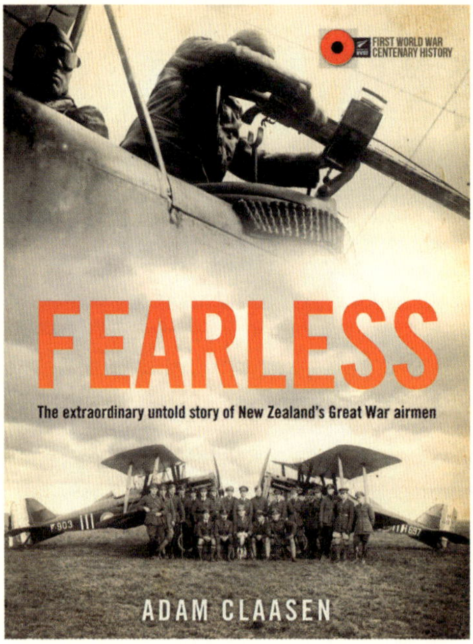

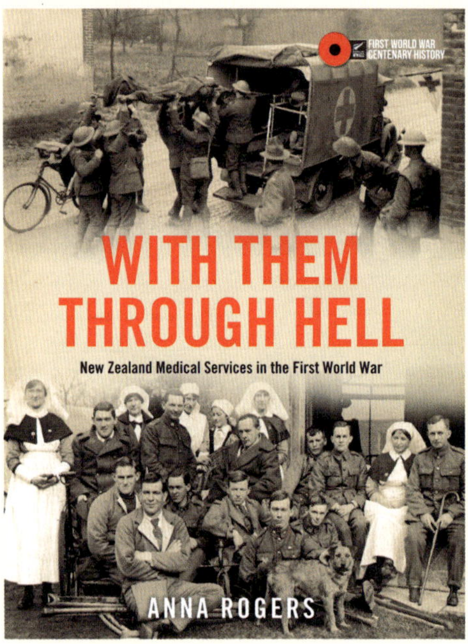

ABOUT THE FIRST WORLD WAR CENTENARY HISTORY PROGRAMME

Massey University, the Ministry for Culture and Heritage (MCH) and the New Zealand Defence Force have joined forces and committed substantial resources to produce a series of authoritative print histories on New Zealand and the First World War. The works in this series are scholarly yet accessible to broad audiences. They draw on an extensive range of primary sources held in New Zealand, Britain and elsewhere, and contain high-quality maps and illustrations. Together they form the first complete and detailed account of New Zealand's First World War experience.

These print histories are complemented by digital resources published through the www.firstworldwar.govt.nz website, part of the Ministry for Culture and Heritage's NZHistory.govt.nz site. The programme's historians have also contributed to other centenary activities, including major international conferences, museum and art exhibitions, television documentaries, heritage trails, and commemorative events in New Zealand and overseas.

The Centenary History Programme Governance Group is co-chaired by Gerald Hensley and Massey University Provost Professor Giselle Byrnes. The group includes MCH Chief Historian Neill Atkinson, Defence Force Historian John Crawford, Massey University Professor of War Studies Glyn Harper, and other representatives of the three agencies. More information about the Centenary History series can be found at http://ww100.govt.nz/first-world-war-centenary-print-histories.

This volume of the Centenary History would not have been possible without generous donations to the Massey University Foundation. It would also not have been possible without Massey University's support to the authors.

MASSEY UNIVERSITY TE KUNENGA KI PŪREHUROA UNIVERSITY OF NEW ZEALAND
New Zealand DEFENCE FORCE Te Ope Kātua O Aotearoa NAVY NZ ARMY AIR FORCE
MASSEY UNIVERSITY FOUNDATION
Manatū Taonga Ministry for Culture & Heritage
FIRST WORLD WAR CENTENARY HISTORY

MASSEY
UNIVERSITY
PRESS

First published in 2019 by Massey University Press
Private Bag 102904, North Shore Mail Centre
Auckland 0745, New Zealand
www.masseypress.ac.nz

Design by Kate Barraclough
Typesetting by Sarah Elworthy
Front cover photographs: Alamy (above) and Hocken Collections, Uare Taoka o Hākena, University of Otago (below)
Back cover photographs: Australian War Memorial (above), Imperial War Museum (centre), Wanganui Collegiate (below)

A catalogue record for this book is available from the National Library of New Zealand

Printed and bound in China by Everbest Investment Ltd

ISBN: 978-0-9951029-9-6